A KENTISH LAD

The Autobiography of Frank Muir

Also by Frank Muir:

THE WHAT-A-MESS CHILDREN'S BOOKS

THE FRANK MUIR BOOK: AN IRREVERENT COMPANION TO SOCIAL HISTORY

THE OXFORD BOOK OF HUMOROUS PROSE

THE WALPOLE ORANGE

A KENTISH LAD

———

The Autobiography of
FRANK MUIR

BANTAM PRESS

LONDON · NEW YORK · TORONTO · SYDNEY · AUCKLAND

TRANSWORLD PUBLISHERS LTD
61–63 Uxbridge Road, London W5 5SA

TRANSWORLD PUBLISHERS (AUSTRALIA) PTY LTD
15–25 Helles Avenue, Moorebank, NSW 2170

TRANSWORLD PUBLISHERS (NZ) LTD
3 William Pickering Drive, Albany, Auckland

Published 1997 by Bantam Press
a division of Transworld Publishers Ltd
Copyright © by Frank Muir 1997

Reprinted 1997

'Red Sails in the Sunset', music by High Williams and words by
Jimmy Kennedy c. 1935, reproduced by permisssion of
Peter Maurice Co Ltd, London WC2H 0EA

A catalogue record for this book is available from the British Library.
ISBN 0593 03452X

Typeset in 11/13pt. Sabon by Falcon Oast Graphic Art
Printed in Great Britain by Mackays of Chatham PLC, Chatham, Kent

For the grandchildren.

Abigail and Gabriel Wheatcroft
Isobel Muir

To give them a whiff of how kind and colourful life
has been to Bummer.

CONTENTS

Unless otherwise stated, photographs are from the author's collection.

Chapter One

SMALL PLEASURES

Good holidays stick in the memory and I have complete recall of one trip which turned out to be quite perfect. I was travelling alone and I packed fussily with care and precision, emptying out my case and beginning again until all my holiday things lay in neat, un-ruffled order.

When the day of departure came at last I bade farewell to my loved ones, picked up my heavy case and off I went. I had three days of good food, late nights, sing-songs, games and laughter and then returned home with happy memories.

I was aged six. I had spent the holiday at the Derby Arms Hotel, Ramsgate, Kent, the pub in which I was born, which was 100 yards down the road and kept by my granny.

A pub is an excellent place for a holiday when you are young and impressionable. The Derby Arms was excitingly crowded and noisy on Friday and Saturday nights with a penny-in-the-slot mechanical piano plonking away and a great deal of loud singing of sad songs; the favourites in the public bar were 'Way Down Upon the Swanee River' and 'There's a Long, Long Trail A-Winding', both sung slowly and sorrowfully with deep feeling. The favourite tipples were pints of mild and bitter (a mixture of the two draught beers), stout, and, for ladies in funds, port and lemon (a tot of tawny port topped up with fizzy lemonade).

My brother Chas and I were not supposed to go into the bar, but we could see in and we would sneak in whenever possible to be nearer the action.

At weekends the bars were packed with sailors from the boarding houses up the hill and miners from Chislet colliery and Irish navvies working on the new railway line; there must have been some outbreaks of rowdyism and violent behaviour but I cannot remember seeing or hearing any in the years when I grew up there. Perhaps because the working man had just survived a war and was not taking his pleasure in a fight but in a bit of fun; the local pub was his equivalent of radio, TV, theatre, music hall and bingo – and his wife was usually with him. Another factor was that our granny had a glittering eye like the ancient mariner and a very powerful, indeed awesome personality when provoked.

The Derby Arms Hotel was well positioned for a pub, being on the outskirts of Ramsgate on the main road to Margate. Just along the road, McAlpine's built a huge brick viaduct to carry the express trains from London over the Margate road to the new Ramsgate station and my brother Chas and I watched it being built.

Better still, we watched when the viaduct was tested by a convoy of six enormous railway engines which, like a family of elephants, huffed and puffed backwards and forwards across the viaduct, hissing steam and blowing their whistles triumphantly. For two small boys – very heaven.

On the far side of the road to the pub stood a grey, granite horse trough, much appreciated in summertime by the huge shire-horses in the brewer's dray when the pub's beer was delivered. It was a long pull from the town. In the granite on the front of the trough a message was chiselled saying that it had been donated by a local resident, the creator of *The Scarlet Pimpernel*, Baroness Orczy.

To my delight, a beer delivery took place on the Saturday morning of my perfect holiday. The dray was backed up to the front of the pub and two enormous draymen, not so much born as drawn by Beryl Cooke, jumped down and hooked back the huge trapdoors in the pavement. A special squat and very strong ladder was then lowered into the cellar; this ladder did not have normal wooden rungs but curved iron bars, which allowed the heavy wooden barrels to be safely slid down.

In the cellar where I crouched, overexcited and probably half drunk from the heavy fumes of beer which permanently hung in the cellar air, all was cobwebs, bent lead piping running from the barrels to holes in the ceiling, wooden spigots and mallets, and a lot of dust.

The massive draymen rolled a barrel off their dray and slid it down the ladder where it thudded onto a sandbag at the bottom. Granny's cellarman Fred then manhandled the barrel up a little ramp onto its rack. Four full barrels were delivered and then the four empties were pulled up the ladder by Spanish windlass (a rope looped round the barrel's tummy with one of its ends fastened to the top of the ladder and the other hauled upon).

During my holiday the weather was warm and sunny and I was taken for walks. Facing the Derby Arms was an old sunken country lane which was my favourite walk. It led through cornfields gashed with scarlet poppies ('Don't lie down and fall asleep near the poppies or you'll be drugged by opium and never wake up'), past St Lawrence College, Ramsgate's public school, eventually coming out on the main road near the Brown Jug pub, Dumpton Park, nearly at Broadstairs. The lane had the ancient and melodious name of Hollicondane.

At the side of the Derby Arms was a road leading uphill to where the new railway station was being built with the help of my father, who had a little wooden hut all to himself and was putting up a mile stretch of iron railings alongside the station's approach road. The hilly road up which my father walked to work every morning went past what was, in the last century, a rough and quite danger-ous conglomeration of lowly boarding houses, slop shops and grocers called the Blue Mountains – a nickname almost certainly bestowed by Australian seamen from Sydney, which has a range of hills behind the city known as the Blue Mountains.

Until recently most pubs were called hotels and years ago they probably did provide accommodation of a modest 'commercial gentleman' nature. The Derby Arms Hotel could well have been built for that kind of trade.

Upstairs on the first floor there was a penny-in-the-slot loo for ladies, and my brother Chas and I, on our way up to bed or bath, grew used to making our way up the stairs alongside cheery ladies breathing out fumes of Mackeson's milk stout and hauling them-selves up by the bannisters towards comfort.

One afternoon I crept into the ladies' loo – utterly forbidden territory – to find out what mysteries lurked there, and managed to lock myself in. As the pub was closed and my granny was resting, I had to cry myself hoarse before rescue arrived.

On the floor above were some small chill bedrooms where commercial gentlemen might once have been thriftily accommodated. At the age of six I thought there were about fifty bedrooms up there, but as I grew older the number shrank to more realistic estimates, until one day I counted them and found that there were three bedrooms, plus a couple of tinier rooms which had a bath and a loo.

In these bathrooms, above each enamelled iron bath crouched a Ewart's 'Victor' geyser, a gas-fired engine of copper and brass which had to be operated with caution and bravery.

The lighting operation was an act of faith. It required a good supply of matches and an iron nerve. An arm had to be swung out from the belly of the machine and the pilot light on the end of it lit. It was reluctant to go 'plop' and produce its tiny blue flame and often had to be warmed up first, which might take half a box of Union Jack matches, though there was some compensation in that the matchbox had a joke on the back. (Sample joke on the back of a Union Jack matchbox: 'Mummy, mummy! Johnny's swallowed a sixpence!' Mother: 'That's all right, it's his dinner money.')

Then the lit pilot light had to be swung back into the stomach of the engine. This action opened up all the main gas jets which hissed threateningly for a moment and then, touched by the pilot flame, exploded with a great 'WHOOSH!' If you swung the arm in too slowly or – and I've never understood the scientific reason for this – if you swung the arm in too swiftly there could be an explosion which charred the eyebrows. Ever since those days I have never been happy putting a match to gas.

After a few minutes of gestation the geyser's nozzle began to deliver a thin trickle of steamy water at a temperature of about 2,000 degrees centigrade.

A huge room which must once have been the function room of the 'hotel' took up most of the first floor. It had a faintly Far Eastern smell to it, probably from the Chinese bits and pieces of furniture with which the room was stuffed: brass gong-like tables on fretworked teak folding legs; huge black-lacquered screens with mother-of-pearl cockatoos flying across them; faded little framed watercolours of junks on the Yellow River and distant mountains capped with snow. The oriental smell probably lasted because the windows seemed to be kept tightly shut even in mid-summer. During the ten years or so when I more or less lived in the Derby Arms I had the feeling that I was the only person who ever went into that room.

I loved the place. When I walked across the floor the joists creaked and the floorboards floated up and down beneath me like a stiffish trampoline. I found all sorts of treasures stacked away in cupboards. There was a fine large musical box which still worked beautifully. It was cranked up by a ratchet handle and offered six tunes, changeable by working a lever which urged the cylinder sideways a tenth of an inch so that a differently arranged set of pins was presented to the musical teeth.

One of the machine's sophisticated extras was a set of large graduated bells. When I had forgotten all about the bells and the box was delicately tinkling away delineating a waltz, a pin on the revolving cylinder would lift a bar of heavy clappers and drop them down onto the bells with a terrific jangle.

I found four enormous volumes of *A Pictorial History of the Great War*. Terribly gripping photographs of Somme trenches and howitzers and mud and early tanks shaped like rectangles squashed sideways.

I unearthed several albums of cigarette-card collections, depicting such excitements as famous British footballers with haircuts like Dr Crippen and long shorts down to mid-shin, and British racing cars painted racing green with spare cans of petrol clamped to their ample running-boards and bonnets buckled down with leather straps.

I came upon albums of early picture postcards, each card held in place by having its corners tucked into oblique slits in the album's black pages. The favourite subjects for the photographers and watercolourists seem to have been pretty girls with their hair piled high, Canterbury Cathedral, cottages with heavily floral front gardens and sailing ships crowded together in Ramsgate's inner harbour, their bare masts and complicated rigging making patterns as delicate as spiders' webs.

It was a mystery how Granny came to amass this odd collection of oriental oddments and local semi-collectibles and I suggested to my mother that they were bestowed by sailors in lieu of bar debts. For some reason my mother was horrified by this and pointed out that Granny's then current husband, known as Pop, was the engineer of a trading vessel plying the China Seas, and Pop had probably brought the Chinese bits home. Seemed a long way to transport furniture.

Pop turned up once or twice when he was a widower and my mother looked after him. He was a very fat man in a pale and crumpled tropical suit. I was greatly impressed by his revelation that he sweated so much in the Mystic East that an expensive leather watch strap rotted on his wrist in a few weeks, so he switched to knicker elastic.

He looked like the American movie villain Sidney Greenstreet, but I did not find him at all sinister. Like so many salts when ashore he flung money around freely, behaviour guaranteed to win the affection of any normally venal small boy.

If the character and shape of a growing lad is determined by a mixture of heredity and environment, then heredity from the maternal side of my family could have played only a small part. I am tall. I was once, some years ago, before I began to acquire a literary stoop, 6 feet 6 inches tall, and my son Jamie is even taller, and my daughter Sal is a good height, whereas my mother's side of the family were (except for my mother) shortish and on the plump side.

Granny was a splendid lady of great character but she was small and stout and she waddled. She had a remarkable goitre like a small dumpling poised on her shoulder, so impressive that it took considerable will-power not to keep looking at it. Granny was not a great eater or drinker but every evening she sipped a half-pint glass of fresh milk – only one – which she had previously spiked with an unspecified quantity of whisky.

Granny was a Cowie from Peterhead in Scotland. The Cowies had always been connected with the sea and sea-going folk. Granny's mother had kept a kind of up-market boarding house in Barking High Street, East London, where she accepted as guests only ships' captains and chief engineers, and our granny continued the maritime tradition, although the life of a sailor was frequently brief in those days. Granny's father, a ship's carpenter, was drowned when the *Union Castle* went down in May 1896. He left six Cowie children, four of them girls. Besides Granny, whose name was Elizabeth Jane, there was her sister Susan, also short and stout, who stayed with Granny most of her life and helped her run the Derby Arms.

During the First World War Susan became engaged to a Canadian who then took himself off to live in Tiverton, Devon. He exchanged letters with Susan regularly for many years, but Mr Green behaved more like a pen pal than an ardent suitor, which was probably just as well as after forty years of correspondence it emerged that he had been married all the time.

Then there was Vera, charmingly bulky, who married a chap with the splendid name of Captain Helmer Augustus Dilner and went off with him to make a home in New Zealand.

And finally there was Adelaide, known as Addie, a jolly lady and nice to have for a great-aunt. Like her bulky sisters, Addie was not avoirdupois-deprived; indeed she was immensely proportioned, with a one-piece bosom which was a cross between a French provincial hotel bolster and a sandbag. In the garden she would lie back in her deckchair and park her cup of tea on nature's shelf; no hands. Addie married Jack Turnage, an Anglo-Indian who was a foreman in a gun and shell factory in Calcutta and they went off to live in India.

Jack Turnage was amiable and kind and Chas and I were fascinated by his ear lobes, which were long and dangly like an elephant's. When I was grown up, Addie and Jack retired from India to a modest house they had built on Ramsgate's West Cliff and here Jack was able to go quietly doolally in comfort (when we called, he would take us aside and whisper that they were coming up through the cavity walls to get him).

Our granny, when aged twenty-one, married a ship's carpenter, aged twenty-four, named Harry Harding, who was a breakaway member of an ancient West Country family which had farmed at Cranmore, Somerset, since before the Norman invasion. The union produced my mother, Margaret (Madge), and then poor Harry Harding, like Granny's father, was lost at sea.

Granny did not languish long as a young widow. She soon married the son of an inspector of lighthouses for Trinity House, Frank Herbert Webber, after whom I was christened (I could have done without the Herbert). In fact Granny and Frank Herbert could not have been legally married as poor Harry Harding's whereabouts and death could never be established. But in 1909 the Webbers moved to Ramsgate and Frank Herbert became the licensee of the Derby Arms Hotel, and there they produced a half-sister and two half-brothers for my mother: my Aunt Mary, Uncle

Jack and Uncle Alex (my favourite of them all). All went well for ten years until in 1919, in the middle of the Spanish flu epidemic, Frank Herbert rather unwisely tried to shovel snow whilst wearing only trousers, shoes and a singlet. He caught flu and died.

Granny persuaded the magistrates that she, widow of the ex-licensee, was quite capable of running a decent, law-abiding public house by herself and she took over the Derby Arms and ran it trouble-free for twenty-two years, assisted in the bars by my mother, Margaret – known as Madge – my great-aunt Susan, and two employees, a French slave-of-all-works named Eugenie and, for the heavy work, a newly demobbed naval petty officer named Fred Pearce.

Meanwhile, in the superior boarding-house in Barking High Street, a young marine engineer from New Zealand booked in. His name was Charles James Muir and he was my father. He and his sister Rose had been orphaned in New Zealand when they were quite young and had to strike out for themselves. My father went to sea as a ship's engineer (a profession which at that time seemed to have consisted almost entirely of Scotsmen), and my Aunt Rose went to work in Christchurch Hospital in a lowly capacity, probably heaving a bumper across the ward lino to bring up a polish. She ended up Superintendent of the Hospital MBE, re-membered by the Rose Muir Society for Nurses, which she founded, and a stained-glass window in the hospital chapel celebrating her contribution to nursing in New Zealand.

In the boarding house in Barking, young C. J. Muir caught a glimpse of the landlady's granddaughter, Margaret Harding, and that was that. He pursued her to the Derby Arms in Ramsgate, wooed her between voyages to and from New Zealand and they were married in St Luke's Church, Ramsgate, in 1916. Chas was born in 1918 and I in 1920.

Dad was tall. He was a lean 6 feet 1½ inches and he was gifted with accomplishments that were dazzlingly impressive to a small son: he could cut hair, repair socks, name the stars, do a little tap-dancing and he never lost his temper or shouted or complained. He was also rather good-looking, as was my mother. I am allowed to say this because physical traits notoriously jump a generation.

Dad found that life with his family was infinitely preferable to life on the ocean wave and he left the sea.

The Muir family moved out of the Derby Arms and along the

road into Thanet Lodge, a pleasant but elderly and inconvenient little house, though with a garden. My mother had to cook on a neurotic kitchen range of great age which needed frequent stoking, and there was an old-fashioned 'copper' in a corner which had to be filled by saucepans and was heated from beneath by a small bonfire. On laundry days, or when a pudding needed a boil-up, a match was put to the bonfire. About an hour later the water began to hubble and bubble, all the windows steamed up and the whole house dripped with condensation.

On the opposite corner of the road to the Derby Arms stood a tiny sweetshop which was owned by my mother, bought with help from Granny. This yielded a small but steady income, very welcome as the depression of the Thirties built up.

It was a bad time for my father to have made his move away from the sea. Jobs on land were increasingly difficult to find and the only work available to him was in unskilled occupations like working on Ramsgate's new railway extension or loading stores onto naval vessels lying off-shore from the First World War 'mystery port' of Richborough. It was called the 'mystery port' (a military secret known to everyone in Ramsgate) because it was the main port from which ammunition, guns and tanks were shipped to France.

For Chas and me those were happy days. One of our occasional pleasant chores was to walk up the hill past the Blue Mountains to the railway site where Dad was putting up his railings and take him his tea makings. This was a spill of greaseproof paper containing a stiffish, unlovely-looking pudding of tea leaves, sugar and condensed milk. In his little hut Dad would boil up an enormous iron kettle, scrape the mixture into a large mug, add boiling water from the kettle and stir the brew into fragrant life.

I have never drunk tea since.

Mother was busy working in the pub and the sweetshop, so she would occasionally hire a very sweet, plump, young local girl named Edie Budd as a minder for Chas and me. Edie would take us for walks along Hollicondane ('I keep telling you, don't lie down near the poppies') or a splash about in the sea from a bathing machine on Ramsgate sands. It was all a bit Dickensian – a family with hardly any money hiring a girl for a few coppers who had no money at all, but it worked amiably.

Edie was a member of a fervent Pentecostal sect in Ramsgate and asked Mother whether she could take Chas and me to a service one

Sunday morning. Mother was delighted to get us out of the house so that she could get on with cooking Sunday lunch, so off we went with Edie.

The vocal enthusiasm of the congregation and the charismatic nature of the service made a deep impression on Chas and me. So much so that back home, halfway through lunch, Chas suddenly leaped to his feet and declaimed very loudly, 'Alleluia!' Then he sat down leaving our two stunned parents looking at each other.

Not to be outdone and now well in the mood of the meeting, a few minutes later I too leaped to my feet, eyes shining with zeal. 'God be praised!' I announced ringingly. 'Can I have another potato?'

On non-Edie days the railway construction depot up the hill provided excellent play facilities; there were tall heaps of sand to run up and down and flatten, bags of cement to jump on and kick into grey clouds, heavy nuts and bolts to hurl at the watchman's hut, and, best of all, an old, slow-moving and bad-tempered watchman to provoke.

One evening Mother asked us what plans we had for the morning. We said, 'We're going to the builders' depot to play with the Bugger-Off Man.'

So much for the influence of heredity. Not much influence, really, or I should be walking with a waddle, sporting a goitre, or at least be able to break into a tap-dance, but all these accomplishments are alien, so perhaps the stronger influence on me when a toddler was environmental; it was being a Kentish lad growing up in Ramsgate and Broadstairs which did the damage.

Towns, like strangers, often seem dull and unattractive at first but become interesting the more one learns about them. Ramsgate is like that. Nowadays one thinks of it as vaguely seaside, something to do with cross-Channel ferries and hovercraft, with a good harbour (some may perhaps even remember that this was a rallying point for the Dunkirk 'little ship' armada), on the whole not a very exciting place. But it was quite a town in its day.

In Tudor times it was a humble fishing village of about two dozen hovels clustered, as with most of the East Kent towns, round the sea end of a natural cleft in the chalk cliffs. This cleft was enlarged to allow carts first to haul catches of fish inland and later to carry into the hinterland much more lucrative goods.

By the eighteenth century the town was beginning to grow and to prosper modestly, due to the development of trade with the Baltic, Europe and Russia, to good fishing, but mostly to the most profitable trade of all – smuggling.

Everybody seemed to be in on smuggling. The gentry, farmers, professionals and tradesmen put up the working capital and they (with the clergy) were the customers. It was a good investment; it has been said that almost every house of any size built along the coast of Thanet in those days was paid for with the profits of smuggling. The actual heavy work on the beach at night – loading the casks and cases onto packhorses, avoiding the occasional officer of the Preventive Service, leading the train of horses up the steep cleft and on to an inland hiding place – was done by farm labourers only too happy to oblige at the going rate of three times their day wage.

A kind of highly profitable reverse smuggling also went on around Ramsgate and the Romney Marshes area in which high-quality, raw English wool, a carefully controlled export much sought after by continental weavers, was smuggled *out* by specialist wool smugglers known as 'owlers'.

There were two extraordinary things about this nationwide criminal activity; firstly it seemed to carry with it no pangs of guilt; almost everybody who could afford to drink tea, which was heavily taxed in England, bought smuggled tea. And secondly, although smuggling was losing the government enormous sums in revenue, the politicians of the day never bothered to tackle the problem seriously. In the eighteenth century there were only fifty mounted revenue officers to patrol the whole length of the Kent coast, ludicrously few when the smugglers could assemble pony trains of 200 armed men.

In the eighteenth century the business of smuggling was called, without irony, 'free trade'. A rather more legitimate source of prosperity enjoyed by Ramsgate in the middle of the eighteenth century came with the invention of the British seaside holiday.

Until the middle 1700s, waves and mountains were not regarded as objects of natural beauty but as dangerous and boring obstructions which the traveller had to endure to get where he wanted to go. Then all this changed. The grand tourists began to enjoy the 'picturesque view' and the medical profession invented the seaside.

Up to the 1750s, citizens suffering from scrofula and various other unsightly diseases were prescribed a course of the waters, which meant taking rooms at a fashionable spa such as Bath or Royal Tunbridge Wells and enjoying a regime of dunking the unsightly body in a public bath of hot spring water claimed to be 'chalybeate' (not a word which passes the lips daily, meaning 'containing iron') and reeking of sulphurous salts, and then drinking a pint or so of the revolting stuff from a fountain.

The trouble with going to a fashionable spa for treatment was that it was like going to a modern health farm: far too expensive for the average citizen with a spotty back. But the sea was free and much more hygienic than cruising around in a hot bath with a batch of other skin diseases.

So wallowing in the briny, which began at Brighton as remedial treatment for the afflicted, became fun for the whole family. The great British seaside holiday was born.

The Isle of Thanet became London's seaside; its three key resorts being Margate, Broadstairs and Ramsgate. The pioneer town of the three was Margate, England's first seaside resort of any consequence. It was the nearest of the three towns to London, so it appealed to rich Londoners travelling by coach and to the poorer East Enders who arrived by the cheapest form of transport, boat. Margate was on the Thames estuary side of the North Foreland and so holidaymakers did not have to endure the boisterous seas which visitors sailing round the headland to Broadstairs and Ramsgate had to endure.

Large, pleasant houses were built at Margate for the *ton*, the town had (and still has) England's second oldest theatre, and bookshops and concert halls abounded. It had a long sandy beach, a sea-bathing infirmary, and it was a Margate Quaker, Benjamin Beale, who invented the 'modesty hood' to fit onto bathing machines. Bathing machines were a breakthrough in seaside decorum, consisting of a horse-drawn changing hut on wheels with Mr Beale's canvas hood at the back. The thing was towed by its horse into the shallows, enabling the lady within to change into her bathing costume, climb down a short ladder and cavort discreetly beneath Mr Beale's canopy in her own little bit of sea without the embarrassment of her wet flannel costume clinging to her form and revealing her intimate bumps and dents.

Gentlemen bathed stark naked further along the beach.

By the early nineteenth century Margate had changed

considerably, moving firmly downmarket; perhaps because the new railways were demonstrating that the big profits came not from milord in his own coach strapped to a wagon, but in the masses crammed onto wooden benches in trucks. Much cheaper accommodation was built and Margate became the seaside success story for the working man and his family.

East End Londoners mostly travelled to Margate by the cheapest and most uncomfortable of small packet-boats, the common hoy (hoy polloi?).

Charles Lamb, aged fifteen, went for a happy week's holiday to Margate with his cousin and later recalled the humble voyage (fare – 2 shillings 6 pence) in his essay, 'The Old Margate Hoy' ('Can I forget thee, thou old Margate Hoy, with thy weather-beaten, sun-burnt captain, and his rough accommodations – ill-exchanged for the foppery and fresh-water niceness of the modern steam packet? . . . Not many rich, not many wise, or learned, composed at that time the common stowage of a Margate packet').

Broadstairs was the permanently genteel town of the three Thanet resorts, appealing strongly to the middle classes and those who wanted to be thought of as middle class, like Mr Pooter who referred affectionately to the town in *Diary of a Nobody* as 'good old Broadstairs'.

It was hardly a resort – no fairground with big dipper, or on the other social level no golf links either – but it did have a Grand Hotel and a pleasant, curved bay and a bandstand and a bit of a pier and a minstrel show on the beach, and it developed a reputation for its healthy sea air so it became a popular site for convalescent homes and expensive preparatory schools; many a union leader recovered his voice in his union's red-brick, neo-Gothic convalescent home on a Broadstairs cliff top, and many a minor royal and future duke began his schooling being walloped in a Broadstairs prep school.

Further lustre was added to the town's reputation when Charles Dickens found it a placid place in which to write. He frequently stayed and worked at the Royal Albion Hotel (still going strong) and at Bleak House, an odd building like a small Scottish baronial castle which overlooked the harbour. At the time it was called Fort House but the name was changed to Bleak House when the novel became successful. It is now a Dickens museum.

Of the three Thanet resorts serving London it was Ramsgate

which managed to be the most comprehensive socially, offering an *Upstairs, Downstairs* arrangement of suitable holidays for both the rich and the non-rich.

The less well-off were tempted with a long, safe, free beach, an army of bathing machines, Punch and Judy shows, donkeys for children to ride, lots of pubs, bracing sea air, inexpensive boarding houses and a view of sailing ships constantly beating up and down the busy Downs (the slightly sheltered waters between the seashore and Goodwin Sands). And early in the century the uncomfortable voyage by hoy was superseded by the railway. Trains from London emerged dramatically from a tunnel cut in the chalk cliffs and disgorged their holidaymakers a few yards from the seafront. Later a new station was built on the edge of the town and the old seashore terminus became a funfair, Merrie England.

Unlike Margate, Ramsgate kept its hold on the affections of the wealthy. Elegant Georgian terraces were built on the East Cliff top, Nelson Crescent, Albion Place, Paragon Place, and well-to-do London merchants took to wintering in fashionable Ramsgate. And during the summer season their good ladies, after a discreet dip from their bathing machine, could drink their (smuggled) tea, tuck up their (smuggled) lace cuffs and enjoy their game of whist far away from both the citizens of Ramsgate, described by a lady visitor from London in a letter home as 'the smelly inhabitants', and the seething crowd of holidaymaking 'Arry and 'Arriets on the beach below, a busy scene captured by Frith in his hugely popular painting of 1853, *Ramsgate Sands*.

It was claimed that King George IV actually deserted his beloved Brighton one summer for a holiday at Ramsgate but I can find no proof of that; however, the monarch did graciously condescend to visit Ramsgate in 1821 when he disembarked from a visit to Hanover. The town fathers, in ecstasies, had 100 tons of Dublin granite fashioned into a copy of a classical obelisk and erected to commemorate this widely unpopular king's gouty foot touching down on Ramsgate soil. Local townspeople referred to the obelisk as the 'Royal Toothpick'.

During my childhood, trams used to grind noisily up and clatter noisily down Madeira Walk, the steep winding hill which descended rapidly from the rich terraces of the East Cliff through an ornamental chine to the harbour. I remember when very young being shown the sharp corner where, I was told, a tram had once jumped the tramlines, tipped over the edge and plunged down into somebody's back garden. I could never pass that corner again without an enjoyable little frisson.

Other frisson-inducers in my early years included the unhygienic-looking iron mug chained to the drinking fountain in Ellington Park, from which, I was informed, a boy of my age had recently caught the Black Death; a synagogue – actually a Jewish seminary and college set up by the Montefiore family – lying behind high walls on the road to Broadstairs where, my brother Chas told me, Jews used to be flogged until they agreed to give all their money to the roller-skating rink along the road and become Christians; and being christened at the age of seven, the ceremony having been postponed because my father was at sea when I was born. I was a bit old to be christened, but queuing up with the babies at the font was not so embarrassing in retrospect as was my appearance. The solemn ceremony marked the first occasion on which I faced the world with my hair stiff and glossy from a generous handful of Field's Lavender Solidified Brilliantine.

King George IV was not the only person of high consequence to enjoy the pleasures of Ramsgate. In 449 AD, Hengist and Horsa (their names translate as 'The Horse Brothers') led the first Teutonic invasion of the island, setting sail from Jutland and landing on a beach, Ebbsfleet, to the west of Ramsgate. The Horse Brothers were followed in 597 AD by Augustine (later St Augustine), sent by Pope Gregory to bring Christianity and Latin verbs to our Isles. Augustine and forty monks managed to achieve this peacefully and he became the first Archbishop of Canterbury.

Princess Victoria, before becoming Queen Victoria, enjoyed a number of visits to Ramsgate, staying at many of the fine houses and meeting everyone of substance. The town also had its odd eccentric resident, such as Sir William Curtis, Bt., who built his estate, Cliff House, on Sion Hill, a splendid site overlooking the harbour. Sir William, a 'very badly educated Tory', made a huge fortune from manufacturing sea biscuits in Wapping. He became Lord Mayor of London and was famous in his day, rather like Lord and Lady Docker were in the 1960s, for his conspicuous wealth. His sumptuously fitted yacht was particularly marked out for mockery by Whig wits. King George IV, though, enjoyed many a luxurious cruise with his rich friend and stayed at Cliff House, Ramsgate, in 1821 when he returned from Hanover.

Another resident, less noble and rich, who made his mark on Ramsgate was the great Gothic revival architect and designer, Augustus Pugin, perhaps most famous for working with Barry as designer of decorations and statues for the Houses of Parliament. Pugin built himself a Gothic house in Ramsgate with its own little church. He was converted to Roman Catholicism in 1833 and made his church into a kind of abbey. His house and the church – St Augustine's, Ramsgate's first Roman Catholic church – are still there, faced with glistening black flints. Pugin died at his house in Ramsgate, insane.

And then there was young Vincent Van Gogh. In 1876 the somewhat muddled young Dutchman, aged twenty-three, recovering from unrequited love for his London landlady's daughter and uncertain whether to become a pastor like his father or an evangelist amongst the working classes, moved to Ramsgate and was taken on as a teacher in a small impoverished school with twenty-eight pupils, run by a Mr Stokes. For four months Van Gogh taught some of the young of Ramsgate their mathematics, French and geography.

My friend Michael Meyer pointed out to me that Mr Stokes almost certainly could not have afforded atlases for the geography lessons, so somewhere in Ramsgate there is probably an old gentleman whose father tucked away in the attic a sketch map of Mesopotamia drawn by Vincent Van Gogh.

Before he left England and went back to Holland leaving school-teaching for more creative pursuits, Van Gogh drew a charming little pen-and-ink sketch entitled *Vue de la fenêtre de l'École. Ramsgate, 31 mai 1876.*

The first school my brother and I went to was not unlike Mr Stokes's academy. Ours was about the same size, was called Thyra House School and its proprietor, headmaster and 50 per cent of its staff was a Mr Rule. Mr Rule, a heavily built man with a Bavarian accent, had a look about him of Field Marshal von Hindenburg, so when the First World War broke out he prudently changed the spelling of his name from Ruhl to Rule.

Chas and I used to walk to school, and a fair way away it was, too, for a couple of ex-toddlers. We would toil up the hill from the Derby Arms to what was the flour mill at the top and down the other side to South Eastern Road where Thyra House was, pausing to hurl a potato in a desultory sort of way at the front door of an old lady who lived in a row of houses on the left pavement. If we scored a hit the lady would hurtle out of her door shaking her fist at us and screeching. It was the kind of mindless bad behaviour which most children seem to enjoy for a while. Perhaps she, too, came to enjoy it as part of life's rich pattern because she never seriously tried to catch us.

The other 50 per cent of Thyra House School's staff was a thin, almost transparent lady who pedalled the harmonium with spirit and taught us to sing hymns, her favourite being 'You in Your Small Corner and I in Mine'. Chas was good at hymns and was nominated Best Singer. I was nominated Best Opener (opening the mouth wide was a much-esteemed virtue in Thyra House hymn-singing). Years later I was delighted to find that the French for 'small corner', *petit coin*, was a popular euphemism in France for the lavatory.

It was in the middle of an arithmetic lesson at Thyra House, taken by the headmaster himself, that I discovered the enormous satisfaction that came from creating laughter and it became the main aim of my working life.

I was sitting at a double desk with a plump fellow scholar who was almost asleep with boredom. To cheer him up I made a humorous remark. He sniggered and whispered what I had said to the boy behind him and he sniggered too.

Mr Rule's fat hairy forefinger bent in a beckoning movement and I slid out from my desk and stood next to him, clutching my pencil, knuckles white with fear.

'Muir, you were talking in class again. That is not permitted, heh? Vill you kindly repeat aloud vat you said to Leatherbarrow? It is fair, is it not, that you share your vit vith all of us?'

'Please, sir,' I mumbled, 'I said, "This pencil top is sir's bum."'

The roomful of children erupted in joyful mirth. It was an intoxicating moment. I had made the whole school laugh.

It might be thought that it was not really much of a joke on which to base a career. It was not even remotely witty, and it was hardly comedy of observation; my pencil top was only half a centimetre in diameter and held one of those useless pink rubbers which smear pencil marks without erasing them, whilst sir was what Americans call a 'lardbutt'; his behind was about a metre wide. But the roomful of children laughed at what I had said and my destiny was fixed.

Chapter Two

BEACH BOY

The parents suddenly upped sticks from Ramsgate and moved to Broadstairs, settling into a pleasant rented house named Fernbank. The move probably came about because Dad had been offered a reasonably good job with McAlpine's, helping to build a factory up in Selby, Yorkshire.

Then things began to go wrong. My father caught pneumonia rather seriously and my mother went up to Yorkshire to nurse him. My brother and I were looked after by Mother's sister Mary and her husband Len (Chas and I were pages in daffodil-coloured satin at their wedding. Yellow Pages?).

Mother was away for months and when she and Dad returned to Broadstairs their savings had all gone and Dad was none too strong. Uncle Len came to the rescue. He had opened a shop near Broadstairs railway station selling electrical goods and was building a business based on the new craze – listening to the wireless.

Dad became an installer of sets and aerials for Uncle Len. He rode around Broadstairs on a curious vehicle called a 'Ner-a-Car', not unlike the outcome of a liaison between a motor scooter and a sway-backed motorbike. Its main feature was a large storage box under the rider's legs, large enough to hold tools and bits of wireless sets.

Wireless was a growth industry and for years things went well for Uncle Len and Dad. One weekend Dad brought home the makings of a crystal set and put it together. I remember moveable coils like a pair of ears, glowing valves, the 'cat's whisker' (very important component), which was a piece of fine wire moved about by a little lever, and the 'mighty atom', a tiny lump of quartz glinting in the light. The quartz was probed by the 'cat's whisker' until a station was located and we could listen to it through the heavy black earphones (two members of the family per headset).

The excitement when Dad first tuned in and we heard sounds coming to us through the air *without wires* was terrific. Never mind that we knew perfectly well the transmission came from the North Foreland Lighthouse a mile up the road and was only a few dots and dashes of morse code – it was magic to us.

We moved to a newish rented bungalow, Adstone, on Linden Avenue, where Mother was able to take in lodgers during the summer season. Chas and I much enjoyed our lodgers, who made a change to our routine. We particularly liked a Mr Sumner and family who were most amiable and came year after year.

With the extra money coming in from the guests, Mother was able to cover the bungalow's floors (almost but not quite wall to wall) with grey haircord, an inexpensive form of carpet which was attractive enough to look at and hard-wearing. Walking on it in bare feet was like strolling across Brillo pads, but the carpet was my mother's pride: people like us – I suppose lower middle class hoping to become middle middle class – did not have carpets in those days, we had bare floorboards, varnished, or lino and rugs.

In keeping with my new role as the family jester, Chas gave me for my birthday a joke ink blot, a piece of metal pressed into the shape of a large shiny blot of Stephen's blue-black ink and suitably coloured. It was startlingly realistic.

Sniggering with excitement I laid it on Mother's new carpet, put an empty ink bottle on its side beside the blot and called out, 'Quick, Mother! I've had an accident!'

Mother shot in from the kitchen, took in the sight of the ink bottle on its side and the large blot on her beautiful new carpet and gave me a whack round the back of my head with her wedding-ring finger which sent me ricocheting off three walls.

This would probably have won her fourteen days hard labour in Holloway Prison in these enlightened times but it was exactly the right treatment then. I have hated the lurking sadism of practical joking ever since.

Adstone had a brick shed at the end of the garden where we could make things. I built a writing desk from plywood with a sloping front, but I was never able to use it: I unthinkingly painted it with a particularly pungent creosote and nobody was ever able to get closer than 6 feet to it.

Our real life was the beach. Or rather 'the sands'; it was rarely called 'the beach' in those days. When we were not at school we were playing on the sands, and swimming. Well-off visitors hired tents for changing and we soon knew which tents were not hired and could be used free by us, though they were hardly luxury accommodation; the green canvas tents were, whatever the weather, oddly airless and smelled heavily of linseed oil and pee.

Swimming costumes were not chic in the late 1920s. Chaps wore a black affair or one with a horizontally striped upper half and a black lower half with an imitation belt with a rusty buckle in between. A semi-exciting design innovation was large decorative holes below the normal armholes. In those days it was the chaps, not the girls, who wore a tiny modesty skirt on the front of their costumes. Made more sense, really.

Swimming caps were definitely *de rigueur*. If you were a swift swimmer, played water polo and were proud of your crawl, you wore a brightly coloured rubber skullcap like half a football bladder. If you were a distance man you wore a heavy black rubber helmet, about a quarter of an inch thick, which had black rubber earpieces vulcanized on. The difficulty was that you really had to be fitted for these. I occasionally found such a helmet abandoned in the sand, but the earpieces never quite coincided with my ears and agony ensued.

The quality of the bathing was hardly Cap Ferrat standard, not that we minded or even noticed (or had even heard of Cap Ferrat). The water normally had a healthy English Channel chill to it and was grey and semi-opaque with bits of dead seaweed and grains of sand swirling about in it.

If you were unlucky enough to be swimming when the *Perseverence*, a large, open, ex-fishing boat, moved away from the jetty in a wide sweep taking visitors on a shilling sick-round-the-bay, for the rest of the morning you swam in and swallowed petrol-flavoured sea water.

I was never a fast swimmer. I developed a labour-saving technique based on an ancient stroke called the 'trudgeon' which seems to have disappeared from the seaside swimmer's repertoire. In my version I lay floating on top of the water face down, occasionally giving little frog-like twitches of the legs as in the breaststroke whilst performing a lazy arm movement on my side as in the sidestroke. These dabs at propulsion through the water occurred only every few minutes and then in as gentle and energy-conserving a manner as possible. Although not yet in my teens, and thin with it, I could swim like this non-stop for an impressive three or four hours at a go. Unless there was a current running I hardly moved from the same spot.

I had lots of friends on the sands and after a swim we would dry off, throw ourselves face down on our towels in a star formation, heads together, and natter away for hours. I would try to make the others laugh, not with comical voices and jokes but with comical notions. I cannot remember these being very successful but neither can I remember any of my friends actually hitting me.

A large proportion of our chat was concerned with sex. We all knew with rough accuracy what happened in the process which Alan Bennett described in a play as 'the docking manoeuvre', but like most boys of our age we spoke out on all the more intricate and subtle nuances of lovemaking with the bold authority assumed by those anxious to hide their pig-ignorance.

One cherished fragment of sex-lore amongst our group was that any Belgian or French girl student who wore a gold cross on a chain was easy game. Easy game for *what* was not clear to us younger members of the group, but we cried, 'Yes, aren't they!' and leered along with the big boys.

The only one of us who achieved an, as it were, 'hands on' experience with a girl student was a senior member of our group. He had taken a French girl to the concert party at the Bohemia theatre in the High Street, which must have been a baffling enough experience for her, during which he established some sort of fleshly contact. He started out telling us the story of his achievement with a kind of boastful enthusiasm, but then this tailed off into a slightly embarrassed mumbling. He had become fond of the girl.

One chilly morning I rose enormously in my group's estimation by becoming the first of us to see a female nipple. Both of the pair, what is more, and only inches away from my nose.

Speculation as to what a girl's bosom actually looked like has fascinated growing lads all over the world, it seems. A few years ago I was on a plane to Mauritius with my wife Polly, who was born there, when an elderly American leaped to his feet, his brow knotted with worry, and shouted above the engines, 'Does anybody here know the lines which follow "Twas brillig, and the slithy toves . . .'?

I did know ('Did gyre and gimble in the wabe; All mimsy were the borogoves, And the mome raths outgrabe'). So I bawled the rest of Lewis Carroll's extremely odd little verse to him and he sank back in his seat, at peace with the world again. I met him later on a beach in Mauritius and learned that his name was Dillon Ripley and he was Secretary Emeritus of the Smithsonian Institution in Washington and probably America's most distinguished ornithologist.

At the time Mr Ripley and I were sitting under one of those thatched parasols on a Mauritian beach, contemplating with aesthetic pleasure a very pretty Italian girl bouncing and jiggling along the beach, dressed entirely in what appeared to be a short piece of string.

'When I was a schoolboy at the beginning of this century,' Mr Ripley said reflectively, 'the entire boyhood of America thought that female breasts were brown.'

'Brown?' I ventured.

'Dark brown,' said Mr Ripley. 'You see, the only breasts American boys ever got to look at in those days were photographs of Far-Eastern tribes in the dentist's waiting-room copy of the *National Geographic* magazine.'

My own first glimpse of the erotic zones happened at Broadstairs when I was busy saving their owner's life.

There were two life-saving measures in force at that time for the preservation of Broadstairs bathers. Somewhere in the bay a small ancient rowing boat was anchored, with a retired salt of great age slumped asleep over the oars. This was known as the safety boat. There was also an anchored raft in the middle of the bay which not only provided a useful resting place for tired swimmers, but also gave purpose to a quick dip; one swam out to the raft, dragged oneself aboard, got one's breath back and then dived off again and swam back to the shore.

On that fateful morning there was a cool breeze blowing across the bay and the water was choppy and chilly. The rest of our group did not fancy swimming so wandered off and busied themselves with another healthy boyish activity on dry land, namely filling empty Andrews Liver Salts tins with thin strips of cordite, used during the war for projecting naval shells and still being washed up on the sands, and sealing the tins to make bombs which exploded most satisfactorily when thrown on somebody else's bonfire.

I was gazing vaguely at the horizon, the way you do when you are at the seaside and cannot think of anything better to do, when I noticed the head of a swimmer bobbing up and down in the choppy water. The bobbing head was making for the raft and seemed to be at the end of a long swim round the jetty. I heard a faint feminine cry for help in a foreign tongue and the head disappeared for a moment or two.

I swiftly removed my shirt and shorts, and now clad only in my swimming costume with the chic four armholes and the rusty buckle, I sprinted to the water's edge. I then sprinted back, took off my wristwatch and laid it on my towel. I went through the same routine with my leather sandals and then I plunged into the cold water and made for the struggling swimmer. In no time at all I had reached the raft. This speed through the water was not because I had up-graded my style from the trudgeon to the crawl, but because the tide was out, the raft was only in 4 feet of water and I could wade to it.

The swimmer was a girl and she really was a bit distressed, gasping for breath, uttering little foreign whimpers and clearly tired. Quite pretty.

'It's all right, madame,' I said, speaking very loudly because I thought she was probably French, 'you're safe now, I've got you.' I swivelled her face-up in the water and held her under the armpits as I had seen the Sea Scouts do in life-saving practice. 'Upsy-daisy!' I cried, trying to get her up onto the raft.

I don't know exactly what happened, but in the course of trying to pull and push her across the edge of the raft her swimming costume was rolled down to her waist.

I stared, goggle-eyed, I am afraid, at this revelation of secret feminine anatomy. My knowledge of what a nipple looked like had been until then largely conjectural, based on saucy stories in furtive American collegiate magazines ('Greg took off his catcher's mitt and slid his hand inside Fran's bra. Her erect nipple bored into the palm of his hand like a flint arrowhead. "Greg, no!" she hissed urgently . . .'). Suddenly I was unexpectedly face to face with the naked reality.

Her breasts (smallish, both about the same size) were not brown like those in the *National Geographic*, but extremely white with a touch of blue due to the cold, and they were slightly puckered from being too long in the water. Her nipples were, rather surprisingly, not brown either but a bluish-greenish colour and wrinkled by the cold water. They were not unlike dried olives.

Teeth chattering but rested, she thanked me charmingly in French for helping her (at least I think she did), pulled up her costume without any self-consciousness, slipped back into the water and swam competently towards the shore.

I waded to the shore, mind spinning, determined not to share with the others my warm and wonderful, very personal experience. Though I eventually gave them an edited version.

One thing about growing up at the seaside in Broadstairs was that come summertime there was little point in going elsewhere for a holiday. I did not 'go away' for a holiday until I was married; up until then there seemed no better place to be on holiday than Broadstairs sands.

Early on in my years as a beach boy I was wrenched away from the sands and taken into the countryside for a day's outing; it was my first close encounter with nature and I was not happy with it.

The occasion was part of a money-making scheme I had going. Our local parish church needed choirboys; it seems they were constantly defecting or metamorphosing into baritones, and the going rate for the job was 5s. a quarter (£1 a year!) so I rushed to join. I have no singing voice as listeners to radio's *My Music* will sympathetically agree, but my proven skill at opening impressed the organist and I was taken on. I turned up religiously (an entirely inappropriate adverb) and hung on to my financial bonanza by lurking in the shadows a lot in church and, during hymn and anthem singing, miming.

But nobody warned me that there was an annual choir outing into the countryside.

For this the vicar traditionally hired a brake, an ancient, Edwardian, horse-drawn, bus-like vehicle which had plodded along for many years between Ramsgate and Pegwell Bay, carrying passengers who were in no hurry, until it became so unroadworthy that no horse could be persuaded to pull it on a regular basis. I sat on a plank seat on the uncovered top deck, well away from authority, happy to be lumbering slowly towards the Kent village of Pluck's Gutter (what magical names these old hamlets have, to be sure).

We arrived late at the meadow where we were to have our picnic lunch because the elderly horse turned bolshie just north of Deal and slowed down to about 1 m.p.h., but the vicar soon had us debussed and sitting in a circle round him on the meadow grass, clutching our official-issue brawn sandwiches.

'Choir!' he cried, ringingly, revolving slowly like a lighthouse so that his words would reach us all in turn. 'Most of your days are spent in the town or playing about on ugly sand. Today is your holiday from all that. Today, Choir, you are in the heart of Beautiful Nature!' In which case, one fake chorister's unspoken thought was, the sooner the holiday is over and we are back to ugly sand the better.

If you are uncomfortable sitting on sand you just wiggle a bit and the sand adjusts itself to the shape of your bottom. Nature does not do this. You sit on a tussock in a Pluck's Gutter meadow and what happens? You wiggle a bit and a needle-sharp piece of long grass goes up the leg of your shorts. You shift sideways to assuage the agony and the suspiciously warm patch on which you are now sitting is a reminder that this is a pasture on which sheep have safely grazed.

Nature, of which the countryside unfortunately has a lot, is not only carpeted with needle-sharp grass and prickly flora which scratches your ankles and becomes lodged in the buckles of your sandals, but is also full of dangerous fauna. The seaside has its little bits of fauna too, but these are harmless and frequently edible, e.g., shrimps.

At the seaside insect life is benign, just a few little hopping things in the sand. Nature, on the other hand, harbours whole regiments of malevolent predators whose teeth cause damage and pain far in excess of the tiny beasts' size and fighting weight.

For anybody collecting this kind of scientific data I am able to report that during about seventy minutes spent in a Kent meadow (the Garden of England) sitting unknowingly on firmish sheep droppings, the following occurred: a very large and shiny black bug, seemingly in drink, flew erratically backwards and forwards in front of me and then thudded into my forehead. A weal arose. A colony of ants invaded my lower legs and scurried about, biting; about 200,000 very small red marks appeared. A cricket levitated in front of me and dropped down the front of my shirt, causing me to utter a thin girlish scream. A squadron of large horseflies with hairy legs and metallic-blue tummies settled on my lunch. I threw away my brawn sandwich.

Soon after that hapless outing, to prevent recurrences I sought out the vicar and resigned from the choir, which came as a surprise to the vicar as he had no idea that I was in it. I did not sever all my connections with the church, though. I contributed 'The Mystery of the Tree Trunk, an Exciting Adventure Serial', to the parish magazine. Like all parish magazines of those days it had a properly printed section dealing with Christian issues, and another inserted section of local interest produced in purple ink on a jellygraph by a churchwarden. This latter section was where my serial appeared, although 'appeared' is hardly the word, as in most issues, due to hot weather hardening the jelly, my contribution was partly or wholly illegible.

It was all rather sad because I much enjoyed writing the serial. It was an ordinary kind of story; some children fell down a hole in a hollow tree trunk and happened upon some Chinese airmen who were villainous dope-smugglers (to me 'dope' meant the pungent spirit which the RAF used to spray on their Sopwith fighter planes to tighten the fabric). I did not plan the story ahead, it just lurched from episode to episode. Unfortunately I never found out how it ended. Owing to lack of support in the parish, the magazine went out of business after four issues, the only time I have ever heard of a parish magazine going bust.

My interest in both reading and trying to write was awakened back in the Ramsgate days when I did well in an exam at Thyra House School and my granny gave me a book prize, the first book I had ever wholly owned. It was a highly popular volume in its day with well-drawn, sensitive illustrations: *The Story of a Red Deer* (1897) by the Hon. Sir John Fortescue KCVO.

As the title suggests, it was the story of a red deer. I read it very slowly, almost learning it by heart as I went, savouring every twist of the story, every description, and believing totally in the reality of the animal. Unfortunately Sir John did a Walt Disney and killed off the deer at the end. I did not actually blub because I was getting on a bit by then, rising seven, but I had a painful lump in my throat for about three weeks afterwards whenever I remembered the noble beast's sad end.

Two or three years later, when we moved to Broadstairs, I was given pocket money lavish enough to buy a weekly comic (3*d*.). The importance of this step to this young reader cannot be exaggerated. A comic once a week gave me entry into a syndicate of eight other comic-fanciers at school, each of whom bought a different comic. Then once a week we all swapped comics on a carefully worked-out rota system. So for threepence I enjoyed eight new comics a week.

I quite liked the *Champion*, which had stirring war stories such as the exploits of His Majesty's torpedo boat, HMTB *Battler*, but my favourite by a mile was the *Magnet*, stories set in a public school, Greyfriars, and featuring Billy Bunter the Fat Owl of the Remove, the peerless Bob Cherry and a cast of a hundred other regulars.

The weekly *Magnet*, usually about 20,000 words, was almost wholly written by Charles St John Hamilton under the pseudonym Frank Richards. Hamilton is in the *Guinness Book of Records* as the world's most prolific author, with a total output of boy's magazine prose equal to a thousand novels. And he lived just up the road from us in a large villa at Kingsgate, a frail old bachelor in his eighties, occasionally to be glimpsed through the front gate pottering about his garden dressed in a skullcap, dressing gown, pyjamas and bicycle clips.

Another local author was Countess Barcynska, a writer of fragrantly romantic novels (*Pretty Dear*, 1920; *Love's Last Reward*, 1921; *He Married His Parlourmaid*, 1929; and many more). The countess, originally from Poland, wintered in the south of France but summered in a modest house on the front at Broadstairs which was proudly pointed out to visitors. She was a sad-looking, rouged old lady in a large and floppy straw hat. I saw her from time to time doing unPolish, non-literary things like buying a dressed crab in the fish shop opposite Marchesi's restaurant in Albion Street.

It was the closest I had ever been to a real writer and I desperately wanted to talk to the countess and seek her advice on professional problems of authorship, like did she happen to know a publisher who might be interested in buying four episodes of a serial about dope-smuggling Chinese airmen who lived under a tree, and would a really good publisher print my work on a jelly-graph efficient enough to deliver at least *part* of it in a legible state. But (thank God) I never plucked up enough courage to approach Countess Barcynska with my problems and she died in 1930.

The family move from Ramsgate meant, of course, that Chas and I had to bid farewell to Mr Rule and Thyra House School and start again at a school in Broadstairs. It has always been a matter of wonder to me (and profound gratitude) that Mother and Dad, neither of whom had much formal education, were absolutely committed to giving Chas and me the best education they could afford. They could not really afford *any*, but somehow each term they managed to save and scrape enough pounds and shillings together to pay the fees and keep us at one of the small private schools which existed (rather than prospered) in Thanet. I think they probably managed to do some sort of deal with the depression-hit proprietors but I have no idea what sort of deal it could have been.

In Broadstairs we became pupils of Stone House School, Stone Road. This was one up from Thyra House School because it took in a few boarders. I cannot think that it was a very agreeable place to board because Chas and I stayed there for just one night when our parents had to go away and we found the food most peculiar. For dinner we had liver which was overcooked to the point of being bone dry. Cutting into the liver was like sawing away at a leather purse, and when I finally made an incision the inside poured out onto the plate like sawdust.

We had several teachers, all faintly odd. One was a rather nervous old man who instituted weekly tests. To avoid mutiny he gave a penny to any boy who answered a question correctly.

Another unlikely pedagogue was Mr Murphy, a teenager who was not really a teacher at all. He had been accepted as a potential steward on the Ramsgate cross-Channel ferry and was filling in his time at Stone House School until a vacancy on the ferry occurred.

Mr Murphy was a cheerful young man and we all liked him, but the learning he imparted to us was mostly off-the-top-of-the-head rubbish. For instance, he taught us in a geography lesson that the west coast of Ireland was rough and rocky because it had been pounded for centuries by Atlantic waves. A moment's reflection might have reminded him that pounding waves tend to smooth out knobbly coastlines rather than roughen them, wearing away the headlands and silting up the inlets.

But we were all sad when Mr Murphy's job as a ferry steward came through and he departed to richer pickings, if only because he was young and amiable and most teachers in our sort of school were old and sarcastic.

Besides French and Belgian girls (with or without gold crosses round their necks) Broadstairs schools attracted children from further afield, particularly from rich Middle-Eastern families who wanted their sons to be able to speak conversational English.

Latterly I had a friend at the school who was Persian (now Iranian, I suppose) whose name I never saw written down so I can only guess at its spelling; it sounded like 'Mossen Sadri'. He had a great sense of humour and we got along very well. I thought I owed it to him to spell his name correctly in these pages so I telephoned a very nice jolly man at an Iranian translation bureau in London and asked him how my friend's name should be spelled. He told me that a man of that name was well-known in Iran and the name was spelled Musa Sadr. He was the leader of a Shiite faction but had been kidnapped a few years ago and had not been heard of since. I can only hope that Musa Sadr is a common name in Iran.

By the time the young Musa Sadr arrived from Persia to join the school, Stone House School had moved to a new home, a large house like a boarding house right on Broadstairs front and near the bandstand. A huge noticeboard on the front of the house proclaimed it to be BRADSTOWE COLLEGE (Bradstowe was the ancient name of Broadstairs). It was a more convenient building for a small boarding and day school, with a brick annexe at the back housing a couple of classrooms, but Chas and I were only there for a short while before our parents moved us on to greater things.

So the few marvellous sand-and-sandals years were beginning to come to an end; it had been a period of steady change and improvement for small boys.

One magnificent advance in our living standards was the arrival in our lives of the Mars bar. Before the launch of this rich and superb orchestration of chocolate, soft toffee and creamy whip, sweets were more basic. Chocolate usually came in a thin rectangle, like a thickish credit card.

Uncle William's Toffee was offered in many flavours (my

favourite was banana) and was not wrapped in chew-sized pieces but came in a 6 by 4 by ½-inch slab which the shopkeeper held in the palm of his hand and smote with a hammer. He picked up the shattered shards of toffee from the floor, wiped them on his pullover, weighed them on worn brass scales and handed them over in a screw of paper. The first fragment you popped into your mouth was usually the biggest piece, triangular with sharp points almost piercing your cheeks. When you tried to talk to somebody you sprayed them with a fine jet of toffee juice.

Liquorice was a favourite, sometimes called Spanish. It came in all manner of shapes including bootlaces, pipes, All-Sorts, and batons, and when stamped into the shape of document seals was known as Pontefract cakes. Although the blackness of liquorice stained small faces and clothes, on the whole parents did not mind children chewing the stuff as, unknown to the children, it was a mild but effective laxative.

Boiled sweets, be they acid drops tasting of car batteries or pear drops tasting of nail-varnish remover, came loose in a jar, but they seldom stayed loose very long as they tended to coagulate into a hard mass which the shopkeeper had to hack viciously with an ice pick (sweetshops were much more labour-intensive in those days). The result was that, to our delight, most sweetshops had a jar filled with clumps of broken boiled sweets which they sold off cheaply.

Another favourite, i.e. inexpensive, chew which has now virtually disappeared was the tiger nut. This fibrous morsel could be described as resembling an owl pellet dropped by a constipated bird which had been feeding solely on the insides of horsehair mattresses and the tufts on top of coconuts, with perhaps a beakful of haircord carpet for pud. You chewed and chewed your tiger nut but it yielded little flavour and did not diminish as the hours went by. I cannot say I miss it.

The chap in the park who sold tiger nuts from a tricycle also sold inexpensive nougat with peanuts in it like gravel, candy twist (a rock-hard spiral of translucent boiled sweet tasting of cloves and therefore associated in the young mind with toothache), and sparkling Fanta, another cheap treat in those days, which came in many flavours and in bright colours not to be found in nature. The chap dispensed this stuff by filling a mug with water, adding concentrated Fanta in the flavour of your choice and tickling it up into bubbles with a huge cylinder of some sort of gas.

Another item which has all but disappeared from present-day young people's balanced diet is sherbet. This sweet fizzing powder used to come in two forms, the sherbet fountain – a graspable cylinder of yellow cardboard with a liquorice tube sticking out of the top; sherbet was sucked up the tube and when it hit saliva, fizzed and tickled the tongue. The other form was the sherbet dab, a triangular paper packet of sherbet with a toffee-based mini-lollipop sticking out of one corner. The technique was to take out the lollipop, lick it until it was tacky and then dab it back in the sherbet and swiftly convey the toffee-flavoured dab to the mouth whilst still fizzing. Delicious.

When we first went to Broadstairs neither Chas nor I had been in a motor car; we did not even know anybody who owned one. The streets were busy with horse-drawn carts, errand boys delivering groceries on bikes which had huge baskets on top of the small front wheel, and horse-drawn milk floats from which the milkman ladled milk into your jug from a churn.

In dairies the produce was also 'loose'. Cream stood on the counter in a wide brown bowl, guarded from air attack by a squadron of wasps. Butter was a huge yellow lump on a marble slab. A half-pound block was shaped up by the shopkeeper by hacking off a suitably sized piece and patting and slapping it very loudly into a rectangle with two grooved paddles. This was the job we all wanted to do when we grew up.

The first motor car Chas and I actually touched belonged to the girlfriend of our nice Uncle Alex. Uncle Alex was only a few years older than Chas and me but he was a very good cricketer and altogether a bit of a goer. It was unnerving for him when cutting a dash on the sands at Broadstairs in his pearl-grey flannel bags and cricket blazer, chatting up a likely lass, suddenly to be addressed by two largish lads as 'Uncle'. He had a threatening word with us.

Alex's permanent girlfriend was Tilly, an archetypal flapper, lean, bony and fascinating, with a tulip haircut and Clara Bow lips. She was an unconventional girl who was, rather surprisingly, a good long-distance swimmer. But unpredictable. She eventually married Uncle Alex's best friend.

Tilly's father was a successful Ramsgate greengrocer, and for her twenty-first birthday he gave her a new Austin Seven Ruby saloon car. This was the late 1920s. Chas and I were not only allowed to run our hands along the Austin Seven's beautiful flanks, but for five wonderful minutes sweet Tilly let us sit in it. The colour scheme was chocolate brown and beige and a little silver vase was mounted on a windscreen pillar with a dead flower in it. There was a ring which the driver pulled steadily and a roller blind rolled upwards over the rear window, shielding the driver from the glare of headlights from the car behind.

During the last of our years in Broadstairs there were noticeably more private cars on the road than there had been when we arrived, and horse-drawn delivery carts had begun to give way to square, sit-up-and-beg vans and lorries like the Foden, with its exterior gate-change gears and solid tyres perforated with big horizontal holes to give the hard rubber some illusion of springiness.

Happily, our Sunday mornings were still occasionally enlivened by a distant cry of 'Hottttttt Rollllls!' and either Chas or I was deputed to dress swiftly and track down the Hot Roll Man by following his shout. The baker carried the fresh warm rolls on a tray covered by a cloth.

When you are very young anything is possible and your personal limitations, if any, have yet to make themselves known. One of the evil effects of growing older is to become progressively aware of the activities in life which you are simply not equipped ever to be any good at.

During my early days at Broadstairs I realized that becoming an architect was not on as a career. What happened was that Mackintosh, the toffee-makers, decided to promote their new wrapped toffees by a series of sandcastle competitions at holiday resorts round the coast. There were glittering money prizes to be won; a whole £1 note for the winner, 10s. and 5s. for the runners-up.

I worked hard on my castle; it had a moat and turrets, a castellated keep and a cardboard drawbridge. I had most intelligently carted damp malleable sand from the edge of the sea, but I had forgotten the sun. By eleven o'clock my entry, bone dry, was crumbling away at the edges. Then as the judging party began its tour of inspection I stepped back to see how far they had got and trod on my castle. And that was that, though some good did come from it: every competitor was given a small scarlet pail of about twelve Mackintosh toffees, by then warm and soft from the sun and most welcome as a mid-morning snack.

In those early days I trod the boards for the first time.
Broadstairs' popular beach entertainment for many years was
Uncle Mack's Minstrels, a wondrously politically incorrect alfresco
concert party which performed on a white wooden stage on the
sands. The cast, dressed in spangly romper suits and black mortar-
boards, sweated behind a faceful of burned cork in the last flutter-
ings of the tradition of 'nigger minstrel' shows. Uncle Mack's
Minstrels was an innocent display of what is now looked upon as
being offensively racist (among my books I have a collection of
classic jokes and sketches taken from those original nineteenth-
century minstrel shows entitled, if you please, *Niggerosities*).

Every Wednesday morning Uncle Mack conducted a talent competition for young hopefuls; the winner got 5s. At the time there
was a play doing the rounds of the repertory companies called
White Cargo, which then became a popular film. It was a throb-
bing story of sex in the jungle, a bit like the work of Somerset
Maugham. A young British planter is tempted by the ravishing,
dusky beauty Tondelayo into joining her in a spot of 'mammypalava' (we all knew what that meant), but she catches a social
disease or is poisoned or something and at the end staggers off into
the jungle, clearly not feeling at all well, leaving our hero to smile
devilishly at the audience and declaim (splendid curtain line), 'If
she lives – she lives with ME!'

I decided that I would sing the audience the theme song from the
film version of *White Cargo*, accompanied by Uncle Mack on his
banjo.

I have a snapshot of myself at the time of what turned out to be
my tragic stage début. I was short of two front teeth and the
pockets of my short trousers were bulging with such boyhood
necessities as a tobacco tin full of worms gathered from the fore-
shore for use as bait, some pebbles for skimming through the
waves, a bottle of iodine in case I cut myself, some useful string and
an orange.

Now the song was a steamy, very sexy ballad, written by, of all
people, Noel Gay, who wrote 'Me and My Girl', 'Let's Have a
Tiddley at the Milk Bar', 'Run Rabbit Run', and about a thousand
other popular hits, and it described the singer's longing for more
mammypalava with the seductive Tondelayo. With an introductory
twang from Uncle Mack's banjo I launched into song.

Sadly, it was not my audience. I had hardly piped out the first few lines when the punters became restive. I think perhaps I put a bit too much passion into it because well before I had got to 'nights of madness' Uncle Mack had taken me by the elbow and propelled me firmly off-stage, murmuring, 'Have another go when you're a bit older, sonny.'

It was a pity because I needed the five-bob prize. I had developed an interest in photography. This was a new thing for families, following a brilliant breakthrough by the Kodak company in making cameras cheap enough for everybody to own and simple enough for anybody to use. Instead of a camera being like an expensive piece of laboratory equipment, all shiny mahogany and brass, the Kodak Box Brownie was made of what seemed to be dimpled black cardboard. It had a tiny reflex viewfinder, which you had to shield from the light with a hand otherwise you could not see anything, and when you pressed the lever to take a photograph a large safety pin moved across the lens opening, followed reluctantly by a sheet of metal with a hole in it. And that is all there was to it.

The film was an eight-exposure strip of celluloid backed by paper and wound on a spool. After taking a snap you turned the Brownie upside down, peered into a little window at the back and wound on for the next snap, being guided by a pointing hand, dots and the number of the next exposure.

I have no idea how much the Brownie cost because Dad got it by saving up cigarette coupons. Tobacconists' shelves were stocked with different names then. Craven A was still going strong with the new cork tip (originally paper printed to look like cork) but there were lots of other popular brands, now rarely seen, such as the cheapest of them all and a great favourite during the First World War, Woodbines, sold five at a time in a flat, green, open paper packet. When we did *A Midsummer Night's Dream* at school, a titter was enjoyed by all during Puck's big speech: 'I know a bank whereon the wild thyme blows' when he got to 'luscious woodbine'.

There was also the modestly priced Turf, Park Drive and Black Cat to choose from, and at the upper end of the market De Reske, Du Maurier and Passing Cloud. This last brand, quite expensive, came in a pink packet with a picture on it of a toff puffing out smoke with a dreamy look, like a deb's delight at a party enjoying a modern-day exotic substance. The cigarettes were oval, as though somebody had sat on the packet.

Black Cat was one of the earliest brands to issue gift coupons to be collected and exchanged for items from a catalogue. Dad was not a heavy smoker so heaven knows how long it took him to puff through enough Black Cat fags to provide us with a Kodak Box Brownie, but he managed it.

I became deeply interested in photography, but there was not enough spare money for the parents to waste on films and processing so I had to be more or less self-financing, hence going in for competitions with cash prizes. The chemicals needed were quite cheap and I taught myself developing and printing, developing my films in a cupboard, see-sawing the film in darkness through a soup plate of developer and then through another of hypo. I adapted an old picture frame to make contact prints.

A good source of money for photography was programme-selling at the annual Broadstairs Water Sports. This was an exciting event in itself. Narrow boardwalks were run out into the bay for the swimming-race contestants to dive from, and there were dinghy races and water-polo matches while a regimental band played marches and 'Gems from *The Merry Widow*'. The high spot of the day was a sea battle between boatloads of white-clad bakers and boatloads of black-clad chimney sweeps. For ammunition the bakers hurled paper bags of flour at the black sweeps and the sweeps hurled paper bags of soot at the white-clad bakers. It ended up as a tremendously satisfying mess, with all the whitened sweeps and blackened bakers swimming around in the water trying to scrape themselves clean enough for their wives to allow them into the house when they got home.

An ambitious young programme-seller, remorselessly aggressive and prepared to trudge all day up and down the esplanade and the sands accosting holiday makers, could earn himself a cool 2 or 3s. commission.

Life for Chas and me was soon to change radically and the good days of slopping about on the sands most of the time and acquiring the minimum of learning were about to change. The parents had decided that we were old enough to go to a real school and they managed to have us accepted for Chatham House School, Ramsgate.

About that time I went through a strange rite-of-passage experience, perhaps preparing me for the rather more earnest existence I was due to face in a more grown-up world.

My love for my mother had never been obsessive; it was the normal warm trust, respect and love of son for mother and vice versa, and I had the same kind of relationship with Dad. But Mother did stand in a slightly different light in that, unlike Dad, who used to be away for long periods, Mother had always been there, a permanent source of comfort and safety in a world often difficult to understand.

Then, lying in bed one night, it occurred to me that Mother would *not* always be there. One day she would die and I would never see her again. This was much too enormous a concept for my tiny split-pea brain to cope with calmly and I simply gave way to inconsolable misery, sobbing into the pillow far into the night, with Chas eventually having to come in and say, 'Oh, for God's sake, shut up!'

But I could not shut up. Night after night for about two weeks, as I lay in bed, the dread black thought crept back that one day Mother would not be there; it was like a medieval nightmare crouching over me. I just did not know what to do but to howl as quietly as possible and hope that sleep would soon bring oblivion.

Mother chose a good moment and gave me a gentle talking-to, explaining that I was quite right about her having to leave us all one day (she actually lived way into her late seventies), but that was how it all worked and I must learn to accept death as a fact that none of us could do much about.

Suddenly, a few days later, as if the sun had emerged from behind a cloud, everything became all right again and life returned to being warm and secure, dread evaporated and my strange emotional and irrational experience was over; it never returned.

For Chas and me life entered a new phase and we cycled off to Chatham House every morning with a packed lunch which we ate from its greaseproof paper in company with lots of other boys in the school dining hall, which smelled of the previous day's in-house meals.

Chatham House was, at last, a real school with properly qualified teachers and opportunities to act and write things and play cricket and rugby and make music; a senior pupil when we were there was a boy from nearby Dumpton Gap, a very good organist named Edward Heath; I understand he later went into politics.

My good friend Uncle Alex had been there and had played cricket for the school. Chatham House was and remains an excellent grammar school by any standards.

But then, a year afterwards, our lives suddenly changed yet again and the Muirs moved away from the sands and the sea for ever and went to live in London.

It was a happy move for Dad. A firm of machinery manufacturers named Belliss and Morcom Ltd, which made turbines and reciprocating engines, had equipped an engine room for a firm named Caribonum which made high-grade typewriter ribbons, carbon paper, and Field's ink. The factory was in a somewhat far-flung London suburb, Leyton, E10. The installation was giving trouble which proved difficult to fix and somebody at Belliss and Morcom remembered Dad, who had worked successfully with their equipment when he was a marine engineer in New Zealand. They traced Dad to Thanet and recommended him for the job of looking after Caribonum's generating machinery.

I went up to London with Dad for his interview. We sailed on the paddle steamer *Royal Sovereign*. A fine way to go. The ship was somehow proud and broad, and the thunder and splashing of the paddles was both exciting and comforting. Dad took me down to the engine room where steam hissed and shiny things went in and out and it was, I remember, very hot.

Dad fixed the trouble with Caribonum's engine, was offered the permanent job of Caribonum's deputy factory engineer and, of course, took it. So quite suddenly it was farewell to swimming in sea water tasting of petrol, and Chatham House School, and lying on the beach with friends listening to a portable gramophone with the Rexine peeling off the lid and the gramophone needle ploughing sand out of the record's groove as the Tiger Ragamuffins, Ivor Moreton and Dave Kaye, played 'Tiger Rag' at hectic speed on two pianos. And the almost erotic luxury of being pink and hot from lying in the sun all day, and then at night sliding between cool, crisp sheets with a new story from the *Robin Hood Library* (4d.).

Could life in London possibly match such delights?

Chapter Three

GROWING UP

Number 28 Church Road, Leyton, E10, was the first house my parents ever owned; they paid for it very slowly over many years. It was in a short terrace of similarly low-priced, fairly basic homes in Church Road built just after the First World War, each with a useful strip of back garden and a useless patch of front garden.

Dad immediately planted grass seed on the near half of the back garden to give us a lawn, erected a rustic trellis screen with climbing roses and packed the far half of the garden with veg.

With Dad in a real job and the kitchen garden flourishing, food was now good and plentiful. It always had been for Chas and me, but during the bleaker years I think the parents exercised a little secret parental hold-back.

Two regular meals I remember with great affection from those early Leyton days: in summer we had huge platefuls of Dad's lettuce dressed with vinegar and sugar, and in winter we had a little joint of lamb or beef on Sundays, the surplus of which was curried by Mother on Mondays.

It was not the curry or the meat which Chas and I enjoyed so much as the copious spoonfuls of Sharwood's Green Label mango chutney which it was our joy to spread over it. But on one traumatic Monday, Mother found that she had run out of the delicious sweet chutney. Chas and I were desolated and stared in dismay at our unchutneyed curried lamb. To us it was like being asked to eat 'sour pork' without the 'sweet and', or Heinz baked beans not in tomato sauce but in hot water. Mother rose magnificently to the problem and graced our curry with liberal spoonfuls of Allen and Hanbury's cod-liver oil and malt. We found it delicious.

The Borough of Leyton once had one foot in Epping Forest and the other in London, but as the years passed the forest withdrew and the London suburbs crept outwards, engulfing Leyton and its neighbours. But when we moved to Leyton in the early 1930s there was still a blacksmith in the High Street with his forge in a white, wooden clapboard smithy, and near us in Grange Park Road lived and worked the Childs, a family of glass-blowers, and at the top of the road in the High Street was a tiny factory which made church organs.

Church Road is a kind of wriggly hypotenuse running from Leyton High Street down to Lea Bridge Road. The purpose-built Caribonum factory lay down a side road off Church Road, about a mile away from us and well within walking distance.

Chas and I were immediately enrolled at Leyton County High School for Boys. The rather longish title was to differentiate the school from its sister establishment, the Leyton County High School for Girls. They were not all that difficult to differentiate as the girls' school was full of girls and was not in Leyton at all but in Leytonstone.

To get to school Chas and I only had to walk about 100 yards up the road to the High Street and catch a tram. Tram tickets were sold at the school at a specially subsidized cheap rate. Of course, being sent off to school on a Monday morning bearing cash to buy the week's tickets was a terrible temptation, and most of us dipped into our tram money for sweets and had to walk to school in the latter part of the week. It was about a mile and a half from us to Essex Road and we developed a kind of shambling jog to avoid being late.

One tiny urban pleasure which partly compensated us for the loss of beach life was the antisocial manner in which we got off the tram, which satisfyingly infuriated the tram driver.

On the floor by the driver's foot was a thing like an iron mushroom. This was connected by a lever to a clapper, so that when the driver stepped on the iron mushroom, the clapper hit a huge iron gong under the floorboards and gave a very audible warning of the tram's approach. A dozen or so of us LCHS lads used to travel to school every morning on the upper deck of the tram. When we arrived at our stop we all streamed down the staircase and jumped the last three stairs, landing heavily one by one on the iron mushroom. The clangour was ear-splitting.

Leyton County High turned out to be an extraordinarily good school. In rank it was not even a grammar school – our nearest local grammar school was Sir George Monoux School (pronounced locally as 'Sir George Monarchs') in nearby Walthamstow – but a county high, a grade of secondary school which provided an almost free education; I think my parents had to find £11 a term (harder to find then than it sounds now). The syllabus was amazingly extensive: French was compulsory and another language had to be taken as well, usually either Latin or modern Spanish or German. There were classes in woodwork and metalwork, there were tennis courts and football and cricket pitches to play on, a dramatic society which performed plays in the school hall, musical appreciation classes, a school orchestra and a gymnastic team so proficient that it made an annual performance tour of Denmark.

A third of the sixth form was expected to win a scholarship to Oxford or Cambridge, and did, and over the years the school notched up an impressive list of distinguished old boys, including John Lill, the classical pianist; Arnold Diamond, smooth villain in many a film and telly play; Levy, a sixth-former (can't remember his first name) who achieved fame in the RAF for being acclaimed the most successful hitch-hiker of the war, reputed to have thumbed his way during one leave to, through and back home again from Canada; John Dankworth, saxophonist and jazzman; Sir Derek Jacobi, actor; and perhaps the best-known face of all, my contemporary at LCHS, the actor John Hewer, who has been on our small screens for many years as the white-haired and curly champion of the fish finger, Captain Birds Eye.

The headmaster of LCHS, Dr Couch, was an awesome figure to us, capped and gowned and ascetic-looking, nephew of the great literary authority 'Q', Sir Arthur Quiller-Couch.

Teachers taught in their gowns, adding their degree hoods at formal events. Wearing gowns in class should not have mattered but it did. We mocked the teachers but we also respected most of them; the academic dress gave them a touch of remoteness and helped them to achieve a natural authority in the classroom.

My attempt to become part of the great gymnastic tradition of the school ended in a little pain, a lot of humiliation and a realization that as well as having no future as a castle architect working with sand, I also had no future as an acrobat. The shame came on me quite early in a gym class conducted by the school PT instructor, a short, stocky, appallingly healthy Scot who busied around the gym in squeaky plimsolls.

The exercise was a forward somersault. My instructions were to sprint down the gym gathering speed, leap onto the springboard and shoot into the air, curl up into a ball and bring both my fists down sharply so that I would spin forward and land lightly on my feet on the mat.

What could be simpler?

Other boys went before me and spun forward in the air with natural grace and dexterity, but they had the short, chunky build of PT instructors, with calf muscles like grapefruit. I had been short and chunky, rather unpleasantly so, for quite a bit of my childhood, but I was now aged eleven and had elongated. I was taller than anybody else in my year and very narrow, about 14 inches at the widest part which was my feet, and I seemed to have no calf muscles at all; my legs were narrow pink cylinders from hip to ankle, the line only broken by bony knees.

My turn came. I pounded forward confidently, my feet making booming noises on the wooden floor of the gym, leaped onto the springboard and hurtled athletically up into the air. That was when I realized that the physical agility game was not for me. Almost fainting with the excitement of flying up towards the roof, I forgot to curl up into a ball. Instead I rose into the air rigid, slowly turned over like a caber tossed at the Braemar Highland Games and landed on my head. I toppled forward on the mat, stiff as a plank and momentarily unaware of where, or who, I was.

The mat was padded to save the necks of unco-ordinated parcels of skin and bone like me, so the result was a brief headache but no blood ('Pity it wasn't cement,' muttered the PT instructor, rather bitterly I thought), and I was given a chit saying, 'Excused all PT classes. Extra Hygiene instead.'

I had greater success in more sedentary areas of effort. During my first year I wrote a one-act play, *Almost a Crime*, which was directed by Collins of the sixth form and performed in the school hall on Parents' Day. I wrote a kind of gossip column for each issue of the school magazine under the pseudonym 'Nuncio' (which I hardly need to remind readers is Italian for 'the Pope's special messenger'), I joined the Dramatic Society and played, in a quite outstandingly hammy performance, the Persian poet Suleiman in *The Poetasters of Ispahan*, but good came of it because I had made a splendidly long and wispy beard out of grey crêpe hair which reached down to the waist and was so impressive that Mr Lewis the English master appointed me the school's official make-up artist (Collins of the sixth form, a tall, thin, funny chap, was good on Mr Lewis, whom we all liked. 'What a fine literary figure,' Collins would say in awed tones as Mr Lewis strode into view down the corridor. 'The Byronic limp, the Shelley-like toss of the head, the Shakespearean semi-baldness . . .').

Woodwork classes were an option which I jumped at. I had just learned how to cut mortise and tenon joints (I still can if given enough time, say about ten times as long as it took me then) when the metalwork master started a class in jewellery-making and I rushed to join. For the rest of my time at LCHS I spent happy hours every week in metalwork class making a pair of silver cuff links.

I must have made about fifteen pairs during that time, or more accurately one pair fifteen times. Cutting the cuff links from sheet silver, engraving them with the letters 'F' and 'M', melting black enamel into the letters and making the chain from silver wire wrapped round a knitting needle were all no problems to an unathletic lad with patience. The snag with the whole process became apparent when the time came to solder the bits together. The method was to warm up the silver with a mouth-operated methylated-spirit blowpipe until the proper temperature had been reached, and then touch the two bits to be joined with a bit of silver solder. Theoretically the solder would then melt, run and join the bits of silver together. Now for the snag. Silver solder melted at about half a degree lower than the silver itself so if – or rather, when – I blew through the blowpipe too strongly, the whole damn cuff link melted into a blob of silver and I had to start again from the beginning.

I did eventually complete a pair of cuff links and wore them proudly in the great outside world when I left school, but silver is soft and after only a few weeks the links of the chain wore through and both cuff links fell to pieces.

Perhaps I should have persevered with forward somersaults.

*

School life was busy and enjoyable, but then so was life outside. I found that the world was full of new interests, the problem was to sort them out and ration time and energy to fit in as many as possible. I became fascinated with the various escapements of watches. I couldn't afford to buy watches, of course, but I could look at them in the High Street pawnshops and occasionally persuade 'uncle' to open up the back of a couple.

I bought, very cheaply, an odd length of brown velveteen which had been salvaged from a fire and made myself a smoking jacket (I did not smoke). I had not realized what an extraordinarily difficult thing it was to attempt. I found a book on tailoring in Leyton Public Library, doggedly read it up and then had a go. Luckily mother had an ancient Singer hand-turn sewing machine with flying cherubs all over it, which was a great help. The finished jacket was wondrously ill-fitting and quite awful, of course, but that was not the point; I had made it.

On the other hand, although I tried very hard, I failed to build a typewriter, which I had planned to assemble from a collection of items including a rolling pin, a John Bull rubber printing set and the wire from a number of straightened-out coat-hangers.

When I was about twelve I took up bell-ringing at our parish church down the road. This was mainly to bring a little diversity to Sundays as Chas and I were shooed out of the house and sent to morning service, afternoon Sunday school and evening service. Bell-ringing was agreeably dangerous for a young person as the bells were extremely heavy and if you pulled one off balance and held on to the rope too long it could whisk you off your feet and crash your skull against the belfry roof.

But there was the annual and wonderful bell-ringers meat tea. This was arranged by our team leader (ringmaster?), Mr Hughes, a printer by trade. We went on a brief tour of several country parish churches as guests of their bell-ringers, rang a few 'changes' on their bells for friendly then sat down with them in a village pub to enjoy the traditional bell-ringers' meat tea of ham and salad and mustard pickles.

The high spot of our campanology year was New Year's Eve. We climbed up the belfry ladder and tied heavy leather muffles to the bell clappers. Just before midnight, we rang a few minutes of softly sounding 'changes' and three minutes before midnight climbed up again into the belfry, whipped off the muffles and scrambled back down in time to welcome in the new year with the brilliant sound of a clear, loud, unmuffled peal.

Photography had to be fitted into this busy schedule. I was by then interested in making movies as well as taking stills, so money had become a grievous problem. There was the usual routine embezzlement of tram-ticket money. Actually, it had now become bus-ticket money as the trams had been superseded by privatized bus services. Our favourite buses were painted brown and had on their sides, in gold lettering, *PRO BONO PUBLICO*. Besides dipping into bus-ticket money I had my pocket money (3*d*. a week), and occasional half-crown tips from relations, but there was a massive shortfall which I decided I could best meet in two ways: one by buying small items and selling them at a profit, and the other by inventing and making the equipment I could not afford.

There were a number of junk shops as well as pawnshops strung along the High Street and I rapidly became Leyton's small-time Arthur Daley, wheeling and dealing vigorously. An early coup was to buy a rusting birdcage for 2*s*. 6*d*. at one end of the High Street, buff it up a bit and sell it for £1 at the other end.

After a series of complicated transactions worthy of a tall thin Medici, I had amassed a working capital of about £5 and I bought an ancient 9.5mm cine-camera from a pawnshop for £2. It was almost a museum piece, hand-operated (two turns of the handle a second), but by an extraordinary piece of luck I found a rusty motor attachment for it in a photography shop which cost only £1 10*s*. I also found a cheap and tinny hand-operated 9.5mm projector, broken but reparable, which cost me 10*s*. I fitted it with an electric motor from a broken-backed Hoover which a dealer let me have for nothing.

To process the 30-foot reels of 9.5mm film, 'reversal' stock which did not need printing, I built a winding drum and tank from plywood and bits and pieces. I fitted the drum with glass rods with elastic bands round them at intervals to keep the wound-on film from sliding about and sticking to itself.

The tank worked rather well until disaster struck. I did the processing in the evening on our kitchen dresser which Dad had covered with a sheet of marble rescued from the council dump. Now the last chemical to be used in developing the film was acid, which dissolved the metallic silver and 'reversed' the image from negative to positive. That evening, working in pitch-darkness, I poured the acid wide of the mark and it sloshed onto the marble table top.

As every child left alone in a school chemistry lab learns, with the possible exception of dropping a pellet of phosphorus into the chemistry master's cup of tea, there is little in science which produces quite so dramatic an effect as pouring acid on marble. The marble hisses, it smokes, it bubbles, it gives off chemical fumes, it produces what is known in the trade as 'vigorous chemical action'. Which is a fair description of what the accident produced in my mother. I had to switch on the kitchen light, which fogged the film, and then swiftly rinse the marble with a bucket of water from the sink, which soaked everywhere. When Mother came in and saw the mess I had made of her kitchen her ring finger went to work again and, big lad that I was, I endured what the French delicately describe as *un mauvais quart d'heure*.

For some odd reason, I had up until then thought that making people laugh and writing prose for them to read were two different pursuits. I was writing busily all the time for the school magazine and for English classes and so on, and a fair bit of it was fiction, but my short stories, perhaps all stories written by boys in their pre-teens, owed more to O. Henry than P. G. Wodehouse; they tended to be deeply dramatic and rely for effect on a surprise ending. The sort of thing was a moody piece about an athlete contemplating losing his record for the 100-yard dash (oh, innocent sporting term) the following day, ending with the revelation that the athlete was actually a felon in the condemned cell.

But I came to my senses one autumn in, I think, 1934, when I nearly died. I had a low-down pain which niggled. We though it might be just a strained innard from hauling on the church bell-ropes, but it persisted and got worse and it became clear that it was something nasty. One afternoon, with suitable dramatic effect, the skies clouded over and the earth went dark and the ambulance came. I had acute appendicitis and was whisked away to Whipps Cross Hospital, where it emerged that we had left it a bit late and the thing had burst and peritonitis had set in. I was in there for months. Recovery was slow and lacked charm, involving a piece of hosepipe inserted in the operation scar for drainage, and prevented by a huge safety pin through the top of it from dropping down

(where to?). I wrote the whole experience up for the school magazine. It was my first attempt at a funny piece and I realized then,
for the first time, how much comedy feeds on serious matters. And
times were becoming serious. I was now aged fourteen and getting
anxious about my future.

Our geography master at school was a small, plump,
Pickwickian figure named Mr Cohen, who used to goad us all to
work harder by staring pityingly at us through his thick spectacles
and exclaiming, 'You'll all end up twopenny-ha'penny clerks,
twopenny-ha'penny clerks.' Mr Cohen was not to know that the
future was going to be even bleaker than that for pen-pushers
because the rise of computers would mean no jobs even for
twopenny-ha'penny clerks.

I enjoyed classes and at LCHS it was OK to do a bit of work,
you were not sneered at or biffed by your classmates and I had no
particular worries at facing the big exam the following year:
Matric. But I had no clear idea of how to go about carving a career
from then on.

Unless we were sons of military men or of doctors, in which case
we knew from childhood that we would either follow our father's
profession or be seen dead rather than follow our father's profession, very few of us had the faintest idea of what we wanted to
do.

In county high schools the thinking was less in terms of a career
as of simply getting some sort of a job with the hope that the job
would develop into a career. All I ever *wanted* to do was be a writer
and amuse people, but in my situation that was about as feckless
an ambition as wanting to become Pope Frank I. I had never in my
life knowingly met a professional writer or publisher or impresario
or agent or comic. How to begin?

I made a start one school open day by finagling a meeting with
the editor of the local paper – I think he was a governor of the
school – and asking him how I could become a journalist. He said
he would consider taking me on as an apprentice if I would come
and see him once I had my Matric exam results.

Was I on my way? No, I was not.

Our family world suddenly changed completely and tragically.
Dad died.

He died in a manner which was very Dad. He was at home in
bed with the flu when somebody arrived by bike from Caribonum,

breathless, with the news that the boiler had developed a fault and had to be shut down, and the factory now had no power. Could he advise? Being Dad, he got up, struggled into clothes, made his way to the factory through the cold air and climbed into the warm boiler to locate the problem. Back home he developed pneumonia and a week later he died.

Chas and I had to leave school immediately to bring in some money and to do this we had to find jobs without having any exam qualifications to flourish. Chas was aged sixteen and a bit and I was fourteen and a half.

The outlook was grim but Caribonum was helpful. It was a family company founded by a Yorkshireman, C. F. Clark, who ran it according to modern American business methods, but with a strong Yorkshire paternalism. Mr Clark was stocky, with an under-slung Habsburg jaw; he was getting on in years but still played cricket on Saturday afternoons at the company's sports ground in Walthamstow and awarded a cream flannel shirt to any employee who bowled him out. Good bowlers dreaded hitting C.F.'s stumps as the shirts were expensive but very thick and tickly to wear.

Once a year we were all invited to C.F.'s house in the country where he held a kind of open day. We were greeted in the Great Hall by church music coming from a huge pipe organ played by C.F. himself, bent over the keys in a scene later to become familiar in Hammer horror films starring Vincent Price.

C.F. sent somebody down to help Mother sort out arrangements for the funeral and business matters, gave her a small pension and found jobs for Chas and me in Caribonum.

So I went to work in a carbon-paper factory, which sounds about as Dickensian as you can get, but was actually interesting and enjoyable. Most evenings I spent Mother-sitting. This suited both Chas and me as Chas, who could immediately play any musical instrument by ear and could draw very well, was al-together a more gregarious and socially welcome person, and I could nip swiftly to and from home and the public library. During the next few years I took out plays and ploughed through most of the middle-of-the-road playwrights, now little read or produced, like John Van Druten and Edward Knoblock (who?), and I read a great number of novels. My taste in humour developed from the *Just William* stories in *The Happy Mag* (a thick magazine seemingly printed on blotting paper) to Dornford Yates's *Berry* stories, to P. G. Wodehouse . . .

Mother would not go out and took to listening to the radio for hours every evening; the regular broadcasters became her friends and she could recognize a voice instantly, even if only heard once and months before. Another unlikely gift Mother had was a natural ability to spell. I only had to sing out a word and Mother would spell it correctly, although her education had been so brief that she had almost certainly never met the word before nor knew its derivation.

Leytonstone Public Library had a small theatre attached to it used by a flourishing play-reading society which read a play (aloud) every Thursday evening to a loyal and appreciative audience of OAPs and vagrants sheltering from the weather. I joined the society and much enjoyed myself, but there was an inherent problem in reading a play rather than learning it by heart, a problem never solved by me, which was how to play either a passionate love scene or a fight to the death whilst reading from a book held in the left hand.

I provoked much merriment when playing love scenes as for some reason all amateur actresses seemed to be short in stature and I was then well over 6 feet, which meant that I either had to woo the beloved by sagging down at the knees like a chimpanzee enjoying his cup of tea, or by leaning forward with my behind stuck out at an acute angle.

I wrote, I think, five one-act plays in all for the society to perform. Shrewdly, love scenes and fights did not occur in any of them, so that the producer could cast me in the lead if she was so disposed.

Sadly, or from another point of view mercifully, none of these plays has survived.

Chapter Four

THE WAR (PART ONE)

Caribonum again behaved generously in Dad's memory when war loomed. The inevitability of conflict in Europe was brought home to us by *Daily Express* headlines stating authoritatively THERE WILL BE NO WAR.

In 1939 I was aged nineteen. To fill in my time profitably before joining up, the company took me off checking invoices in the general office, put me through their training course for salesmen and sent me out on the road with a bag of samples, a Homburg hat and a card index of customers on my territory, which was mainly a length of the Commercial Road in East London. The point was that the job of salesman carried with it much more money, no less than £4 10s. a week plus commission.

The training course was interesting. It taught the sales force to wear a clean white shirt, scrub its fingernails, display an expression of happy confidence at all times and to say nothing in the sales pitch which the 'prospect' – the potential victim – could answer with a 'no', like, 'Can I interest you in a new sort of carbon paper?'

I was hopeless at it, but no matter. Customers knew that very soon it would be virtually impossible to buy any stationery at all, and coaxing office managers into ordering an extra typewriter ribbon or box of carbon paper was about as difficult as persuading a spaniel to accept an extra chocolate drop.

One of my customers decided to befriend me. She was a Miss

Cohen, a very large genial lady who ran a somewhat unconventional business from under a railway arch; she bought second-
hand uniforms of no further use to the post office and exported
them to India.

The business thrived (I gathered that the red piping round the
jacket and down the trouser seams was much esteemed) and when
I was part of England's might, kindly Miss Cohen sent me comfort
parcels – socks and chocolate and Penguin paperbacks – every
month for two or three years.

With a teenager's deep concern for personal comfort rather
than for the war needs of the nation, I opted for service in the
RAF rather than the Army or the Navy, because it seemed to me
that in the RAF I would get to sit down more. Propaganda films
and newsreels showed that the Army went in for a great deal of
marching up and down carrying heavy rifles and haversacks, and
my father, who was a professional sailor, was sick every time he
went to sea, and as no doubt he had passed on to me some of the
relevant chromosomes, I thought it would be wise to avoid a life
aboard ship. Also, although a flying job was the objective, there
was such a long wait for a training course that a 'trade' had to be
taken up first, and the RAF, alone of the services, wanted photographers.

The first few months of service life in uniform, square-bashing,
learning how to drill and to march and to do without privacy and
swallow the basic service philosophy of 'if it moves salute it, if it
doesn't move, paint it' was an educational experience, and not all
of it was unpleasant; only parts of it were.

For instance, ritual humiliations. During square-bashing training
we slept on three tough little square mattresses known as 'biscuits'
on folding iron bedsteads. In charge of our hut was a chunky and
dismal physical training corporal who had his own little room at
the end of the hut. When the post was delivered in the morning we
had to line up in front of this oaf, and if he called out our name
we had to raise a hand. He would then toss our envelope into the
air so that it fluttered under a bed and had to be grovelled for on
hands and knees.

I had a problem from time to time with service language. I had
never in my life heard such a concentration of profanity and
obscenity. About my fourth day in uniform our drill sergeant disliked some manoeuvre our squad had messed up and shouted at us

in fury, 'Jesus Christ Al-f***ing-mighty!' My blood froze. But eventually one got used to it.

There was, too, a communication problem, which was not a class matter (I was educated in E10 not Eton) but simply a difficulty in understanding what was required of me when the pronunciation was homely regional rather than standard English.

One morning we were all paraded to tidy up the bits of greenery and garden round the huts for a visit from some bigwig, and a sergeant with a sheet of paper was singing out the duties we had each been allocated.

'Willis!'

'Sarge.'

'Paper picking-up, you. Right?'

'Sarge.'

'Challis!'

'Not on parade, Sarge. Had to report sick.'

'Got no business reporting sick when the grass 'as got to be tidied for the air commodore. Doesn't 'e know there's a bleedin' war on?'

The sergeant, a regular, sighed at the pathetic standard of conscripts he was supposed to train into magnificent fighting machines.

'Muir!'

'Sarge.'

'Do the edges. Right?'

'Right.'

But it was not right at all. As I made for the tool store I realized that I didn't know whether I was supposed to trim the edges of the grass, or cut the hedges? 'Edges or (h)edges? I could hardly go back and ask the Sarge whether he meant an aitch to be present.

Willis J. was in the tool store signing for a sack, hemp, waste paper for the putting into, and I asked him whether he thought Sarge meant the hedges or the edges, and Willis J. said, 'You got cloff ears? 'E said, "Do the *Adj's*." That's the flower bed in front of the adjutant's office with the rope round it painted white. You repaint the rope. Gottit, berk?'

The service mind revealed more of its individuality when I was posted to RAF Farnborough to take my photography course.

The teaching was conducted by four almost identical, late-middle-aged instructors with very short, brushed-down hair. They wore those long beige overall coats associated with carpet ware-housemen. All four instructors were civilians, retired regular sergeants from various RAF photography sections. Their method of instruction was by means of monologues committed to memory (I think probably with some difficulty). The method bore oddly little relation to teaching, but then RAF photography bore little resemblance to civvy photography. Aesthetics played no part. The cameras, which were bolted into the aircraft, looked more like large domestic mincing machines than cameras: grey metal castings with a heavy hood protecting the lens. The film inside was 5 inches wide and provided the photo reconnaissance intelligence officers with a series of 5 x 5 inch prints of the territory flown over.

'On removing your camera from the appropriate aircraft once it's landed and the engine has been discontinued,' the instructor would recite in a rapid, expressionless baritone, 'you will hold the camera firmly against your chest or up your tunic and proceed rapidly with it to the photography section darkroom, taking care whilst *en route* not to wallop the camera against nothing solid or fall over thus causing damage to Air Ministry property for which you will be held financially responsible. Once within your dark-room, switch the top light off, the red light on, and holding the camera firmly in your right hand, repeat RIGHT hand, you will activate with your left thumb, repeat LEFT thumb, the sliding but-ton "G" which I described to you where it was yesterday after-noon. For purposes of committing the button to memory, you will find it marked "G" in diagram 804A in your instruction manual, volume four, page two hundred and forty-seven.

'Operating button G will cause the back of the camera to be released from its locked position and thus be openable at will. Insert the fingernail of your right hand into the crack in the side of the back opposite to the hinge and ease the back open. Carefully, repeat CAREFULLY, remove the spool of exposed film with the right hand without, if possible, touching it. Once you have the film in your grasp, don't for Christ's sake drop it in the sink or tread on the bloody thing or the pilot'll have to go back up and fly the sod-ding sortie again, won'e? Is all that crystal clear?'

At the end of the course we had to undergo an exam called the TTB (Trade Test Board). It was very important to get high marks in this as a brilliant result would earn a posting to a crack squadron.

I failed the test.

My nemesis was the mime sequence. Looking back over the years I even now find it difficult to think of any test quite so pointless, but then I suppose I would think that having failed it.

For this piece of what I still think was archetypical service idiocy, I had to close my eyes and, in broad daylight, mime developing a film in the unit darkroom, each movement of which I had been made to learn by heart and practise endlessly under the piercing if somewhat lunchtime-beer-dampened eye of my instructor.

I thought I worked well in the test. Neatly, rapidly, concentrating on getting all movements in the right order. I finished, as taught, by miming pinning up the film to dry on a line, rather like hanging up a wet bathing costume.

I opened my eyes, returned to my chair and waited while the bunch of visiting examiners conferred like boxing-match judges. I felt confident. In the oral test I had, I thought, got the chemistry answer right: 'At what temperature does a solution of hypo recrystallize and become unstable?' And also, 'Which RAF camera should be used for which particular job?' ('The recording of the effectiveness of a fighter aircraft's machine-gun fire requires the fitting, in the fitting provided in the aircraft's leading edge, port wing, of a loaded cine-camera, model CC/A/804/MK/624.')

'Aircraftsman Muir, rise to a standing position', said the head warehouseman in a sepulchral voice, like an eighteenth-century hanging judge addressing a doomed felon who had been caught nicking a handkerchief. I stood up. 'You done well in the early tests, Muir, but you let yourself, and worse still your instructor, down in the last test by a gross piece of forgetfulness. We have no other alternative but to pronounce you as having failed.'

I was stunned.

'What did I do wrong?'

'It's not what you *did* do, Muir, it's what you *didn't* done,' said the hanging judge. 'What you forgot to perform was to *mime switching off the top light when you entered the darkroom*. As you know well enough, with the top light on, as soon as you opened the back of the camera the entire film would have been fogged and ruined.'

'But . . .' I said, 'it was *mime*! If it had been real I would have *seen* the light was on and switched it off, wouldn't I?'

'That is supposition,' said the judge. 'Cap on, about turn, by the left – quick march!'

So, instead of developing cine-film shot during the Battle of Britain or printing out 5 x 5 inch prints of German cities, I was posted to RAF Warmwell, Dorset, where at the time they had no accommodation for a photography section and I was allocated a chair and table in the armoury, where I spent months watching armourers pouring boiling water down rifle barrels.

To cheer myself up I wrote a three-act farce. It was titled *Bishop's Leap* and was one of those pieces which began with the title and then had to have a story invented to fit the title. The play was so awful that merciful memory has obliterated the details, but I recall that the first act ended with a plump but sporty bishop, for charity, sprinting across the church-hall stage about to perform a back somersault. The curtain descended quickly before the bishop actually rose into the air. The following two acts explained all.

Barrack-room life was quite jolly. There were various traditional japes which we were taught by old hands and they all seemed to contain a streak of cruelty. One game was to argue some non-sensical point with a recruit who knew with absolute certainty that he was right, which he was. It was possible, eventually, to make him break down in frustration and burst into tears.

For instance, one of the group, who was pretending to read a newspaper, would say, 'It says here there's a new breed of killer slug which attacks red cabbage.'

Shouts of scorn.

'Get art of it! There's no such thing as *red* cabbage!'

The victim, a country boy or a lad whose dad grew vegetables, takes the bait.

'Course there's red cabbage. My mum pickles it.'

Howls of laughter.

'Cabbage is green, mate, everyone knows that! How can you have *red* cabbage? You'd believe anything, you would.'

'But I've seen it growing! I've picked it! I've eaten it!'

More corporate mirth.

'Cabbages is *green*! It's a law of nature! You don't have red lettuce, do you? Admit it.'

The victim is now near tears.

'There *is* red cabbage! There *is*!' he shouts and runs to the safety of his bunk.

Another version of the game denied the existence of pit ponies.

'Ponies down a coal mine? How do you get 'em down there –

drop 'em down the shaft? And how did they see where they was going – were they issued with torches? If so, how did they sign for them?'

'I tell you they *did* have ponies down pits.'

'Never!' And so on.

Another game, doubly effective when played on a victim with a weak heart, was popular when rumours were rife that the Germans were about to invade the South Coast. A dozen pranksters got up in the middle of the night when the victim was asleep, silently put on their gas masks and gathered round his bed, their black, rubber-clad faces pressed only a few inches from his. One of them would then shake the victim awake, and as he recoiled from the ring of horrible masks surrounding him, everybody shrieked in simulated terror: 'THEY'RE *'ERE!*'

But there were also gentler activities in the social life of RAF Warmwell.

Local Devon ladies had banded together and opened a canteen where, mid-morning, they served the most wonderful doughnuts I have ever eaten. Without slobbering too much over the memory of those perfections, I have to report that they were British, not American doughnuts, in that they did not have a hole in the middle like a deck quoit but were classically spherical, fried to a golden brown and rolled in soft sugar so that the outside was crunchy. They had a gobbit of strawberry jam in their centre (how did they get it in there?) and were served warm.

I was glad to discover that RAF Warmwell had an active dramatic society, run by the entertainments officer who, after the war, became a colleague and a personal friend, Flight Lieutenant Arthur Howard, father of the actor Alan Howard and brother of the famous film actor Leslie (*Gone with the Wind*) Howard.

Arthur was a very funny comic actor in the dithering tradition and he had a beautiful speaking voice. He encouraged me – no, in fact he bullied me – into writing innumerable comedy sketches for the station concert party which was invaluable experience, and he made me act as compère for the concerts, work for which I developed a morbid affection and which proved again to be excellent experience.

In the middle of 1940 I bought my first car from a garage in nearby Dorchester. It was an elderly Triumph saloon, a tad larger than an Austin Seven with a rather chic, fabric-covered roof (with the fabric mostly rotted off) and no dynamo. The asking price was £15, but the garage man let me drive it away for a down payment deposit of £5 in cash.

I learned to drive by simply watching closely for a week or so beforehand how drivers drove – when they pressed the clutch, when they pushed the gear lever – and I felt confident that I had mastered the technique and could drive the car back to Warmwell without bother.

The journey of 6 miles took me over three hours. I did not know about letting the revs drop when changing up so I never got beyond second gear, and getting into second gear was so difficult that most of the time I stayed in first gear and ground noisily and very slowly back to camp.

The garage man prudently retained the logbook in the hope that I would eventually pay the other £10. Without the logbook I could not apply for petrol coupons and so had to rely on help from my flight-mechanic friends to 'liberate' the odd gallon of RAF petrol. This was coloured with green or red dye which stained the carburettor and so gave the game away to the station police, but the fitters had found a way of neutralizing the dye, so finding the small amounts of petrol needed to occasionally take a carload of aircraftsmen to a Dorchester pub or cinema was no problem.

The lack of a dynamo to recharge the battery was more of a problem. We put the battery on to an RAF trickle charger as soon as we returned from a spin, but the car would sometimes lose power alarmingly.

One night we were on our way back from a trip to the cinema in Dorchester, the car bursting with humanity like a passenger train in Calcutta, and had reached the perimeter road of the airfield when the battery began to fail. The car faltered to a stop in the middle of the road and all the lights went out.

We sat there for a while in the pitch-dark, wondering what on earth to do, when we heard the dread sound of an approaching vehicle. When our eyes got used to the darkness we could see that lumbering straight for us was a huge, heavily armoured defence vehicle called an Armadillo which must have weighed at least a couple of tons.

'Lads,' said Corporal Tyzack, quietly and sincerely, 'I think that as trained fighting men we all know how to deal with a crisis like this. Right?'

And they all began to sing with fervour, 'Abide with me, fast falls the eventide . . .'

The Armadillo ground to a halt a few inches away from our radiator and the driver gave us a tow back to camp.

London was being blitzed, but life was comparatively peaceful at RAF Warmwell, Dorset. It was a fighter station and most days we could see the German bombers, very high over us, crossing the Channel and making for targets inland. Our Spitfires and Hurricanes were scrambled immediately, but mostly they took so long climbing to the height of the bombers that by the time they reached the right altitude the German planes had disappeared.

A year or two back, when I was working at Caribonum, I had the chance of bringing a touch of serendipitous pleasure to an old lady on top of a bus. I had been presented with a liqueur chocolate by an aunt who had been given a box of them for her birthday. The chocolate, I remember well, was in the shape of a tiny bottle, and on its label it claimed to contain real green chartreuse. I put it in my pocket, waiting for an occasion momentous enough to celebrate by drinking a tiny chocolate bottle of liqueur.

A few days later I was on the top deck of a bus when two elderly ladies on the seat behind me began discussing, quite loudly, what they had always wanted from life but had never achieved. One said, 'A fur coat – anything but rabbit.' The other said, 'All my life I've thought that luxury was having a liqueur chocolate all to myself. Not just a nibble of somebody else's; not sharing it with the grandchildren or letting my husband suck the booze out of the bottom. All to myself.'

It was an extraordinary situation for me, and irresistible. I reached into my jacket pocket and took out my liqueur chocolate, twisted round and said to the lady behind me, 'Look, I have to get off the bus here and this chocolate will melt if I leave it in my pocket any longer. Please will you have it?' The lady looked at the liqueur chocolate in her hand in utter disbelief and I rushed downstairs and off the bus before she could mutter polite refusals.

I found myself standing on a pavement in Leytonstone with a light drizzle falling when I should have been warm and dry on a bus taking me to Caribonum's branch office in Woodford, but Dame Fate knew what she was doing.

At RAF Warmwell my tiny scrap of impulsive generosity on the bus in Leytonstone found a mirror image and I was the grateful recipient of a much more generous gesture.

The fifth of February 1941 was my twenty-first birthday. What to do to commemorate this deeply important milestone? I decided to drive into Weymouth for a hell-raising night of wild pleasure.

This proved difficult to achieve. For one thing my car, the dynamo-deprived Triumph saloon, became engine-deprived on the way back from watching an interstation footer match when the sump plug unscrewed itself, the oil glugged out and the engine seized up. On 5 February 1941, my engine lay in bits on a hangar floor being worked on by my friends, but I found there was a wartime bus service which ran every three hours from RAF Warmwell to crazy, fun-loving Weymouth. The last bus back left at 8.15 p.m.

Also, I only had £1 to fund my Babylonian evening and at the last moment I was put on fire-picket duty – which meant patrolling the station all night making sure it had not burned to the ground unnoticed by the official fire brigade – and it cost me 10s. to bribe a corporal with girl trouble and concomitant money problems to do my fire-picket duty for me. So I arrived at Weymouth with not a lot of money left for hell-raising.

This was just as well as there was nothing to buy. It was a dark night, the seafront cafés were shut and boarded up, the beach ugly with huge iron anti-tank spikes sticking up from the sand as Weymouth braced itself for invasion. I couldn't even find a cinema which was open. I had a beer at a pub, but this was a cheerless experience so I just walked the deserted streets. I knew how chilly in spirit out-of-season seaside resorts can be from my years in Thanet, but Weymouth in 1941 was a very great deal gloomier than anything I had experienced.

To my great relief I noticed that it was just gone half-past seven, time to make my way to the bus station and the last bus home to Warmwell and the warmth of the familiar.

Opposite the bus station was the possibility of some sort of birthday pleasure to be had: a brightly lit milk bar.

Milk bars were an odd phenomenon of those days. I suppose nowadays they would be denounced by newspaper health corres-pondents as 'temples of cholesterol' and 'purveyors of mad cow juice', but in the war days they were bright, cheap and cheerful places to sit and enjoy a cheap sandwich and a drink. The drink was always milk, usually in the form of a milk shake, a beaker of chilled milk which was flavoured and then fluffed up by an electric whizzer. Milk bars were everywhere; there were many in London's West End and every resort had plenty of them, so there was clearly a strong demand for that kind of informal café. Why have they virtually disappeared? Did we all go off milk because of the postwar fad for dieting, or was it just that we developed a distaste for the stuff?

I went into the milk bar opposite the bus station in Weymouth and sat on a tall stool at the counter. I was the only customer. There was a plump lady with orange hair behind the bar, clad in the blue and white uniform of the milk-bar chain. She was smoking a cigarette, occasionally tipping the ash into a milk-shake beaker.

'What's up, love?' she said. 'You look like a bloodhound what's trod in something.'

'It's my twenty-first birthday,' I said.

'Christ!' she said. 'You poor bugger! Now, I wonder . . . Hang on a sec . . .' She got off her chair and rummaged for quite a long while in the back of a huge refrigerator, eventually producing a half bottle of champagne, giving me two thirds of it.

'There you are,' she said, handing me my glass. 'It was give me years ago by the deputy area manager who was after my body. Happy birthday, love!'

So I celebrated my twenty-first birthday by drinking champagne with a warm-hearted lady in a milk bar at the royal seaside resort of Weymouth, where in the eighteenth century the middle-aged King George III is said to have caught his first glimpse of the sea ('Is that all it does, Charlotte?).

I was still a cuckoo in the armoury waiting for the photography section to be completed when I was joined by another graduate from the Farnborough course, A/C 1 Bickerstaffe, an important figure in my service career.

Whilst on leave in London, A/C 1 Bickerstaffe was sent a telegram by the Warmwell adjutant ordering him back to Warmwell immediately as he had been posted to Iceland. Bickerstaffe replied by telegram to the adjutant: 'Cannot return. Fell down a bomb hole in the Haymarket and best blue uniform at dry-cleaners.' This does make a kind of service sense as we were forbidden to travel in civilian clothes.

So the next day I was sent to Iceland in place of Bickerstaffe.

The journey from Dorset to Iceland was not enjoyable. The train up to the Scottish embarkation port, Gourock, on the Firth of Clyde, seemed to take about three weeks with its long halts and brief spurts of movement and total lack of lighting and heat. The servicemen packing the carriages lapsed into a kind of hibernation, a temporary moratorium on living.

The midwinter voyage on a troopship across the North Atlantic was also less than charming, although in spite of my morbid fear of being seasick I was about the only person on board who wasn't. It was a close-run thing though when we were on parade on deck for lifeboat drill and some idiot opened the door from the galley. The smell of boiling cabbage wafted across our nostrils and the entire parade broke ranks and lurched for the rail. I only avoided being sick because all the places at the rail were taken and I was unable to get in.

A sergeant gave us a stern educational talk about the importance of personal hygiene when we disembarked at Reykjavik, which he referred to as 'Reek-JAR-vick' (normal pronunciation, 'Recky-a-vick'). His hilarious lecture was mostly inaudible due to a boisterous wind sweeping across the deck, but I caught his warning, rather Old Testament, that most of us would probably catch VD, so we should report to the medical officer as soon as we sighted a red blotch because there was a new ointment. And we were to avoid spitting. This was meant literally, i.e., to take evasive action when walking busy Reykjavik pavements. According to the sergeant the air contained volcanic dust and Icelanders of both sexes spat copiously and frequently. Oddly, this turned out to be quite true and had been true for well over a century because in *Travels in Iceland*, published in 1812, the scientist Sir George Mackenzie noted, 'The unrestrained evacuation of saliva seems to be a fashion all over Iceland.'

A group of us were posted to a new RAF station being built at Kaldadharnes, a flat area beside the sea about 70 miles up the road from Reykjavik and rumoured, without truth, to be sinking into the sea. We were installed in a new wooden hut with an iron stove in the middle and that was all. Home comforts had to be foraged for, i.e., stolen. My bed was four empty petrol tins supporting a brand-new door with a sign screwed to it reading 'Your Chaplain – Knock And Enter At Any Time'. On this I placed my Lilo, an inflatable canvas and rubber mattress which I had carried all the way from England, and Lilos weighed heavy in those days.

On about the third evening I sat comfortably on the bed darning a sock. When I had finished I thoughtlessly parked the needle by sticking it into the Lilo. Realizing what I had done, I even more foolishly yanked the needle out. Later, in the middle of the night, my hip grounded on door; the Lilo had deflated. However carefully I searched I never did find the puncture; even when the Lilo was pressed under water the pinhole was too small to release tell-tale air bubbles, so during the eighteen months I spent in Iceland I had to get up every night at about three in the morning and go dizzy blowing into the Lilo.

The station's runways and hangars were already completed and in use and a section of Royal Engineers was busy putting up the station's living accommodation, NAAFI, admin offices and so on. This was a lengthy process, as during the hours of darkness a third of the new doors and floorboards disappeared. Well we, the established residents, had to have beds to lie on and it was our duty to find wood to burn in our stoves to stop us from freezing to death (we were, after all, Air Ministry property). So by the time a new hut had been erected it had taken three times the material it should have done and taken three times as long to put up. But nobody seemed to be bothered much.

Eventually we managed to make the huts comfortable and warm, which led to inquisitive visits from small furry things. My bedside table was a pair of square empty petrol tins balanced on one another, which brought the top to the same height as my face. One night I brought back a bar of chocolate from the NAAFI, took a bite before going to sleep and left the rest on my table. In the morning I woke to find only half my bar of chocolate left. It had been nibbled all the way round, and according to the size of the fang marks, by a sizeable rat or a small wolf. The chocolate was an inch from my nose.

Photography was not a very vital part of our squadron's activities. The aircraft were mainly Hudsons, chunky, medium-sized reconnaissance planes, and their function was to make painstaking anti-submarine sweeps, depth charges primed, over the northern approaches of the Atlantic.

The squadron had one remarkable and famous coup when a German U-boat, trolling along on the surface for a breath of fresh air, its crew fed up to the teeth with the war and their dangerous and uncomfortable job, surrendered to one of our planes which then, to its annoyance, had to fly patiently round and round the slow U-boat to escort it back to Reykjavik harbour and peaceful captivity for its crew.

As most of our aircrews' time was spent searching for the enemy on the North Atlantic's waves there was not much point in them repeatedly photographing stretches of heaving sea, so although a handsome darkroom cum caravan arrived from England, once again I was underemployed.

Soon after the British had moved into Iceland to stop Germany grabbing it as a U-boat base, a small force of Americans arrived. We helped them land on the quay and carry their stuff to waiting lorries. When they arrived back home in the USA they were given a medal, which is more than we were.

The GIs were different from us in many ways, the most immediately striking being their startlingly clean, white, high-necked vests which peeped above their open-necked shirts. We must have had some sort of laundry arrangements of our own but I cannot remember ever changing my one vest, a greyish, friendly garment which also kept me warm in bed during the Icelandic winter and was useful for blocking out draughts from an ill-fitting window near my bed and for acting as a back-up towel.

As soon as our rich allies had settled in, our ground crews started schemes to separate them from some of their surplus dollars. The lads' most successful swindle was to acquire a chunk of aluminium, machine it into a crude cigarette lighter and sell it reluctantly to a GI as a personal souvenir to take back home to the USA, made from a German Messerschmitt fighter shot down by Uncle during the Battle of Britain. The demand was so brisk that the fitters and riggers laboured far into the night at their workbenches, and suitable lumps of aluminium were like nuggets of gold.

There was a constant flow of jeeps and trucks between Kaldadharnes and Reykjavik and it was easy to cadge a lift. It was a curiously alien journey, about 70 miles through a barren landscape surrounded by glaciers and a variety of different types of volcano, including the great, still occasionally erupting, Hekla. Hot springs were everywhere and the hot water was piped into villages and towns for heating; every village seemed to have nearby a small and rather ugly concrete open-air swimming pool, like a static water tank, steaming away in the cold air, and ranges of naturally heated greenhouses abounded. I read somewhere recently that Iceland was the second largest exporter of bananas. Well, well (if true).

Near at hand, too, was the huge and famous spouting hot spring, the Great Geysir (whence our word 'geyser', as in Ewart's 'Victor' geyser, came). Much of the farmland which the road to Reykjavik passed through was once lava fields and still looked like a moonscape with 10-foot-high broken lava bubbles scattered around.

The farmhouses were shack-like, made with cement and corrugated iron, many with turf propping up the sides and holding down the roof. There were small flocks of huge sheep nosing about for blades of grass, and many grey ponies and a white hen or two. Outside most farmhouses there was a complicated structure of poles and wires from which stockfish hung to dry. Occasionally one glimpsed a small church painted white. There was little vegetation and no trees at all. It was rumoured that Akureyri in the north of the island possessed ten trees with real leaves which anybody could look at and even touch, but we put that down to boasting.

Nightlife at RAF Kaldadharnes tended to be on the quiet side, usually spent lying on our beds talking and reading, only springing into action when an eldritch howl rent the night air as some unlucky lad, weaving his way back to his billet after a couple of pints in the NAAFI, broke through the ice covering a ditch and had to be swiftly hauled out before he froze rigid, which took about two minutes.

Compared with Kaldadharnes, Reykjavik was a combination of Babylon, Las Vegas and Sin City. There was a popular Salvation Army canteen known as the Holy Grocer's, two cafés which sold real cream cakes and two cinemas built some years apart, called, with cool Scandinavian logic, the Old Cinema and the New Cinema. Both of these dream palaces had frequent trouble with their projectors. The audience sat in total darkness except for the scrape and sparking as thirty or forty GIs tried to get their souvenir aluminium cigarette lighters to light.

Taking a taxi out of Reykjavik was a physical experience. The taxis looked as though they had come from some early Hollywood gangster film, battered and bulbous old American Chevies with their gear lever on the steering column. Every time I saw one I expected Edward G. Robinson to be crouched in the back cuddling a Thompson sub-machine-gun.

Reykjavik was then quite a small city, and when a cab reached city limits the concrete road ceased and there was a sudden 8-inch drop onto a dirt road. The local cabbies took the drop at speed and all the passenger suffered was a traumatic bounce and a bang as the car's suspension touched bottom. Returning to Reykjavik was more difficult, but most cabbies kept a few bricks in the boot to help the car climb up the concrete step into town.

I discovered to my delight that in Reykjavik there was a forces radio station. It was actually Iceland's national radio station which – Oh, how British – was hired by our conquering occupying force for quite a large sum of money to broadcast to its own troops for an hour or so every afternoon.

I made contact with the officer who ran it, Major Roberts-Wray, a kind man, and infiltrated myself into his operation as a scriptwriter and occasional broadcaster, in neither of which disciplines I had had any experience at all.

On my first visit to the studios I began my study of the Icelandic language by learning the Icelandic word for 'recording studio', which was written above the door. It is *Rikisutvarpssalur*, and it took a bit of learning. It turned out to be the first of only two Icelandic words I ever did learn during my eighteen months there. The other was the Icelandic for 'journalist', a much better word than ours, *bladamadur*, pronounced 'blather-meister'.

My superiors at Kaldadharnes seemed only too glad to get shot of me. I was allowed to shunt backwards and forwards to Reykjavik more or less whenever the forces radio needed me there. And they had many needs. There were several good readers, including the Navy's flag-lieutenant, to cope with news items and scripted talks, but the station was woefully short of light entertainment. There was an Iceland Forces Orchestra but nobody knew what to do with it apart from getting it to play interminable Glenn Miller numbers at unit dances.

The Americans had a showbiz saying that a beginner starting a showbiz career needed first of all to have 'somewhere to be lousy in', a luxury denied most present-day comedy writers because very high minimum fees mean that radio and TV producers are understandably reluctant to take a chance on an untried talent who costs them almost as much as an award winner.

Iceland Forces Radio was my opportunity to be lousy and I seized it gratefully, being energetically lousy over quite a large spread of programmes. There was acting as compère to the band and giving the concerts a little humour; there was a music programme I invented called *Once Upon a Time* in which I linked the musical numbers the band wanted to play into adult fairy stories of a rambling, shaggy-dog nature, which were read admirably by the flag-lieutenant; there was a piano programme with commentary written and spoken by me called *Ivory Interlude*; there was a music cum comedy sketch show called *Roadhouse* in which the band played being the roadhouse's band and I mainly ad libbed most of the roadhouse's staff and guests; and there were little comic serials inspired by (i.e., stolen from) strip cartoons in the *Daily Mirror*.

I got on very well with the forces orchestra. The musical director was Sapper Edwin Braden, a friendly Northerner who was an unbelievably badly designed human being, ginger hair, a stained and tangled moustache like an old toothbrush used for cleaning eggy spoons and a body shaped like an unpeelable potato. But a fine professional musician, unflappable, right on top of the job, frequently still finishing off an arrangement as the band's coach pulled into an army camp for a concert.

I had so much writing to do that it was easier working at a table in the NAAFI than crouching on my bed, so I plugged away at the funnies with conversation surging round me and the bellowing of complicated orders only heard in NAAFIs, e.g., 'Hey, Mave – cup o' char and a wad (cup of tea and a cake), hussif ('housewife' – i.e., sewing kit in a roll), packet of envelopes and a pork pie. Ta, luv.'

And I much enjoyed visits to the Forces Dance Orchestra in the hut where they lived in Reykjavik. They were quite a distinguished bunch in the dance-music world: besides Edwin Braden there was Cyril Stapleton as lead violin, later to form his own orchestra with great success on the radio. We had two vocalists – essential to dance orchestras at that time – the deservedly popular and famous Denny Dennis, and the equally so Sam Costa.

Denny, real name Dennis Pountain, a quiet, dull man with a beautifully deep and true voice, was supposed to be Britain's answer to Bing Crosby, in much the same way that later, Matt Munro was supposed to be Britain's answer to Frank Sinatra. They were both excellent singers but wrong answers.

Sam Costa, a good jazz singer and a funny man in the showbiz style, always seemed to be sitting on the end of his bed grooming his feet. He took enormous trouble with his toes, clipping the nails, buffing them up with a buffer, massaging them for hours. After the war he was a great success, firstly as the third star of the comedy show *Much-Binding-in-the-Marsh* and later as a disc jockey on BBC Radio 2. Not as a dancer. Interesting, that. Could a job not have been found for Sam's excellent feet on Radio 2?

When I first arrived in Iceland I found that among our superiors in the chain of command were a few quite elderly officers, delightful old boys but long in the tooth, if any. I worked out the reason. They were survivors of the First World War who were keen as mustard to do what they could for the old country in its Second World War, and the authorities had to take notice as the old boys still had about an hour and a half to go before reaching the age when they were too old to be recommissioned and could tactfully be sent out to grass.

The veterans were duly welcomed back into the services, but what to do with them?

The answer was to post them abroad to non-trouble spots, to areas where crises were unlikely to occur and where young station commanders could find odd jobs to keep the old boys busy without them actually clogging up the war effort. The perfect non-trouble spot to post the old warriors was, of course, Iceland, and we had our due share of them.

One of the German pocket battleships, I think it was the *Scharnhorst*, slipped through the net of Allied naval vessels penning it in a fjord and steamed straight for Iceland. What it hoped to do when it got there I have no idea but there was no panic in RAF ranks. The RAF regiment at Kaldadharnes had fifteen rifles and these were coolly issued to airmen to defend the airfield to their last gasp should the battleship be foolhardy enough to attack.

I was broadcasting in Reykjavik at the time, where the Army, which proudly produced a Bofors anti-aircraft gun, was a bit more excited. I was issued with a rifle and ordered to man a sandbagged observation post on the airfield perimeter and shoot on sight any battleship which did not reply satisfactorily to my challenge, 'Who goes there, friend or foe?'

The only good thing which came out of all this was the marvellous view I had that night of the aurora borealis, the northern lights, a breathtaking sight like a Dada-esque firework display in very slow motion.

During this I leaned my rifle against the sandbag wall of the bunker in order to find a hanky and have a blow. Suddenly before me, coming up to the waistband of my tunic, stood a tiny bald figure with a captain's pips on his shoulders. I was young then and nowadays I might judge differently, but at the time he seemed to me to be about 104 years old and frail with it, like a pensionable stick insect.

'Whar's your wifle, airman?' he demanded in a high quavery voice.

'There, sir,' I said, pointing at it.

'Nevah be parted from your wifle, man,' he said. 'Don't you wealize I could overpaar you?'

There was another golden oldie at Kaldadharnes, a wing commander who always wore his old Royal Flying Corps uniform, which he must have cleaned and brushed daily since 1918. He strode about in his ancient jodhpurs, high brown boots and Sam Browne belt with a pistol in the holster. This he rested his right hand upon and occasionally slapped. He looked like Biggles.

The wingco was not Biggles, but according to William Amos in his book *The Originals: Who's Really Who in Fiction*, Biggles was in Iceland at the time. He was the air officer commanding Iceland, Air Commodore Cecil Wigglesworth, by all accounts the man on whom the author Captain W. E. Johns based Biggles.

The wingco painted beautifully sensitive watercolours of the volcanos and glaciers which surrounded us and he gave them away to anybody, of any rank, who wanted one. I think his official function was education officer but he seemed to spend a great deal of his time flying the station Gypsy Moth upside down over the runway.

He died suddenly. His funeral was in the station all-purpose chapel, but he was buried near a forlorn little church about 7 miles away in the middle of an old lava field, now a farm. Considering the transport difficulties of getting there, there was a surprisingly large turnout of volunteers from all ranks to give him a decent send-off.

Another elderly gentleman (laundry officer) promoted me, for quite the wrong reasons. Promotion was most welcome to me, not as a matter of prestige but because the promotion, aircraftsman first class to leading aircraftsman, represented in material terms something like an extra three cream cakes, four pints of NAAFI bitter and six cups of café coffee per week.

It came about because I was doing a broadcast of *Roadhouse* at the *Rikisutvarpssalur* (how the word trips off the tongue) in Reykjavik and I had a lift back to Kaldadharnes in the 15 cwt. Commer truck which had been recently instituted as a shuttle service for RAF personnel. It was a dark cold night in March and the roads were gleaming with frozen snow and ice.

About 20 miles out of Reykjavik, in the middle of nowhere, as we in the back were harmonizing an emotional version of 'You Stepped out of a Dream', the Commer, being nursed by the driver slowly round a bend, began to slide sideways towards the edge of the road. It continued to slide sideways until it reached the edge and slid into a ditch.

This was not high drama, not a Formula One racing car hitting the crash barrier at 232 m.p.h.; the Commer simply came to rest slowly and gently on its side like an elephant succumbing to a tranquillizer dart. None of us were injured, just slightly shocked and not at all happy at being stranded on a very cold night far from home.

I was unanimously voted the honour of walking to the nearest farmhouse and ringing the station duty officer for help; it was a long walk. Volcanic earth was not fodder-friendly and the farms had to be enormous to support just a few sheep and a cow or two, and the farmhouses were miles apart.

I picked my way across the rock- and lava-strewn land towards a light. Luckily there was a moon and I only fell over about thirty times before arriving at the farmhouse. The farm family were very kind and after I had mimed the Commer sliding over and the need to phone, they led me to the telephone and I rang the duty officer.

'RAF Kaldadharnes,' said an unlovely voice.

'Is that the duty officer?' I asked.

'The duty officer's off-duty. It's Sergeant Meadows 'ere!' said Sergeant Meadows irritably. I knew the horrible sergeant well. He had an inch-high forehead and a personal grudge against Hitler because the war had postponed his retirement and his plans to spend the rest of his life peacefully making his wife's life hell and bullying the children.

'Well, what do you want?' he barked down the phone.

'It's A/C 1 Muir, Sergeant, nine-three-one-one-one-zero' (you never, ever forget your service number). 'I wish to report that the Commer's come to a full stop.'

He put me on a charge.

The charge was 'dumb insolence to a superior', a magnificent example of the service mind at work. How can somebody be accused of dumb insolence because of something he said?

It seemed to me that I should not have much difficulty in getting off the charge when my case came up. I sailed through five years in the RAF and several petty charges without being found guilty by simply listening to the wording of the charge and replying to it rationally. At Warmwell I was put on a charge when an officer could not find me. The charge accused me of being 'absent from my place of duty'. I explained to the 'judge' that as the photography section had yet to be built, I had no place of duty. And got off.

And I once lost my RAF identity card. The charge read, 'Carelessness in losing identity card,' and I argued that the charge as written could not be proved until circumstances of the loss were determined, e.g., it could have been stolen by a master pickpocket, in which case it was not carelessness on my part but a matter of him being better at picking my pocket than I was at preventing my pocket being picked. I got off.

But it was a dangerous game. At any moment word could have gone round the officers' mess that A/C 1 Muir F. 931110 was a smart-arse, a barrack-room lawyer who should be taught a lesson. On the other hand, as far as I was concerned, any gamble was worth a try rather than being given 'jankers' on some feeble charge and having to scrub the guardroom floor at dawn every morning for a month.

A few days later my case came up and the dread Sergeant Meadows marched me smartly into a room to face the duty officer: 'Lef'-right! Lef'-right! Right turn! 'At orf.' Sitting behind the table was a white-haired old gentleman with wings on his uniform breast and an herbaceous border of medal ribbons. He looked at the charge sheet, put on spectacles and had another look, 'Ah,' he said. 'Muir.' He looked at me hopefully. 'Muir?'

'Sir,' I said, adding helpfully, 'nine-three-one-one-one-zero.'

'Hah,' he said. 'Commer truck. Reykjavik, eh? Why? Eh? Duty, what?'

'Sort of semi-duty actually, sir,' I said.

His brows corrugated with thought.

'You. Muir,' he said after quite a pause, 'in Reykjavik for . . . eh?'

'I was broadcasting, sir. On the forces radio programme.'

'Great heavens!' he murmured. He polished his glasses on his tie and stared at me with interest. 'Broadcasting? You mean you . . . talk things and . . . sing music . . . and . . . similar?'

'I try not to sing, sir.'

'But talk? Into a whatchamacallit – microphone? Chat on about this and that . . . and so forth?'

'Yes, sir.'

'Great heavens!' He leaned back in his chair, stunned. It occurred to me that the reason he was so impressed was that he himself was not a talker. A man of action, yes, but he clearly had only a very limited vocabulary at his command, and if everyday expressions like 'pass the marmalade' and 'does this train stop at Tunbridge Wells?' were excluded, he probably got through a normal day on about 120 words.

'Sergeant,' he said. 'What rank he? . . . er . . . broadcasting air-man?'

'It says it clearly on the charge sheet in front of you, sir. See, sir? Aircraftsman first class.'

'Have him promoted!'

Sergeant Meadows, his face a mask of venom, marched me smartly out of the room and shortly afterwards I became Leading Aircraftsman Muir F. (931110), and *slightly* richer.

The tour of duty in Iceland was only for one year because cook-house food was none too nourishing over a long period; fresh vegetables were unobtainable and every meal consisted of a chunk of sheep cooked in a simple and semi-edible fashion, a couple of slices of tinned beetroot and an ascorbic-acid tablet to prevent scurvy. Pudding was usually industrial apple pie and custard substitute. The technique when dining was to queue up for the first course, find a place at a table and eat the sheep and beetroot while they were hot, then turn the tin plate over and collect the pud on the back, thus only having one tin plate to sluice in the communal bucket of tepid water on the way out.

The Icelanders ate a tremendous amount of fish, usually dried in hunks and a challenge to the teeth, or dried whole and a challenge to the nose. W. H. Auden wrote in his *Letters from Iceland*, 'The tougher kind tastes like toe-nails, and the softer kind like the skin off the soles of one's feet'.

I tried eating in a restaurant in Reykjavik but it was not an unqualified treat. Icelanders like their soup sweet and mine turned out to be hot cocoa with grains of uncooked rice floating about in it. The main course was the choice of either dried fish or sheep and beetroot. The pudding, which was a cream cake, and the coffee were both delicious.

I was so involved in enjoyable tours round army camps introducing the forces orchestra and writing and performing in about five series of radio shows that I volunteered to stay in Iceland for a further six months, which I found was possible if your reason was deemed worthy enough, which mine was judged to be.

In between the two tours I returned to England for a short leave and was interviewed about forces broadcasting in Iceland by Alan Keith on a new BBC radio programme called *In Town Tonight*.

In the hospitality room after the show the producer pointed out to me a smallish lean figure in army uniform and a warm British camel-hair overcoat. He was slumped in a chair, tapping his leg rhythmically with a swagger cane. He had a Mediterranean face and complexion, and when he stood up and went over to the sandwich trolley he walked with a rather dramatic limp.

'That's Philip Ridgeway,' explained the producer. 'I rather think he's a captain. He's some kind of a roving army entertainments officer and he's going to Iceland with you; that's why I invited him here.'

The figure limped back clutching about eight sandwiches wrapped in a paper doily.

'Captain Ridgeway?' I said.

'Major,' he said. He sat down, sticking out his gammy leg to make sitting down possible. His trouser leg rode up and a curved dagger in a jewelled sheath fell out of the top of his sock. He picked up the dagger and jiggled it back into place.

'One of our undercover chaps in Cairo gave it to me when I managed to get him out of a spot of bother in a cellar,' he said, quietly. 'I've only had to use it once.'

This was preposterous, B-picture stuff, but I realized that it could *just* be true. The Ridgeways were unconventional: the major's father, also named Philip Ridgeway, was a pioneer radio impresario who as early as 1930 produced a new sort of radio variety show called *The Ridgeway Parade*, which combined cabaret, variety and revue in a highly entertaining mix. He had great success with it in the theatre, too.

Philip Ridgeway, junior (the good major), tried for a while to follow in his father's footsteps but found his chance of making a reasonable living lay in more fringe showbiz activities; he did a bit of acting in his father's shows, but concentrated more on becoming a public relations and publicity man for film companies and a minder for stars at first nights.

'You did *quite* well in your interview, Muir,' he said to me mid-sandwich, 'but from a professional point of view, don't sound so enthusiastic. It's very amateur to show enthusiasm.'

With this dubious advice ringing in my ears we set sail back to the Land of the Midnight Sun.

Back in Iceland I did not see much of the major as his duties lay more with army unit concert parties. But I saw enough.

I have always wanted to declare an Ad Libber's Charter, which would establish that if a good ad lib is only heard by three people then the ad libber is entitled to repeat his ad lib later to a wider audience.

For instance, years ago I was at a local dinner party and the lady next to me said, 'Do you cook, Mr Muir?' I replied, 'No, I'm afraid I don't. I eat a bit but I don't cook at all.' 'You should learn,' she said. 'There are some very easy-to-understand recipes on cards by that man with the nice grey hair who runs restaurants and cooks on television. You know, Robert le Carré.' And I said, 'Oh, yes, didn't he write *The Pie That Came in from the Cold*?' Only that one lady was within earshot and she had never heard of John le Carré.

A choice instance of my credo not working at all occurred years ago during the run of the BBC2 television game show, *Call My Bluff*. Patrick Campbell and I, the team captains, were taken to lunch by a publisher, Geoffrey Strachan of Eyre Methuen, to discuss putting together a book based on the programme (we did it, too, and illustrated it ourselves, revealing to our great surprise that neither of us could draw).

The lunch took place at one of the first of the trendy trattorias, Mario and Franco's in Soho. I ordered something not very Italian but trustworthy like grilled sole and Paddy Campbell ordered quenelles – those bits of fish mucked about with in a frying pan. It was an expensive item on the menu in those days, £15.

When the food was served Paddy saw, sadly, that he was only given four bits of the very expensive mucked-about-with fish.

I said to Geoffrey, 'Well, really! Four quenelles for fifteen quid?' Then imitating Paddy's Irish accent, 'Four quenelles!'

Paddy always said it was the best pun he had ever heard. As he lived in the South of France where quenelles were often on the menu, he tried to appropriate my pun and dazzle his friends, but, alas, life is not as compliant as that. Whenever Paddy entertained in a Nice restaurant he would hopefully order quenelles and they were duly laid in front of him; sometimes there were three quenelles on the plate, frequently there was a more generous helping of five, six, or seven quenelles, but never, ever, was Paddy served four quenelles.

I now lean on the Ad Libber's Charter to support me in retelling an ad lib which I made many years ago. It was only heard at the time by the one person to whom it was said, that delightful, blonde, cheerfully sexy singer, Frances Day.

The plot started a couple of months after I returned to Iceland on my extension six-month tour of duty. I began to feel ill. Most of the day I had a kind of V-shaped ache in the groin. I had a very busy schedule of shows to write and as usual with any sort of illness, my way of coping with the problem intelligently was to ignore it and hope that it would go away. But it did not go away; it got worse.

I eventually reported sick and was immediately sent to the Army hospital at Reykjavik. It seems that I had developed a tubercular infection of a testicle which was growing to the size of a King Edward's potato and would have to come out. The operation had a beautiful name: orchidectomy.

Life in the hospital was rather pleasant. An elderly American GI in the next bed fed me endless Camel cigarettes. A bottle of Guinness was served to us morning and evening to build up our constitutions after living so long on sheep and beetroot, and the surgeon, Major Edwards, was not only efficient but cheerful with it. He told me not to worry or get a complex over the op. It was a tiny op, he assured me, and was like having an ear off: nature had provided a second ear and the body soon adapted to working on only one. I was not too happy about the analogy of my extremely personal operation being like having an ear off but his manner was reassuring.

On the days leading up to the operation the only book I could find to read was James Joyce's *Ulysses*. Not perhaps an ideal choice under the circumstances but there you go.

The op itself was no problem. It only required a local anaesthetic, so I chatted to Major Edwards while he busied himself. While he was at it he also removed a rather volcano-like boil which had suddenly popped up on my neck.

After the operation, drowsy from medication, I was slid into a bed in a ward and, as a new boy, inspected by Matron.

'And what have they been doing to *you*?' she enquired cheerily, reading my clipboard for details.

'Had a boil removed,' I mumbled drowsily.

Matron froze. 'We prefer the word "testicle",' she said.

Major Edwards sat alongside my bed many times over the next few days questioning me to find out how I had become infected. No doubt worried about a possible epidemic.

Eventually he found what was almost certainly the answer. In our hut was a corporal cook in charge of disposing of the considerable mass of waste food collected in bins at the back of the cookhouse. He did a deal with a local Icelandic farmer to exchange bins of pig food for churns of the farmer's fresh milk, which the corporal parked in our hut for us all to dip into, and enjoyably thick and creamy milk it was, too. But the milk was not pasteurized, and I drank a lot of it every day.

QED.

By an extraordinary coincidence, I found many years later that my experience was not unique.

The cast of the BBC radio show, *My Music*, which Denis Norden and I had been in for ever, was invited to record a special edition of the show at the Hong Kong Arts Festival. Also in the show were, of course, Ian Wallace and John Amis. On our free weekend, we were all sitting on a luxury junk belonging to our rich hostess, clutching half litres of gin and tonic, when I found myself talking to Ian in a rambling sort of way about Iceland. And I told him about the tainted milk and the op.

'But this is remarkable!' said Ian. 'I had the same thing! Early part of the war. Stationed in a lonely bit of Dorset farmland. Drank lots of milk more or less straight from the cow. Hospital and the same operation!'

What is more, John Amis reminded us that Sir Malcolm Sargent also endured the same loss. Could it be an affliction which haunted only the highly musical?

And so to the ad lib which laid for me the ghost of this otherwise not very humorous medical experience.

The year was about 1952. The scene was the stage of the BBC radio's audience studio at Aeolian Hall, New Bond Street. The show we were performing was *The Name's the Same*, a confection in which a panel of grown-up and fairly intelligent people like Denis and me spent an hour or so of our lives, lightly paid, deciding whether the chap standing before us, who played the double bass in a nightclub, was really named Julius Caesar, or if he was was bluffing (his name really *was* Julius Caesar).

The guest member of our panel for that show was the lovely Frances Day, then mature and all the more attractive for it.

Before the show, the cast regulars were gathered together in an ante-room waiting for Frances to arrive – we had not met her before – chatting away and sipping our room-temperature white wine from the hospitality trolley. I was standing with one foot up on a chair, expounding away to Denis about something boring when, from behind me, a hand came between my legs and grabbed my vitals. I turned round, considerably shocked, to find Frances Day looking up at me with her cute little pixie smile.

Still holding on: 'Hello!' she said.

But I had my moment after the show.

We are all standing about signing autographs for the contestants ('For Marie Antoinette – all good wishes for the future,') when a little old lady gave me a card to sign. I drew a heart pierced by an arrow and added the words, 'You are ever in my memory: the stranger who blew you a kiss from his Rolls-Royce on St Valentine's Day.' The old lady was thrilled.

Frances said, 'You really are diabolical!'

'Actually,' I said, 'I'm monobolical.'

Chapter Five

THE WAR (PART TWO)

I was to find that RAF Ringway was different, very different, from RAF Kaldadharnes. There was not a volcano in sight nor one smelly fish drying on a clothes line to disturb the neat greenery of the gardens and parks and trees around RAF Ringway, which was and is again now the civil airport, situated on the pleasant Altrincham side of Manchester.

To my surprise I felt quite an emotional twinge leaving Iceland. Thanks to the warm Gulf Stream (every English child is taught at school about the benign influence of the Gulf Stream; even our nice Mr Murphy, geography master/ferry bar steward at Bradstowe College, Broadstairs, managed to get it right), Iceland was not all that icy. Perhaps I was just so much younger then but I do not think of it being unbearably cold, although I do remember standing at the window of the NAAFI drinking a beer on Christmas morning and the froth freezing on my new and already rather revolting moustache.

There really was a midnight sun in the summer, but not every day, only when the weather was right, whereupon we all rushed out with our cameras and photographed each other with a clock tower in the background showing round about twelve o'clock. It could have been midday, of course, but no, it was midnight all right because the shadows were different. The trouble with all that bright sunshine was that sleep became difficult and we began to look forward to winter and a bit of good old relaxing night.

Unhappily, winter with no sunshine at all turned out to be gloomy and progressively dispiriting. The days never became really light, except for a glimmer or two around midday, and it was not relaxing at all but deeply depressing.

I liked the Icelanders. Their blonde girls were often astonishingly beautiful, which helped, and I found that most of the population, as so often happens in a land where living is hard, were noticeably hospitable and friendly. But they were not exactly zany funsters. In his *Letters from Iceland*, W. H. Auden wrote to Christopher Isherwood that he thought that Iceland was the place for enjoyable but brief visits. 'I think that in the long run, the Scandinavian sanity would be too much for you.'

In his book, Auden presented what he claimed were translations of a number of Icelandic sayings including, 'Every man likes the smell of his own farts.' And, 'Pissing in his shoe keeps no man warm for long.' At a poetry reading in London I accused Auden of inventing these, but he insisted that they were genuine, sane, Icelandic proverbs.

There was no prospect of my volunteering for a third term of duty on the island, particularly after having had an operation because wounds healed extremely slowly out there, so I packed my kitbag (almost tearfully) to go home.

I gave my heavy Lilo to a newly arrived airman who was pathetically grateful, not knowing of its need to be given the kiss of life in the middle of the night. I could not get the second-hand portable typewriter I had bought out there into the kitbag, so I made a rope loop and when embarking on the troopship for home wore the typewriter round my neck, balancing the kitbag on my shoulder. Climbing the ship's ladder with that lot made me feel like an Egyptian slave humping a 6-foot cube of stone up the side of a pyramid.

On my last night at Kaldadharnes I found sleep difficult. The sun was shining brightly through the window and my mind was busy remembering. I remembered that before leaving RAF Warmwell I had been rehearsing one of the leading parts in a play which was a great favourite with amateur dramatic societies at that time, *Outward Bound*. It was one of those 'well-made' plays in which a group of assorted characters with heavy problems were closely confined together, in this case on a cruise liner, and eased their problems by thrusting them on to one another. The big twist in *Outward Bound* was that everybody was dead.

I played a decent, stiff-upper-lip sort of chap. All was going well and I was word-perfect in my part when I had this sudden posting to Iceland.

Reykjavik had a theatre and in my first week there I discovered to my astonishment and delight that an Icelandic amateur company was playing *Outward Bound* in Icelandic. I went. It was a weird experience because I knew almost the whole play by heart in English.

The Icelander playing my part of the cool British gent was short and tubby with a Ronald Colman moustache, plus-fours, cricket blazer, clip-on bow tie and a deerstalker hat; he looked like the comic in Butlin's holiday camp 'Family Variety Hour' in Bognor Regis.

And then in my bunk just when I was at last happily nodding off, I sat bolt upright and wide awake again. I had remembered my car. My beloved Triumph saloon! Short of a dynamo and roof fabric but *my first car* and I had left it, forsaken, forgotten in my rush to catch the train to Iceland.

I left the Triumph parked on the grass verge about 100 yards on the Dorchester side of the main gate of RAF Warmwell, and it should still be there. As far as I am concerned anybody who finds the car may keep it, it's just that in the glove compartment there should be a partly consumed packet of Victory-V extra-strong throat pellets – real killers – and my local chemist has never heard of them. The packet may be sent c/o my publisher.

The voyage home from Iceland was without incident and I had great pleasure in finding a post office back in Gourock and sending Mother a telegram: 'FATTED CALF FOR ONE TOMORROW EVENING?'

I hesitated before sending it because I knew Chas was abroad; he had been posted to India, and there still lingered from the First World War the dread of seeing a postman at the front door bearing a buff envelope; it was the War Office's way of notifying that a next of kin had been killed in action or was missing believed dead. But I was glad I did send it because when I arrived home I found that the telegram had given Mother no dreads, just pleasure.

The fatted calf was a piece of cod escorted by parsley, mashed potatoes and fresh beans from the garden, a dinner which was caviar and pâté de fois gras after eighteen months of sheep and beetroot. And not an ascorbic-acid tablet on the premises.

My two weeks leave at home produced some surprises. Unlike Kaldadharnes, Iceland, where life was peaceful and mostly routine, Leyton, London, E10 was in the middle of the war. To observe blackout restrictions was tedious but vital, and to walk outside at night, with searchlights sweeping the sky, lighting up barrage balloons and picking out the high silver slivers which were enemy aircraft, was to walk suddenly into a gloomy, lonely and noisy world. No cheerful lights shone and anti-aircraft guns thumped away all round, and even a quick dash to the postbox on the corner was accompanied by the 'ping' and 'tinkle' of chunks of jagged metal from spent anti-aircraft shells falling about one's ears.

When the sirens began wailing, Mother, like all the wives and families who endured the bombings almost every night, became expert at judging from the throb of the aircraft's engines whether the planes could well pass directly overhead and be a real threat or were moving away.

If the enemy throb was ominous we rapidly trooped out into the garden and down into the air-raid shelter. The shelter was a little triumph of wartime invention, cheap and easy to erect; it looked like an arched hut made from bent corrugated-iron sheets bolted together. Once it was half buried in the garden and the curved roof covered with a foot of earth and planted with potatoes it was protection against almost everything short of a direct hit from a landmine.

These shelters started out as grim little cells of damp darkness but the process of cheering them up soon began. The floor soil was trodden hard, duckboards were laid and bits of old carpets were cut to size and nailed down. Heavy curtains of anything to hand from sacking to moth-eaten velvet were made into draught-excluders for the shelter's entrance. Old deckchairs and benches were brought in, and cushions and some form of lighting. And the shelters could be warmed up quickly with a small paraffin heater if some source of paraffin could be located. Bookshelves were erected and a torch was kept in a cupboard.

No bombs fell alarmingly near during those two weeks, the bombers' main targets being the City and the docks, but for various reasons, such as bad navigation or the need to conserve fuel to get home, the bombers would sometimes empty their bomb bays indiscriminately over a suburb, and one exciting night Church Road, Leyton, E10 experienced the sprinkling upon it of a load of enemy incendiary bombs. These had been horribly successful when used on the City but we were luckier.

I think they must have been seconds. Half of them didn't ignite and were carried off by neighbours as extremely dangerous souvenirs, and many of the bombs ignited but only fizzed and sparkled in a desultory sort of way, like fireworks bought from a damp sweetshop. Some of the bombs did their job well and produced immense heat very quickly, but most of these seemed to land in the middle of the road or in a field, which I believe both sides found could be the problem with incendiaries unless they were scattered over crowded inner cities.

I wistfully hoped that a stray incendiary might land on Laurie's Preserves, the marmalade factory about 100 yards upwind of number 28 – as long as it was empty and fully insured, of course – because when it was boil-up day at Laurie's, the tingly acrid smell of the hot marmalade could penetrate reinforced concrete at a thousand paces.

One well-made incendiary bomb did land on the church roof and ignite but the voluntary services dealt with it promptly. There was a patrol already up there in case of trouble, and while we service personnel on leave were in the street below bumbling into each other in the half light from smouldering privet hedges, the Civil Defence and fire-pickets were rapidly dealing with the incendiary on the church roof with the regulation-issue bucket of water, stirrup pump and small length of garden hose.

The only really tragic moment in the night's excitement came when all of us had at last bored each other rigid with our own experiences ('We were in the shelter and I said to the wife, "Something fallen on my cabbages." She said, "Never!" I said, "I deffnly heard something fall. I'm going to take a look".') We quietly slunk back to our own houses.

A pale, anxious young lad in khaki was waiting for me at the gate of number 28. 'Excuse me bothering you,' he said, 'but have you by any chance seen a rifle? Lee-Enfield, bolt action? I rested it against a fence and I can't seem to find it . . .'

I could, of course, have overpaared him, but to what end?

On the train up to report to No. 1 PTS, RAF Ringway, kitbag on rack, I tried to conjecture what the letters No. 1 PTS stood for.

Nobody had told me when my posting notice was handed to me in Kaldadharnes. They probably did not know – initials proliferated in the services – but it was where I was bound and I was keen to find out the activity going on there, in which I would be heavily involved for perhaps years.

It was quite a long train journey in wartime from Euston to Manchester and as I dozed, my mind drifted away in search of possible meanings of No. 1 PTS.

No. 1 Paper-Tearing Secretariat? Something to do with spying? The Far East? Don't the Japanese call it 'oregano' or is that growing miniature trees? Anyway, no.

No. 1 Pupil-Teacher Symposium? Could be. Everybody in the services, corporal and above, seemed to spend half their time teaching colleagues how to do something. Perhaps the teachers get together with their pupils in a symposium and learn from the pupils how they think they should be taught? No.

No. 1 Pentecostal Tabernacle and Synagogue. No.

At New Street Station, Manchester, I had to sign for another travel warrant from the Transport Office to get me on to Ringway so I asked the duty travel officer the vital question.

'Parachuting, lad,' he said. 'That's what they do at Ringway: parachuting. Teaching the Army how to jump out of planes and float down to earth as light as a lump of thistledown. Ringway is Number One Parachute Training School for the whole of the British armed forces, so stick your chest out proudly and pray that *you* don't have to jump. Four fifteen p.m., platform three and don't miss it.'

After RAF Warmwell and RAF Kaldadharnes, RAF Ringway was a luxury billet, warm and comfortable and busy; not a new shanty town built on commandeered farmland, but a going concern newly borrowed by the RAF from the civic authorities, with comfortable brick barrack blocks. The NAAFI was on one side of the main road to Altrincham and on the other side the guardroom guarded a number of enormous aircraft hangars, admin buildings and workshops, including – at last – a well-equipped photographic unit. On the opposite side of the airfield stood a factory belonging to Fairey Aviation where Fairey planes were assembled and tested. Never a dull moment on the runways.

Britain was the last of the great powers to go in for dropping troops into action by parachute and it completely changed the established technique of landing. Films of German and Russian (and American) pre-war mass drops showed that the soldiers were trained to land with their feet apart, if possible in a standing position, so that in theory they could then sprint swiftly into battle. The snag to this was that the parachute's direction and velocity of landing in those days was not easily controllable and the parachutists frequently landed more heavily on one leg than the other and it then bent or broke; the number of such minor casualties was formidable.

The British authorities, rather brilliantly, decided that as the RAF was going to have to fly the troops into action it might as well train them how to drop as well, so the British army was taught their parachuting by RAF physical training instructors. The RAF's PTIs' greatest improvement was to change the other nations' method of landing from an attempt to achieve a standing position to curling up with feet and knees together and rolling over, thus avoiding a shock impact. In a short while most other nations switched to our technique.

There was a graver problem. Sometimes the parachute failed to open. The unfortunate trainee fell swiftly to earth, his parachute clinging tightly to itself, a narrow column of white silk instead of a billowing umbrella. This fatal occurrence was known, and dreaded, as a 'Roman candle'.

But miracles do sometimes happen. The late Roland Gant, who was my editor at Heinemann the publishers, spoke perfect French and had a dangerous and secret job operating in occupied France. He told me that one night he had to rendezvous with a British radio operator due to be dropped from a Lysander plane at 1,000 feet onto a secret dropping point in Normandy. The Lysander was on time, its navigation was spot on and all was going well until the agent jumped. Roland, to his horror, saw in the moonlight that the parachute was not opening; it was a Roman candle. The dark figure hanging beneath the white silk streak gathered speed and finally hit the earth with a sickening thud. As Roland ran towards the parachute, the parachutist suddenly rose up and called out, 'That you, Roland? Fuck this for a game of soldiers!'

By a million to one chance the agent had landed in a soft peat bog. He had broken bones but he had survived.

Too many Roman candles occurred during the intensive training courses at No. 1 PTS and the boffins brooded. Tests were made on the possibility of static electricity sticking the silk together and it was decided that more hard information would be helpful, e.g., does the parachutist's manner of exit from the plane have a bearing? Are there rogue parachutes which deploy in the wrong manner? It was decided that the photography section would photograph *all* training drops on Bell and Howell amateur 16mm cine-cameras filming at their maximum speed (producing slow motion) of sixty-four frames per second. Which was when I arrived on the scene.

The aircraft used at the time for training drops was the old Armstrong Whitworth, 'Whitley', a heavy, ponderous bomber which was ideal to jump from as it could stay airborne at low speeds. But where could the camera be mounted?

I was unanimously elected by the photography section to volunteer to be the one to undergo the experiments.

The first bright idea was that I should film drops from the unused bomb bay, so two planks were roped to the bay and I was laid face down on them and strapped in place, pointing forwards, looking downwards, camera in shaking hand. It was dark and nasty in there but terror was to come. The plane took off well enough; noisy and draughty but tolerable. And then . . . and then the doors of the bomb bay slowly opened beneath me and I lay there, hanging from my ropes, with nothing between my face and the surface of the earth. I might well have screamed.

The whole terrifying experience proved to be a waste of time. When we landed it was realized that the aperture in the floor of the aircraft through which the parachutists jumped was aft of my bomb bay, so they all jumped out behind me and there was nobody for me to film.

The boffins' second bright idea was to remove the rear-gunner's turret at the back of the Whitley and for me, clutching the Bell and Howell, to lie on the floor in a prone position where the turret once stood, facing to the rear and taking up a bent posture not unlike a wasp's sting.

The plan was for a colleague to sit on my ankles to prevent me falling out of the plane, and when jumping commenced I was to lean downwards at right-angles, with the camera pointing forwards (into the slipstream, note), and film the squaddies as they emerged from the jumping aperture ahead of me.

There was so much wrong with this plan that I can hardly

believe we eventually won the war. For one thing, when I tried bending down and pointing the camera forwards towards the aperture the slipstream took my breath away and almost tore the camera from my grasp. And once bent over, I found that, like doing a forward somersault, rearing back up again required powerful, well-exercised muscles which I did not possess. So I just dangled there like a rag doll over the side of a pram until my colleague managed to pull me up into the aircraft by the back of my flying jacket.

This suggested a method and I lowered myself again into the slipstream. But this time my colleague had looped my long woollen scarf around my neck, hanging on to both ends. A parachutist jumped and my colleague hauled on the scarf and drew me up as the parachutist passed below me and drifted rapidly away behind the aircraft. It was painful on my Adam's apple but I managed to get a reasonably good shot of the parachute deploying.

It was when the film had been developed and we were all gathered round the projector to view it that the asininity of the method became apparent. Firstly, as I was upside down when I began filming, the parachutist apparently came out of the aperture upside down on the screen. As he passed beneath me and my colleague hauled on the scarf, the parachutist appeared to gently turn over and drift rapidly away, the right way up. Worse, the parachutists jumped in a stick of ten at a time and all I had time to get on my film was the first man out. The method was totally impractical for recording mass jumps.

It was our officer i/c photography unit who came up with the solution. This time the *front* gun turret was modified. A wooden camera-mounting was devised, which held the camera pointing backwards below the belly of the Whitley and towards the jumping aperture. The camera was instantly removable so that its spring could be wound up by hand (no electronic gadgetry in those days) and reloaded with film.

My colleagues and I had to lie prone in our turret, forefinger on the camera button, and when we heard through our headphones the despatcher screaming, 'Action stations! – GO!' begin filming. It all worked well. We had to keep careful records so that we could develop any specific drop the boffins called for, and the boffins had a library of thousands of slow-motion picture sequences of deploying parachutes to study.

After a couple of years of this and other lines of research, Roman candles became a satisfactorily rarer phenomenon.

Monitoring every training jump meant a great deal of flying for the five of us in the photographic unit. I recently found my old flying logbook and was reminded that a normal working day started about 0730 and consisted of anything from ten to twenty flights to and from the dropping zone. But the dropping zone was Tatton Park, a large country estate only a few miles away, and an average flight took only fifteen to twenty minutes. I saw in the logbook that by 28 October 1943 I had clocked up 1,000 flights.

The dropping zone had a different atmosphere to the airfield. To have jumped and still be alive, no bones broken, was such an exhilarating experience that Tatton Park, with a good canteen run by local ladies, was a happy place. Not without an occasional problem, of course. I was there on some kind of duty one day and a matronly lady in tweeds grabbed my arm rather painfully in the canteen and drew me to one side. 'I am the volunteer regional organizer, food and comforts,' she said. Her voice dropped to a commanding whisper and she looked away as she spoke. 'It's the chemical lavatories. Would you be good enough to ask your commanding officer to arrange for them to be emptied more frequently. They are, well, let me just say that the chemicals in them are odorous . . . and my volunteer ladies find them offensive to dignity and hygiene and try not to use them, which causes problems . . .' She paused, in a sudden agony of embarrassment at talking so frankly to a peasant, and then recovered. 'Doesn't bother *me*, of course,' she added with a bright smile, 'hunting woman, you know!'

I did not know that ladies who hunted had a more convenient system of plumbing than lesser mortals, but it was an interesting thought.

In those early days parachutists launched themselves into space through a hole cut in the floor of the Whitley aircraft halfway down the fuselage. The hole was lined with a deep wooden collar, of conical shape, about 2 feet deep and about 5 feet wide at the top, narrowing down to about 3 feet.

The trainee wore a quick-release harness with his parachute at the back of it, and he hooked the static line, which tore the parachute pack open automatically when he jumped, on to a cable which ran down the length of the fuselage at shoulder level. When

'Action Stations!' was called he sat down with his legs dangling through the hole, his hands gripping the edge, looking straight ahead. On the command 'GO!' he went. He did this by pushing off smartly with his hands and jerking to attention. This resulted (with a bit of luck) in him dropping cleanly through the centre of the hole, whereupon his static line would pull the cover off his parachute, which would deploy into the slipstream and be blown open.

Jumping through the aperture was in practice a bit trickier than it sounds. If he did not push off hard enough, his parachute pack caught on the edge of the aperture behind him and tipped him forward so he went into the slipstream upside down – not nice. Worse still, if he pushed too hard, his face hit the aperture facing him and he left a couple of his front teeth imbedded in the woodwork. This painful misfortune was quite frequent and was known to the troops with grim jocularity as 'ringing the bell'.

I made my first jump from a barrage balloon and it was an abysmal effort. I was up in a balloon which had a jumping aperture fitted to the floor of its cage for training purposes. All soldiers made their first two descents from a balloon. I finished filming a stick of Polish trainees jumping through the aperture, happily singing (I think Polish troops sang in their sleep), and the sergeant instructor suggested that as I had a parachute on, as required when up in the balloon, it would be easier and quicker for me to jump rather than wait for the balloon to be slowly wound to ground level by winch.

He yelled, 'Action stations!' and I sat gingerly on the edge of the aperture as I had seen the trainees do. He moved me to a less suicidal position and told me not to worry, it was a piece of cake. The opposite side of the aperture looked very close and I thought I saw a tooth in the wood, but it was probably only a knot. On the scream of 'GO!' I went rigid as instructed and dropped, unwounded to my surprise, through the hole.

The descent was not at all what I expected, not that I knew *what* to expect. It is quite a long drop from a balloon before the parachute opens, about 200 feet, because unlike an aircraft drop there is no slipstream to whip the silk quickly into action. There was no feeling of dropping through space, just a very strong, not disagreeable, but wholly novel physical sensation, not unlike beginning to feel the effects of an anaesthetic. After quite a while the chute billowed open somewhere above my head with a loud welcome crackle and it was as though a hand had grabbed my harness and was holding me safely and firmly.

It was a terrific moment. There I was, suspended on a sky hook with nothing but air between my boots and the world. And there was no feeling of descending, instead the earth was very slowly rising up to meet *me*. And then the world rose at an increasingly rapid rate until I thudded quite heavily onto the Tatton Park turf.

I had a colleague down below, chortling, taking photographs of my descent. Oh, dear. My landing looked like a shop-window dummy falling off the back of a lorry.

Some time later the PTS commanding officer decided that it might be a good idea for somebody from the photographic section to go on an official parachuting course. My colleagues (as all my colleagues everywhere seem to have done during my war service) unanimously decided that it was I who should have the honour of breaking a leg or two for the war effort.

The training programme turned out to be forward somersaulting all over again, slightly glamorized.

We were trained by RAF physical training instructors, mostly sergeants, for whom no praise can be adequate. They were physically impressive, of course, tough and indestructable; one felt that if they jumped out of a plane without a chute they would just bounce twice and stroll to the NAAFI for a pint, but they had humour and character as well, and we trainees clung to their strength and reliability as one used to depend on one's bank manager.

In fact, the instructors did jump without chutes by tradition on Christmas Day, in sticks of ten from upstairs windows of a barrack block onto the rose beds below.

Another Christmas tradition was to have a drunken afternoon swim in the static water tank near the main gate. This was covered with green and slimy algae and was colder than anything I had known in Iceland. As I have a touch of Raynaud's – that thing where your fingers go bloodless in cold weather – I stayed in the water for about a second and a half. Even then I emerged with chattering teeth and my whole body was the bluish-white colour of the French girl's bosom at Broadstairs.

We were split into groups of ten and began with 'synthetic training' in one of the big hangars. On a busy day the hangar was like an Hieronymus Bosch picture sprung to life: the air was rent with great echoing shouts of, 'ACTION STATIONS! – GO!' Figures flew through the air clinging to pulleys and swooping down cables; bodies thudded onto mats as they practised their rolling; they clung to trapezes and jumped down from the top of the hangar to make whirring descents by a frightener called 'the Fan', so called because the speed of descent was (slightly) diminished by a large fan on the end of the drum of cable.

At this time the lumbering old Whitley Mk. V warhorses were gradually being replaced by the smart new Douglas DC-3s, 'Dakotas', from America. The great change for the better was that Dakotas had no hole in the floor to be jumped through; the parachutist now hooked his static line onto the wire and ran out of the door.

On their morning drop to work at Tatton Park the instructors had a small competition amongst themselves as to how quickly they could launch ten men out of the door. They found that the best technique was for the man with the longest arms to stand back from the door gripping the sides whilst three or four of the thinnest instructors in his stick squeezed in front of him, holding on to each other. The rest of the stick lined up behind. At the cry of 'GO!', the man with the long arms gave a mighty pull, ejecting the men in front of him and himself, and the rest sprinted down the aisle and hurled themselves almost as one through the door. The point was to determine how to drop a stick of parachutists onto the smallest possible landing area.

Life at RAF Ringway for Leading Aircraftsman Muir 931110 became increasingly busy and rewarding. Besides the flying and the other photographic duties, I wrote a moving story entitled *Return to Sheol* (the title is the only thing I can remember about it), and a play in the Terence Rattigan mode about a young Hudson pilot in Iceland whose radio went wrong on his homeward flight and he completely missed the island. It had a happy ending but I cannot imagine what it was. How on earth did I get him home in one piece?

My ambition to get on an aircrew course came a step nearer. I was summoned to RAF headquarters, Adastral House, a large building at the bottom of Kingsway which later became the offices of the commercial television company Associated Rediffusion. (James Thurber, on his last visit to Europe, thought the name Associated Rediffusion sounded like a complicated nervous disease. On that visit he also said, 'A woman's place is in the wrong,' and when a lady at a reception in Paris gushed that she had read all his books in both English and French and, oddly, preferred them in French, he murmured modestly, 'I guess I do tend to lose a little in the original.')

In the Kingsway building I was interviewed by a board of mature RAF officers and probed as to my zeal and general airworthiness and given a small medical, which seemed all right, and my height was measured with some difficulty, as the arm of the measuring gadget did not go up that far; it stopped at 6 feet 3 inches, and in those days I stood a weedy 6 feet 6 inches. Alas, no longer. A literary stoop and natural shrinkage of the spinal discs have brought about a diminution. It seems that one's discs dry out with age, and there are a lot of them back there. I have now stabilized at a bent 6 feet 4 inches.

My eyes were also tested. Good result, 20/20, but again measured with difficulty as my eyes were, and still are, of course, unusually wide apart. The eye chap was fascinated with how wide apart they were and kept saying, 'My, my,' and checking the measurement with his calipers.

'Does it matter that my eyes are unusually wide apart?' I asked, a bit nettled. 'Is there any significance to it?'

'Well, yes,' he said, 'it's more or less accepted that eyes which, unlike yours, are close together indicate a person who will tend to be a little more cunning and untrustworthy in his dealings than a person with an average eye-separation measurement.'

'I see,' I said, thoughtfully. 'And what do eyes as wide apart as mine indicate?' I asked.

'Er – stupidity,' he said.

I returned to Ringway to await my call to higher things. The call did not come, so for something like three more years I walked about with a curved white flash tucked in the front of my forage cap which indicated to the world that I was potential aircrew waiting to be put on a flying course. By the end of the war the flash was about as white as my beloved old vest, which my mother eventually scraped off me, making me wear a dauntingly white, crisp but unfriendly new one. The new vest was never as warm as the old one, nor as effective in cold weather when worn as a hat.

Then life at Ringway began to warm up. The RAF High Command, with an eye to the future when the tide would turn and our forces would invade Europe, rashly decreed that ground crew tradesmen like photographers should learn to be more generally useful so that they could be called upon to drive heavy-goods vehicles and troop-carrying buses.

And so another terror was added to Ringway's parachuting course. In spite of never having been taught how to drive anything and my experience limited to main-road runs from RAF Warmwell to Dorchester in my Triumph saloon, I was cheerfully added to the list of volunteer auxiliary bus drivers.

My approach to driving a bus full of parachutists back from Tatton Park to Ringway was one of blithe, unwarranted confidence. There was, of course, no period of training because there was nobody trained to do the training, so on my maiden trip I just climbed into the driver's cab, glanced round to see where everything was and kangarooed off.

I found that hauling the bus round corners was hard work and I had to learn that a bus is very long and it is necessary to steer wide round sharp bends because the back wheels tend to cut the corners. Happily, on my first couple of trips the trainee parachutists were Polish and sang so spiritedly after their drop that they did not hear the rear side of the bus side-swiping bushes, trees and the occasional wall.

The troops (and some instructors) put in a petition to the transport officer asking for me to be put on to other duties because, they said, travelling back from Tatton Park in my bus was more terrifying than the jump. So that little bit of fun came to an end.

Another and far more interesting bit of fun soon replaced it. The Air Ministry issued a memo telling squadron commanders that those airmen waiting for a pilot's course should be given as much flying experience as possible.

This move was warmly welcomed by the Ringway pilots because they were mostly ex-bomber types who had survived their tours of duty and were bored to sobs making twenty-minute flights all day like air taxis, and as I seemed to be the only potential aircrew eligible I had a great time. Between them they gave me a complete flying course.

A typical entry in my logbook reads:

24 June 1943. 1500–1705. MENTOR training plane. Dual instruction: Flt. Lt. Hooper. Taking off and landing, flying straight and level, rate 1 turns, climbing, flying on course.

That was straightforward enough, but the following day's log entry read:

25 June 1943. 1520–1630. Whitley. Dual Instruction: WO Blake. Straight and level. Flying on course. Rate 1 turns. Climbing and gliding.

The Whitley was another matter. WO Blake would have flown it on the outward leg and dropped his stick of ten trainees. This could not be left to a learner pilot as it entailed flying the plane as slowly as possible for the parachutists' sake without the plane falling out of the sky, and anyway I had to be up front, face down, filming. After the drop I would get up and race back to the cockpit and take the co-pilot's wheel (there were no co-pilots) and WO Blake would say, 'It's all yours!' and I would bring the empty plane home and, after a bit of experience, even land it. The controls were heavy and responded slowly. Making a three-point landing meant hauling the wheel back as far as it would go at exactly the right moment – it felt as though the wheel was attached to heavy industrial elastic – and the beast would gently subside onto the runway, as though glad of the rest.

The flashiest entry in my logbook was the day I flew what was perhaps the heaviest aircraft then in service, followed by the lightest. The heavy job was a Stirling bomber, full of parachutists newly arrived at Ringway and being given 'air experience'. This was the most boring of all the Ringway pilot's duties, as all he was required to do was fly the trainees anywhere for an hour, straight and level, and then fly them back. So the pilot was perfectly happy for me to fly the plane up and down the Welsh coast on his behalf while he put his feet up on the instrument panel and wrote to his wife.

On landing that day I then climbed into the station Tiger Moth for some dual-control with WO Curtis. The Moth was so light to handle after the big one that I flung it around a bit at first, but settled down eventually. Unlike the old Whitleys you could land it with a finger and thumb on the control stick. We looped the loop, which was a simple, fun manoeuvre and centrifugal force kept everything in place, but then WO Curtis flew the plane upside down like the nice old wingco did at Kaldadharnes and that was not fun at all. There was no centrifugal force and one dangled dangerously upside down from the safety straps while dust, dead spiders and other detritus on the floor of the cockpit dropped down one's trouser leg and lodged in the catchment area of the crutch.

Warrant Officer Curtis, soon Pilot Officer Curtis, gave me as much flying instruction as he could. In return I used to babysit so that he could take his wife to the pictures. He had been a commercial artist before joining up, and together we made a huge wall-newspaper, changing it monthly. It became quite popular. I wrote the text, which was largely made up of limericks and clerihews featuring station 'characters', jokes, spurious official notices like, 'In future all beds must be made up as laid down in standing orders,' and each edition had an episode of a serial parodying some genre of popular literature; our first target was James Hadley Chase's *No Orchids for Miss Blandish*, a cunning and hugely popular mix of soft porn and violence.

Our version, which featured in its plot that pioneer of contraception, Dr Marie Stopes, was entitled *No More Kids for Mrs Blandish*. My typed sheets of text (I still had the portable typewriter) were pasted onto a huge stretch of paper pinned to the NAAFI noticeboard and PO Curtis brought the whole presentation together with some inventive and funny artwork.

And so, in this fashion, the days and months passed. Then a year and then another year. It was known as having a 'soft war', that is to say being warm and fed and still alive.

But there were occasional little hiccups in the steady breathing.

I notice in my logbook that the entry for Christmas Eve, 1942, reads:

Whitley. PO Bruton. Dropped stick of ten, then forced landing. Starboard engine on fire.

And on 24 July 1943:

Whitley. PO Bruton. One stick of ten and then forced landing. Starboard engine cut out.

After taking the jumping course I made a total of eleven jumps. The first two were, as required, from a balloon, but these were now equipped with a door frame to jump through rather than that beastly hole in the floor, and when the despatcher bellowed, 'GO!'

in my ear, my reflexes worked well and I shot through the door as though voice-propelled.

I was allowed to make the second jump immediately, a great treat as the euphoria of having survived the first overcame the awful anticipation of the second. The balloon was winched down, I put on a fresh chute, climbed in and we floated back up to 600 feet. 'ACTION STATIONS!' roared the instructor. I stood tall in the doorway gripping the sides of the door frame, the picture of an intrepid and confident parachutist waiting for the 'GO!' to propel him on his way.

It did not come. The instructor decided to play a little sadistic trick which instructors sometimes did to cheer themselves up after a hard day of shouting soldiers out through doors.

'OK, Lofty,' he said in a quiet kindly voice. Lofty was my wartime name. 'No hurry, old lad, just go whenever you feel like it.'

It was awful. I drew back from the doorway, twitching, then moved resolutely forward, then retreated again, and then dithered on the edge. And I realized how much of a parachutist's training was to accustom him to leap automatically on the shout of 'GO!' without any kind of thought process holding things up. I eventually fell out.

When I made my last balloon jump much later I sustained my one and only war wound, but I suspect that it does not count as it was self-inflicted. I forked myself in the behind.

It was a murky November day and I was up in a balloon with a boffin and an instructor, filming some experimental parachutes being hurled out of the balloon attached to rubber dummies which weighed the same as a human being.

A fog came up and we suddenly seemed to be suspended in damp cotton wool. The drop was cancelled and the instructor telephoned the winch-lorry below to find out what it was like down there and the winch-man reported that a breeze had cleared the fog away at ground level. The instructor decided that he and I should jump. Me first. So out into the damp cotton wool I stepped.

Very odd sensation. No feeling of height whatsoever because there was nothing in sight to tell the brain that it was not at ground level. That strange powerful feeling overwhelmed me again, of being weightless, non-human, then the welcome clacking, crackling sound of the chute opening.

It was traditional in the lower echelons of the RAF to carry the personal knife, fork and spoon (the 'irons') in the right hip pocket at all times, so as to be able to cope instantly, anywhere, if somebody offered food. I had my irons in my right hip pocket when I landed backwards, in a rolling movement as taught, and the fork's four prongs stabbed into my bottom, drawing blood. Not enough blood for me to put in for a Purple Heart, or even a morning's sick leave, but for a year or more afterwards my right buttock bore an honourable scar in the form of four dark-blue dots. But to whom could I, with pride, display my war wound?

I made nine other parachute leaps at Ringway, all of them water jumps into the large lake in Tatton Park. The excellent thing about jumping into water was that it was really very difficult to break a leg on landing and quite impossible to stab yourself in the behind. Thus it was the preferred sort of jump to offer elderly visiting brass hats, like General 'Windy' Gale who made many drops into the lake. The visiting party was usually only the brass hat and an aide, so the stick was usually beefed up by the inclusion of Wing Commander Kilkenny, who was the training school's headmaster, any instructors to hand and occasionally, at the last moment if nobody else was available, me ('Busy, Lofty? Wanna water jump? Grab a chute from the packers and see you on the tarmac in a couple of minutes. Hurry!').

Jumping into water was relatively harmless but called for new skills. The parachute harness felt safe and indeed was safe because the wearer sat in a loop of webbing and was held in place by other webbing which clicked into a junction box on his chest. All he had to do to get out of the harness was to thump the quick-release catch on his junction box which released all the retaining straps and left him sitting in the loop.

On a water jump the parachutist had to detach himself from his harness before hitting the water or the silk might settle over his head and drown him. The technique was for the jumper, at about 10 feet up, to bang his quick-release box and so release the lateral straps, then, clinging on like grim death to the harness straps above his head, slip out of the loop in which he was sitting, let the parachute go, and drop the last few feet into the water unencumbered. The parachute would drift along on its own for a little way and then settle into the water, vast and translucent like a huge silken jellyfish. The trick was to judge accurately the moment to let go.

*

I finished writing another unproducible play, a thin cautionary comedy of a frightened German spy, a conscript, staying in a country house hotel near an RAF bomber airfield and, mid-spying duties, falling in love with his aristocratic landlady. I called the play *The First Casualty* from a good line attributed to an American senator: 'The first casualty of war is truth.' And I wrote a number of humorous monologues about parachuting (in verse, too, of a sort) which the padre and I recited at the drop of a hat and at the top of our voices at boozy PTS end-of-term parties.

Another episode in my war which was a good thing rather than a hiccup was the experience of first love, although I was a bit old for that sort of thing. I was no longer a gangly youth with spots but a grown man in my early twenties with spots, the owner of a small fawn moustache, a Morris open two-seater car with a drop-head hood and a hernia.

The object of my affection was a slim, intelligent, sweet young girl named Joan Young, who helped out as a volunteer in the Ringway canteen run by local ladies. Joan had just finished school and was waiting to go up to university.

For something like a year we had a most enjoyable friendship, not meeting very often because it was not possible, but finding much pleasure in each other's company when we did. It was totally innocent, a fun affair but not an *affaire*, and when it reached its natural end we parted as equably as we had met. We never saw each other again but I have always been grateful to Joan for making me consider somebody else's feelings other than my own and for opening my eyes to the richness that a close relationship can bring to day-to-day living.

Before I met Joan I found that I had this hernia, which hardly came as a surprise the way I jumped. The condition manifested itself as a smooth bump which popped out from time to time in the groin area. It could be fingered back to whence it came but would emerge again, particularly during one of the rare occasions when I was being energetic. No pain. As ever, my way of coping was to hope it would go away, which of course it did not. So I went into the RAF hospital to have it darned back into place.

Just before the surgeon came to inspect the damage, I hung a sign over my bed: 'Does my hernia concern ya?' but Matron made me take it down. After the op I had to try to live for a week or two without coughing or laughing, both of which induced sharp pain, but that was about all the suffering involved. On the credit side I was given post-natal contraction exercises by a beautiful, muscular little blonde WAAF sergeant physiotherapist.

After a couple of weeks in hospital I was sent off with two or three others to convalesce in a boarding house in Blackpool. The town was then empty of people and deep in gloom beneath scudding rain clouds; I sent a picture postcard of the trams on Blackpool front to my sergeant physiotherapist and wrote on the back:

> Those blue lagoons
> And tropic moons
> Are nowhere near Blackpool,
> H. de Vere Stackpoole.

One of the surprisingly few rackets operated by the photographic section at Ringway was the developing and printing of the station's snapshots. These were almost always rolls of 120 film. By working in the evening we could give a swifter and cheaper service than Boots the chemist or their rivals Timothy White's, and besides speed and economy our service could offer discretion. In other words, we would discreetly process any naughty pictures which Boots might refuse to print, or, worse still, hand over to the police.

Just such a roll of Kodak 120 film was passed to our sergeant by a pretty WAAF officer. He developed and printed it in secrecy and it turned out to be a series of flashbulb snaps of the pretty WAAF officer and another pretty WAAF officer larking about in the bath. Nothing at all sordid, just two girls giggling and fooling about, but a wartime bath was quite revealing as Ministry regulations allowed a maximum of only 5 inches of bathwater, which wasn't much cover for a couple of bouncy WAAFs. One snapshot was an echo of that famous School of Fontainebleau painting of the two naked, po-faced aristos, the Duchesse de Villars and Gabrielle d'Estrées, sitting very upright in a bath, one of them holding delicately 'twixt finger and thumb the nearest nipple of the other, as though switching off the bathroom light.

The sergeant quickly printed a couple of sets of prints for the WAAF officers and then spoiled any good name our section might have had for discretion by printing off fifty more sets to sell in the sergeants' mess, and he told A/C 1 Clive Cook to hide the negatives under the darkroom floorboards for use if demand grew for more copies.

Clive came back to the section day room where we were all cleaning cameras and loading film for the morning. He was clutching a box.

Clive said, 'I found these under the floorboards.'

He put the box on the table and opened it. Inside were about thirty or forty glass negatives and their contact prints. They were all portraits of a plumpish girl with no clothes on sitting on our office Windsor chair, her legs immodestly arranged.

The lads whooped and wolf whistled and settled into the traditional services method of looking at rude photographs. The owner or custodian sat in a chair and the others sat on the floor round him. The owner counted the pictures out one by one and counted them back.

We grabbed the pictures eagerly and went, 'COR!' but not for long. The trouble was that nothing happened in the photographs, just a tubby girl slumped in a chair; missing was the usual lean, dark-haired gentleman wearing only shoes, socks and sock-suspenders who usually provided some action. The sergeant's pictures of the same girl became a bit boring after the initial excitement and there were too many of them.

Then somebody said, 'I know her! She's that WAAF who doles out the breakfast porridge! You know – Spotty Dotty!'

'So it is!' somebody else said. 'Well, well. Spotty Dotty! Should be Spotty Botty.'

Horseplay ensued, during which Clive carefully slid the photographs back into their box and took them back to their hiding place under the darkroom floor.

One of the great parental warnings in those days, meant to terrify – and a great favourite with my mother – was, 'Carry on the way you're going and you'll end up in the *News of the World*.' Which is just what happened to our sergeant. A year after I was demobbed, Clive sent me a cutting from the *News of the World*. RAF SERGEANT IN NUDE WAAF PHOTO SCANDAL rang out the headline. It seems that our sergeant had become careless in pursuing his little hobby and had been shopped by the aunt of one of his WAAF sitters. The WAAF was so pleased with her portrait, which from the neck up made her faintly resemble Betty Grable, that she took it home and rather carelessly left it on the sideboard where it was spotted by her aunt. The sergeant was successfully prosecuted. Thus, it could be said, does retribution eventually overtake the ungodly hobbyist.

Over on the far side of Ringway's airfield, almost hidden amongst trees, stood a large Edwardian house. This was where the men and women of Special Operations, the SOE, the saboteurs, wireless operators, regional organizers and so on lived for a few days while they took a brief intensive course in parachuting by night. They were not allowed to come near the NAAFI or the camp cinema or the rest of us. Nobody saw them arrive or train or jump or depart.

In charge of this operation was a Major Edwards (most of the army men I came up against during the war seemed to have been named Major Edwards, e.g., the army surgeon in Reykjavik).

This latest Major Edwards had a profitable sideline in civilian life writing a form of popular song known as the 'novelty foxtrot'. I was told he wrote the hugely successful novelty foxtrot of the Thirties, 'All By Yourself in the Moonlight'. I can still remember the melody but not the words, which is probably just as well.

The unit's second-in-command was Captain Dalton. My connection with the group was acting as their photographer when they needed one, e.g., taking identity photographs for their forged passports. I was lent an album of continental mugshots to study so that I could reproduce the slight differences in lighting, the way the subjects sat, how they arranged their faces (they tended to be more po-faced than the Allies), and so on. And, most impressively, I was given a box of real continental photographic paper to print the mugshots on.

Almost exactly fifty years later, in autumn 1994, I was ambling across the *place* in Monticello, a hill village in Corsica of which more later, when an Englishman and his wife came out of the small hotel and he waved at me and called me by name (actually he called out 'Lofty!'). The Englishman was Captain Dalton of the special agent section on the other side of the airfield at RAF Ringway.

We stood and had a good long natter – long nattering was normal in Monticello; it could take an hour to cross the 50 metres of *place* if you met somebody – and our nattering about those colourful special-agent days at Ringway produced the riveting information that Captain Dalton's son was the actor, Timothy

Dalton, who had recently played James Bond, Special Agent 007, on our silver screens. A happy coincidence which rounded off rather neatly my memories of RAF Ringway. Except for just one more happening.

The general atmosphere in the forces at that time was not jolly. It was like a heavy industry awaiting takeover and bracing itself for huge redundancies. The Arnhem drop was over, VE and VJ day had come and gone, and the large number of airmen and back-up ground staff who had been fed (and well fed, on the whole) would soon have to feed themselves, and find themselves a job. Being demobbed, once so eagerly looked forward to, was being viewed with increasing apprehension by many of the younger servicemen now it was about to happen.

One result was the proliferation of little training courses which the authorities set up to help ease the problem. Anybody who had been a teacher in civvy street was asked to arrange a course in any subject he was capable of teaching, or incapable but interested in. There were courses all over the place in everything from whippet management to operatic singing.

At Ringway, where I and everybody else was waiting to be posted or demobbed or something, a course was started in practical geography, which turned out to be map-reading. The instructor was an elderly retired photographic intelligence officer and he was deeply bad news; a real pill, arrogant, sarcastic, humourless and pompous. Most of our section joined his class because it was vaguely to do with photography and got us off a morning parade, but we suffered for it in being humiliated and patronized and demoralized by this dreadful man.

Ironically, he was extremely good at his job. He really could read a map like a newspaper and could pinpoint an aerial photograph more swiftly and accurately than anybody else in the RAF. We knew this because he told us so. Miserably, he was probably right. He offered a £5 note (in those days a huge crisp white document which had to be unfolded) to any of us who could show him an aerial photograph taken within a 10-mile radius of Ringway which he could not identify on an Ordnance Survey map within an hour.

One of our section produced a 5 x 5 inch print of a piece of woodland near Wilmslow and the flight lieutenant had his finger on it on the map in about thirty seconds.

I think it might well have been A/C 1 Clive Cook, later a freelance journalist, who devised a devilish scheme of revenge. Suffice it to say we gave the flight lieutenant a 5 x 5 aerial print to pinpoint. Minute after minute went by as he repeatedly peered from photograph to map and back again. When the class came to an end he grabbed the map and the print and strode out without a word.

News reached us that the flight lieutenant had become obsessed with our challenge, and even during meals in the mess would sit there with a small magnifying glass, trying to match the rivulets and coppices on the photograph with features on the map.

And then I was suddenly posted off to RAF Henlow to spend my last months before being demobbed.

Arriving at a new station is a tedious business as everything is unfamiliar and you don't know who anybody is or where to find them and you have left all your friends behind you so you have nobody to moan to. But I was fortified in spirit during that difficult period by the knowledge that, back at RAF Ringway, the frightful flight lieutenant was trying very hard indeed to plot on an Ordnance Survey map a 5 x 5 photographic enlargement of a square inch of Spotty Dotty's pudenda.

Chapter Six

'HEIGH-HO! HEIGH-HO! IT'S OFF
TO WORK WE GO'

The beginning of my career as a professional writer was a heady moment at RAF Henlow when I first received money for a script instead of a pat on the back and a spam fritter in the NAAFI.

The year was 1945; the war was over and demobilization was the only thing that seemed to matter; there was little serious parachuting photography going on at Henlow and that work was done by two experts. One was a small hypochondriacal sergeant – when he had to drive me to RAF Farnborough in his own car he brought along gauntlets for us both to wear, cough sweets to suck, a rug to go over our knees, and he had cut and fitted domestic patterned carpet to prevent killer draughts from rising through the floor and giving our legs bronchitis.

His colleague was a vast, elderly, white-maned and duffle-coated ex-army man named Major Court-Treatt. The major, brother-in-law of the great W. O. Bentley who designed the early classic Bentley cars, had returned to Britain from being a cinematographer in Hollywood to do his bit for the war effort and seemed happy to stand for hours on a Henlow runway in ferocious weather which would have carried off the delicate sergeant, patiently operating a highly technical 35mm Newman-Sinclair cine-camera on a tripod.

As once again there was little official photography work for me to do, I looked about to see what was going on in the way of station entertainment. I did not have to look far. One of the first

111

people I bumped into at Henlow was my old entertainments mentor from RAF Warmwell, Flight Lieutenant Arthur Howard. Arthur had been posted from Warmwell to Cairo, where he said he had found a much more interesting young protégé than me to help on his way, a young airman who was determined to become a straight actor. Arthur said that he was a very promising young actor indeed. At this point the hairy hand of coincidence touched us.

Arthur said, 'His name's Richard Gale.'

He was my cousin.

Richard did become a professional actor and a good one, but later, when he was married and had every hope of a decent career ahead of him, he was taken ill and died appallingly young.

Arthur was determined to put on a sophisticated revue at RAF Henlow, I think mainly because he had a close friend, Derek Waterlow, who wrote brilliantly clever and tuneful revue songs.

This immediately post-war era saw the rise of the 'intimate' or 'little' revues; they provided the kind of charming musical numbers and 'camp' humour which the public seemed to enjoy after years of more basic entertainment.

The big success in London at that time was Alan Melville's witty revue *Sweet and Low* with Hermione Gingold, followed in due course by *Sweeter and Lower* and *Sweetest and Lowest*. I saw *Sweet and Low* and, inspired, wrote Miss Gingold a deftly grotesque monologue. Brimming with quiet confidence, I sent it to Miss Gingold. She sent it back.

I toiled and produced the book of the revue which Arthur so wanted. I was quite pleased with one sketch, a proposal of marriage that might have been written by August Strindberg, Beatrix Potter and Noel Coward. I played the part of the chap in the three playlets and the girl was played – beautifully – by our best actress at Henlow, LACW Gabrielle Hamilton.

The camp's verdict on the revue was that it was not at all that bad but, on the whole, not much good. One trouble was that our amateur actors, including me, were just not up to that kind of delicate playing, moreover most of the sketches were much too flimsy for the taste of our service audiences, which was still for more boisterous comedy.

Flight Lieutenant Arthur Howard departed to civvy street to resume his acting career, ENSA shows came and went, and then another impresario set about producing the sort of show that Henlow audiences really wanted. His name was A/C Dave Aylott, a large, gentle man who, pre-call-up, had been a make-up artist at MGM Film Studios, Elstree. After demob, Dave started a firm called Eyelure, which made and marketed false eyelashes with great success.

Dave's closest friend and aide at Henlow was an airman named Charlie, who used an unlikely chat-up routine on his partners at NAAFI dances. As they waltzed dreamily to 'Who's Taking You Home Tonight?' Charlie would murmur to the girl that he was now fully recovered from an early bout of VD which had left him impotent. Charlie's conquests were a Henlow legend.

Dave's idea for the new show was breathtakingly ambitious; he wanted to build an authentic old time music hall auditorium inside one of the empty hangars, serving beer throughout the performance and a cold supper in the interval (supper to be included in the price of admission, which was 1s. 6d.), with a proper stage and scenery, flanked by boxes filled with Victorian roisterers.

And Dave Aylott succeeded. One key to success was that hundreds of ex-civilians waiting to be demobbed and with nothing much to do had in their midst useful talents and experience which Dave could put to work. For instance, in charge of all aspects of scenery was Corporal Johnny Russell, a month or two short of returning to his old civvy job of being one of Jack Hylton's production directors. Dave's house manager was A/C Ben Arbeid, whose ambition was to be a film producer, which he later became. Warrant Officer Parsons assembled and rapidly trained a full-sized pit orchestra. The dances were arranged by an excellent comic in the Danny Kaye mould, who had a splendid bass-baritone singing voice. He also had huge feet but was, oddly, an excellent dancer. He was LAC Alfred Marks ('Alfredo' in the programme). I sorted out the songs and put together the continuity and Dave gave me a thump on the back and bought me a spam fritter in the NAAFI. Best of all, Dave's connection with Elstree film studios resulted in them lending us lorryloads of props, plaster pillars and other assorted scenery.

Four or five of us took turns at the table to be chairman. This was necessary because controlling a hangar full of happy, yelling, beer-primed airmen and women played havoc with the vocal cords, and I was also singing some of the songs on stage (I was the Great Gus Herbert).

I recently found the menu for the cold supper served during the interval. For 1s. 6d. the punter not only enjoyed the show but also: 'Assorted Cold Meats. Sliced Beetroot' (was I never to escape it?) 'Vegetable mayonnaise. Cold Baked Beans. Bridge Rolls – Biscuits and Cheese, French Cakes and Pastries. Sausage Rolls – Minerals 6d. Best Beer 1s.'

No wonder we ran for two weeks (an enormous run for a camp show) and were packed out every night.

The show's success attracted some enjoyable publicity. Terry Ashwood came down and filmed Alfred Marks doing his 'Alfredo' act for showing in cinemas as an item in *Pathé Pictorial*, culminating in a colour spread and story in the weekly magazine *Illustrated*. The story was written by a young journalist soon to be snapped up by the BBC as a cricket commentator, Brian Johnston.

Encouraged by all this, I read in an evening paper that an agency for hopeful radio comedy writers had been set up by Ted Kavanagh, a pear-shaped New Zealander who was the founding father of professional British scriptwriting. He wrote the great wartime radio comedy *ITMA* and became as famous and respected as the show's star, Tommy Handley.

Ted gave the calling of scriptwriter some prestige and dignity. Before Ted Kavanagh, scriptwriting was a somewhat nondescript occupation and comedy writers were often a touch furtive. Ted Ray told me that when he was playing the London Palladium, a small cabby in a raincoat used to sidle into his dressing room regularly with foolscap pages of jokes, most of which were topical, witty and thoroughly usable. Ted accepted them and then had the greatest difficulty in getting the writer to accept any sort of realistic payment. Eventually the cabby accepted 5s. per foolscap page; less than a shilling a joke.

I sent some samples of sketches and bits to Ted Kavanagh Associates and Ted replied in person accepting me as a client of the agency and giving me my first job, to write a six-minute radio script for a clarinet player who wanted to be a comic (in those days almost everybody seemed to want to give up what they did well and be a comic). I worked hard on the clarinet player's script and sent it in.

A few days later a letter arrived from Ted Kavanagh saying that the clarinet player had changed his mind about being a comic and had been persuaded by his wife to join his father-in-law as a French polisher. Enclosed was a cheque for £20 in payment, which I later learned was Ted's own money.

Pre-Ted Kavanagh and *ITMA*, and indeed for some time after, scriptwriters simply did not exist in the public mind. A year or so later I was driving home after watching a radio show, *Monday Night at Eight*, for which I had written a routine for Jimmy Edwards. During rehearsal Jimmy played a funny piece on the trombone and Geraldo, the great band leader, said words to Jimmy which etched themselves on my memory:

'Jim,' he said (nobody called Jimmy 'Jim' in those days except Geraldo), 'Jim, you're playing much more betterer.'

I was driving home after the show when I was gonged by a police car (I was driving at about 31 m.p.h.). I apologized to the officers for my dangerous turn of speed and explained that I was driving home with my mind rather occupied with how well the script I had written had worked on the air.

The two police officers were stunned. 'What do you mean – script?' one said. 'Don't they make it up as they go along?'

To avoid them turning ugly and arresting me, I said I would send them tickets to a performance of *Monday Night at Eight* so that they could see for themselves. They turned up on the night, un-mistakable in their huge boots and identical mackintoshes, and afterwards, having seen the performers reading everything off their scripts, were a little like two elderly children who had discovered that there was no Father Christmas but were not going to show their bitter disillusionment.

The first time I worked for the BBC was in 1947, as a performer on television rather than as a writer. I was demobbed by then and had collected my chalk-striped grey flannel suit – not all that bad a fit – a pork-pie hat made of stiffish cardboard and a gratuity of £40. All were most welcome.

The television job was compèring a revue celebrating the BBC's twenty-fifth anniversary. It starred Claude Hulbert and, according to the front of the script, a leading comedian from the Players Theatre, Olive Dunn. 'Olive' turned out to be a missprint of 'Clive'.

Before the war, the BBC led the world in providing a public tele-vision service, but the war put a stop to it. The corporation was keen to get the pieces together and open up a TV service again, which they did in 1946 with magazine programmes, much music, lots of news and one or two variety shows.

The receiving sets in use were like huge veneered filing cabinets with a little screen in front the size of a birthday card. It was a limited service because it could only be satisfactorily received in the London area. A television executive told me that in the first few months television was only received by about 200 wireless dealers and, inexplicably, the late Queen Mary.

The studios were at Alexandra Palace in North London, a huge building in a large public park which had never quite worked successfully in any activity it had been put to. But BBC TV now had a centre and the transmission masts worked well because of the park's high location.

Not that the BBC's bit of Ally Pally was all that suitable for conversion to studios. The rooms were too small and a drama production which would normally have required a large studio had to be split between two small studios. It was quite usual to be ambling peaceably along the corridor towards the bar and suddenly have to squash flat against the wall as a fully armed centurion and his cohort belted out of Studio 1 and clattered past, jangling and sweating, to their next scene in Studio 2.

It was relatively easy in those days to get some kind of booking on BBC TV if you had anything at all to offer. The BBC's system of auditioning was comprehensive and generous, and almost anybody demobbed from the services who had done some troop shows could get a chance to show the BBC what they were worth. Most of these hopefuls were more extrovert than gifted and soon dropped out of show business, but some are happily still with us – the golden oldies of broadcast comedy.

Television auditions were managed by the splendid Mary Cook and took place in rooms off the Tottenham Court Road above the Theosophical Society. Mary Cook not only coped with new talent when it applied to the BBC but also looked for it, in that she provided a supply of volunteer singers and comedians for a services canteen in the old Café de Paris nightclub. Her brilliant method of attracting talent for her shows was to supply performers with an enormous tray of marvellous free sandwiches; gourmet delights unobtainable elsewhere such as lettuce and shrimp paste or blue cheese and banana. The attraction of Mary Cook's sandwiches should not be underestimated in any serious social history of this period of television.

Most of my colleagues were like me, hopeful writers, or

performers or writer/performers, without a spare twopence between us, constantly bumping into each other in our search for eateries where food was just a little bit cheaper. For instance, word went round that sandwiches in The Black and White Milk Bar in Leicester Square were a halfpenny cheaper than elsewhere because they were spread with cream cheese instead of butter, and all BBC canteens were cheap and good if we could avoid being thrown out – we had no real right to be in them in the first place.

Mary Cook offered us not only endless and delicious sandwiches and the experience of performing at the Café de Paris, but if we were any good the chance of a BBC TV audition above the Theosophical Society.

I had my audition. I traced the gifted Gabrielle Hamilton; she joined me, and for our audition piece we played my showy, three-part 'Engagement' sketch from the RAF Henlow revue.

They booked Gabrielle.

But all was not lost. The BBC's twenty-fifth anniversary revue came up, and as it seemed to its TV producer to be the sort of show I could probably cope with, and I was cheap, I was offered the job. Then followed an offer to compère a Saturday afternoon telly series set up to display the talents of the best of the new performers sieved out by Mary Cook's auditions. The series was called *New to You*.

Among the young stars-to-be I introduced on *New to You*, making their first television appearance, were Norman Wisdom (achingly funny; fifty years ago his falls were, naturally, that bit crisper and more startling) and Ian Carmichael, who did a delightful song and dance à la Jack Buchanan in full white tie and tails.

The enjoyable thing about working on television in those days was that it was very intimate and nervy. A satisfactory method of recording programmes was not to be invented for many more years, and until then TV was gloriously 'live' and dangerous. But not frightening. When a camera broke down, a frequent occurrence, viewers were immediately on your side. I used to chat to them and say things like, 'You're no doubt wondering why Ian Carmichael has just disappeared in his best clothes. It's because we are experiencing one of those famous BBC events known as a "technical hitch" and you are very privileged to be in the middle of one. Mr Carmichael will be back again very soon unless you see two men turn up in white coats and attack the camera with screwdrivers. This means that its boiler has gone out or something and we're in trouble.'

Two men frequently did turn up and take off the top of the camera. This meant a long delay, so I would advise viewers to put the kettle on and my place in front of the one still-functioning camera would be taken by a tank of goldfish wheeled in on a trolley.

I did find danger in another aspect of early post-war television: the make-up. Before the war it had been hideous and unnatural, greens and greys because of the odd colour sensitivities of the early cameras, but by the time I joined the colours were fairly normal, just rather unnaturally bright, like the make-up of the soubrette in an end-of-pier concert party: pink face, scarlet lipstick in a cupid's bow shape, blue eyeshadow, carmine dots at the corners of the eyes (what on earth were they for?).

One Saturday, after presenting *New to You*, I was due to go to a party with friends in the beautifully named old Essex town, Theydon Bois – pronounced 'Theydon Boys'.

It was one of those shows when cameras fused one after the other and the goldfish cavorted heroically and everything ran very late. So when I was finally allowed to go I didn't waste time taking off my make-up but rushed down to my open sports car and roared off. At Ilford I realized I was lost, so I cruised up to a policeman and stopped the car.

'What can I do for you, sir?' he said amiably.

'I'm looking for Theydon Bois,' I said.

The officer gazed at me steadily for a moment and then said, 'Well, you won't find any round here, ducky.'

The finale of my first fine flourish as a pioneer telly performer came soon after the conclusion of the run of *New to You*. The show's producer was the veteran Bill Ward, one of the world's first ever television producers, who asked me if I could think hard and come up with some sort of original solo act which I could perform in a show he was lining up. I told him, with that mindless confidence of the young which is so infuriating to the no longer young, that it would present no problem.

I then forgot about it because my mind was busy on other important tasks like devising a style and writing the trial script for a semi-known, nightclub band leader who wanted to be a comic, and doing something about the exhaust system of my car, which had fallen off at Dalston Junction.

I came to with a jerk when a letter arrived from Bill asking me whether I had any special production requirements as the show was three days away. I rang back and said I hadn't and that I was a bit tired from rehearsing my act but was eagerly looking forward to the show.

After about ten minutes of deep thought I went on a tour of the junk and bric-a-brac shops along Leyton High Street and bought odd-looking, incomplete and broken pieces of pottery, china statues and vases, in fact any lump of something which did not clearly look like anything specific. I also bought a porcelain paperknife in the shape of an Indian army cutlass, and an ancient lace doily, partially torn.

My plan for the act was to display my rubbish to viewers as exceedingly rare and ancient artefacts of enormous value. Staring unblinkingly at the camera as lecturers did in those days, I would talk about the museum treasures and hold them up to view, and then as I fumbled about I would drop them on the floor or knock them over and eventually destroy the whole tableful. As it was obviously an act impossible to rehearse, I put all my rare bits into a carrier bag ready for the show and went to the pictures.

I thought up what I was going to say on the way to Ally Pally in the BBC's free green minibus service from Broadcasting House and formulated the significance of my items. For instance: the old and torn Victorian cake doily was a religious Tibetan prayer shawl crocheted by nuns from the softest wool tweaked by priests from the armpits of young albino goats found only in the Himalayan village of Pawa. They were exceedingly rare. The tall thin vinegar bottle (cracked, from a boarding-house cruet) was an Aztec tear vase used by Incas to collect their weepings after losing a religious battle. The tears inside the vase (Stephen's blue-black ink) traditionally went dark with age, and the present fluid was believed by British Museum carbon-dating experts to be about 1,204 years old.

The idea of the act was that I would begin by expatiating first on the history of the doily/prayer shawl and its rarity and value. I would then put it down carefully, without looking, on the table. Then I would start talking about the vinegar bottle/tear vase, and, in reaching for it, accidentally knock it over. As the ink flowed over the table I would grope around, still talking straight to camera, pick up the priceless Tibetan prayer shawl and mop up the blue-black ink with it, finally dropping the soiled fabric onto the floor like a spent Kleenex. And so on. I would end with just the porcelain paperknife and a large blue china vase which once held stem ginger (rare Transylvanian burial urn). Then came the really difficult bit. Without taking my eyes off the camera lens I had to position the paperknife so that it was balanced on the near edge of the desk, half on the desk and half off it. Then on the far end of the paperknife I had to casually position the ginger jar/burial urn.

'. . . and so', I would say, 'my time is up. I only hope that I have not only given you some pleasure, but that I have struck a BLOW – for the cultures of the past.'

On the word 'BLOW' I would bring my fist down heavily in a gesture. It would strike the protruding end of the paperknife, and the vase resting on its other end would shoot high into the air, disappear over the top of the scenery and be heard smashing to bits against the studio wall.

And it all happened beautifully on the live broadcast. At the end the table was bare and bits of broken crockery and glass were everywhere. I still think that on screen the act *sort* of worked.

One of the good things about people who work in television is that when you have done something which was a bit of a disaster, they do not rub salt in. They do not come up and say, 'Did you really think that was going to be funny?' They do not say anything. They just try not to meet your eye.

I negotiated the dangerous corridor to the bar without being trodden on, but when I reached the bar, which was busy after the show, I knew how well the sketch had gone down because nobody at all spoke to me, or even looked my way.

I suddenly felt my elbow gripped. 'Well done!' It was the nice Bill Ward, speaking quietly. 'Bit ahead of its time, that's all.'

Something like twenty years later, Bill Ward was setting up a BBC TV commemorative show at Lime Grove Studios and he asked me to perform my lecture on antiquarian artefacts once more. Understandably excited by this, I stocked up with another carrier bag of assorted broken rubbish from along the Shepherd's Bush Road and devised colourful provenances for them.

The lecture went off without a hitch. The china bits broke on cue and at the end the vase went sailing up and over the scenery like a kamikaze owl. As I was picking up my shards after the show, nice Bill Ward came down to the floor. He gripped my elbow. 'Still a great sketch, Frank. Lovely. Well done!' he said, and looked away. 'A little ahead of its time, that's all.'

With a wisdom beyond my years, I realized that my chances were slim of earning enough money from performing comedy on television to live comfortably and buy a younger car with treads on the tyres, and I made the decision to concentrate on being a radio writer. Not that I was one yet, but I had at least had a tiny whiff of that side of the game.

My first professional experience of writing radio comedy to suit an established comedian happened at RAF Henlow when I went to an ENSA concert starring a conjuror turned comedian named Peter Waring.

It was said that ENSA stood for 'Every Night Something Awful', but ENSA shows were put on with professional entertainers and actors and many were excellent. I think that (sometimes) it was a demi-semi-affectionate jibe, rather as the NAAFI was described as 'where you can eat dirt cheap'.

I was attracted by Peter Waring's style of humour, which was cool, deft and witty, quite different from the robust material of the usual stand-up comic of those (and these) days. Waring was one of the new 'class' acts, a slim, good-looking thirty-something, with the shiny, slightly wavy black hair then much admired, a good dinner jacket and a cork-tipped cigarette, which he held a little awkwardly because of a badly wounded right arm.

ENSA's programme notes explained that Peter Waring's real name was Commander Peter Roderick-Mainwaring DSO RN, and that he had been invalided out of the Navy after an enemy shell had smashed his right arm in a naval action on the Murmansk convoy run. As it happened, Peter Waring was in need of a scriptwriter. He was getting some radio work and each broadcast needed something like eight minutes of new material.

Most music-hall comedians began by writing their own scripts, or more usually remembering, pinching and adapting jokes from other comedians. When starting out in the game this one act would do them for a long while in the music halls, or, like Peter Waring when I first met him, performing mainly on a live circuit of hunt balls, company dinners and deb dances. Radio was another matter. Every performance needed a fresh script, and as this effort was beyond the range of most comics, the need for professional comedy scriptwriters came into focus.

I found Peter Waring's style fairly easy to pick up. I wrote a sample radio script for him which he liked and accepted thankfully. He was reluctant to part with any money for it to a uniformed airman, but I now had the Ted Kavanagh Associates agency to collect my fee, and so at last I lost my writing virginity, as it were, and became a money-earning pro.

Radio immediately after the war was a growth industry for comedians and writers. The Forces Programme – later called the Light Programme and now, I suppose, the cheerful end of Radio 4 – was stiff with variety shows such as *Music Hall*, *Workers' Playtime*, *Calling All Forces*, *Variety Bandbox* and *Garrison Theatre*, which used not only a star comic but also one or more newcomers who were given shorter spots earlier in the show. So short sometimes that the Australian comedian Bill Kerr, who later joined the Tony Hancock team in *Hancock's Half-Hour* and then went home and became a fine character actor in Australian films, began his radio act by announcing lugubriously, 'I've only got four minutes . . .'

One of the happiest of the smaller shows was a confection named *Caribbean Carnival*, a joy to all writers and performers as almost nobody heard it so the material could be used again elsewhere. The show was produced in the best of the BBC's audience studios, the Paris Cinema, in front of a mostly silent audience of Caribbeans and OAPs, but Edmundo Ros and his band played cheerfully and singers sang calypsos in between the comedy acts and the show had a happy air.

It seems that the programme was beamed solely to the Caribbean and so could not be heard distinctly by any other far-flung listeners. Moreover, according to legend, the broadcasts did not even arrive in the Caribbean, the signal weakened on its way like the light from a torch growing dimmer, and it finally expired completely just west of the Azores.

There was a lot of BBC radio work to be had in those days but not a lot of money. Unlike the present day, writing for radio in the 1940s provided bread and butter and occasionally jam, but not cake.

The usual fee offered to a new comic for a six- or eight-minute spot was £10 and he almost certainly had to buy a script which would have cost him his £10. So how did the economics work?

The answer lay in song. In those days it was the custom for a comic to end his act by singing the verse of a popular song of the day such as, perhaps, 'All By Yourself in the Moonlight' or 'Ever So Goosey'.

Some old time music-hall double-acts found this new discipline difficult to adjust to; it did not fit comfortably into the way they had worked all their lives. A comic often did not learn his stage act in a word-perfect way nor read his script for radio as written, but left it to his straight man to prompt him along, which gave the performance a more impromptu feeling.

Radio producers met the problem by flashing a green light to the comical duo when it was time for them to end their patter and go into their finishing song. So post-war listeners became used to comedy acts finishing like this:

STRAIGHT MAN: You were telling me about your mother-in-law.
COMIC: What about her?
STRAIGHT MAN: Isn't she fat?
COMIC: Fat?
STRAIGHT MAN: Yes, fat.
COMIC: (*light shining*) Did I ever tell you about my fat mother-in-law?
STRAIGHT MAN: (*amazed*) You've got a fat mother-in-law?
COMIC: My mother-in-law, she's that fat – when she sits on a bar stool it's like batter spreading.

(*possibly some laughter*)

STRAIGHT MAN: How's your dog?
COMIC: 'E's a funny dog is my dog. Do you know 'e doesn't eat meat?
STRAIGHT MAN: Your dog doesn't eat meat! Why doesn't your dog eat meat?
COMIC: I don't give 'im any!

(*perhaps a little more laughter*)

COMIC: 'Ere, I'll tell you another funny thing about my dog, he can play 'Star Spangled Banner' on the piano-accordion. All you do is give 'im a kick in the . . .
(*a green light starts flashing urgently*)
STRAIGHT MAN: (*ruthlessly cutting in*) Well, it's certainly a

funny old world we live in, but as a wise man once said . . .

(*a note is struck on the piano and both sing romantically, in creditable harmony*):

Red sails in the sunset,
Way out on the sea,
Oh, bring back my loved one,
Home safely to me . . .

Music publishers, most of the smaller ones located in Denmark Street, London's Tin Pan Alley, encouraged comics to sing the song they were currently trying to make into a hit by employing song-pluggers. These were personable young men whose job was to persuade the BBC producer of the show to feature the song, or to pay the comic to sing it.

A typical successful song-plugger was young Bill Cotton, partner with Johnny Johnson of a small music publishing firm in Denmark Street. Young Bill was called 'Young' to differentiate him from his father, the veteran band leader (and racing motorist) Billy Cotton.

Young Bill was good at plugging songs because he was gregarious, cheerful and an irrepressible teller of stories and so was welcome as a ray of sunshine in most of the dark offices of the BBC Variety Department at Aeolian Hall, New Bond Street. Bill's style was to play the record and if the producer was not impressed, say something like, 'Yes, it *is* a bit of a bugger, isn't it? Never mind, I'll drop in tomorrow morning with a ballad. You'll like it.'

Young Bill moved onwards and upwards to become a television producer, then BBC TV's Head of Variety and eventually Managing Director of BBC Television. A nice man and very good company.

So the comic had his original BBC fee of £10 and now had another £10 from the song-plugger, 'plug money', to buy himself a script. And in those days a young writer like me with few financial responsibilities could exist on writing two or three such scripts a week.

The hope of a writer was then to make himself so indispensable to his up-and-coming comic that if and when his comic was given his own series by the BBC, he would want his own writer to write it. Which is what I had well in mind when, lately retired from the complicated new world of television, I discovered that Peter Waring, my first, indeed only client for my scripts so far, was now doing his conjuring/comic act at the Windmill Theatre.

Peter gave me an enthusiastic welcome in his dressing room, not because he had missed me personally but because he was beginning to get a diaryful of guest appearances on radio and was in desperate need of a writer who was familiar with his style and was available and cheap.

I think that, inexperienced though I was, I was able to help Peter Waring quite a bit during the following year. In those days, scriptwriters thought of themselves as comedian's labourers. They tended to be writers who had little they wanted to say but were skilful in how to say things, and their concern was to build up those aspects of comedy for which their lad had some talent and to obscure his deficiencies.

I managed to wean Waring off the bits of conjuring in his stage act, which were really only a kind of crutch for use when the laughs were not coming. The trouble was it was not real conjuring, just the operating of simple tricks bought from the joke shop that used to be on the corner of Old Compton Street and Wardour Street in Soho. His main illusions were the egg-in-the-bag trick (a china egg and a black velvet bag covered with invisible pockets) and the magic cube (a boring box which the magician looked through at the audience to show it was empty and then from it produced a series of tatty cardboard dice).

He liked to conclude with a comical monologue, which was no problem, but then he would sign off with a benediction to the audience which I loathed but to which he was attached. He would smile his charming sexy smile, hold up his wounded hand over the audience like an army bishop and say, 'Good night, good luck (and then quietly and with deeply bogus sincerity) – *God bless.*'

After a few months of being a guest comic on other people's programmes, his fresh, upper-classy style grew in the affection of post-war listeners and Peter Waring suddenly became a hot property. The BBC offered him his own comedy radio series, and he asked me to write it.

So I worried out of the typewriter (the same old rattler) the trial programme for what is now known as a situation comedy, which I called *Heigh-Ho!*, with the subtitle *It's Off to Work We Go*. The idea was topical: a demobbed naval commander (Peter Waring) tries to get a job, not helped much by his uncle (Kenneth Horne) or his girlfriend (Charmian Innes). The series was to be produced by a youngish Scot, Charles Maxwell, who had come to the BBC from working across the Channel with Roy Plomley as a producer and announcer for the pioneer commercial radio station, Radio Luxembourg.

Each programme of the six would find our hero applying for, and failing to get, a different kind of job. And in the middle of the show Charmian Innes would sing a relevant original song (lyric by me – delivered to the composer by Tuesday morning at the latest, please).

The trial programme went on, light laughter occurred, and the show, with the three stars working well, showed enough promise for the BBC to commission a series of six. This was pleasant and gratifying. I had spent the dry run crouched at the back of the auditorium, panicking at the way things were happening so quickly.

From the riches I had earned during my late television career I had saved nearly £100 and I had lashed out and bought an open Singer Sports car of some age for £35. It was a bit slow for a sports car and tended to come apart. On rounding Trafalgar Square at a steady but exhilarating 15 m.p.h. one day the gear lever came away in my hand. Happily it was nine o'clock in the morning and there was hardly any traffic (ah, memories) and I was able to cruise safely to the side of the road and stop. I managed to fiddle the gear lever back into its hole and keep it there until I found a garage.

Like most old bangers of the period, the door catches had come adrift and driver and passenger were prevented from being pitched out onto the road on sharp corners by ordinary domestic brass bolts screwed to the doors. There was sometimes a bonus to this arrangement. When giving a lift to a girlfriend it was clearly one's duty to ensure her safety by reaching across her to check that the bolt on her door was safely home . . .

My old banger had now become a necessity because I was busy at all sorts of hours and I could just make my petrol ration last if I drove maddeningly slowly to and from the BBC in Bond Street, Peter Waring's place and 28 Church Road.

Peter Waring's house, which he rented, was a tiny mews cottage buried in the hinterland of West Kensington. He was looked after by Bill, a very un-Jeeves-like driver-cum-dresser-cum-drinks-pourer.

When I was in conference with Peter in the morning it was quite usual for a prettyish girl in a dressing gown to wander in from the shower, eyes still puffy from the previous night's vigorous pleasures, squeaking in a voice you could engrave glass with, 'Will you get Tom or whatever his name is to drive me to the station, Peter darling, I must get back to Cirencester before two o'clock or Mummy'll kill me.'

These *Country Life* one-night stands of his had expensive tastes, as indeed did he; he was always short of money and was amazed how little I (and my mother) could live on.

One day he said he was in a bit of trouble and could I lend him a few quid. I told him that I had £70 in the world and he was welcome to borrow £35 of it. He said it was only for a couple of weeks and he would return it with interest.

I found the first two or three scripts of *Heigh-Ho!* fairly easy to write and the songs not difficult, but then it all became progressively harder and daunting, I think because I was inexperienced and working alone. Being in a partnership halves the fees but it also halves the worries.

The day of the first transmission arrived. Rehearsals had gone well and Kenneth and Charmian were delightful to work with. Kenneth Horne was doing the show in between seasons of the hugely successful *Much-Binding-in-the-Marsh*. He was also the sales director of Triplex Glass. Kenneth was an immensely likeable man, the kindly old uncle, the decent officer, and he and Richard Murdoch brought to broadcast comedy an intelligent charm and insouciance which has never been equalled since; perhaps not even wanted nowadays.

They usually met and worked on the *Much-Binding* scripts over lunch in the RAC Club in Pall Mall, which was near Kenneth's Triplex office in St James's Street. Kenneth and Dickie would tip-toe respectfully into the vast morning room past snoozing members towards the magazines and reading matter arranged on a table. It was then Kenneth's pleasure to sprint past Dickie towards the table with a cheerful yell of, 'Bags I the *Port of London Authority Quarterly*!'

One of the standard devices used by comedy writers is the social introduction made funny by wordplay with names, for instance one which Denis Norden and I wrote for an early *Take It From Here*: a lackey announcing guests began with 'Sir Filthy and Lady

Lucre!' One of my favourites from Dickie and Ken's *Much-Binding* was 'Mr and Mrs Sam Wanamaker Junior!'

Dickie Murdoch told me of a time when the two of them were trying to think up new announcements on their way to performing in a Sunday concert. They were deep in thought when Kenneth suddenly said, 'How about "Mr and Mrs Tittybelt and their son Chas?"'

Heigh-Ho! was broadcast from one of the minor studios rented by the BBC, formerly newsreel cinemas which showed only non-stop news and short cartoon films, highly popular with children on holiday and parents too early for trains. Our studio was the Monseigneur Cinema, one of two or three which the BBC leased in Oxford Street.

During the rehearsal in the Monseigneur on the afternoon of the first *Heigh-Ho!* broadcast, our producer Charles Maxwell was called to the phone. We waited for him and when he rejoined us a few minutes later he seemed a bit distracted. We decided that it was probably some small domestic problem and thought it best to carry on as normal.

That evening the performance went well. The show got its laughs and the audience seemed to like it, as did the critics in the next morning's papers. We all took it for granted that the BBC would want a second series and planned accordingly. But there were to be no more radio shows starring Peter Waring, or even with Peter Waring as a guest.

Charles Maxwell later told us the extraordinary truth. The phone call he had received which interrupted rehearsals of the first *Heigh-Ho!* was from Pat Hilliard, then Head of the BBC Variety Department. He told Charles to go ahead with producing the six programmes of *Heigh-Ho!* because they were contracted, audience tickets had been issued and so on, but there were to be no more. Peter Waring was not to be employed again by the BBC.

It seems that Commander Peter Roderick-Mainwaring DSO RN had never existed. He was bogus, an identity which Peter Waring, in reality not a comedian but a small-time conman, had invented for himself. The Navy would never have recruited Waring because of his injured arm, which was not caused by an enemy shell but by a burn resulting from Waring leaning against a hot steam pipe on a pre-war cross-Channel ferry.

A few years previously Waring had worked as a clerk in a BBC office and had absconded with the cash box. In true BBC tradition he was not prosecuted in a splash of unwelcome publicity but discreetly sacked.

When awkward questions about his family arose he would quietly explain that his distinguished father, the admiral, and his dear mother, the pianist, had been killed in a car accident in Greece.

At the end of his radio series Peter Waring disappeared completely from public view, eventually surfacing at Blackpool months later in prison. Newspapers reported that he had been arrested on a charge of fraud.

He hanged himself in his cell.

My lasting memory of that charming, lightly talented, doomed petty crook who played such a part in my early career was him borrowing that £35 from me, half of all the money I had in the world, and promising to return it in a few weeks with interest.

Two weeks later he handed me back £50.

Chapter Seven

TAKE IT FROM HERE,
Don't go away when you can
TAKE IT FROM HERE,
Why don't you stay and maybe
Join in the fun, now the show has begun.
Half an hour of laughter beckons,
Every minute packed with seconds . . .

After Peter Waring's second sacking by the BBC and miserable end, I returned to freelancing and found that useful small writing jobs were forthcoming from BBC producers I had worked with, especially Charles Maxwell. And through many visits to Peter Waring at the Windmill I was judged to be harmless by the Windmill Theatre's short but fierce ('They Shall Not Pass') stage-door keeper, and he allowed me to have a coffee in the canteen with the new comedians starting their careers at the theatre, one of whom I hoped would have a style which needed my sort of writing.

The Windmill was an extraordinary part of the theatrical scene; more than just another nude show, it grew in stature during the war to become a semi-cherished London institution.

The performances were continuous as in a cinema, five shows a day, featuring brand-new comedians, a small resident ballet, a

The older lad, who looks like a Swedish goalkeeper, is my brother Chas. I am the one clutching an unidentifiable lump of knitted wool and looking up expectantly for food, which I clearly do not need.

All mothers are beautiful and ours most certainly was.

Our happy family in the sunshine. This was taken at Fern Bank, Broadstairs, just before Dad went up to Selby in Yorkshire to find work. The result was a well-paid job but also, unfortunately, double pneumonia.

Dad. Unflappable. Totally reliable. I think the portraits of both Dad and Mother date from the First World War.

Leyton County High School's talent-free production of *The Poetasters of Ispahan*. Playing Suleiman, the poetaster clutching the scroll, was my first disastrous taste of the thrills of ham acting, from which I have never escaped. Note that to my left is the long beard that I teased out from crêpe hair and which greatly impressed Mr Lewis, our English master.

One of my weekly letters to Dad in Yorkshire when he was lying in bed steaming with pneumonia. This one told of our school sports and must be one of the few fervent descriptions of a potato race to be found in English literature.

Littl kogg
89 RAMSCAT
Broadst
here
Engl

Dear mother and dad
                    you can see
that this letter is all over the place
because I am writing it in bed
Today the half-holiday, there wa
sport there were first of all a potat
race, there were six caps likes this
in that pacture you will see six cap
and then you see six lines of potat

            the picture you see six roes
        If dad to rams to the
        to and put it in the ca
        then go and get the scat
        otato and put it in the cap
    so on when we had brecke

Do not be misled. This is not a small rodent in the RAF Photography Section, it is me. No.1 Parachute Training School, Ringway, Manchester, c. 1945.

Ringway. 'It'll be a bit cold filming on top of the van, but as long as you don't forget to take a ladder...'

The best part of parachuting: packing up the chute after surviving.

1947. A slim Jimmy Edwards posing with Joy Nichols for a *Radio Times* picture promoting a new series of *Navy Mixture* (radio, of course). *BBC* ©

I can't remember much about this except that it was a production still from a little film I co-starred in, in about 1947, entitled *The Clouded Crystal Ball*. Don't know what happened to the film; had I won an Oscar I think I would have remembered.

A study of two fine 1950s haircuts (and suits). The full ashtray hits the eye, but Den used to take only a couple of small puffs and then mash the rest of his cigarette into extinction. He must have been quite rich in those days. *BBC* ©

Another jolly little pic to herald a new series of *Take It From Here*. Time has elapsed; it is 1954, Joy has left and June Whitfield is now in the company. *BBC* ©

A party in a café in Old Cannes to celebrate the wedding of one of Polly's French cousins. I seem to be entertaining the company with a wildly feeble impression of Charles Boyer.

A rare picture of Polly looking dangerous, taken during the war when she was in the WRNS and being used as a model. *Basil Shackleton*

Very newly-wed (2 mins).

1949. On honeymoon in the South of France.

Polly loathes this photograph. Might have been better if the lighting had not made me appear to be wearing a Thai gent's evening skirt, but it does show what the British used to wear in the 1950s when seeking tempestuous fun on a sultry Mediterranean night.

Back room Boys
by Cott

A cartoon from the cover of the Australian radio magazine *The Broadcaster*. Denis is the one who looks like a political spin doctor and I am the bent head waiter.

Another exciting picture from the Australian magazine advertising our radio series.

Take It From Here takes to the stage. Did rather well. *Mander and Mitchenson Theatre Collection*

The Cleopatra sketch from *Take It From Us* at the Adelphi (in those days all stage revues and comic films seemed to include a Cleopatra sketch). Jimmy Edwards and Joy Nichols are working strongly. *Mander and Mitchenson Theatre Collection*

1953. For some reason (public clamour?) somebody decided to take a photograph of the Muirs and Nordens back from Australia.

Jamie and I pretending we love gardening. Actually, now that Jamie has his own garden he has broken ranks and become a bit of an enthusiast. Well, you do your best, but eventually they go their own way...

At the flat in Addison Road just after I had half drowned Jamie in the rubber bath.

Tom Blau/Camera Press

Outside Anners with two large poodles, Polly and an exciting new fast car. There seems little more to be said. *Cyril Baker*

Polly and I posing on a canal hire craft just before we had our own *Samanda* built. They were, in the main, great holidays on the 'cut': vigorous yet restful, exciting yet peaceful (and dry land was only about 4 feet away). *Bernard Alfieri*

singer or two and, of course, the famous nudes. Indeed, as far as the general (male) public was concerned the Windmill meant nudes and not much else, certainly the comics had a tough time trying to hold the audience's attention between the fleshly *scenae*.

It was the only theatre in London to keep open throughout the war and its proud slogan, 'We never closed', was immediately modified by wags to 'We never clothed'.

When I squeezed past the girls on the narrow staircase up to the canteen, they mostly wore bullet-proof tartan dressing gowns and hair curlers. The legend – put about by the management? – was that the nudes were really prim, middle-class girls, many of them daughters of the clergy, but I never met any of those. The girls I knew were much like any group of busy working girls, though prettier than most, and had the normally complicated private lives of pretty girls.

One luscious dancer was the resident nymphomaniac (if there is such a thing as a nympho she certainly *was* one) who was obsessed with the leading male dancer, and when he leaped on stage she would swoon with lust and slump to the floor, which was dramatically unhelpful and physically quite dangerous for the other dancers teetering about the tiny stage on their points. Sadly, no sexual liaison between her and her loved one was feasible, but many Windmill girls, in the Gaiety Theatre tradition, married admirers.

The Windmill was owned and run by a small neat man smoking a cigar, Vivien van Damm, known affectionately but unfortunately as V.D. He was tremendously important to hopeful comics and writers because his policy was to audition pretty well everybody who applied and then give any new and unknown talent he discovered a chance on his stage.

In Piccadilly one day I met a disconsolate Alfred Marks ('Alfredo' of the Henlow Music Hall). He was demobbed and could find no opening at all in show business so was going to try his luck in America. It was extremely difficult to get any kind of permit to work in America so a number of what seemed to me to be tricky deals had to be arranged through friends to acquire the papers. I begged Alfred, whom I knew, liked and admired as a performer, to have one last go over here and apply for an audition at the Windmill.

He went for an audition, V.D. booked him, and Alfred stayed as resident comedian at the Windmill for twenty months. This was the beginning of his fine career in theatre, television and radio.

Besides Alfred Marks, performers who began their career playing some kind of part in Windmill productions included Kenneth More (song and dance man), Bruce Forsyth, Jimmy Edwards, Michael Bentine (part of a double act, 'Sherwood and Forest'), Michael Howard, John Tilly, Peter Sellers, Eric Barker, Harry Secombe, Arthur English, and many others too humorous to mention.

All were only too happy to begin at the Windmill where they were lightly paid but, as Jimmy Edwards put it, were able to scratch a bare . . . living. The productions were not variety shows but complete revues in miniature called *Revuedeville*, devised and produced by V.D. and his team of a resident composer, lyric-writer, costume designer and choreographer. A new *Revuedeville* was staged every few months.

The Lord Chamberlain's Office ruled, surprisingly, that the girls could be completely naked so long as they did not move. So the high spots of the show for the punters, in fact the whole reason for the punters buying tickets in the first place, were the three or four production numbers based on themes like classic paintings brought to life, or vaguely religious medieval groupings, in practice any theme which could include a rigid nude pretending to be part of a stained-glass window, or a Greek slave standing in an alcove balancing a vase of paper lilies on her shoulder.

Rather sweetly, although modesty would seem inappropriate to the work, the girls (unlike Spotty Dotty) had a code of prudery. Although they had permission from the Lord Chamberlain to display their all in static attitudes, they were unkeen to expose to the punters their most private part. So when a girl had to assume a new pose, her colleagues would observe her in rehearsal from all parts of the small auditorium, stalls to balcony, to reassure her that her stance of one leg forward and knee bent, or whatever, did the trick and she was, as the girls called it, 'safe'.

When one performance finished, the lights came on and there was vigorous movement in the auditorium as those patrons who had seen enough, perhaps three performances, filed out and the queue outside surged in. Some of the regulars stayed behind to watch another performance and as they were scattered all over the auditorium, they pushed forward eagerly to occupy newly emptied, better-situated seats, preferably in the front row.

There are lines which can encapsulate a person or an event in a few words. I was once told a story, allegedly true, which demonstrates the point.

It seems that Ethel Merman, the strong-voiced and hugely successful American musical comedy star, retired to California where her pleasure was to take her best friend, a largish lady, to all the opening nights of comedians and singers in the cabarets of Los Angeles and around.

Miss Merman was a popular and recognizable star and when fans came to her table to pay their respects, her routine was to say to them all, 'Hi, sit down and have a drink.' One such admirer was a filthy-rich elderly Texan, with the big hat and thin tie and bits of silver all over him. He sat down and had a drink, in the course of which Miss Merman spotted, with interest, his cuff links, which were miniature pistols. 'They work,' he said, 'try one.'

He proffered his wrist. Miss Merman carefully took hold of one of the tiny pistols and pulled the trigger. There was a sharp 'crack', a little smoke and Miss Merman's best friend let out a loud yelp and clutched her large bosom. The wad of the blank cartridge had struck her painfully.

Miss Merman, who thought it was a live round, let out a shriek of anguish which, taking into account Miss Merman's formidable vocal chords, might well have put a wobble on all the roulette wheels within a square mile, and howled what is perhaps the definitive line expressing middle-aged Californian culture of the 1960s: 'Shit – I've just shot my best friend in the tit with a cuff link!'

The Windmill line is a lot less colourful but might in its own way indicate something about class and British nudity.

During the hurly-burly of audiences changing over at the Windmill, a slide came up on the screen reading: 'GENTLEMEN ARE REQUESTED NOT TO CLAMBER OVER THE SEATS.'

It's the word 'gentlemen' that does it.

In spite of the work insecurity, they were happy days for me. I drove home to Leyton every night, a fair old way in the Singer Sports, tooting when I passed 28 Church Road to let my mother know that I was nearly home. She was always in bed by then but never went to sleep until I was back. I parked the car in the forecourt of a garage in the High Street.

Caribonum had always said that they would have a job for me

when I was demobbed and I did some agonizing over whether I owed it to my mother to go back there and give her some financial security, but my mother would have none of it. I knew she deeply distrusted the entertainment world of which she knew nothing (I knew very little more), but she insisted that I had a go at what I wanted to do and if it came unstuck – well, I could try something else.

I had several fledgling writer and writer/performer colleagues similarly brimming with the same hopes and the same cheerful camouflaging of worries and we all got along well. I was never aware of any deep jealousies or bitter rivalries between any of us. Our main hang-out was Daddy Allen's Club, a modest, first-floor drinking club and restaurant above a shop in Great Windmill Street. It was a prime position because it overlooked Archer Street and the stage door of the Windmill.

Archer Street was the headquarters of the Musicians' Union and the street itself was a market place for instrumentalists looking for gigs. The way it worked was that orchestras had one member who was known as the 'fixer'. The fixer's function was to hire musicians when his orchestra needed them to augment the regulars, or to act as substitutes. He would know most of the lads chatting in the middle of the road and would pass among them offering, perhaps, 'Ted, guitar doubling trumpet? Bar mitzvah, Bournemouth, Thursday evening?' Or, 'Trombone? Pit orchestra at the Finsbury Park Empire. Charity concert, Sunday? Anybody?'

The club's proprietor, Daddy (or Papa) Allen, spoke with a thick nobbly foreign accent, perhaps Hungarian, but his pretty daughter had married an absurdly handsome RAF Spitfire pilot who helped serve in the bar when on leave and the family was becoming more British every day.

The club had a licence to serve drinks all afternoon, plus Jenny Bell, a plump and pretty young restaurant waitress with what Terry-Thomas described as 'knockers like vintage Bentley headlamps'. Those delights, together with roast lamb and two veg at 1s. 9d., were an irresistible combination to growing lads.

One could tell when somebody in the club was working at the theatre by a movement of the wrist known as the 'Windmill Twitch'. With five shows a day and several appearances in each show, a performer never had more than a few minutes completely free all day and was forever twitching his wrist over to check the time on his watch.

There was a sad illusionist whose task of frantically stuffing his feather flowers back into slits in his dinner jacket and folding his silk flags-of-all-nations and ramming them into pouches in his shirt took so long that he had only *just* finished when it was time for him to go back on stage and pull them all out again. He eventually suffered a comeover and, reluctantly, gave up the glitter and tinsel of show business.

Spike Milligan was an *habitué*. At the time he was playing the guitar and trumpet in a funny lugubrious musical act called the Bill Hall Trio. Spike found the showbiz at Daddy Allen's (and the delightful waitress) happily stimulating after surviving unpleasant war experiences in Italy and fourteen days in the army prison, Preston Barracks in Brighton, for not treating his rifle with enough love and respect. Even in those days Spike fizzed with original comedy ideas. In Daddy Allen's bar one wet afternoon, Spike said, 'We're in an audience in a theatre, full house, staring at the curtain. Fanfare. The curtain slowly rises. On the other side is another audience staring at *us!*'

Cripplingly expensive set to build just for one laugh, but no matter, plenty more ideas where that one came from.

And there was Terry-Thomas, escapee from the meat trade at Smithfield market and working as a singing impressionist at the Prince of Wales Theatre. In his act, set in a BBC studio, he played a DJ who has mislaid his records and in desperation has to sing them all himself.

Terry stood with me for almost the whole of one afternoon in the bar of Daddy Allen's clutching his half pint of bitter, at blood heat like everybody else's after being frugally nursed for two or three hours, and said to me with deep sincerity, 'I can create *anything* to the sound of Mexican music.'

And then, very shortly afterwards, a new young comic began work at the Windmill. He was a stout figure with a handlebar moustache and an educated voice. He came on stage lugging an empty beer crate in one hand and a large euphonium case in the other. He wore crumpled sponge-bag trousers with bicycle clips, morning coat, winged collar and gold pince-nez specs. He put down the beer crate and sat on it. Opening the huge euphonium case he took from it a small penny whistle and played a sprightly tune. He then said, 'Encore,' pushed the mouthpiece up a nostril and played the tune again. Then he tucked the penny whistle away in his top pocket and announced, 'The second encore has been banned.'

He was 'Professor' Jimmy Edwards. At our first meeting in the Windmill canteen, I realized that he was in need of a writer, and his seedy schoolmaster act on radio with its fake erudition was the sort of stuff I would enjoy writing. It was a key cup of coffee in both our lives. I became Jimmy's scriptwriter.

Jimmy began to get more radio guest spots. Pretending to be a schoolmaster taking a class was a useful formula and one with which the audience could immediately identify – they had all been to school and been shouted at. It was relatively easy stuff to write because the built-in setting meant that about a tenth of the script was more or less written.

For instance, Jimmy would begin with some vigorous school-masterly commonplaces like, 'All right, pay attention! Sit up straight! Don't fidget! That boy – you're chewing in class. Spit it out. NOT IN THE HAIR OF THE BOY IN FRONT OF YOU! Write out a thousand times, "I am a mindless pain in the sphincter and spotty with it." Now let's get on. Those of you able to read might have seen in the newspapers that the prime minister . . .'And then on to the topical jokes with the useful saver that if a joke flopped, Jimmy could cover up by bellowing, 'WAKE UP AT THE BACK THERE!'

Meanwhile, Charles Maxwell was about to produce the final series of a wartime show entitled *Navy Mixture*, so called because it was aimed at the Royal Navy. This targeting of a particular service seems a mite odd now but it made more sense during the war when a show like *Navy Mixture* would include items of specific interest to its own particular service. By the last years of the war the services each had their own series: the RAF had Dickie Murdoch's and Kenneth Horne's *Much-Binding-in-the-Marsh*, the Army had Charlie Chester's bright and breezy *Stand Easy*, the Merchant Navy had *Shipmates Ashore*, presented by Doris Hare, with lots of messages from sailors' families, and civilians had *ITMA*.

Then Dame Fate stepped in and set Jimmy Edwards on the road to a successful career, and, in a smaller way, me too.

Charles Maxwell decided to cast the last series of good old *Navy Mixture* with some new talent. He had already found a girl presenter, a singing and comedy girl freshly arrived from Australia, Joy Nichols, and he now needed a new funny man as resident comedian.

The previous series of *Navy Mixture* had been written by Eddie

Maguire, a pleasant and helpful writer who was planning to take things easier and lead a country life. Through the producer's grapevine, Charles heard that there was a new comic at the Windmill, Jimmy Edwards, who seemed to have good potential for radio and should be looked at, so Charles asked Eddie to go and see Jimmy at work and report back.

It was at this point that Dame Fate started playing her tricks. She arranged for Eddie Maguire to shoot himself metaphorically in both feet (not that Eddie minded, he wanted to retire anyway).

The first shot Eddie misfired was when he went to the Windmill, sat through the comic's act and then reported to Charles that the act was no good. But he had watched the wrong comic.

The second shot, in the other foot, was his report on the comic he *had* seen. He told Charles that the act involved a razor and lots of lather, demonstrating how different men shaved differently, and ended with a bit of singing. Eddie found the act messy and the comedian not interesting. It was Harry Secombe.

So after due consideration – and things did get their due and proper consideration from Charles – he contracted Joy and Jimmy for the final series of *Navy Mixture*, and as he knew my work from *Heigh-Ho!* and I was now writing Jimmy's material, he contracted me to write the scripts.

So for a few months I was earning regularly what seemed to me a huge sum of money. The *Navy Mixture* script paid something like £35 a week. This sounds a skinny sum, but I recently rang the Bank of England information service and the good man there told me that the equivalent of £1 in 1946 is now £19. 95p. So my £35 was equal to a present-day £694. 75p per week.

The series was easy work, taking about three days writing a week; a fairly straight but chirpy continuity for Joy, a comic solo routine for Jimmy and some sort of sketch for the two of them. The show also had musical items, plus a bit of singing from Joy or a close-harmony group, and a guest comic.

The most successful guest comedian we had was a newly arrived, middle-aged Australian named Dick Bentley. On stage Dick did the popular stand-up act of playing a few bars of music rather badly on his violin and then stopping to tell a joke, but his radio routines were another matter; topical, self-deprecatory, crisp and witty.

Navy Mixture finished its long and honourable life and I was out of work again. But not for long. Ted Kavanagh Associates arranged for me to co-write with an experienced old hand of the game, Dick Pepper, a new and eventually long-running radio series for the American comedian Vic Oliver. It was given the dreadful title of *Oliver's Twists*.

Vic Oliver was (not that it did him much good) Winston Churchill's son-in-law. He had a mid-European-cum-American accent and in retrospect I do not think that I was a good choice as a supplier of comic material suitable for Mr Oliver. Most of my stuff seemed too English and local in allusion for him to understand, and he was clearly more comfortable with simpler comicalities. When he had read through my contribution for the first script of the show he laid it down for quite a while, rubbed his eyes and then explained patiently the kind of material which he preferred. As an example he told me a sure-fire gag which for years had never failed to cause audiences throughout the world to fall about with helpless laughter.

His humdinger went, 'When I sang in the church choir, two hundred people changed their religion.'

I was hardly either prospering or advancing my career during those Vic Oliver years – about two years of jollity-writing in all – but I was surviving. And much brighter prospects were beginning to build up back at the BBC Variety Department, Aeolian Hall, New Bond Street. The last series of *Navy Mixture* had produced surprisingly good figures and Charles Maxwell was pressing his bosses to let him produce some sort of new comedy series starring the successful newcomers who had done so well in *Navy Mixture*, Joy Nichols, Jimmy Edwards and Dick Bentley.

Charles was given the go-ahead, and as I had written Joy and Jimmy's material and Dick's very good guest appearances were written by the Kavanagh office's staff writer, Denis Norden, Charles took Denis and me to lunch at an expensive Italian restaurant in Jermyn Street and asked us if we would try to knock out some sort of a show between us.

Denis worked in a large room in the Kavanagh offices in Waterloo Place, Lower Regent Street, just down the road from Jermyn Street, so we trailed down there after lunch for a get-together talk. Denis proved to be almost as tall as me but two years younger and better dressed; I recall a modish 'drape shape' suit and a sharp hairstyle reminiscent of Tyrone Power in *Lloyds of London*.

It was rather a gloomy meeting. Both of us already had un-interesting but time-consuming writing commitments – I had *Oliver's Twists* and Denis had a number of Kavanagh's comedian clients to keep funny – so we decided we had better write this new show for Charles in the evenings. Denis was married to Avril and had a baby son, Nicky, so the sensible solution was to work in his flat, which was just to the north of Regent's Park, and Avril would most kindly feed me supper along with her family.

The show was given a starting date in 1947 and Denis and I got down to the problems of setting up the show. We were not certain of Joy Nichol's potential so we went to see her performing at the Finsbury Park Empire. With her brother George she did a good old-fashioned, song-and-dance double-act.

We thought, beforehand, it might be a good thing to book George to do the odd-voice parts, but it turned out to be rather a bad idea. Brother George was deeply into mystic beliefs and at one point in the evening said to us rather alarmingly, 'I could destroy myself with a single thought.' Brother George went home to Australia shortly afterwards and disappeared from show business and from view. Perhaps he thought his thought.

My memory is a bit hazy on what we actually turned out for those early *Take It From Here* programmes but the series certainly went through structural changes as soon as we got to understand our cast's great capabilities and grew a little more confident ourselves.

I do remember that the setting for the first shows was something to do with being a commercial radio station and that Maurice Denham played a character named Major Network (this he denies!). And Clarence Wright, who was in *ITMA* and was an original Ovaltiney on Radio Luxembourg, sang 'Transatlantic Lullaby' in a high tenor voice with a gentle, built-in bleat.

The first series limped to its finish to modest listening figures, and there it would all have ended had Charles Maxwell not had faith in all of us and argued with the Head of Variety Department, Michael Standing, that we should have another chance. Which, thank God, he gave us.

In the months before the next series went on air, Denis and I found the odd-voice character man we needed working in a revue (written by Eric Maschwitz) at the Playhouse Theatre, the brilliant Wallas Eaton. And we listened closely to American comedy shows transmitted on the American Forces Network in Europe. We had a lot to learn from American radio comedy in those days, such as Fred Allen's brilliant use of odd but real characters popping in, and fresh satirical techniques from Henry Morgan.

The second series of *Take It From Here* was quite a different set-up. We dropped the commercial radio idea and arranged the show in three parts. The brief opening spot featured Joy, Dick and Jimmy being themselves and swapping topical banter. Then a current popular song from Johnny Johnson's close-harmony group The Keynotes (originally and improbably named The Harmony Heralds), then the middle spot which we called the 'gimmick', which consisted of 'idea' sketches which our cast played brilliantly.

The 'ideas' ranged from *Hamlet* played as a pantomime, the London Passenger Transport Board Operatic Society's version of Gilbert and Sullivan ('Don't cuss the poor old bus, swearing at the drivers, wanting change for fivers. Up the LPTB, it's quicker to get out and walk'), to the operatic weather forecast ('Taking the temperature with a thermometer, Fahrenheit, Centigrade, where's the barometer? Check the velocities, what a dead loss it is, mucking about on the ministry roof. The mercury's sunk to the figure 0. Figure 0? Figure 0, Figure 0, *Feeeeger* 0!').

After the 'gimmick' came a song from Joy, or perhaps Dick, sometimes a duet, then the last spot, which was a longish parody of a genre of film or play or book. This last part was something of a small breakthrough in radio comedy because as far as we knew it was the first time in a prime-time series that the listener was credited with having been to school, taken a newspaper and read a few books.

Radio was advancing rapidly on all fronts from the mid-Forties on, finding its own voice in drama, pioneering a style of documentary programme which only radio could produce, and *TIFH* (as our programme soon became known) made its small contribution by attempting a humour different from end-of-pier, music-hall material ('when I sang in the church choir . . .'), and presenting instead parodies of films and literature.

Our approach was to take a well-known book or a period of history or a type of popular film, sort out in our minds what the subject immediately suggested, the clichés in fact, and work up the jokes accordingly.

For instance, we wrote an episode set in Roman Britain, a period remembered from school by most people for having dead straight roads, which were built by Romans with strange names that sounded like Anonymous, Lascivious or Titus Anewticus, and Roman numerals which looked more like letters of the alphabet than numbers. We had our Roman platoon being drilled by the centurion:

CENTURION:	'Roman soldiers, by the left, *numbah*!
1ST SOLDIER:	'I.'
2ND SOLDIER:	'I, I.'
3RD SOLDIER:	'I, I, I.'
4TH SOLDIER:	'I, V.'
5TH SOLDIER:	'V.'

John Watt, who was a notable early Head of BBC Variety Department (heads rolled rather frequently then due to retirements), said that the Roman soldiers numbering off was the first new joke he had heard on the air since the war.

Dick Vosburgh, the American writer of comedy and musicals who settled in England with his family, to our enrichment, always referred to *TIFH* as 'The Source'. Certainly some of the wheezes in those early shows seem to have passed into common use, which is a pleasing thought. For instance, we parodied the fashion for films and books about North Country factory owners facing industrial action and called our parody *Trouble at t' Mill*, a title which lives on.

Most radio humour is by its nature ephemeral and it is rewarding to find that quite a few effective lines from *Take It From Here* have been preserved on film and are still quoted. This happened because a close friend and colleague of ours, Talbot 'Tolly' Rothwell, was signed up by Peter Rogers and Ralph Thomas to write the *Carry On* films, which were very much like a cinema version of our radio parodies of popular literary genres in *TIFH*.

Tolly ran out of time and asked us for help, so Denis and I dug out those of our early *TIFH* scripts which ended with a film or book parody and passed them to Tolly to borrow from.

The pleasure which Denis and I have of seeing our early quips and fancies preserved on film is tempered by the irony that it is an old *TIFH* line which is quoted as the archetypal *Carry On* line: Dick Bentley as Caesar, attacked by Brutus and Co, cries, 'Oh, infamy! Infamy! They've all got it in for me!'

At the end of the series Michael Standing summoned us into his office and made a statement which Jimmy Edwards later said was one of the high spots of his whole life. 'I am very happy to tell you', said Michael, 'that we have a hit on our hands.'

And so *Take It From Here* settled into its eleven-year run. Denis and I worked to a routine: the show was first transmitted live, and then, with a workable recording machine at last available, recorded on Sundays. On Monday morning we started on the next week's script. We never in eleven years had a spare script standing by.

We began by writing the last spot, the dramatic or literary parody. We would settle on a subject, inspect it from all angles, discuss what must inevitably be included in some form, think up an opening and then start getting it on paper, discussing each line as we went. Denis did the actual transcription because his rapid writing was more legible than mine, but it was not a grievous chore; even on a smoothly productive day only three or four pages were produced.

The next day we tackled the 'gimmick' spot. This could be time-consuming. For instance, one of our techniques was writing what we called 'mathematical dramas'. A typical example would be three Noel Cowardish playlets performed by our three stars which were so unfunny that Jimmy (say) would suggest that they interleave the three playlets into one. This produced a totally different (hopefully funnier) play.

The last item to be written was the brief opening sequence, usually quips exchanged by the stars as themselves, e.g., (as a general election loomed):

JIMMY EDWARDS: I am considering entering politics and being the Grand Old Man of the Conservative Party.
DICK BENTLEY: Watch it, Jimmy. Politics is a dirty business.
JIMMY EDWARDS: Then I'll be the Dirty Old Man of the Conservative Party.

It was a punishing regime for Denis and me. One night when I was driving back from Denis's flat at midnight in my Singer Sports along the deserted Essex Road I fell asleep at the wheel. I woke up to see a lamp-post approaching me at speed. The lamp-post either dodged out of the way or I managed to swerve, but no impact occurred, and after a rest and some deep breathing I cautiously drove home with the windows open.

Then, breakthrough. Denis and I managed to slough off our other commitments and from then on put in a full working day together on *Take It From Here*, no evenings, on either side of Denis's desk at the Kavanagh offices.

For the next few years our lives were lived to the same pattern; meet and write all week, have Saturday off, do the show on Sunday, start the next week's script on Monday. On Sundays, show days, we met just after lunch at the Paris Cinema, Lower Regent Street, and chatted for a while. Dick would be very funny about his Pekinese dog, Yulu, which he seemed to spend most of his week taking for walkies in Regent's Park.

Dick was always fascinated by Jimmy's extraordinary honesty; Jimmy seemed to be incapable of telling even the whitest of lies. When asked how his week had gone playing variety in Glasgow he would say to Dick, 'I think they actually *hated* me.'

Joy Nichols became romantically involved with a baritone cowboy in the London production of *Oklahoma*, a quiet American (when not singing) named Wally Peterson, and with matrimony in view Joy had a gynaecological examination which resulted in bits of her having to be adjusted. One Sunday afternoon's whole pre-show chat was taken up by Joy describing to us in candid detail exactly what had to be rearranged within her and how it had been done. Wallas Eaton – who never married – was beginning to turn green when Dick said to Joy with deep sympathy, 'You poor thing. And my Yulu's got diarrhoea . . .'

At the end of that series Joy resigned from the cast to wed her Wally and go back to the States with him to become, she hoped, a star of Broadway musicals. When she came to say goodbye she gave us little presents.

Joy settled in New York with Wally, had a daughter, Roberta, but the marriage was uneasy, perhaps because she never did get anywhere in American show business. Eventually she drifted back to England, but could only get small parts. Just before she died she was working behind the counter of a Mothercare shop. Wally was with her at the end.

Replacing Joy in the show presented difficulties because Joy really was very good at comedy as well as being a useful singer. We had to replace her with two girls, a singer and a comedy actress.

143

For our singer we were lucky to sign up Alma Cogan, a large, happy girl who was beginning to make her mark with records and international cabaret appearances (in wondrous 'gowns') and her swinging, chuckly style of singing was just right for a comedy show.

We auditioned many girls for the actress job and had pretty well settled on Prunella Scales, whose readings were excellent, when we heard one last girl, a singer/actress from the chorus of *South Pacific* named June Whitfield. And so June joined the show as our actress. Her range of voices, even then, was extraordinary. She did a particularly wonderful 'debby' screech and was also a very good mimic.

With our two excellent additions to the cast, *TIFH* began to collect awards. The first prize we won as a comedy show was a life-size silver microphone from the *Daily Mail*; each of us was also given a tiny silver replica about an inch and a half tall, too small to mount on a stand and too big to make into a cuff link, but encouraging to have.

Then in 1950 the show hit a kind of jackpot when a new voice was heard in the land: 'OOOOOOooooooooooo, Ron!'

Eth and the Glum family began as a one-off sketch in the 'gimmick' segment of *TIFH*. At that time BBC Radio was having success with a warm-hearted series about nice families such as the Huggetts in *Meet the Huggetts*, which featured the formidably lovable team of Jack Warner, Kathleen Harrison and a very young Petula Clark. As an antidote we invented a repugnant family.

In the original sketch Alma Cogan played Ma Glum as a grumpy matriarchal figure permanently sunk in an armchair by the fire, and Ron and Eth had yet to emerge in their true relationship. Pa Glum was always the same, the pioneer male chauvinist pig, years before Andy Capp made his appearance.

That first sketch went so well that Denis and I realized we were on to something. We changed things round and made Eth a plain girl whose only hope of getting married was to stand up to Pa Glum's dreadfulnesses and hang on like grim death to her fiancé, the terminally dim Ron. For example:

ETH: Oh, Ron, nobody's perfect!

RON: *You* are, Eth.

ETH: (*purring with pleasure*) I'm not, Ron! I have faults like everybody else. Tell me one.

RON: You haven't got any faults, Eth.

ETH: Of course I have, Ron! Come on, there must be *something* you don't like about me. Something tiny.

RON: No, Eth.

ETH: Some little thing . . . ?

RON: Well, there is *something*.

ETH: (*roguishly*) Come on, then – out with it!

RON: You're a bit ugly.

We realized that the state of being engaged had not been overused and had interesting comedy potential. In the 1950s it was still an unnatural state of suspended animation, a social arrangement not found in nature which had its own rules of semi-permissive behaviour. To the boy it was like driving with one foot on the accelerator and the other on the brake.

We banished Ma Glum from the room and only heard her from afar shouting and screaming incoherently as something awful happened, usually caused by her husband.

For example, there is a loud thumping and banging and a scream from Ma Glum followed by incoherent wailing (Alma was very good at this):

PA GLUM: (*sighs*) I dunno – that woman! I ask her to do a simple task like getting the garden roller down from the loft . . .

We evolved a formula. Each Glum episode began with Ron and Eth on the sofa. June did her wonderful Eth voice and began, 'OOOooooooooh, Ron!' and Dick Bentley – after a pause and he was a master of pauses – said in Ron's extraordinary flat Australian accent (Australian!):

RON: Yes, Eth?

And Eth would start the plot rolling, saying something like:

ETH: I do think you should try again to get a job, Ron. It is four years since you last tried. And when we marry I want to feel secure.

RON: (*uncomprehending, repeats dully*) Secure.

ETH: Yes, Ron, secure. You do know what 'secure' means, beloved?

RON: Of course I do, Eth. It's that metal spike that keeps the Sunday joint from unwinding.

ETH: No, beloved, that's 'skewer'. 'Secure' means having money coming in regularly . . .

Ron was a randy lad and Eth was definitely not at all in favour of that sort of thing. Halfway through her argument to persuade Ron to get a job, Ron would suddenly say:

RON: Give us a kiss, Eth!

ETH: Don't, Ron! Ron, get off! You know how this skirt seats . . .'

As they grappled Pa Glum would burst in, see them struggling and say something like:

PA GLUM: 'Ello, 'ello, 'ello! All-in wrestling? Break clean!

And then he would explain why he had rushed in:

PA GLUM: Ron, run upstairs and fetch me your mother's toothbrush – I've got my new suede shoes on and I've trodden in something.

Or:

PA GLUM: Ron, have you seen the *Radio Times*? – the boiler's gone out.

The expanding success of *TIFH* brought Denis and me to the notice of other producers and we now had no problem finding work to fill in the six months of the year when *TIFH* was not on the air. One interesting new sideline was rewriting scenes in comedy films, particularly for the Norman Wisdom pictures. The producer would find that a scene was not working and would ring us and ask if we could sort it out ('by tomorrow').

In one Wisdom film the producer, Hugh Stewart, urgently

needed a big comic catastrophe, full of as much physical action as possible. We set to and in an hour had mapped out and phoned through to Hugh Stewart a sequence set in a theatre in which a symphony orchestra was giving a concert. It was a huge orchestra and it was seated on a revolving stage. When the scenery had been built and they were about to shoot the scene, Den and I went down to the studios to watch.

For reasons of plot – Wisdom was probably trying to escape from villains – we had our star frantically crashing about backstage amongst the switches and levers which controlled the stage effects. So the symphony orchestra, which doggedly played on throughout, began to revolve. Then all the lights went out. The lights came on to reveal that it was raining heavily on stage. The orchestra revolved faster and faster. The rain stopped and thick snow began to fall. Dry-ice mist spread. Cannon, as in the 1812 Overture, boomed. The scene ended in what might be described as orchestrated chaos.

'To think,' said Den to me, thoughtfully, 'that fifty-thousand-pound charade took us just an hour to write.' And we crept away.

It was an era of rather colourful radio producers. One, Vernon Harris, was successfully writing feature films on the side (one of them was *Three Men in a Boat*, which starred David Tomlinson, Jimmy Edwards and Laurence Harvey). We met Vernon in the lift as he came down from a high-level Variety Department meeting and he was ashen-faced. 'They've given me a *programme*!' he muttered desperately. 'This is going to seriously interfere with my work.'

The Assistant Head of Variety was an ex-Indian army officer, a really delightful man named (Major) Mike Meehan. At that time the still very Reith-minded BBC management had just issued to all its Variety producers a book of guidelines to what was broad-castable and what was subversive filth. This was the famous *Green Book*. It warned against such evils as saying that BC stood for 'Before Crosby', and cold weather meant 'winter drawers on'.

Mike Meehan went into hospital with a respiratory problem and to cheer him up Denis and I wrote to him asking if, in light of the *Green Book*'s guidelines, he would kindly OK the enclosed script.

The script began: '"C-C-C-Christ!" said the king to the one-legged nigger.'

It took us half a morning's work, but in this splendidly politically incorrect sentence we managed to get five infringements of the *Green Book*'s dicta into eight words.

One of the most unconventional producers was Pat Dixon, pushing retirement age and a rebel by nature, apt to turn up to departmental meetings carrying an American Civil War Confederate flag. Over the years we wrote several series for Pat, including *Listen My Children*, *Third Division*, which was the first comedy series for the BBC's new arts network, the Third Programme, and a number of hour-long monthly revues. Pat was always happy to try out new talent and the young comedians he booked for these shows were cheap to hire at the time but would cost a fortune a few years later, e.g., Benny Hill, Peter Sellers, Michael Bentine, Harry Secombe . . .

An interesting innovative series started by Pat Dixon, which Denis and I helped him push into shape, was *In All Directions*, starring Peter Ustinov and Peter Jones. In this the two Peters were supposedly wandering about London trying to find their way to somewhere called Copthorne Avenue. On the way they asked various people how to get there, thus setting up a number of character conversations and sketches. It was an innovative show because nothing was written down. They improvised the dialogue and Pat recorded the items in takes, as with a film.

Another bright but none too successful idea of Pat Dixon's was to send Denis and me to Paris with a new invention, a portable tape recorder. Ours was called (I think) a Soundmirror, and was a large heavy mahogany box with two tape spools which whizzed round, controlled by a kind of sturdy gear lever. Pat's idea was to call the programme *Ça c'est Paris* and Denis and I would go behind the scenes at the fashionable Parisien *haute couture* salon of Pierre Balmain and discuss this and that with the models changing in their dressing rooms. We were nothing loath. It seemed to us to be an excellent idea, in fact, quite the best that had been put to us for years.

Pat set it up in the summer months when *TIFH* was off, put in for the tape recorder and in due course BBC Accounts paid us, as was usual, an advance on our fee.

Pat Dixon had organized matters so that we would linger around the supermodels' dressing rooms with our tape recorder in mid-July. In fact 14 to 16 July. The truth then dawned on somebody that this was the great French holiday, the *quatorze juillet*, and everything would be shut, especially the fashion houses. Paris would be empty.

Pat had to cancel the whole enterprise.

Then Den and I received a memo from the BBC Accounts Department asking us to repay the advance they had given us. Den and I considered this request most carefully and then sent a letter back to BBC Accounts saying, 'Thank you for your memo requesting the repayment of the advance we received for the *Ça c'est Paris* project. We regret that we have no machinery for returning money.' The BBC Accounts Department was perfectly happy with this.

The great Peter Sellers was then an unknown at the Windmill doing an act which consisted mainly of a very long story about various dodgy street-market characters with funny voices selling each other a tin of sardines. The pay-off was that the man who ended up with the tin opened it and the sardines had gone mouldy. He protested to the chap who sold it to him who pointed out that the sardines were for buying and selling, not eating. This story, in various versions, has since become an urban myth but it may always have been one.

Den and I wrote a spot each week for Peter in *Third Division*; he played all the street traders in what we called *Sellers' Market*. We also used his extraordinary gift for character voices in sketches, one of which was a parody of those Fitzpatrick Traveltalks which seemed to be a part of every cinema programme in those days ('. . . and as the sun sinks slowly in the west we bid farewell to Bali, Isle of Enchantment . . .'). We called our version *Bal-ham, Gateway to the South*.

Peter was very quickly taken famous and was persuaded by George Martin (who later produced the Beatles' records) to record a comedy LP. Peter asked us if he could include three of our sketches which he had enjoyed performing: the mad headmaster of a progressive school talking to a timid potential parent, an interview with a moronic pop star and his gaoler/manager ('Come back here! I've told you repeatedly, where the carpet starts, you stop!'), and *Bal-ham, Gateway to the South*.

Some forty years on, in 1990, a group of Balham businessmen known as the Triangle Action Group, bent on making the centre of Balham an even more attractive place to shop, decided that as *Bal-ham, Gateway to the South* had more or less put Balham on the map for the tourist trade, they should erect a statue to its begetter, the famous Peter Sellers.

The *Evening Standard* got to hear of this and it made a good story, which Denis and I read with some alarm. Sellers was not the begetter, he was the actor who performed it, and there is often an assumption (rather dangerous to writers) that somebody as famous as Sellers wrote his own material and owned it. We had recently had an altercation with the late Peter's American lawyer, who had graciously handed out permission to a book publisher to include the script of *Bal-ham* in a book, on the quite baseless assumption that the copyright belonged to Peter's estate.

So Den and I, anxious to affirm our copyright in this curiously long-lived and quite famous piece for which we have considerable affection, wrote a letter to the *Standard*, which they published. The letter read:

> Further to your article (Balham calls for a statue, 15 February 1990), while we are all for putting up a statue to Peter Sellers, we may be able to save the good burghers of Balham a bit of money.
>
> It wasn't Sellers who dubbed their fair suburb *Gateway to the South*. The sketch was one of several we wrote for him in a Fifties radio series called *Third Division*, some of which he included on his album. However, this does not mean that the Triangle Action Group must now involve itself in the expense of putting up *two* statues.
>
> For a trifling sum, we would be prepared to go along to the new shopping centre and stand there personally.
>
> Frank Muir and Denis Norden

After forty years the LP is still selling, gently but steadily.

Again for Pat Dixon, Denis and I wrote a new sort of relaxed, early morning radio series starring a recently arrived Canadian named Bernard Braden and his wife Barbara Kelly. We called this show *Breakfast with Braden*. Braden was a brilliant broadcaster and the show achieved a kind of cult status. We followed the original series with a late-night version, *Bedtime with Braden*, and then *Between Times with Braden*.

The various Braden series were major series which meant that they went out in the autumn and winter when *Take It From Here* was also on, so our working week in the winter was busy.

We now had an office in the maid's quarters at the top of a building on the corner of Regent Street and Conduit Street. On Thursdays we would stroll down to Maddox Street, have a snack-bar lunch and then cross New Bond Street to Charles's office in Aeolian Hall and read him the *Take It From Here* script we had just finished (Denis would read it, it was after all in his own writing, and I would 'laugh it up a little' as American writers say). Then we would spend Thursday afternoon doing such rewriting as Charles called for. He called for quite a bit from time to time which we tended to resent. Later we worked for a producer in television who never queried anything and treated our scripts as Holy Writ. We felt lost and insecure.

On Fridays we wrote the Braden show. We only had a day to write this, so we evolved techniques like interrupting pieces of comedy rather than having to give them an ending. A typical example in a Braden show went:

BERNIE: So to this week's recipe, which is for oxtail soup. Bring a saucepan of water to the boil. Get an ox and back it slowly towards . . .

BENNY LEE: (*breathless*) Sorry I'm late, Mr Braden. I'll sing my song faster to catch up . . .

One Thursday, after lunching as usual at the snack bar, Denis and I strolled over to Aeolian Hall only to find, to our dismay, that neither of us had the script. We rushed back to the snack bar but it was not there. In something of a state we went back to our eyrie in Conduit Street wondering what the hell to do, whether we should try to remember the entire script and type it out, or what? About an hour later a man telephoned us from his office in a factory in Surrey. He had found our script in his briefcase and had kindly put it on a passenger train back to London.

It seems that Denis had parked the script on the shelf under the plastic tabletop and the man sitting opposite us had also parked *his* papers there, and he scooped first. On leaving he had slid all the papers on the shelf into his briefcase.

An agitated Charles rang. 'It's gone four o'clock! *Where's the script?*'

Denis said, 'It's in a small umbrella factory just outside Reading.'

It was at about this time that we experienced our first important newspaper interview. We were taken to lunch at the Connaught Hotel and interviewed in depth by two of the most powerful feminine journalists of the day, Anne Edwards and Drusilla Beyfus, then of the *Sunday Express*. The lunch was delicious, ending with sliced bananas poached in red wine.

The ladies wanted to know everything about us and wrote away briskly in their notebooks: how we each started, how we met, the sort of comedy we enjoyed, the comedians we did not enjoy, early mistakes, ambitions – it was about four o'clock in the afternoon when we staggered back to the office, exhausted and a little hoarse, but glowing with satisfaction that we had at last been recognized as worth interviewing by a national newspaper.

On Sunday morning we both dashed out and bought a *Sunday Express*. Yes, there was the column, and there, at the end, was the interview with us. It read, in its entirety:

Pudding of the Week. Lunching at the Connaught with writers Frank Muir and Denis Norden, we finished off the meal with a delicious new entry on the menu – sliced bananas poached in red wine.

With work now coming in from all directions and the prospect of ending in a debtor's cell receding, I thought that now was the time for me to move my life forward a large notch.

I decided to get married.

But to whom?

Chapter Eight

THE PLIGHTING OF TROTHS

I first saw Polly McIrvine in the BBC canteen at Aeolian Hall. I was queueing right behind her, clutching my tray as we reached the coffee urn, my face about 6 inches above her blond hair (naturally blond, I noted, rather unromantically, as if it mattered). She had on her tray beans on toast and an apple.

I was immediately attracted, surprisingly strongly, not by Polly's good looks but by her voice. An attractive speaking voice seems to me to be being bred out of the British, which is a pity. It is not at all a matter of accent or not dropping aitches but of timbre, of a musical sound, which is still occasionally present in the voices of older folk but rarely in the young, and never in the voices of present-day presenters of children's television programmes, on whom children model themselves.

It was summertime and Polly was wearing a cotton dress with wide horizontal stripes of bright blue alternating with white, like an old-fashioned milk jug. I watched her every move beadily from a safe distance as she ate her beans and apple, and then I followed her into the lift at Aeolian Hall – the biggest and slowest lift in the Western hemisphere, built to elevate grand pianos to what was once a concert hall on the first floor – and trailed behind her stealthily along the third-floor corridor, flitting from one doorway to another like an inept private eye, eventually seeing her disappear into the Bookings Department, the office which issued all our contracts (which were in lovely guineas in those days).

Polly was hardly a BBC career girl. Labour was directed then, and unless a girl could get a job with a corporation like the BBC, which was deemed a public necessity, she could theoretically end up down the mines or weighing fish on Grimsby docks. Polly, newly demobbed from the WRNS, was fortunate in getting an extremely dull job at the BBC typing contracts for the Variety Department's bookings manager (and Gilbert and Sullivan enthusiast) Pat Newman.

A couple of days later I made my first move, and a shrewd gambit it was, too. *TIFH* was by then a much-talked-about new hit and tickets to see the show going out live from the Paris Cinema were much in demand. Those of us connected with the show were allowed a small ration of tickets.

A few days later I watched Polly's office door for quite a while before I decided the coast was clear, then I knocked gently and went in. There was the milk-jug dress sitting at a typewriter. She looked up.

I cleared my throat a couple of times and went suavely into the speech I had rehearsed for an hour or two. 'Er – I wondered – er,' I said, putting the *TIFH* ticket on her desk in front of her, 'whether you – if you haven't actually got anything better to do, of course, which you probably have, and why shouldn't you? – Whether you – er – would like to come to this?'

She picked up the card and read it. I felt wholly confident because offering a *TIFH* ticket to a keen listener was like offering a cup-final ticket to a football fanatic.

'What's *Take It From Here*?' she asked, curiously.

My heart sank. It was clear that if my prey had never heard of *Take It From Here*, my trump card was worthless. In the long reaches of that night I realized that it was stupid to expect an attractive girl to spend her evenings glued to the wireless.

'I'm so sorry,' she said, 'but I've arranged to spend that evening with a girlfriend.'

'Bring her along!' I blurted. 'I'll book a table for dinner at the Screenwriters' Club.' This was a splendid private restaurant and bar in Deanery Street at the back of the Dorchester Hotel, set up by the screenwriter Guy Morgan and others. The club bore about as much resemblance to Daddy Allen's Club as the Dorchester did to the Union Jack Sailors' Mission, but much of the overheard conversation at the Screenwriters' was just as unlikely. At lunch there one Saturday I heard one mink-clad lady discussing a famous violinist with another mink-clad lady. She was saying, 'Then they moved to New York, I remember that. But what became of *her*?'

'She was murdered.'

'No, the *other* one, his second wife?'

I remember little of my first date with Polly, which is perhaps all for the best because I heard many years later that when I dropped the girls off at the block of flats where they both lived, Polly's friend said to her, 'He seems awfully keen. Are you interested?' And Polly said, 'Good God, no!'

But I persevered. This was not wholly due to love at first sight, although there was a lot of that, but it was also due to my ignorance of the practice of wooing. I simply did not know the rules of the game and did not recognize the codes which Polly was probably issuing – she had plenty of casual boyfriends – to warn me not to nurse more serious ambitions. So I blundered on.

Brother Chas would have played it like the game it usually was. He would have known the rules and the codes because he had always had stacks of girlfriends and was much experienced in complicated flirtations. My few experiences always seemed to consist of taking a liking to a girl because of her nose or something and then going off her bit by bit as I got to know her. Naturally I expected this diminution of ardour to happen with Polly, but it did not. Polly was not just a pretty voice; the more I got to know her the more I found to admire and like, and then love. It began to get serious my end.

With more money coming in I was able to part-exchange the Singer Sports for a drop-head Frazer-Nash BMW. This sounds grand but it was actually a very old car; the hood leaked, there was so little pressure in the cylinders that I could crank the engine holding the starting handle between finger and thumb, and it had been rebored so many times that the garage said that there was no more metal left for another rebore. On the bright side, it had real door handles and looked quite sporty on a dry day.

With a bit of research I managed to establish Polly's hours of work, so when she emerged from Aeolian Hall at about six she would find me parked outside, elbow nonchalantly stuck out of the car window. I would exclaim, surprised, 'Hello again! Look, I'm going west, can I give you a lift home?' and I would rush round and fling open the passenger door.

My journey home to Leyton was actually to the east but what matter? I was beginning to establish a bridgehead in Polly's awareness.

The recurring coincidence of finding me parked outside when it was time for her to go home lasted a month or two and then we progressed to occasionally going to films and events together and we began to draw closer.

One chilly Saturday we drove down for a day's excursion to Brighton and Hove. On Hove front we ran into Ted Kavanagh. I was alarmed because Ted was strongly Roman Catholic, as was Polly (Ted was a member of the Knights of St Columbus), and I did not want him to think that Polly and I had nipped away for a dirty weekend, so I introduced Polly carefully.

Ted took a photograph of us on my camera and I sent Polly an enlargement on which I wrote:

> *Don't laugh at my jokes too much,*
> *People will say we're in Hove.*

At the end of one of my lifts home, Polly invited me upstairs to her flat (her mother was out), pinned me down safely to the sofa with two or three heavy family photograph albums and I learned about her background. About the same time that my grandfather sailed for New Zealand, Polly's grandfather left Aberdeen University with his degree, swiftly married, and in 1856 sailed with his bride, a cradle and a huge mahogany dining-room table to the island of Mauritius in the Indian Ocean, a journey which took six months by auxiliary sail. There he began his work as the island's first Presbyterian minister.

Their son, Polly's father, was born in Mauritius, became a businessman in the capital, Port Louis, exporting and importing. When on leave in France in 1914 (because of the slow travel they had terrific leaves in those days; usually a whole year every three or four years) he married a French girl from the north of France. They just managed to escape from France and get back to Mauritius before the Great War overwhelmed Europe.

Polly was born in Mauritius and managed to survive the high infant-mortality rate of the sub-tropics. An elder brother, Brian, and an elder sister, Isabelle, known to all as 'Pigeon', also survived. Brian became an actor and Pidge became a nun at the IBVM convent and girl's school at Ascot, later Reverend Mother for a couple of tours of duty.

This background was somewhat different from mine and I am eternally grateful that my ignorance of courtship practices meant that I did not realize that my determination to marry Polly was an almost hopeless dream. So on with it I went. As far as I was concerned I had found the girl I wanted to grow old with and that was that. The example of my own parents had shown me what a good thing marriage was and I was not going to be put off by theoretical problems.

I told my mother that I wanted to marry a girl I had met at the BBC and that she came from Mauritius. 'Oh, dear!' said my mother, not even knowing where Mauritius was but fearful of complications. 'She's a natural blonde,' I went on. 'Huh!' said my mother.

One evening I took Polly down to 28 Church Road to meet my mother, and it must have been an ordeal for both of them. Polly and *her* widowed mother lived in North End House, a block of large modern flats with flowers in the vestibule, a lift operated by an attendant and the flats had a short corridor of small rooms off the kitchen to house the staff (not that there were any after the First World War). Twenty-eight Church Road was not quite like that. Polly was marvellous, but when I saw her home on the tube she was unusually quiet and thoughtful.

My mother, typically, changed her tune completely after meeting Polly and from then on sided with Polly against me for the rest of her life. 'Have you asked Polly what *she* wants to do? No, you just go your way without giving her a thought . . .' Or, 'What does Polly think about it? You might give her *some* consideration . . .' Or, 'How Polly puts up with your selfish behaviour . . .'

To smarten myself up, a long-overdue move, I bought a cheap off-the-peg tweed jacket from Austin Reed which, by a miracle, happened to fit. My mother commented, with that kind of affectionate injustice which one never forgets, 'Spending more money? Oh, well, easy come, easy go.'

Easy come!

My campaign moved forward a notch when Polly disclosed that she and her mother were going to France to visit a French aunt and various relations.

'But that's marvellous!' I exclaimed, starting back in surprise at the good news. 'I have to go to Paris to see a man. Let's arrange to meet!'

How much Polly realized that she was being wooed with a string of blatantly fake coincidences has never emerged. She probably enjoyed the whole charade.

Polly and her mother were going first to Vouvray, the town of wine caves, and then on to Paris to stay at a Benedictine convent with one of Maman's nun sisters, Tante Isa. It was arranged that when I had booked into a hotel in Paris I would send a telegram to Polly in Vouvray with my hotel's phone number and Polly would phone me when she and her mother arrived back in Paris.

I had never been to France before and spoke only schoolboy French. It was an extremely tedious business shipping the car over, with great wads of forms. No fancy drive-on ferries; at Newhaven the car was hoisted off the quay by a crane and lowered roughly into the forward hold of the small cargo ship.

The drive to Paris was fascinating and exciting. Many of the roads were still cobbled and had a terrific camber so that the car heeled over at an alarming angle when close to the kerb, almost hitting its head on roadside trees. I stopped for petrol at one of the strange, very French kerbside petrol pumps which had huge glass vases on their tops. When I ordered my precious litres – special cheap coupons for tourists – a crone in rusty black, bent with age and arthritis, painfully worked a handle to and fro and petrol rose into one of the glass vases. When enough had been pumped, she pulled a lever and the petrol golloped down the hose into the car's tank.

I hadn't the faintest idea where to stay in Paris, but I happened upon a tiny square up in Montmartre which seemed to consist entirely of small hotels and I booked in for the night at a safe bet, the Hôtel d'Angleterre. There was a very sweet and helpful African receptionist who sorted out my passport and the various personal details then officially required and I went to bed. In the morning a very pleasant African girl brought me coffee and a croissant. I went downstairs and in the hallway was a coachload of friendly Africans queueing to book in. I realized that for my one-night stay I had chosen a hotel entirely manned by, and catering for, Africans.

I drove along the almost deserted Champs Elysées and parked the car at the kerb. The morning was warm and sunny and I sat at a pavement table at the elegant café, Fouquet's, and enjoyed that

French civilized pleasure of a glass of chilled white wine at eleven in the morning (it was actually champagne but sipping champagne mid-morning sounds too dissolute to admit to).

I had an urgent problem. Polly and her mother were due to leave Vouvray at any moment for the Paris convent and I had promised to send a telegram to Polly telling her in which hotel I was staying, but I now had no hotel. I looked about me for help.

The pavement tables were almost deserted, but a few tables away sat a pleasant-looking Frenchman, a bit older than me. He smiled, stroked his tie and then pointed at me. I was wearing a striped RAF tie. I went over to his table to get some advice on hotels. He was drinking a glass of white wine (non-bubbly) and invited me to join him. In excellent English he asked what I did in the RAF and parachuting at RAF Ringway came up. An extraordinary coincidence emerged.

My French friend had also been at Ringway. He had been recruited into the SOE and had been sent to learn night parachuting at the course for agents at Ringway run by Major Edwards and Captain Dalton.

He told me stories of his spy days, of walking into a café full of Germans just after being dropped into Normandy and inadvertently pulling out of his jacket pocket with his handkerchief a packet of twenty Players cigarettes, which clattered to the floor. He passed the cigarettes round to the German soldiers as souvenirs liberated from a captured British colonel.

I managed to interrupt my friend's sparkling stream of reminiscences long enough to ask him to recommend a modest hotel for me for a couple of nights. No problem. The address he gave me was about a quarter of a mile away, just down from the Arc de Triomphe. Hôtel les Acacias, rue des Acacias.

Seeing me into the car with his chatter back on full flow, I learned that he lived in a flat near the Louvre and was back at his old trade of designing nightclub decors. He said that he had several old SOE friends and resistance colleagues whom he would invite that evening to a party at his flat to meet me and celebrate whatever any of us could think of to celebrate.

Exhausted already by his nervous energy and relentless charm, I drove round to the Hôtel les Acacias which was exactly right. Small, family-run, cleanish, cheapish. Polly and I used it many times later and we were treated as regulars.

On one visit we coincided with an international rugger match, France versus Wales, and a batch of Welsh fans had booked into the hotel. Wales won and that night the Welsh fans sang in triumph, emotionally and very loudly. They seemed to be set to sing all night. About three in the morning Madame, in dressing gown and hairnet, knocked on our door and asked me whether we would be kind enough to do something to diminish the noise coming from room 2-10 (by then the boyos were treating the whole arrondissement to 'Land of My Fathers', fortissimo and *con amore*). I knocked on the door of room 2-10, not that they could have heard me above the din they were making, and went in. There were extraordinarily few of them making all that noise and they were not all that drunk, just dog-tired and in a kind of ecstasy of patriotic pleasure at their team's victory.

'Lads! Lads!' I shouted. 'You must stop this singing, you're keeping the whole hotel awake! Next thing is, they'll call the police and then you'll be locked up in the Bastille, and once you are in the Bastille *you'll never be heard of again*!'

This got through. Three or four of them mumbled apologetically and quietly trailed back to their own rooms, leaving just their host lying on his bed. He looked up at us and said, in a gentle Welsh tone of infinite sadness, a line which is now part of our family's private language: 'There's no 'arm in being 'appy.'

On another of our visits to Paris and the Hôtel les Acacias a further family code expression was born. The hotel did not serve food other than a continental breakfast (with croissants never older than an hour away from the local baker's oven, where they were baked in small batches all day), but there was a little café/restaurant just along the road and there was a small underground garage where we could leave the car.

One morning we went to collect the car and found that a customer with his thoughts on a higher plane had left his large Citroën car at the foot of the ramp, blocking it off, and had gone away with the keys. The garage owner, a small plump man in blue overalls, was in a paroxysm of rage, jumping up and down and flailing his arms. He stopped eventually, breathing heavily, banged his hand down on the car's bonnet and delivered judgement: '*Cet homme, il est véritablement LE ROI des cons!*' This, abbreviated to '*il est véritablement . . .!*' has proved a useful code message between Polly and me ever since.

I settled in at the hotel, sent a telegram to Polly at Vouvray giving the hotel's name, address and phone number, unpacked – which took about forty seconds – wandered round Paris a bit, had a rest on the bed and drove to my French friend's flat for his party of ex-resistance men.

The evening, which went into the early hours, produced a great deal of storytelling and bellows of laughter and champagne. It was a gay party (I think probably in both senses) and when I woke up in the late morning I was in a huge and very chic bedroom wearing putty-coloured silk pyjamas. I dressed with great speed and rushed back to the hotel.

I was too late. Polly had already telephoned, twice, and madame had reported, no doubt with relish, that I had been out all night. No, monsieur did not say where he was going, or with whom. And I had still not returned . . .

I begged madame to ring the convent's number for me immediately.

The line was engaged.

Standing there in the hotel's tiny foyer I started to sweat at the delay. It wasn't a question of explaining what I was doing out all night, I just suddenly had this strange deep longing to *see* Polly.

In Paris, of all places, I should have been able to make considerable progress towards wedded bliss, but I seemed to be making a porridge of the whole thing.

I then realized how much I disliked the courting process. I have never been very competitive and for months I lived with the constant fear that any moment I might lose Polly to somebody she liked better – when we first met there were several eligible young men circling in the background. And losing Polly was simply too disastrous a possibility to even contemplate.

This way of thinking was of course insulting to Polly, seemingly treating her as a pawn in a game and taking little account of her own wishes, but I was feeling very jumpy and scared as I paced the tiny lobby.

Then madame got through to the convent. Polly and her mother were out shopping. I left a message with the duty nun that unless I heard from Polly that it was inconvenient, I would collect her from the convent after Mass the following morning – a Sunday – give a toot on the car horn to announce that I had arrived and then whisk her off to coffee and lunch *chez* Fouquet's and in the afternoon a drive along the river to St Cloud.

Tante Isa's convent was in the suburb of Asnières, not too far away, and the roads next morning were almost empty of traffic, so I arrived comfortably early. I felt a quiet confidence that this was going to be a good day.

As I drew up in the car I tooted a modest toot on the horn to announce my arrival.

The horn stuck.

It is quite extraordinary how deafening a noise an elderly Frazer-Nash BMW's horn can make on a quiet Sunday morning in a narrow French street outside the high wall of a convent. I prayed that Mass had finished. I was also interested to note a scientific phenomenon which I might designate 'The Muir Effect'. This states: the longer a stuck horn blares, the louder it becomes.

Then Polly emerged from the convent's front door and jumped in beside me. Conversation was impossible, so I put the car into gear and, with the horn still blaring as though warning the citizenry of an invasion, drove off.

Just along the road the horn unstuck as mysteriously as it had stuck and the blissful diminution of noise made speech possible. Polly looked terrific and at last here I was, sitting close to her, and we were *talking*. It was a good feeling. I explained what had happened, apologized like steam and did what I could towards what would nowadays be called damage limitation. I think I was slightly forgiven.

The rest of the day went (fairly) well. At Fouquet's a gypsy lady with a huge flat basket of cut flowers went on a semi-begging tour of the pavement tables, dragging a dirty, large-eyed little girl behind her. I bought a spray of red roses which I formally presented to Polly, meeting her eye and giving her a deeply significant look.

In the European language of flowers, the gesture of presenting Polly with red roses represented a floral declaration of my love. But Polly grew up in Mauritius. Years later Polly told me that when I dropped her back at the convent that evening she gave my roses to the Reverend Mother, who liked flowers.

'But you must not give me your roses!' protested the Reverend Mother. 'Do you not know what it means when a young man gives you red roses?'

'Well, actually, no I don't!' said Polly cheerfully.

*

Back in England, autumn set in and a new series of *Take It From Here* was scheduled, and Denis and I had to begin thinking about what we were going to do with the show. New ideas had to be found, old characters replaced.

The preparation of the first show of a run of *Take It From Here* was nerve-racking. The problem was that although we got down to it and produced the first script a week before the show, the *Radio Times* had to have information about it for their publicity three weeks ahead, so we fed them generalizations along the lines of, 'Jimmy Edwards is as outrageous as ever and Dick Bentley is as cool and calm as ever. Watch out for fun with the Glums,' and more of such waffle.

The awful part came when the *Radio Times* was published ten days before the show. There was – probably on the cover – a photograph of our stars looking comical and an article inside welcoming the series back, which would include new problems for the Glum family, Jimmy being as outrageous as ever, etc. And not a word of it was yet written.

Polly and I were by now going almost everywhere together and one day I blurted out a desperately unromantic half proposal which was more like a declaration of intent to merge – with conditions. I said that I would very much like to marry her but we would have to wait until next summer because of *Take It From Here*.

As the weather worsened and moved into winter, the sun came out figuratively for Polly and me when we admitted being in love with each other. I then met many of Polly's family friends, mainly ex-pat Mauritians who had retired to England, French families who traditionally ran the sugar estates and Brits who ran almost everything else – it was still a British colony then. We made plans to get engaged at Christmas; in those days an engagement was like a mini-marriage in the social pattern, an important formal step.

In the run-up to Christmas we wandered through Burlington Arcade and chose the engagement ring, which Polly had to hide away in a drawer until the engagement was announced. This pre-engagement period sounds very unromantic and non-Barbara Cartland, with no blurted proposal coming as a total surprise to the lady, or the sudden whipping out of an engagement ring from a little box and the ring fitting perfectly, but for us it was a magical period when we planned our immediate future and exchanged long-range hopes.

Next I had to formally declare my intentions to Polly's mother. This turned out to be trickier than I imagined.

I liked Anna McIrvine very much. I think I always puzzled her a little by my deeply English way of not being very serious and using irony a lot, but she called me her *géant* and we always got on extremely well. My problem was that the time I had arranged for our formal meeting was not well chosen.

It was on her return from a drinks party given by an ex-Mauritian friend for fellow ex-Mauritians. I suppose Maman, as I now called her, had enjoyed one glass of sherry – no more. She asked me into her room, sat at her dressing table and had a good look at herself in the mirror. 'Do you like my hat?' she asked, pushing it about a bit as ladies do with hats.

The elegant phrases I had prepared, like, 'requesting the honour of your daughter's hand . . .' and, 'would make me, and I hope Polly, very happy if you . . .' withered on the lips. I was in deep trouble. I knew nothing about hats and I did not much like Maman's. In fact, I thought it was not a good hat at all; it seemed to me to be a bit too dark and formal.

I later learned the tradition of hat maintenance which French ladies practised earlier in the century. One good hat was bought of strong and classic structure and then, as the years passed, was retrimmed in the current fashion by those ladies – pretty well all ladies then – who were nifty with a needle. So I was being asked to pass judgement not only on Maman's taste in hats but also on her colour-sense and needlecraft. In a panic it occurred to me that the coward's way out would be to lie and praise the hat warmly.

What to do?

I praised the hat, of course.

I explained to Maman that the work I did gave almost no financial security but it was going very well at the moment, Denis and I had a hit show and there was every chance of work coming in steadily for the next year or so. I regretted my lack of capital – I would bring to the marriage about £80 in cash and a second-hand freezer (actually a flip-flop ice-cream container bought from a sweetshop), but Denis and I were winning some sort of a reputation, which was how the system worked, and there was money due to us from repeats and royalties, and by the summer I should have saved quite a bit towards a flat.

'But supposing,' said Maman, twitching her hat and looking at it in the mirror, and innocently asking the question which puts the fear of God into every writer, 'supposing one day you can't think of anything to write?'

That stopped me in my tracks. I had no idea how I would then support Polly. What were the chances of Denis and me drying up? Did it happen frequently to comedy writers? I did eventually stifle the panic and that Christmas Eve, in a small room off Maman's kitchen, I proposed to Polly – on one knee and rather emotional about it, too, I am glad to remember – and I was accepted.

We went out to a nightclub to celebrate. It was about eight o'clock in the evening, too early for the night people, so Polly and I were almost the only clubbers, but Edmundo Ros and his band played for us, and when we told him what we were celebrating he arranged for the waiter to pour us wine from somebody else's bottle (I did not know that customers then had to bring their own wine and leave their bottles in a storeroom, with a pencil line on the label showing how much they had drunk. The pencil mark was, of course, easily repositioned lower down by a bent waiter).

The following six months were rather blissful. Except when the bliss almost turned to fury when, in a burst of foolhardiness, I decided to teach Polly to drive. I do not think I have done anything quite as silly before or since.

'Gently,' I would say soothingly, 'let the clutch out now . . . MIND THAT BUS ON THE LEFT!'

'DON'T SHOUT AT ME!'

'Brake! BRAKE!' . . . and so on, both our nervous systems in tatters.

Common sense prevailed in time to save our marriage and Polly went to a professional driving instructor ('Ease out into the main road now, Miss McIrvine. Keep creeping. That's good, keep creeping . . .')

Polly booked our wedding for 16 July 1949, at the Church of the Holy Redeemer, Cheyne Row, Chelsea. The priest was Father de Zulueta, a well-known name in Catholic circles. Ours was a 'mixed' marriage, Polly being RC and I being ostensibly C of E, but really a lapsed agnostic – my doubts were beginning to waver – and I had to agree that our children, if any, would be brought up as

Roman Catholics, which I was happy to do. I also had to attend a course of instruction from Father de Zulueta on the beliefs and practices of Catholicism.

My instruction took place on Thursday afternoons after work, in Father's small, book-crammed study in Cheyne Row. As it was a little chill the gas fire purred away, raising the temperature to about 95 degrees Fahrenheit and consuming most of the oxygen in the room.

Father was a good deal older than me and it was the end of his day's work as well as the end of mine. I only hope that he was the one to nod off first, and nod on again (as it were) last. I cannot honestly remember one item from my course of instruction.

I hired my thick otiose wedding suit from Moss Bros. It was the London season and I was amid impatient queues of honking and braying young men (a line of Oscar Wilde's sprang to mind which, given a little tweak, became, 'The unbearable in full pursuit of the unwearable').

Polly had prudently chosen a high lacy head-dress which, with high heels, enabled the photographer to get both our faces into the same picture.

Before the day I had a small panic about Polly's passport – we were planning to spend our honeymoon in Cannes. The drill was for the bride's passport to be sent to the authorities to be altered to her new married status. It was then lodged with the vicar or priest who handed it over to the bride after the ceremony. Just before the day I checked with Father de Zulueta.

'Ah,' he said. 'Yes. Polly's passport. Yes, I have it. The complication is I have to go to Cambridge tomorrow and I just might not be back in time for the wedding. But have no worry. I have an old friend standing by to marry you should I not be back in time. I have told him about Polly's passport which I have left for him on the mantelshelf in my study – no, it's not there, I put it for safety in the bottom – no, top drawer of my desk. But I shifted it. I thought I might forget it there, so I rather think it's on the hall-stand, or did I hide it amongst my books? You will like my old friend, but I should warn you, I'm afraid he tends to be a little vague.'

We found a flat. It was in Addison Road, West Kensington, and was the top floor of a largish house which had been bombed. The building was being repaired and converted into flats with a government grant by a Mr Waite, a small builder in a bowler hat whose first burst of free enterprise this was, and he was finding it a strain. Mr Waite may have been a dab hand with a putty knife, but setting up a business was another matter. He seemed to have no capital at all; several times he borrowed money from me to pay the weekly wages of his two workers, and when Polly and I sought him out on some decorating point we would sometimes find him leaning against a wall quietly sobbing.

Father de Zulueta managed to get back from Cambridge in time to marry us and bore such a startling resemblance to our eccentric and maverick producer Pat Dixon that the large BBC contingent in the congregation burbled and snorted throughout with suppressed laughter.

We had a spot of thunder and lightning and rain at one point, but as an omen on our future it was hopelessly wrong. Then the sun came out and we all went down to the Embankment for the reception at the painter and wit James Abbot McNeill Whistler's house in Cheyne Row. There were speeches in the book-lined drawing room (Ted Kavanagh expressed his pleasure at speaking in the middle of Whistler's gag library) and then Polly and I rushed back to Maman's flat, changed and started out in the car, hood down, for the Royal Albion Hotel, Brighton, and on the next day to the Newhaven ferry and our Riviera honeymoon.

Immediately becalmed at the traffic lights into North End Road, an elderly neighbour came over to the car and said to Polly, 'Hello! And what have you been doing recently – anything interesting?'

Exchange control was very tight and we could only take out £45 each for our month in the South of France. Various schemes were tried by others to defeat regulations, the only effective one being to borrow francs from a Frenchman over there who was coming to England and pay him back here in sterling. A well-off friend of ours, Johnny Johnson, the music publisher and leader of The Keynotes singing group, tried to smuggle out a wad of £5 notes stuffed into his shoes, but the weather was very hot and when he arrived at Villefranche he found that each shoe contained a rigid papier mâché inner sole.

Pol and I had decided that the best way to have a relaxed honeymoon was to make it the best holiday possible.

We had a dodgy start. Polly's girlfriend, the one who came to dinner with us on our first date, knew the South of France well and kindly booked us into a cheap, clean room along the road, past old Cannes. The weather was very hot so she sensibly booked us twin beds. For our honeymoon! Twin beds!

There are times when being sensible is so utterly senseless. Of course we clambered into one bed, which was very French, short and narrow. For night nourishment we had brought with us a bottle of Cointreau that a wedding guest had given us and which Polly had on her bedside table. Five minutes later we saw an army of ants marching in Indian file up from the garden, across the tiny balcony, through the French windows, along the floor, up the table leg, and then each having his (or her? – one doesn't often hear about female ants but they must exist or there would not be any ants at all) share of the sweet orange liqueur lurking round the cork of the bottle, and then they had their long march back home, quite a bit of it clambering over the backs of incoming millions of their relations.

This was the beginning of our honeymoon and to make as much room as possible for my bride, I eased well over on my side of the single bed until I was half out of it. To stop myself thudding to the ground, I put my arm down on the floor to act as a prop and went to sleep. When the sun woke us quite late the next morning, my arm had stiffened, locked and was devoid of feeling. When I got up it hung down rigidly at my side like an oar. It gradually came round, of course, and by lunchtime it tingled but was back in service as an arm.

It was a good month. We spent most of our time on the beach on a hired mattress beneath a hired parasol. These mattresses, the beach leaseholder's main income, were only about 4 inches apart and it took a long time to teeter between the mattresses to have a swim. The bit of leasehold beach we favoured was called Les Flots Bleu, kept by a most pleasant late-middle-aged, white-haired couple, Monsieur et Madame Barrioz, whose obligatory bikinis were pathetically inadequate to control their rolls of sun-burned, late-middle-aged body.

Swimming was taught by their resident *Professeur de Natation*, Monsieur Maurice, a handsome young blond hunk, but nice, and good at teaching swimming. My demonstration of the British trudgeon stroke came as a profound culture shock to him.

For food we went each morning to the market, *en route* to the beach, and bought two or three slices of cold veal, a pocketful of *salade Macédoine* and a length of bread. A treat was a brace of bananas and a little tub of sour cream. An excellent invention of Polly's was the in-car picnic, which could be eaten whilst driving along. This was a baguette of bread with a slab of chocolate broken into strips and stuffed down the middle of the bread.

In the hot evenings we would sit at a seafront pavement table at Chez Felix, a popular and rather chic café on the Croisette, and we found that we could make a shared *orange pressée* last a whole evening. It's a wonder the Café Felix did not take legal proceedings.

And then our lovely month was over. On the way back up France to the ferry the Frazer-Nash BMW stopped going. It was on a long straight road in the middle of a forest. I struggled with the carburettor, hitting it with a shoe and swearing professionally, when by an extraordinary piece of luck two slightly shifty-looking men appeared on bicycles with sacks on their handlebars. The sacks moved. It emerged that the men were car mechanics from a nearby Citroën factory who were moonlighting for a day's sport in the woods with their ferret. In a moment they had got the car going and we were smoothly on our way again. But not for long. A terrible grinding noise started up from a rear wheel. With the confidence of the lightly knowledgeable I diagnosed that a ball-bearing had cracked and was breaking up.

It was a horrible noise. My diagnosis was correct but there was nothing whatever we could do about it except pray that the bearing held up and got us home. And so the young marrieds, Mr and Mrs Muir, too broke to stop at a café and eat, feeding each other bites from a baguette with chocolate stuffed down its middle, both of us bronzed from the sun and very, very happy, drove slowly up France to the Dieppe ferry, the off-side rear wheel scrunching and crunching like a coffee grinder.

I will now state, hand on heart, that most important of all the many good and happy things which happened to me as a growing lad, the years that I have been married to Polly, getting on for fifty of them, as compared with those early empty years when I was *not* married to Polly, have been, to borrow Geraldo's masterly phrase, much, *much* more betterer.

Chapter Nine

THE FITFUL FIFTIES

Australia.
The arrival (late) of a son, Jamie.
A real home at last: Anners, Thorpe.
And . . . 'We made a sudden Sally.'
     (see Tennyson's 'The Brook')

My marriage to Polly in 1949 made such a happy curtain, act 2, for the 1940s that it would have been helpful to this chronicle if I could have picked up the momentum with a bright crisp assessment, excitingly labelled, of the predominant mood of the 1950s. But no mood seemed to predominate, so I have called the decade 'fitful', which at least reflects its unsettled nature as far as we were concerned.

Polly and I were not yet in our flat in Addison Road, although Mr Waite, the tearful builder, seemed to have accidentally completed his conversion work and had sold the building as an investment to the owner of an Indian restaurant in Kensington High Street. The restaurateur and his family took up residence in the ground floor flat.

We were short of furniture so Maman, with heroic indulgence, allowed me to construct a rectangular oak footstool in her kitchen. Now there was a mother-in-law to cherish.

It was a horrific job, sawing 2-inch-square sections of oak

lengthwise on her kitchen lino without a workbench or a vice, and fitting in stout, bought-in bow-legs which seem to have been designed for supporting Dutch hotel wardrobes. Polly made a tapestry cover for it, then a second, and she is, as I write, needling away at a third. Tapestry does not wear out, it just shrinks and becomes too grubby to live with, like old husbands.

We eventually moved into the Addison Road flat and immediately acquired a dog, the first of a great many dogs (and latterly cats). She was a huge beige standard poodle with a wonderful nature and we named her Pastis, after – call us sentimental if you will – that cloudy drink which, in the South of France with the Mediterranean sun shining on it, tastes like a romantic blend of oil of aniseed and torpedo fluid.

Although Polly had taken a domestic science course at St Mary's, Ascot, was an excellent cook and dietician and was familiar with all those vital modern kitchen skills which are taught at finishing schools such as 'nurturing your stockpot' and 'keeping your teak sink fresh and hygienic', she naturally wanted to extend her horizons and so joined a brief, two-day course in European cuisine run by an ample Hungarian lady named Madame de Biro from her own kitchen in Phillimore Gardens.

Polly spent the first day learning to make *apfelstrudel*, which she then tried out at home. This involved plonking a lump of short dough on the kitchen table, rolling it out into a huge circle and then shuffling slowly round and round the table, pulling gently at the dough's skirt for four or five hours.

The pastry was delicious, of course, so Polly immediately had a go at another delicacy, which proved to be even more desperately labour-intensive: Maids of Honour – elegant, subtle tartlets of cream cheese made by hand from curds and whey, lightly flavoured with freshly ground almonds and encased in the product of another afternoon's trudge round the kitchen table, incredibly light and airy puff pastry.

It was the sort of laborious task which had it been prescribed for the punishment of Victorian burglars would have been instantly denounced by the Howard League for Penal Reform, but Polly completed her batch of tiny *bonnes bouches*, twenty-four of them in all, and beautiful they were to see and smell.

That evening Jimmy Edwards called in for a quick whisky on his way home and Pol put the plate of Maids of Honour at his side.

Jimmy took a bite and started talking. An hour later, after much laughter and so on, Jimmy left. The plate was empty.

Jimmy had eaten all Polly's Maids of Honour *without even noticing what he was eating*. But our marriage survived, and if it could survive that it could survive anything, which indeed it has.

As far as work was concerned, the 1950s began interestingly. *TIFH* was making a breakthrough overseas, particularly in Commonwealth countries and especially – having Dick and Joy in the cast – on the ABC in Australia. And from Australia came a newspaper report on *Take It From Here* which was, quite simply, as gratifying, appreciative and encouraging a piece as we could ever have hoped to read:

Australia Can 'Take It . . .'

Every Sunday night there occurs in Australia one of the strangest phenomena in the whole bizarre history of show business. A BBC radio show called *Take It From Here* goes on the air and all Australia stops to listen. What's so phenomenal about that? Just the fact that *TIFH* runs head on against every important dogma in the textbooks of variety entertainment.

Any Australian producer or entrepreneur will tell you, without qualification, what is needed to make a variety show click here. It must have Australian significance, it must have Australian gags, delivered in the Australian idiom. It must be topical, but above all else it must not be too clever. These are the inflexible axioms.

But *TIFH* has lost all its topicality months before the transcriptions arrive here; the gags, so far from being local, are invariably aimed exclusively at British audiences, and are quite often so subtle, so casually thrown away that only a tiny minority of our audiences can possibly appreciate them. Yet everywhere on Monday morning, in all our coastal capitals from Perth to Brisbane, you will hear people asking, 'Did you hear *Take It From Here* last night?' and then they will start exchanging the wisecracks that made them chuckle.

Whether they realize it or not, Muir and Norden emancipated the radio listener when they hatched *TIFH*. They defied the ancient shibboleth of the trade that you must blunt your wit to suit the mentality of the dullest member of the audience. They worked on the brave new concept that audiences have minds; they gave their listeners credit for some small smatterings of intelligence, and listeners appreciated the compliment.

How could an all-scripted, slick, sophisticated half-hour recorded overseas hope to win the approval of a people whose sense of humour was believed to be stubbornly wedded to the banana skin and the custard pie. It couldn't, of course, but it did. Gags that were topical in Britain six months before, and which should have been quite incomprehensible to us, brought gales of laughter, *TIFH* gag lines slipped easily into everyday conversation, and the throwaway technique, allegedly poison ivy to us, tickled us as we had never been tickled before.

By the end of the last series we had reached a stage where the *TIFH* half-hour was taboo for phone calls and visits. It just didn't, and doesn't, make sense, but somehow, without benefit of claques, or cheerleaders, or prizes, this British show, produced I suspect without even a thought for overseas audiences, has firmly planted itself on the Australian hearth and in the Australian heart.

. . . *Take It From Here* has taken.

Kirwan Ward

If much, or any, of that was true reporting, then it was not perhaps surprising that when in 1951 the Australian Broadcasting Commission decided to celebrate its jubilee, they invited Dick Bentley, now through *TIFH* a big star in radio, to return home to broadcast a special series of ten half-hour comedy programmes. They hoped it would be written in Australia by Denis and me.

This was not a wholly welcome idea as I was not at all keen on leaving my bride on her own for three months and Denis and Avril were equally unkeen to leave their four-year-old son Nick and his baby sister Maggie, so we tried to get out of the trip by asking for a large fee, expenses, a rented flat each and our wives and Nick to be with us. To our dismay our terms were accepted and we had to go.

The flight from Heathrow to Sydney took five days. The plane was a BOAC Super Constellation, a large airliner shaped like a banana. We landed in Rome at midday and all piled into a coach clutching a packed lunch in a cardboard box (like the Institute of Directors at their Albert Hall AGM) and were conducted on a tour of the Holy City by a sweet Italian girl student ('Roma was-a beelt on seven eels'). In the afternoon we flew on to Cairo where we disemplaned again and spent the night in Shephard's Hotel.

We began to get to know some of the other passengers. In the seats behind us was a pair of prep-school boys on their way home, unaccompanied, to holiday with their army parents in Sydney. The taller of the two looked after his younger brother's welfare in exemplary fashion. When exchange control asked us if we had any sterling currency to declare, the senior brother's voice piped up fearlessly, 'Please, sir, yes, sir! I have two pounds fifteen shillings and my younger brother Robin has three and tuppence.'

Next to the boys sat Mrs Macnamara, a broad elderly Irish lady not enjoying her first taste of flying. Her fare had been paid by her son and daughter-in-law, who had emigrated, so that she could see her grandchildren in Melbourne.

It was a long way from Dublin to Melbourne and as we flew eastwards, Mrs Macnamara suffered more and more from the heat. All her belongings seemed to be crammed into a huge string bag which she wedged on the empty seat between herself and the boys, but every time we disembarked to refuel or eat or sleep, Mrs Macnamara's ankles grew thicker and her string bag grew thinner.

We asked Mrs Macnamara whether she had enjoyed her night in Cairo.

'No, I didn't enjoy it, I didn't, no,' she said. 'What with the heat, and the flies, and the soft-walking natives.'

Next day on to Calcutta, where we changed aircrews. This was an alarming experience, as while we were pretending to enjoy our lunch in the airport restaurant, we watched a happy crew of mechanics in dhotis sitting on top of one of our plane's engines, laughing and chattering and banging vaguely at the engine with spanners.

As we were called to board the plane for its long next leg to Singapore over the shark-infested Timor Sea, the captain and crew stood up and the captain called out to us, rather pointedly I thought, 'Good luck!'

We had to sleep in flight that night, which was comfortable enough, though an electric storm with lightning was unnecessarily Wagnerian.

Our overnight stay the next day at Raffles Hotel, Singapore (in an annex at the back), was memorable on two scores. Polly had bought me one of the new nylon shirts for travelling. The good thing about a nylon shirt was, of course, that it dried quickly in the hotel room after being washed. The bad thing was that in Singapore it dried *too* quickly. I washed it in our bedroom basin, wrung it out and by the time I had hung it up in the wardrobe to dry, it had dried and become a wrinkled crumpled mess like a used face tissue. I tried again and sprinted across with the damp shirt to the wardrobe, but on arrival it was again bone-dry and unwearably twisted.

The second Singapore memory was having drinks in the famous Raffles Long Bar with a friendly bear of an Australian who was the editor of a Brisbane newspaper and a most generous host. When he at last called for the bill he told the waiter to charge it to room 141.

When the waiter departed I asked, 'Are you sure there *is* a room one-four-one?' 'Never failed me yet, mate!' he said.

We took off the next morning for the last leg of the journey, refuelled in sub-tropical Darwin and then flew on, flying south to lob down at last, on our fifth day, in Sydney, New South Wales.

The two schoolboys behind us were ecstatic at glimpsing their parents waiting on the tarmac, he in his rather grand uniform and she waving emotionally at every plane which taxied anywhere near her.

Mrs Macnamara was still not enjoying herself much. She had mislaid her huge straw hat in Asia and had spent the last leg of the journey fanning herself vigorously with BOAC's instruction card on how to put on your life jacket when the plane fell into the sea. Her string bag was worryingly empty.

Denis and I reported to the ABC the next afternoon (tired from the journey but jet lag had yet to be invented), meeting the British ex-actor who was going to produce our show, and Harry Pringle, Head of Variety programmes, who showed us round the offices of ABC in Pitt Street. Just before six o'clock, when all the grog shops and pubs had to close for the day, Harry took us downstairs for a quick drink down in the 'hotel' next door. Keen drinkers were standing about on the pavement knocking back schooners of lager as quickly as they could get them refilled at the bar.

A lean leathery character, looking like a sheep shearer, staggered out carrying a glass in each hand and sipping carefully at them in turn so that he wouldn't spill too much. Harry introduced his colleague, who was wearing a flat pork-pie hat with a wide brim. He was having some difficulty with his balance.

Harry said, 'I'd like you to meet a colleague of mine, ABC's Federal Director of Education.'

The ABC was Australia's leading promoter of classical music, mounting concerts and arranging visits from important international soloists. Tickets could be bought by the public at the counter in ABC's Pitt Street offices.

It seems that the ABC once arranged a tour for the pianist Solomon and the ABC's chief, Charles Moses, went to the airport as usual to welcome the great man personally. They met in the VIP lounge. The famous pianist took the ABC chief's hand and bowed slightly.

'Solomon,' he said.

'Moses,' said the ABC's chief, bowing back.

'I do not think that is very funny,' said the great pianist.

Charles Moses was then in late middle age but still relentlessly athletic. He was shortish but barrel-chested and devoted to tree-felling.

Chopping up fallen trees into two lengths was an Aussie competitive sport. The feller stood on the tree bole sideways, swung his axe and whacked a wedge out of the side of the tree between his feet. He then leaped into the air, spun round 90 degrees and whacked a wedge out of the other side of the tree. He repeated this as swiftly as possible until the job was done or he went dizzy and severed a foot. It took quite a few whacks to bisect a thick gum tree.

One Sunday Charles and his wife kindly drove the two Muirs and the two and a half Nordens up into the Blue Mountains for a purist barbecue lunch. Purist because Mr Moses was not one of those urban softies who used firelighters to get the show going, or used already prepared logs, or charcoal, or indeed a barbecue machine itself. He preferred to practise survival techniques.

Mr Moses felled a medium-sized gum tree, axed it to pieces in minutes and arranged the logs and twigs in a hollow in the ground. Then, eschewing the effete use of matches, he spun a twig between his palms until, much, much later, a wisp of smoke arose. We were now about two hours into the afternoon and a light drizzle was falling.

Denis, with a display of woodsmanship which made me proud of him, whispered to me to lure Charles and his wife away towards the panoramic view of Sydney. When we were out of sight, Denis dipped Avril's handkerchief into the car's petrol tank and urged it under the bonfire with a twig. We heard a 'whoosh!' and when we returned from contemplating the rooftops of Sydney there was a huge cloud of smoke billowing up from the damp boskage and in the middle a tiny flame flickered, like the pilot light of the ancient Ewart's 'Victor' geyser at the Derby Arms Hotel.

It was not exactly a gourmet lunch which we eventually sat down to eat in the rain, but the partially burned and partially raw chops were redeemed by plenty of powerful Aussie red wine and a warm feeling that we were being pioneers. Which indeed we were. It was the first barbecue in which we Pommies had ever participated, in fact it was the first barbecue we five had ever *seen*. Meat rationing was still going strong in England and you could not barbecue 'a book and a half of mince'.

The ABC had found Polly and me a small pleasant flat in Pott's Point, which was the property of the gay son of the owner of one of Australia's hamburger chains. It was well furnished except, perhaps, for a tad too many portraits on the walls of heavily muscled, Bambi-eyed young men.

The Nordens were just round the corner in a comfortable flat in Elizabeth Bay. Unfortunately their daughter Maggie was too young to be taken on such a long trip, a sensible decision which she resented at the time, and, now that she is more mature and wiser, still does.

It was in Sydney that we first heard real local radio, neighbourhood stuff. The first radio commercial we caught was an announcement between records of popular music (as distinct from 'pop') that 'Dexters Caff on the corner of Market Place has just got in a delivery of that chocolate cake of theirs, so you'd better get round there right away – I warn you, mates, it'll all be gone by five o'clock!'

The Sydney of forty years ago has changed so much that it is almost unrecognizable now, except for the bridge, the harbour and Bondi beach. It was always an energetic, busy sort of city, but now it has become (which large capital city hasn't?) more international than national. Back in 1951 it seemed more Australian and friendlier. Sydney had just two expensive restaurants and it was a tiny adventure for a visitor to cross over to the North Shore; they had huge ticks there, we were told proudly, which could kill a dog.

We noted with pleasure the tiny differences in English usage, like a placard for an evening paper we saw when we arrived which read, 'OLD MAN BASHED IN PARK'.

As soon as the weather came good the working population tended to drift off to the beach for a swim. Even waiters were known to disappear mid-meal. The effect of this was that 'refos' (refugees from Europe) who continued to trundle their sewing machines in back rooms making handbags when the sun shone were gradually taking over the retail trades.

It was early spring and although the sun was hot the water was too cold for us to cavort happily in the briny and be flattened by huge unpredictable Pacific waves ('dumpers'), but while Den and I were writing, Polly and Avril and small Nicky sat happily on the beach, and the sand was excellent for construction work (Nick is now an architect).

We had left an England still in the grip of restrictions; items such as meat, sweets and clothing were still rationed, and it was a joy for us to be able to buy as much meat as we wanted. But Australia also had its problems; there were odd little strikes and some strange items were in short supply: potatoes, for instance. Hotels and restaurants coped with this by serving well-boiled rice pressed into shape by an ice-cream scoop, so that it looked like mashed potato. And there was a shortage of beer. Beer!

Australia was still a beer-drinking society then (changing to enjoying its own wine in recent years) and one result of this beer shortage tragedy was that the champagne bucket on restaurant tables held ice and, nestling amidst the ice cubes, a bottle of Fosters lager.

With 'Time gentlemen please!' being shouted at six o'clock in the evening and the sun still hot overhead it is hardly surprising that a small web of illegal drinking places sprang up, known as 'sly grog joints', where you could drink on into the night. Denis and I were deeply impressed by these because we were brought up on early Hollywood films when Prohibition was very much a subject for drama, and here it was in reality, life imitating art.

The door of a sly grog joint had an iron grille protecting a sliding panel, so that the owner of the face which appeared on the sly grog side could not be dragged through the hatch by a thirst-crazed non-member of the club. I actually had to say to the face through the grille, 'Rupe Dumbrell sent us,' before bolts were withdrawn and we were allowed in.

Rupe, really Rupert (almost all given names were shortened in Australia, e.g., 'Ian' became 'Ee'), arranged the music for our programme; he was Canadian, cool and a very amusing talker. His father was an archbishop.

Another relic of old Australia which was still around was the illegal gambling game of Two-Up. In this, a couple of punters bet on whether two coins spun into the air would both come down heads or tails (I think that was what it was about). There was a neutral third party who spun the coins. This he did on hearing the punters utter the great old Australian cry, 'Come in, spinner!' It does not sound all that exciting a game but it was.

A more sophisticated and much cheaper method of acquiring grog than in a sly grog joint was demonstrated by the producer of our programme, a very British ex-actor who had emigrated from England when the going became tough and was making himself less than popular in Australian circles by coming out with observations like, 'How I miss my little flat in Half Moon Street and Morny soap.'

Before the run of our show, which we called *Gently, Bentley*, this man kindly invited Dick and the cast, plus Denis and me, to a Sunday lunchtime bottle party. 'Bring a bottle of anything, whisky, champagne, even wine would do.'

On arrival everybody dutifully handed over their bottle which soon formed a colourful collection on the sideboard. When we had all gathered, our host disappeared for a moment to check, he said, how the cooking was proceeding. He returned a few minutes later haggard of face, biting his lip and clearly bearing bad news.

'Dreadfully sorry, loves,' he said, 'I'm afraid lunch is off. The lady wife . . . the dreaded migraine has struck again . . . poor old dear will be in a darkened room for hours, in agony. If you hurry you should be able to get some lunch in a pub downtown.' We found ourselves being hustled out of the front door. 'Don't bother about your bottles; you can leave them where they are . . .'

Gently, Bentley took to the airwaves at 7.15 p.m., 31 August 1951, for ten weeks, and on the whole did its job well. In those days radio acting fees were low and Australian radio actors had to cram a lot of shows in per week to make a decent living, so we found our supporting cast extremely swift in finding the right voices for their characters and bringing the characters to life.

The show had good reviews, Dick Bentley and his wife Peta enjoyed a paid working holiday – they travelled from England comfortably by sea – and due to forethought on our part in taking with us some spare unused ideas from *TIFH* and *Breakfast with Braden*, the Muirs and the Nordens too managed to have an enjoyable three months semi-holiday.

A lack of stress was important as Pol and I were beginning to worry about not producing a baby and we had hoped that our three months of serious meat-eating might have helped our chances. A few days before our flight home Polly needed to rest all day, feet up, and this was not at all easy to arrange in our schedule. But fate leaped to our aid. The key day turned out to be Yom Kippur, a day on which Denis was then unkeen to work, so we took the day off and Polly rested.

As Australia is about as far as you can fly before you start flying back home again, it costs no more to make the round trip, so we all came home via Fiji, Hawaii, San Francisco and New York. The flight across the Pacific was memorable for its comfort. It was a night flight and in a few minutes the cabin staff converted the whole plane into sleepers; seats became bunks and an upper row of bunks hinged down from the ceiling. Each bunk had curtains to draw for privacy and everybody changed into pyjamas, climbed between sheets and had a good night's kip. A wonderful way to travel.

Polly found that she was indeed pregnant – good old Yom Kippur – and as we only had a short stop of a day or so in New York we rushed to Macy's to buy American nappies – designer nappies compared with austerity British equivalents. In the Expectant Family-Maker's department the sales assistant, a plump white-coated American Mom-figure, helped Polly carefully across the carpet.

'And how far are you into your pregnancy?' the Mom-figure asked discreetly, letting Polly sink slowly into a chair.

'About four days,' said Polly.

The pregnancy held firm and when we arrived back at Addison Road there was a lot to do. Polly wanted to have her baby at home and she was recommended a splendid female gynaecologist, Dr Mary Adams, who in her turn recommended a monthly nurse, Sister Toft – the late dear Tofty.

The baby arrived on Saturday 4 July at 19 Addison Road, West Kensington (top flat).

I had been banished to the drawing room, to my great relief as I would have keeled over at the first sign of anything, and I would now be able to watch Drobny play in the Wimbledon men's final on television. But it was not to be. As Drobny pottered onto the court clutching his five or six tennis rackets, Dr Adams shot in.

'Have you got the phone number of the blood bank?'

'Er – no,' I muttered, switching off the telly, 'I'll look it up in the directory.'

Dr Adams shot back to the action.

I found the directory and began feverishly searching.

Dr Adams shot in again.

'Hot-water bottles!' she said. 'Quickly! As many as you can find!' And away she went again.

I stumbled around and found one hot-water bottle, which seemed a bit inadequate, so I ran downstairs to see if I could borrow more from the flats below. Nobody was in. I rushed back upstairs, almost knocking Dr Adams over in the corridor.

'Don't bother about the hot-water bottles,' she said, 'or the blood bank,' and she went back into the bedroom.

I slumped down in front of the telly and switched on, nerves jangling. 'Play!' said the umpire. Drobny bounced the ball five or six times, threw it high in the air and was about to wallop it when I heard the thin, not unhappy, first cry of a new baby.

He was 10 pounds 2 ounces, quite an achievement for small lean Polly. He had to be helped out with those pastry tong things, which gave him blue bruises here and there and a black eye which, combined with some dark, greasy-looking hair, made our son and heir look like a heavy-weight boxer who had just lost his title after fifteen gruelling rounds.

We wanted to christen him Jamie, but as this seemed in those days an obscure and slightly pretentious name, we decided to call him Peter James and leave it to him to choose which name he preferred when he reached the age of reason. At school he asked to be called Peter and then mysteriously changed into Jamie on his twenty-second birthday.

Once I almost drowned the infant Peter James. I was bathing him in a rubber portable bath arrangement, supporting his neck in my left hand in the correct Norland Nanny manner when the lad turned over, rolled off my hand and disappeared under the soapy water. However, no lasting harm was done (I think). I fished about in the water for a while and retrieved him; he was a bit green and blowing bubbles but seemed otherwise intact. I was not much help to Polly, not that fathers were expected to be all that helpful in those days; Denis and I were working rather hard.

I was reminded just how busy Denis and I were in the mid-1950s when Denis recently found his working diary for 1950-something-or-other and rang me in awe at the amount of work, meetings and interviews which we got through in a working day. And this was in the summer when *TIFH* was not on air. But then we were both semi-young, just into our early thirties (except Denis who was still clinging on to his late twenties) – a sketch which then would have taken us an hour to write would take us about six weeks now.

A typical entry in Den's diary was July 1955, 'Lunch with Jack Waller. Savoy Grill. 12.45.'

Jack Waller was a successful theatrical impresario who had just produced a smash-hit farce, *Sailor Beware* by Philip King, starring Peggy Mount in her first appearance in a West End play. We presumed, rightly as it turned out, that Mr Waller was hoping that Den and I had a couple of brilliant farces in the middle drawer of our desk waiting to be produced. He soon realized that we did not have anything in our middle drawer except some indigestion tablets (we tended to have hot bacon sandwiches for lunch when pressed for time) and lots of bits of paper covered with once urgent, but now meaningless notes.

Jack Waller was a small, neat, quite old man, and as soon as he realized that we had no play to offer him, nor time to write him one, he relaxed and was rivetingly interesting about his early life in show business. He had begun at the end of the last century as a musician in a minstrel troupe and he composed music for many of his own later productions. He was an actor and a music-hall performer before becoming a 'producing manager' and organizing extensive tours of plays and musicals in what were then known as the British Dominions.

His stories of touring small towns in the hinterland of South Africa – the 'dorps' – before the First World War were notable for the colourful excuses given to him by local theatre managers for the small audiences which had turned up at their theatres. Such as:

'You picked the wrong time, Jack. Everybody stays behind locked doors when the elephants are in must.'

(*OED: MUST / n*. A male elephant on heat and in a state of dangerous frenzy.)

Another theatre manager: 'Trouble is, Jack, we had a troupe of Swiss handbell ringers here only a month ago. This town is over-entertained.'

I was never very good at working lunches. A bit like President Ford of the USA who was accused by a political enemy of not being able to chew gum and fart at the same time, I have always found difficulty in simultaneously chatting and eating.

Denis's diary revealed that when Kenneth Horne and Richard Murdoch's radio show *Much-Binding-in-the-Marsh* was at its peak, the highly successful British film-maker, Sydney Box, invited Denis and me to lunch at his Lime Grove studios to discuss the possibility of us writing a film version of *Much-Binding*. It was all rather splendid. The dining room, just along the corridor from the front door, was handsomely panelled and the long table was brilliant with linen, silver and glass.

We were joined for lunch by the studio's producers and directors, some of whom we knew, and I was for once talking wittily to Sydney Box whilst helping myself to Brussels sprouts from a dish held by a waitress when a quiet fell and I noticed that I was being looked at.

Whilst talking wittily to Sydney Box I had inadvertently helped myself to all the Brussels sprouts. With mantling cheeks I spooned them back.

A few evenings after the Lime Grove embarrassment, I was with Polly at the Caprice restaurant and we were sitting just a table away from Sydney and Betty Box. We had ordered steak, asparagus and peas. My steak was on the tough side and I was sawing away at it when Mr Box gave a friendly wave. Put off my rhythm, my knife slipped and I sprayed both Sydney and Betty Box with a machine-gun-like burst of hot peas.

Denis and I never did work for Sydney Box. Nor did he eat near me again, come to think of it.

Many years later my unhappy knack of doing something silly whilst trying to eat and think at the same time surfaced again one lunchtime (like chickenpox, the virus never dies; it just lies dormant for ages and then reactivates).

This time I was Head of Entertainment for London Weekend Television and I had unwisely agreed to have an important working lunch in the Park Lane Hotel Grill with Yorkshire Television's Head of Comedy. It was unwise because I was breaking in a new little dental bridge.

My big mistake was to begin with prawn cocktail, which was half a dozen violently pink prawns with reproachful eyes lying on a bed of strips of lettuce in a wineglass, the whole lightly sprinkled with an 'exotic sauce', actually a mixture of bottled mayonnaise and tomato ketchup (£8.50 – not including tip). I was talking vehemently when I noticed that my companion was watching my mouth with a kind of fascinated horror.

Looking downwards as far as I was able, I could see that I seemed to have grown a new tongue, much longer than the old one, and narrower and bright green. Whenever I began talking, it shot out and fluttered like a yacht burgee in a good racing wind at Cowes, and as it fluttered it made a kind of low buzzing sound.

I sucked it back in several times, but it blew out again whenever I tried to keep our important conversation going. What had clearly happened was that one end of a strip of lettuce had become trapped beneath my unfamiliar bridgework. The low buzz I was making was attracting considerable attention from the other eaters, as was the fluttering length of lettuce, and swift action was called for.

I hissed sharply. The green strip blew out and trembled in the wind, 'zzzzzz'. I reached up, grabbed it and gave it a discreet pull. My two new teeth in their bright metal setting shot out and dropped into the butter.

Much-Binding-in-the-Marsh cropped up once more when Dickie Murdoch was commissioned by *Lilliput* magazine to write some short stories based on the radio series. Once the contract was signed, Dickie went off the whole idea; he did not enjoy writing prose and he asked me to ghost write the stories for him, which I was quite happy to do, reckoning it would be useful experience, my first bursting into print since my parish magazine serial about the Chinese airmen. Dickie then lived in Staines, just by the river, and I went down there one evening to discuss payment.

Absolutely typical of Dickie – a charming and delightful man – was that he could not bear to talk money face to face, so he waited until it was dark, drew the curtains, switched off the lights and we discussed my fee in pitch-darkness.

Denis and I were beginning to do quite a bit of writing for stage revues, mainly sketches for George and Alfred Black and Jack Hylton summer shows. One of the first of these jobs was to write a revue for Jack Hylton starring Jimmy, Dick and Joy. It went on at the Piccadilly Theatre and was called, inevitably, *Take It From Us*.

Jimmy by then had become a very strong theatre performer, and his schoolmaster act – which Denis and I helped put together for him – was successful and reliable. For theatre purposes we had given him much more visual comedy. He strode on stage in gown and mortarboard, swishing his cane and glowering at the audience as though they were a difficult class, and went straight to a tall stand-up desk which had two handbells on its top. He took one of these off and rang it vigorously, shouting, 'Quiet, everywhere! Fags out! Pay attention!' He put the handbell back and pulled at the handle of the other bell. It was a beer pump. He pumped a few strokes then lifted the desk lid and produced a frothing half pint of bitter. 'Cheers!' he said.

He glanced out of the window and noticed somebody. 'It's our dear matron!' he explained to the audience. 'She's going to watch the cricket match sitting on her shooting stick.' He smiled benignly and looked out of the window again. Shock, horror!

'Matron! *No!*' he yelled out of the window, then mimed turning the shooting stick round the other way.

George and Alfred Black booked Jimmy for many of their Blackpool summer seasons and before the first of these shows Denis and I went up there to see the theatre and generally get the feel of Blackpool. We were wandering along the Golden Mile one afternoon when we idly wandered into one of the sideshows: it was the World's Fattest Lady. She was probably not in fact the world's fattest lady – in Russia there is usually somebody fatter or hairier or older than anybody else – but she was a vast enough person, slumped in a strong chair in the corner of a small room. There was nobody else in the room. The gentleman who had taken our half-crowns had nipped along to the pub.

It was difficult to know where to look. It seemed rude to stare at her rolls of fat, yet those were her contribution to public pleasure.

''Ow do,' she said in a friendly way, after an agonizing ten minutes or so of silence. 'It's took warm again, 'ant it?'

That was a tricky remark to reply to. 'I suppose you feel it more than most of us . . .' would have been insensitive. Den said, 'Yes, the chap on the radio said it's set in for a couple of days,' a long pause, 'which brings us to next Friday.'

'Good Lord!' I said. 'Does it?' I examined my watch. 'Then it's time we got going.'

We went.

Jimmy was now well established as a top-of-the-bill comic. He had bought a 2,000-acre farm in Fletching, Sussex, which was run by his brother Alan, and he kept his own hunters and polo ponies. He loved playing polo but there was not a lot of it happening on a Sunday in Blackpool, and Windsor Great Park, Cirencester and most polo grounds were an awkwardly long way away from Blackpool for Jimmy to get a game in on his one day off, so he bought himself a plane. It was a little Cessna which he flew carefully and safely, very Bomber Command, straight and level and no showing off.

I went on a few trips with him and occasionally he let me have a go at the controls which was exhilarating. Flying a plane is a bit like riding a bike (only more expensive); once you have done it you never forget how to do it, and a plane is a little like a boat – slow to react, no brakes.

He kept his little plane at Blackpool's Squires Gate airport, from which field modest airlines with small planes such as the de Havilland Dragon, which had about ten seats, flew holidaymakers to the Isle of Man.

These small airlines had to be careful with money, and when a pilot left to better himself they tried to find a replacement who would fit the other man's uniform (like dance orchestras in those days which wore expensive uniforms and whose trade papers carried small ads such as, 'Violinist doubling sax wanted urgently for prestigious Manchester nightclub; 48-inch chest.'

Jimmy told me of a legendary character at Blackpool Airport, an Irish pilot who had newly joined the airline and was too big to fit into his predecessor's official kit so had to wear his own clothes.

One summer morning, in a checked shirt and shorts, he joined a planeload of sunseekers off to the Isle of Man for their holidays and sat himself down in a seat at the back of the aircraft. After a few minutes waiting he muttered very loudly, 'If the pilot doesn't turn up in two minutes, begorra, I'll fly the thing meself!'

Two minutes later, he cried, 'Time's up!' strode down the aisle, squeezed through the narrow doorway into the pilot's compartment and flew the planeload of petrified passengers to a perfect landing at Douglas, IOM.

There is a PS.

Jimmy Edwards told this jape to a group of us after lunch at the Savile Club, and the Scottish novelist Eric Linklater suddenly said, 'But I know him; he's a legend in the Highlands. A friend of mine was on an Islander plane well on the way to the Outer Hebrides and on automatic pilot when the pilot's door opened and the pilot, our large Irishman, backed out slowly, unwinding a ball of string as he went. He stopped at a frail old lady, gave her the string to hold and said, "I've got to take a wee-wee at the back there, me lovely. The plane's nice and steady at the moment, but if her nose starts to drop just give the string a steady strong pull. Will ye do that for me?"'

Jimmy eventually gave up his plane because it was noisy, bouncy in boisterous weather and it was slow. The decision came one summer evening when he was flying back to Blackpool after playing an afternoon's polo in Windsor Park, and the headwind was so strong that quite small cars on the Great North Road beneath him were going north much faster than he was.

One of the best things about Jimmy was that he was excellent company. He loved amusing people, not by telling jokes (which are frequently little nuggets of malice) but with humour, recounting gently amusing things he had heard people say and which he wanted to share.

He was one of those rare comics who could say unconventionally provocative things without raising hackles. Playing polo once against the Duke of Edinburgh's team and being ridden off the ball by the duke, Jimmy cried out, 'Stay close to me, sir, and you'll get your face in the newspapers!' (perhaps a small royal hackle might have lifted a little).

And during the warm-up before a recording of *Take It From Here*, Jimmy would indicate his huge tummy and explain to the audience, 'It's only puppy fat. I had a puppy for lunch.'

How many comics could get away with that without being lynched?

Many of our Sunday-afternoon get-togethers in the Paris Cinema before recording *TIFH* were lit by Jimmy's reminiscences of his week in the country. Like when he held a rough shoot over the farm with some friends in the hope of a pheasant or two and they accidentally shot one of the beaters. He had been banging about the undergrowth with his stick and had put up some pheasants, but the birds had flown low and the guns had winged the beater.

Jimmy rushed forward to see what damage had been done to the wounded man, who lay writhing face down on the ground.

'It's all right, sir,' groaned the beater, 'only shot me in the arse. I were born lucky.'

And a truly memorable occasion one winter when Jimmy, newly engaged, arranged a small, very rough shoot in a waterlogged wood on the farm.

His fiancée, Valerie, sporting an engagement ring with enormous diamonds glinting in the cold sunshine, thought she would make herself useful by joining the beaters, so off she sloshed through the mud. A little while later we heard her give a shriek. Then she shouted, 'Jimmy! I'm in deep mud and sinking! Quick, help me!'

Jimmy shouted back, 'Listen very carefully. Take off your engagement ring and THROW IT AS HARD AS YOU POSSIBLY CAN IN THIS DIRECTION!'

From 1950 to 1955, Jack Hylton starred Jimmy in a series of revues and variety shows at the Adelphi Theatre, London, for which Denis and I wrote Jimmy's material, Jimmy's co-stars ranged from Tony Hancock to Vera Lynn. Vera was off one week and Hylton replaced her with a new, young, strong-voiced singer he had found in Cardiff; it was Shirley Bassey.

Jack Hylton was an impresario of the old order, an ex-highly successful band leader, shrewd, dictatorial, coarse-textured, given to eating fish and chips in the back of his Rolls followed by a pound or so of grapes, the skins and pips of which he spat in the direction of an ashtray. But with all that he was a remarkably good judge of popular taste.

The Crazy Gang were just back from a tour of the Far East and Jack Hylton, anxious to get a new show together for them, asked Denis and me to write them some sketches and pieces. This we did and read them over to the assembled Gang at a planning meeting.

An interesting point emerged. The Crazy Gang shows were essentially ribald, smutty in the good old English music-hall tradition, so we had worked touches of this kind of colour into the scripts. The Gang was shocked. And so, at this response, were we. The group of funny old men who ten minutes before had been gleefully showing us the porno souvenirs they had brought back from the Far East – playing cards with explicit nudes on the back, handkerchiefs with a little border of crude drawings of couplings, rude matchboxes – were taking offence at the harmless saucy lines we had written for them.

'I couldn't say *that*!' said Nervo (or Knox), vigorously scratching out the offending line with a ballpoint pen which revealed a naked lady when turned upside down.

Back at the office Den and I tried to work out their curiously paradoxical attitude and light eventually dawned.

'I think', said Den, 'the problem is that they feel a bit insulted when given smutty lines, as though we think their comedy is built on that kind of humour . . .'

'Which it is,' I said.

'Which it is,' Den agreed. 'But *they* have to put in the smut themselves.'

Which is what eventually happened. The Gang started out not using our pieces in the new show, but then they worked them in, and Denis and I were interested to see that the pieces were now rich in little smutty jokes which were not of our making.

Months later Jack Hylton asked us to call in at his office.

'I haven't paid you enough for those bits you wrote for the Gang,' he said.

Not paid enough? Was this the great Jack Hylton, notably careful with money, speaking? Denis and I looked at each other fearfully. Were we somehow being manipulated? Was it a trap?

He gestured towards the safe on the wall and his general manager, the genial and gifted Hughie Charles (he co-wrote Vera Lynn's 'We'll Meet Again' and many more wartime songs of cheer and encouragement), drew out a packet of banknotes. Mr Hylton took two bunches and gave them to us. 'A hundred each,' he said. 'Unless . . .' he said, raising his eyebrows, 'unless you'd rather have equity shares in the new Rediffusion Television Company?'

Associated Rediffusion had just won their commercial TV licence and Hylton was in the thick of it, promoting profitable ideas and acting as Rediffusion's Head of Variety.

Denis and I, clutching our lovely banknotes, exchanged glances. Green we may have been in money matters, but we knew instinctively when taking a risk would almost certainly be financial suicide.

'We'll take the money!' we said, smiling quietly to show that we knew better than to be palmed off with a few dodgy shares.

Some forty years later, Denis had lunch with the late Lord Willis, plain Ted as he was back in 1951, a very successful TV writer – *Dixon of Dock Green, Taxi!* – who had just been signed up by Hylton to provide ideas for new light-drama series for Rediffusion. Ted had been made the same offer as us and had chosen the shares.

Den told Ted about our canny decision to take the cash. Ted did a sum on the tablecloth. 'If you, like me, had taken the shares,' he said, peering at his sums, 'they would now be worth about fifty thousand pounds to each of you.'

As the 1950s progressed, Denis and I wrote all manner of shows, *TIFH* in the winter and then other radio shows in the summer break; and there were the usual requirements of summer-season sketches, and Adelphi shows for George and Alfred Black from 1950 to 1955, and comedy film scenes to rewrite.

At home on the top floor of 19 Addison Road, Polly was finding that a small flat three floors up was not the perfect place to bring up a large child. It meant leaving the pram – a large-wheeled gondola in those days – by the front door and carrying the heavy lad up the three flights of stairs.

The nearest stretch of healthy air and greenery was Kensington Gardens, which was quite a long trudge with a big pram and a big baby and a big dog, so we decided to find a house with a bit of a garden which was within our somewhat slender means.

It took a year.

Jamie was still young enough to need close attention, so it was mainly my job on Saturday afternoons to work through the estate agents' lists, driving briskly from 'small family house of character, would respond to improvement' (ex-railway worker's cottage with dry rot in Ruislip) to 'modern chalet-style architectural gem, divided for convenience, close to quiet railway line' (semi-detached bungalow near Woking with tremendously busy railway line to Waterloo running past the bottom of the garden).

It was a depressing exercise. Finally, just to reassure ourselves that there was somewhere in the world a house in which we would like to live, we upped the top amount we were prepared to pay from £4,000 to £6,000. From Harrods, of all people, came details of what they called 'a small manor house' (which it never was; it had always been a farmhouse) in the quiet village of Thorpe, which lies in the middle of Staines, Egham, Virginia Water and Chertsey. The ancient, listed, Grade II house belonged to a lady who had just got divorced, and to get rid of her unhappy home quickly she had whitewashed the beautiful old red-brick exterior, and this could not be economically removed.

The house, named Anners (originally Gorings Farm), lay in 2½ acres of farmer's uncared-for, overgrown land with about fifty scabrous apple trees, lots of ancient wooden outbuildings about to fall down and a coach house/garage. A dirty grey horse peacefully grazed on the rough meadow grass which should have been the lawn, and a neighbour's rusty car was permanently parked in the driveway.

I peered through the kitchen window. An ancient ATCO lawn-mower was standing in the shallow sink and the stone floor was a-swim with silverfish. Further inspection revealed that many windows were broken and the lead had been stolen from the roof.

We had found our dream home.

I drove Maman down and excitedly showed her round, and then Polly was able to get away from Addison Road domesticity for an afternoon. It was agreed all round, albeit reluctantly, that Anners had capability.

The price asked was too high for us, but the unhappy lady was open to a lower offer to get rid of the place and we bought it for £4,500. Oddly, for a house which had seen much unhappiness, it has always been a most happy home for us, seeming to exude calm and friendliness from its bricks.

As the house had been derelict for a couple of years there was quite a bit of repairing and decorating to be done. We hired a small local builder to do it. Wallpaper and glossy paint and Wilton carpeting were beyond our means – we had hardly any means at all after buying the house – so we began life at Anners with the walls painted with faintly tinted distemper (which we bought wholesale from a friend of a friend) and art felt floor covering. Art – short for 'artificial' not 'artistic' – had curious non-qualities. Unlike real carpet it did not recuperate. When the huge poodle peed on the blue-grey felt, which she did hourly being an urban dog and dis-trustful of grass, the large stain grew darker and then settled down to become a bright orange-yellow. Nothing at all could be done about this. And where one turned on one's heel, as at the foot of the stairs, a large hole immediately began to wear through the felt. Nothing could be done about that, either.

I had one rather bright idea. To put on a shelf next to the bed in our guest bedroom a selection of the sort of reading matter which would discourage guests from making their stay with us a long one (Benjamin Franklin wrote in *Poor Richard's Almanack for 1735*, 'Fish and visitors smell in three days').

The title of some of these (they are all genuine books) should have had the average visitor backing the car out before breakfast on day two:

Teach Yourself Practical Concreting (A. E. Peatfield)
Hiawatha, Rendered into Latin (F. W. Newman)
Hull Celebrities from 1640–1858 (W. A. Gunnell)
The Poetry and Philosophy of Sewage Utilisation (E. D. Girdlestone)
Little Elsie's Book of Bible Animals (1879)
Effective Punting (James Pembroke)

And lastly – slightly worrying?

Hindustani Self-Taught by the Natural Method (E. Marlborough)

The bright idea did not work because the books were old and curious and rather fun to leaf through.

Two and a half acres of garden – actually 'rough meadow' would be more accurate – was something of a nightmare to me with only Saturdays to do anything about it, but sheer delight for Polly whose priorities I believe to have been (1) flowers and any other kind of beautiful or useful bits of nature, (2) our poodle, or any other make of dog, cat, or small furry mammal, (3) me.

Polly was the horticulturist, I was the labourer. I bought a huge and ancient lawnmower, a Dennis as used to trim Lord's Cricket Ground before a Test. It weighed about a ton and seemed to have been lightly converted from a First World War tank. I also bought a petrol-driven Allen scythe. With these I set about subduing the vast stretches of nettles, cow-parsley and rough tufts of grass, and I hacked down, Charles Moses fashion, dozens of spindly, half-dead fruit trees. I tackled the bumps and dips in the ground by mixing together a small mountain of peat, top-soil and a bit of sand and, helped by friends, spread and pushed it about all over the grass with the back of a wooden rake. The treatment worked rather well.

In February 1953, on a bright and clear day with the sun shining, we moved into Anners, and we are still there, and what is more we have almost got the place straight.

The sun continued to shine on us in that following year, and in December 1954, Polly had our second child. This was not a home *accouchement*, for which I was profoundly grateful. After the previous little problems with producing Jamie, Dr Mary Adams thought it wiser for Polly to go into a nursing home this time and arranged a bed in a clinic in Queen's Gate, London. I remember little about that establishment except that in those more innocent days Polly's staff nurse went about her healing duties with a cigarette permanently on the go, an inch of ash trembling on the end.

The night the baby was expected, I was due at a dinner at Claridges for show-business folk thrown by Sir Bernard and Lady Docker, the entertainingly flamboyant, wealthy, ageing couple who were the great standbys of 1950s tabloid newspaper tut-tutting headlines. I was not allowed to stay at the nursing home and wait for the baby, I was sent off to Claridges. Dr Adams and Tofty wanted a full report of the dinner, who was there, what we ate, what Lady Docker was wearing . . .

The next morning I was allowed into Polly's room. She lay in bed cuddling her daughter. My first sight of Sally was not of a battered and bruised baby like poor old Jamie had been, but of a daughter who was neat, totally feminine and, well, perfect.

'We'll have a marquee on the lawn for her wedding!' I cried out to Polly in a kind of wild surge of happiness.

Chapter Ten

A WIND OF CHANGE WHISTLES
THROUGH THE AERIALS

I happen to be a shower person, believing that having a shower is not only much quicker than taking a bath but is more hygienic. Swishing life's detritus away with running water must be better than scrubbing it off, together with the skin's natural protective oils, with a chemical cake of rancid grease boiled up with caustic soda, and then wallowing in the unholy mixture. We all agree with John Wesley that 'cleanliness is, indeed, next to godliness', but he was talking about clothes.

Anners did not have a shower so we had to install one. It is an ancient house and the header tank in the loft is only about 18 inches above the shower-head, so one was not exactly clubbed to the bottom of the bath by the force of water. He who took a shower (women usually prefer baths) was required to stand patiently beneath a misty trickle which dropped like the gentle rain from heaven upon the earth beneath, until we could afford to put in a small electric pump.

All this domestic detail, as you must have instantly twigged, is a mood-setting prelude to the night of 15 December 1955 when Jimmy Edwards, Alma Cogan and I, with Polly looking after us, took part in the cabaret at the Christmas Staff Ball held in the Waterloo Chamber, Windsor Castle, in the presence of the royal family.

An invitation to entertain at the castle was, of course, an honour, and was arranged by a kind of royal talent-procurer general. For many years this was Peter Brough, an elegant amiable man whose day job was manufacturing shirts, but who was a ventriloquist at night. His dummy was a schoolboy character named Archie Andrews. I always thought that, technically, Peter was not a very good ventriloquist, his lips moved almost as much as Archie's, but his routines with the boy, and he in person, had considerable charm.

Perhaps due to the success in MGM films of the brilliant American ventriloquist Edgar Bergen with his dummy Charlie McCarthy, interest in vents ran oddly high for a while in Britain and Peter Brough and Archie were given their own series on radio, *Educating Archie*. Peter was Britain's first radio ventriloquist starring in his own series. A strange turn of events really; not only did he not have to bother about moving his lips on radio, but strictly speaking he did not even need to have a dummy. *Educating Archie* was well produced by, amongst others, Eric Spear, who later wrote the signature tune for *Coronation Street* and retired to a Channel Island. *Educating Archie* became hugely popular and ran from 1950 to 1960, winning two National Radio Awards for Best Comedy Show.

The set-up was that Peter Brough tried to have Archie educated at home by a succession of tutors. These were played by comedy actors and comics just beginning to make a name for themselves. The show helped them all to prosper. Hattie Jacques was in the Brough household and Julie Andrews played Archie's young girl-friend. The actors who played tutor to Archie included James Robertson Justice, Bernard Miles and Warren Mitchell; and among the up-and-coming comedians who took a turn were Max Bygraves ('I've arrived, and to prove it I'm 'ere!'), Dick Emery, Tony Hancock, Bruce Forsyth, Sid James, Alfred Marks and Harry Secombe.

Peter Brough was an excellent choice to put together entertainment for the Queen. Not only did he know pretty well everybody in the business, but he was personable, discreet, and perhaps most importantly, was not an agent or impresario and therefore had no axe to grind in selecting performers. I cannot think that he ever had much difficulty in assembling the entertainers he wanted. I wonder if anybody who was free on the date ever turned down an invitation to play to the royal family and their guests?

We accepted the invitation happily enough, and Jimmy and Alma changed at Anners and stayed overnight as we are only twenty minutes from Windsor Castle.

The huge and noble Waterloo Chamber was full. For the cabaret, there was a row of gilt chairs in front for the royals and everybody else sat on the floor. Alma sang and bubbled with happy laughter, and Jimmy and I exchanged some topical patter which I had knocked up for the occasion (at one point, after a royal joke, I said, 'I didn't write that line, ma'am, it was written by a man called Les Majesty.' The Queen looked worried and Prince Philip leaned across to her and explained).

Then Jimmy and I launched into the operatic weather forecast, *TIFH*'s attempt to make opera more popular by combining it with the very popular radio weather forecast. The opening item was sung to 'Libiamo', the rousing drinking song from Act I of Verdi's *La Traviata*:

> South Cones,
> Have been hoisted in areas Tyne,
> Dogger Bank, Hebrides and Thames,
> Dover Straits and Portland Bight.
> The wind's
> Veering north to the Firth of the Forth,
> But it's bright,
> Nearly every night,
> Round the Isle of Wight . . .

After the cabaret, dancing was resumed and I found myself partnering Her Majesty the Queen in the Palais Glide.

Oldies will remember that the Palais Glide was a novelty dance, highly popular in the Fifties at boozy works outings and holiday camp gala nights. It required the participants to put their arms across each other's shoulders and form a line, rather like that Zorba dance with which waiters in Greek restaurants tended to spoil one's moussaka. We all then pointed a hoof and tapped the floor this way and that in the manner of a dressage horse, did little runs forwards and then backwards and, I seem to remember, stamped energetically.

Dancing, like making sandcastles and somersaulting forwards, is yet another natural gift which I lack. I am exhausted by a slow foxtrot after a minute and a half and I cannot waltz because my feet keep kicking each other, and anyway I go dizzy.

After half a lap of the Palais Glide I said breathlessly to Her Majesty, 'Can we please sit down now, ma'am? I'm a bit exhausted . . .'

Her Majesty's answer was entirely feminine, even wifely: 'No, you can't,' said Her Majesty. 'Come on, you can keep going a bit longer.'

Afterwards, when we lined up and were presented to the royals by Peter Brough, the Queen Mother said to Polly, and this is the point of this rather tortuous anecdote, 'Does he think up funny things in the bath?'

To which my little wife, my loyal helpmeet, said to the Queen Mother, 'It's all I can do to get him *into* a bath.'

During the next year, 1956, Den and I took on something quite new to us. Tony Shryane, radio producer at BBC Birmingham, and Edward J. Mason, writer, were principal begetters of the long-running daily radio serial *The Archers*. They decided that for a change of pace they would devise and produce a new kind of not-very-academic literary quiz. It was to be produced as a Midland Regional programme recorded in hospitals and town halls in the region, but the pilot programme was to be recorded at 6 p.m. in London at the Aeolian Hall studio, Bond Street, just down the road from our office in Conduit Street.

One of the wordsmiths invited to take part in the pilot was the dramatist and journalist, Lionel Hale, a man of lively wit. It was Lionel who christened the Brendan Behan kind of aggressively Irish play, 'the sod-em and begorra school of drama'. He married A. P. Herbert's daughter Crystal, who had parted from her husband, the poet John Pudney. Soon afterwards the newly-weds turned up at Covent Garden Opera's annual fancy dress ball with Crystal dressed as the Bartered Bride.

Lionel was notoriously late for appointments but compensated for the trouble this caused by brilliantly inventive excuses.

The cast for Tony's literary quiz had been called for 5 p.m., but there was no sign of Lionel until five thirty, when he telephoned the studio and apologized for not being there. He explained that he had accidently bitten a piece out of the tumbler in which his gin and tonic reposed and a tiny sliver of glass had lodged between two of his front teeth; he had to go immediately to casualty at Bart's Hospital to have it removed.

There was also a problem with the other chap. I cannot remember quite what the problem was (or who the other chap was), but having problems with the cast of trial recordings was not unknown as they were paid a specially modest recording fee which was just about enough to cover their bus fare to the studio.

At about 6 p.m. on the evening of the trial recording, while Denis and I were trying to finish a script, Tony Shryane rang and pleaded with us to drop everything and race down to Aeolian Hall, a couple of hundred yards away, and sit in for his two missing contestants.

We explained to Tony that our workload was hideous and the last thing we wanted was to add to it by having to perform in a weekly radio show, that our few remaining free evenings were precious, etc., etc. Tony assured us that there was no obligation for us to be in the show should 'the powers' want a series, it was just to help him out of an emergency; the invited audience was already queueing outside, etc., etc.

We galloped down to Aeolian Hall and did the show. As we were not going to be in the series should there be one, we touched the whole thing lightly, fooling about with the answers and not treating literature, especially poetry, with the kind of po-faced reverence which nourished the attitude that it was élitist and irrelevant. Instead, Tony and Edward J. encouraged us to indulge in what Robert Frost called 'perhapsing around'.

In the last round of questions, Denis and I were given a quotation which we had to identify and then explain how and when it first came to be used. My quotation was, 'Let not poor Nelly starve,' and Den's was, 'Dead! . . . and never called me mother.' As the first was too easy and the second too difficult as to names and dates, we invented answers. (1) 'Let not poor Nelly starve' was first said by the chef at the Savoy when, late at night and short of puddings, he poured bits of this and that over a peach, hastily christened it Peach Melba and sent a waiter out with it to Dame Nelly Melba who was famished after her concert. (2) 'Dead! . . . and never called me mother' was first said by a lad reeling out of a vandalized phone box after failing to telephone his parents.

The audience liked the show to an agreeable extent.

I would say that the definition of a good radio or television producer is somebody who manipulates you into *happily* doing something which you had no intention whatever of doing in the first place. Tony was a very good producer. In spite of his promises not to involve us if the trial recording went into a series, and in spite of our firm resolve not to be trapped, a week or so later Den and I were happily signing our contracts for the first series of *My Word!* It ran for thirty-four years.

As time went by, the explanations given by Denis and me to explain the origin of our given quotations grew longer and more elaborate and the puns at the end, apart from giving pleasure to listeners who had guessed what the puns would be before we got to them, became less important and more desperate. Also, flexible quotations which lent themselves to our treatment were becoming increasingly difficult to find. For some reason proverbs proved the best source, but as the years sped by Edward J. Mason was running out of them.

Tony Shryane also had his problems with our stories. The early ones were not really stories, just one or two sentences – as above – which talked the listener into the pun, but after a year or two the stories, lengthened to around about six minutes each, were complicated and appallingly difficult to ad lib. Tony's problem was that if one of us failed to get our story to work there was no show. Reluctantly, he asked Denis and me to find our own quotations and to do some groundwork on the stories so that the show was safe for transmission and the evening would not be a total waste of BBC money. He also altered the chairman's dialogue from, 'I will now give Denis and Frank the lines on which they will base their stories,' to, 'Here are the two lines which have been given to Frank and Denis . . .' No listener seems to have noticed the change.

Our weekly chore of finding a well-known line to pun upon and dreaming up a fitting story to be ad libbed on the air was a nightmare which we lived with all those years. Keen listeners kindly sent us quotations to base stories upon but, strangely, they rarely worked. We must have received only about a dozen usable suggestions during all those years.

One of the few good ones sent to me was the notion that a story might well be based on a twist of the title of James Hilton's novel, *Good-bye Mr Chips*. My helpful friend explained that the idea came to him when he was driving home with his wife from a holiday in France. They bought pork pies in a pub in Dover, and near Maidstone pulled into a lay-by for a snack lunch.

'Did you enjoy it?' his wife asked, back in the car.

He said, 'Good pie, missed the chips.'

I think the problem which faced listeners wanting to be helpful is that puns are tricky things, not as easy as they might look with which to beguile an audience. For some reason the British public loves to boo and hiss puns and moan and groan at them, which is a bit dispiriting. But then many puns are intellectually clever without being at all funny, e.g., the following very clever American triple pun:

A rich Texan has four grown-up lads who live in Argentina and breed cattle for the Chicago beef market. He calls their ranch *FOCUS*, because it's where the sons – raise – meat.

I do not think that any of our *My Word!* puns achieved quite that height of arid perfection; ours tended to be shaggier and, I hope, jollier, as demonstrated by a couple of examples.

Geoffrey Strachan of Methuen Books persuaded us to put the stories into book form. He published five slim volumes and then an omnibus edition of all five volumes called *The Utterly Ultimate* My Word! *Collection*, whence I give you the following samples, chosen more or less at random and mercifully abbreviated:

DENIS: 'The least said, soonest mended.'

Charles Dickens, *Pickwick Papers*

Denis's story told of a lady who rented a house which had a sauna under the stairs in which the previous tenant had accidentally locked himself and steamed to death. The lady insisted, as a condition of the lease, that the sauna was made safe before her family moved in. Then followed a romp in the sauna between the son of the new occupant and an Italian girl (both unclad, of course), who wilfully got themselves locked in and . . . Well, anyway, the girl's Sicilian parents were all for revenge, blaming the unsafe sauna for their daughter having to marry an Englishman, but the new lady of the house insisted that they had no case against her. As she pointed out: *'The lease said sauna's mended.'*

FRANK: 'There's many a slip 'twixt the cup and the lip.'

Proverb

In my story it emerged that *Déjeuner sur l'herbe* was painted by Edouard Manet in the Bois de Boulogne in a remote glade between a carp pond and a heap of rocks known as Lover's Leap. When exhibited, the painting was hissed and booed for being decadent. Poor Manet, bitterly disappointed, went into hiding. His friends searched Paris afraid that he had committed suicide, then Mr Rory Bremner (an English Impressionist) suggested that they look at the spot where Manet painted his picture. And indeed, there in the Bois was a figure lying in the long grass, clutching an empty wine bottle and snoring. *'Voilà!'* cried Mr Bremner (in perfect French): *'There's Manet, asleep, 'twixt the carp and the leap.'*

I was told recently that the novelist J. G. Ballard much enjoyed the *My Word!* stories, and after hearing a story of mine in which, for purposes of the plot, I extolled the virtues of living in beautiful Shepperton, Surrey (Thorpe is about 5 miles away) – I described Shepperton as 'the Malibu of the Thames Valley' – he was moved by this warm recommendation and drove over in his car, liked what he saw and bought a house there, in which he still lives.

Could this be true? I do hope so.

Recordings of many BBC radio programmes, mainly classical music and drama and some comedy, were sold to other countries by a department known as the BBC Transcription Service, a valuable contribution to keeping the rest of the world aware that Britain was still a force in broadcasting and doing some things rather well, the sort of things which other nations had given up attempting.

After *My Word!* had been on the air for a year or two, the department announced in its international sales brochure that *My Word!* was the most popular radio programme in the world.

We thought this was going it a bit so we got on to the

Transcription Service. They were unabashed, pointing out that the BBC was the only worldwide exporter of radio programmes and *My Word!* was its most popular export, bought by over thirty-five countries including Chile, Germany and Russia. 'QED,' they said. 'Well, well,' we said.

One thing which Denis and I learned, and appreciated, during those early years of *My Word!* was how much the success of the show depended on the inconspicuous skill of the man who compiled it, Edward J. Mason. He had a gift for the common touch which is rare in areas like literary quizzes. He worked within the general awareness of listeners who had been to school; most of his poetic questions were to do with poems in Palgrave's *Golden Treasury*, most quotations were semi-familiar and in most books of quotations. We reckoned that 80 per cent of listeners felt that, given a bit of time for thought, they could answer almost 80 per cent of the questions.

Then in 1967, Tony Shryane struck again. He decided to set up a sister show to *My Word!*, hoping that Denis and I would join the team and bring a similar attitude of unapologetic semi-ignorance to the subject of music.

Tony had signed up the completely professional Steve Race, jazz pianist, accompanist, author, composer, to set the questions and be question master, and he had begun casting the contestants by signing up the bass and broadcaster, David (Bill) Franklin, and the Glyndebourne bass-baritone and splendid raconteur, Ian ('Mud, Mud, Glorious Mud') Wallace. Would Denis and I consider . . .?

Of course, it was out of the question. *My Word!* was a big success and fun to be in, apart from those damned stories hanging over our heads all week, and now Tony was proposing that Denis and I enter another tunnel, because the new show was to end with all four of us singing a song in turn. This meant that every week Den and I would have to find a song each and learn it, all in the midst of much writing work.

'Sorry, Tony,' we said. 'It just simply is not *possible*! Many thanks for thinking of us and all that, but it's not on, and anyway we don't know anything *about* music!'

'That's all right,' he said, 'don't worry. No pressure will be applied. If you can't do it, that's that! When Steve has finished the first script in a couple of weeks' time, I'll drop in and show it to you for interest's sake.'

'Yes, of course,' we said, relieved that Tony was not going to give us a big sales pitch or appeal to our better natures, if any. It was a grave error of judgement on our part.

Tony came and talked gently and reassuringly about the show, and a week or so later Denis and I happily signed our contracts for the first series of *My Music*. It ran for twenty-four years.

My partner in the show, Bill Franklin, died, and in came the splendid John Amis, music journalist, broadcaster, critic and administrator; a large, colourful personality whose striking manner of dressing made him seem not so much clothed as upholstered. John brought to the show a plethora of excellent anecdotes (musicians seem to have even more stories than actors) which he told in an admirably crisp style. He also sang in a high tenor voice, which the rest of us did not dare to attempt for fear of injury, and he whistled beautifully.

Ian Wallace, Glyndebourne bass-baritone, actor in musicals and famed impersonator of a singing hippopotamus, is a pleasure to be with on any show, or even just to be in a room with. So many times during the series Ian embarked on what seemed to be a rambling anecdote, not leading anywhere in particular, only to bring it suddenly to a totally unexpected and hilarious finish. The only thing wrong with the man is that he is far funnier than a singer has any right to be. It is simply not fair.

It was only when Denis and I took part in *My Music* that we realized we could not sing. It had not occurred to us before because it had not arisen. We were writers not vocalists, our job was to sit down and write, not to belt out a chorus of 'Burlington Bertie', but as our singing was part of the programme, and we were being lightly paid for it, we had to ignore our humiliation and sing.

One of Denis's problems was that his voice drifted mid-song from one key to another, as though it was hoping to find a key which would produce a more bearable sound. In the old *Twenty Question* terminology, I would describe Den's voice as an unreliable, domestic baritone with vegetable connections.

Den overcame his disability by searching out and singing obscure (and funny) Victorian comic songs which could be half sung, half croaked in the manner of Rex Harrison in *My Fair Lady*. A particular favourite with listeners, which he was repeatedly requested to reprise, was the romantic ballad (meant to be sung by a woman): 'He Was More Like a Friend than a Husband to Me'.

John Amis pointed out to me recently that Denis's singing had improved enormously over the years. But why? Had he been going in for clandestine singing lessons? Herbal tablets? Meditation? It was a riddle inside an enigma.

My own trouble was not being able to stay on a note without sliding off it. This is quite different from not being able to keep in key. I could put a fair amount of fervour or pathos into a performance, I could do a number con brio to order, as long as I was not required to hang on to a note for longer than half a second; after that my voice developed a vibrato and went wandering.

My solution to the problem was to avoid all songs which had to be properly sung and to choose those with a meaningful lyric which I could concentrate on delivering with poignance, as though it were an item in a rather noisy poetry reading.

The ignorance of classical music which Denis and I brought to the programme was mitigated by two circumstances. Whereas questions on *My Word!* were general and could have been asked of any of us, Steve Race tailored his questions to the four of us individually so that we could show up to best advantage. John Amis would be asked about, say, orchestral history and music-makers' eccentric behaviour and Ian might be asked questions about experiences in opera, Denis was asked about music in films and stage musicals, on which he was sound, and I might be given questions about musical history, which I had written about. Also, Denis and I were saved from humiliation when Steve hopefully gave us the odd question about classical music (we knew the piece so well but what was its *name*?) because we both had chaps beside us who knew *everything* about classical music, and they either scribbled the answer swiftly and slid it across the desk to us, or whispered it. Denis made no attempt to hide this help. 'Just a mo,' he would say to Steve, 'I've got a spirit message coming in from the right.'

A typical Denis ad lib came when Ian described a small crisis during a performance of Mozart's *Don Giovanni* at Glyndebourne. Apparently the producer had altered a sequence but had forgotten to tell Ian, who was singing away in the graveyard scene.

'Suddenly,' said Ian, 'I saw that behind the commendatore's statue the stage manager was crouching. "Psssst!" hissed the figure urgently, "Psssst!"'

'And were you?' asked Denis.

The influence of the two radio shows abroad was extraordinary.

When Kenneth Adam took over as Head of BBC Television he went first on the customary tour of the BBC's overseas offices. On his very first day back at Television Centre he nipped into our office to tell us of an experience he had had whilst *en route* to Australia.

It seems he stayed overnight in a hotel in Fiji. Early in the morning he was wakened by a cheerful Fijian, about 9 feet tall, holding a cup of tea. As he carefully positioned the saucer on the bedside table, the Fijian, smiling happily with all his thirty-two magnificent teeth, said, 'And how is your dear Queen and the noble Duke of Edinburgh, sir?'

'Very well, both of them, as far as I know, thank you,' Kenneth managed to mumble, struggling to sit up.

'And how are dear Mr Muir and Mr Norden of *My Word!*?'

Kenneth said that it was such an extraordinary thing to hear under those circumstances that he had to tell us as soon as he arrived home.

'Well, our billing was about right,' said Denis to me.

And much more recently, in the early 1990s, I was at the Author of the Year party given by Hatchards the bookshop. The guest of honour was the bestselling American writer Kitty Kelley, whose highly successful approach to her work is to write steamingly frank biographies of famous people such as Frank Sinatra and Nancy Reagan.

Miss Kelley was late. Eventually she arrived, a little iron butterfly in powder blue, almost hidden midst a posse of her publisher's publicity staff, like a serial adulteress being hustled into court to protect her from enraged wives.

A few minutes later one of Miss Kelley's young publicity persons came over to me and said, 'Would you like to meet Miss Kelley?'

'No, not much,' I said, after some thought. 'Well, she lives in a different sort of world to mine.'

'But she wants to meet *you*,' he said.

So, intrigued (to say the least), I allowed myself to be steered across to the corner where wee Miss Kelley was holding court. I was introduced and she immediately grabbed my hand in both of hers and pressed it to her bosom.

'This is wonderful!' she cried. 'Nobody told me *you* would be here!'

It was, as far as I was concerned, inexplicable behaviour. Then it all became a little clearer.

'That voice!' she cried. 'As a schoolgirl back home in Washington I used to listen to you under the bedclothes. And now I'm actually talking to you!' She really was genuinely moved, even a little moist-eyed. 'Frank, I want you to know I grew up listening to *My Music*.'

She asked for a signed copy of my book and off she went clutching it happily. I was happy, too.

Both *My Word!* and *My Music* produced much correspondence, some of it testimony to a wavering standard in the teaching of English in our schools. For instance, the beginning of school holidays always seemed to produce a little rush of notelets reading something like:

You are a great fan of mine and my sister, please would you send her and I a singed photo.

Then there were the hopelessly demanding letters which would take about a week to answer properly:

I have for many years been an admirer of yours and Mr Nordern's scripts and it is my earnest wish, also, to become a successful BBC comedy writer. Will you please tell me how you managed to get in? How do I set about writing comedy? Is it any different from homework? What books have you read? Who have you met? Have you got an animal? – I have got, until she died last week of a complaint, a gerbil. What's your family like? . . .

Another favourite went something like:

As you can deduce from the address at the top of this letter, my husband Ralph and I have emigrated from Herne Bay and are now happily ensconced in Toronto, Canada. Imagine our pure pleasure when we turned on the radio last Sunday morning and heard you and your friend (sorry, I cannot remember his name) in *My Music*. The series was about five years old, but at the end of it your friend sang a comic love song about a cockney boy and girl. Will you please send me a copy of the music and the words. Also will you please tell me who first sang it and where? Trusting this will not prove a bother, Kindest regards . . .

The worst ones read something like:

I enclose the first draft of my novel. I wish you to read the book carefully and tell me frankly whether I have the touch of comic genius which my friends and my aunt assure me that I am in possession of. I should explain that the novel is set in the gas showroom of a town in Durham where I live, and the humour arises naturally from the variety of local people who drop in to order a fitted kitchen or a gas poker. The hero is Matt who wants to be a poet but stutters (which I do a little). Please return the manuscript to me with your *constructive* comments by Thursday.

But there are the other kinds of letter. I have a slim file of these, labelled '*Belles Lettres*'.

There is an early one from a lady who was driving down the M1 with *My Music* on her car radio when she heard me wrestling with my song at the end, that old sad Irving Berlin song, 'What'll I Do?'. It seems that I had put into my singing some of the passionate emotion which had lain dormant since my erotic rendition of 'Tondelayo' in Uncle Mack's kiddies' competition on Broadstairs sands those many years ago. The lady was so moved to tears that she had to stop the car and have a little sob.

After reading her letter I rang Tony Shryane. 'What did I *do* with the song?' I asked. 'What was it about the way I sang it which made the lady burst into tears?'

Tony could not remember. 'Perhaps she's a music lover,' he said.

Appreciative letters did not exactly choke the letter box; they came in thinly and slowly rather than thick and fast, but one did float in from time to time.

Another I kept was from a lady, Mrs Brendan McCluskey of nearby Staines, who was expecting her third child, which she was warned might turn up early. She already had two girls and was hoping for a boy. By accident she turned on a radio programme which had Alfred Marks and me in it, called *Frank Muir goes into . . . parties*, and laughed so much that she went into labour. The baby turned out to be another girl, so Mrs McCluskey named her Francesca.

My favourite unsolicited testimonial was a postcard from a lady explaining that her best friend was a nun in Rome. Her friend was ill in hospital, so to cheer her up she had sent her a copy of my book, *The Frank Muir Book: An Irreverent Companion to Social History*. A little while later the nun wrote back thanking her friend for the present. She said she was enjoying the book so much that she had given it up for Lent.

Radio comedy matured in the first ten years of peacetime radio, and by the early 1950s the older formats like *ITMA* and Charlie Chester's *Stand Easy*, which depended on techniques inherited from the variety theatre such as quick-fire entrances and exits and rapid little topical jokes enacted in funny voices, were giving way to character comedy, as in the superb *Hancock's Half-Hour*, written by Ray Galton and Alan Simpson, and for many listeners rising above them all was *The Goon Show* – noisy, irreverent, cunningly smutty, brilliantly inventive and dotty.

The show's original title was *Crazy People*, and the pilot script was written by Spike Milligan, Michael Bentine and a new writer full of odd ideas named Larry Stephens, who was working as a kind of assistant to Spike. This post did not carry a salary because Spike had no money. He also had nowhere to live. But he met Harry Secombe's half agent, Jimmy Grafton (who shared the other half of Harry with another agent), and Jimmy Grafton owned a family pub in Westminster, the Grafton Arms. He also wrote comedy. Thus the ambitious and gifted little group suddenly had somewhere to meet and write, and Spike had an attic to sleep in.

The producers of *Crazy People* were Pat Dixon and the very young and wildly enthusiastic Dennis Main Wilson. In 1952 the first programme was made. It was not quite right, so back to the drawing board (i.e., pub) they all went, changes were made and the first series of the programme, now produced solely by Dennis Main Wilson, went out on the air with a range of eccentric characters who lasted throughout *The Goon Show*'s long life. These included the cheerful, heroic idiot, Neddy Seagoon; Moriarty the perpetual villain; Colonel Bloodstock; Spike's simpleton character Eccles, whose voice, perhaps unconsciously, echoed Disney's cartoon dog Goofy, etc. These inventions, plus bizarre plots and lots of explosions and vigorous sound effects, dismayed, delighted, worried, puzzled and intrigued listeners according to taste. The style came as a breath of stimulating air to broadcast comedy and probably had a greater influence on later generations of writers and performers than any radio comedy programme has ever had.

My only criticism of *The Goon Show* is that the cartoon-like comic voices were dangerously easy to imitate. Indeed, throughout the Fifties and Sixties, breaking into a comical Goon voice in the course of ordinary conversation (to the amusement only of the breaker-inner) was practised by a great many citizens who should have known better, including, alas, Prince Charles.

Although by the 1950s radio had developed its own techniques and was a genuine art form, in that it had an important limitation – there was nothing to look at – it was about to be replaced as the public's favourite mass entertainment by a gadget called television.

I think a tiny tragedy of the twentieth century, very tiny indeed when compared to the big ones, but nevertheless in its own world a tragedy, was that just when radio had matured, found its own techniques and knew what it could do better than film or the theatre, it was suddenly overwhelmed by television.

Television is a technical miracle, but it is, unlike radio, fundamentally a gadget. It is not as precise to work with as film; you cannot iron a shirt or read a newspaper while it is on and still enjoy it as you can with a radio programme; it engages the eyes but rarely the imagination; it does not have the interplay between actor and audience which distinguishes theatre; it is the only medium in which the performers rehearse for hours beforehand, sometimes all day, and then perform the show itself dog-tired; and it presents a number of new hazards to the writer. Radio is a medium of the imagination and the writer can write, 'Over to the doge's masked ball in Venice,' and you are there. The writer in radio speaks straight into the ear of the listener.

Television had grown slowly but steadily in the years since those dear pre-war Ally Pally days when, according to the BBC's distinguished Head of Audience Research, Robert Silvey, the TV service was able to invite its entire audience to tea in one studio. What a splendidly British thing to have even *thought* of doing.

In the very earliest of the pioneering days in television, problems arose which had to be solved by *ad hoc* ingenuity, there being no precedents to help. Such as what to do when the delectable Joan Miller, introducing *Picture Page*, could not hear the floor manager giving her a cue because of the loud introductory music, and could not see him because of the set she was sitting in. The problem was solved, as usual, by the engineers. They devised a gadget like a small electric cattle probe which they wired up to Miss Miller's ankle, so that when her beautiful 1938 vowels were needed for an introduction, the producer only had to press a button and Miss Miller received a short sharp electric shock to prompt her into action.

Early television sets were expensive and, perhaps as a defensive measure, were widely regarded by the public as being a bit 'common' ('We don't have television in our house. What civilized person wants to sit and watch footer or a concert party of an evening?'). Then in the early 1950s the public attitude to television changed and it began to become a symbol of social affluence, of having 'got on'. It was rumoured that many homes displayed a TV aerial on their roof to impress neighbours but had no TV set below. It became normal to see a crowd gathered round a television dealer's shop window in the high street, peering in and blocking the pavement as they enjoyed a free gawp at a display of screens transmitting something exciting like Wimbledon tennis or a uni-cyclist in a variety show.

All the screens showed the same black-and-white picture because at that time there was no colour and only one channel: BBC. ITV did not set up shop until 1955 and BBC2 even later.

Then in 1953 came the big event which accelerated the rate of sale of new sets from a trickle to an avalanche: the televising of the Coronation.

Almost everybody in the country wanted to see the pomp and majesty of the Coronation on television, and almost all seemed to manage it. Owners of television sets found themselves immensely popular in their neighbourhood, and on the big day their front rooms were crammed with neighbours sitting all over the furniture, on kitchen chairs they had brought with them, or the floor, any-where so long as they could wallow all day in the joy of watching a great ceremony which but for television they would never have even glimpsed. And television hire firms did great business.

With more television sets being sold every year, the BBC's income from TV licences went up steadily and they could afford to pay high fees for virtuoso musicians and could attract big-name American performers to star in more complicated and expensive variety productions.

Comedy shows had always been a large and successful part of

the BBC's radio schedules and as television grew and many of the younger BBC producers moved across from radio, they naturally continued this tradition and from, say, 1952 to 1955, the last of the comfortable BBC's monopoly years, when every viewer who was watching was watching your show, there was a natural drift of top-of-the-bill comics and their writers from the quiet backwater of radio to the expanding excitements of telly.

The first serious go at television which Denis and I had came in 1956 when we wrote a sketch show for Dick Bentley which we called *And So to Bentley*. It went out from Lime Grove studios which BBC Television then occupied. Lime Grove was, of course, the scene of my toe-curling Brussels sprout affair, the first of the two gaffes I committed within shooting range of Sydney Box.

Dick's chief support was Peter Sellers and each programme ran for forty-five minutes every other week. The fees in those days hold a kind of melancholy interest in these days of huge payouts. Our fee was a guinea a minute, plus a little bit more because there were two of us, which came to £105 between us, once a fortnight.

It was not a bad show. Dick was fine. Self-deprecating, the kind of understated performance he gave in *TIFH*, which made many sensitive listeners prefer him to the more boisterous Jimmy Edwards. Sellers was, of course, excellent. And that was the problem. Dick became painfully aware that he, nominally the star, was overwhelmed on screen by the charismatic brilliance of the versatile Sellers.

And So to Bentley did not go into a second series, but Denis and I had learned a great deal about the problems and possibilities of working in television, and it was clear that the time had come for us to take the plunge. In a way this was a realistic decision as we had had a good innings with *TIFH* – eleven years – and now there was a temptation to ease the pressure by living off our fat a little, to rewrite past episodes of the Glums and pretend to ourselves that they were new, or improved, and to tart up old sketches.

We decided it really was time to call it a day and we wrote a letter to the Head of Radio Variety explaining that we thought, with great regret, that the time had come for us to stop writing *TIFH* and to move across into television, beginning with a series for Jimmy Edwards.

The BBC Radio Variety Department's reaction was of dismay. *TIFH* was still pulling in good listener figures and a bit of prestige, and for the bosses, not being writers, that was the main (if not only) consideration. We held firm. They asked us whether they could continue *TIFH* with other writers (the copyright of a show was held by us, the writers; we legally owned the show, the BBC only paid us a fee to broadcast it). We agreed to this and a new series of *TIFH* was written by two established comedy writers.

It was astonishingly naive of us not to have asked for a copyright fee, after all it was our show, but it simply did not occur to us. It might have been an expensive blunder had *TIFH* run on for another ten years, but under its new writers the show just managed to complete the one series.

The question of what Jimmy Edwards' television series would be about was simple enough to answer; he would revert to his original comic character of a venal, boozy, devious and incompetent head-master of a small, tatty public school. We invented a name for his school which sounded vaguely unreliable – Chiselbury – and we called the series *Whack-O!*

We began casting and found a very good Taplow (the schoolboy character who outmanoeuvres the headmaster at every clash), and we amassed a useful team of masters. We were particularly happy with having Edwin Apps to play Mr Halliwell, who was young, upper-middle-class, kind to the boys, loyal and incorruptible. The headmaster *loathed* him.

Jimmy had to have an assistant master, and I remembered Flight Lieutenant Arthur Howard whose speciality in comedy was being dithery and dim. Denis agreed that we might give him a go, so we wrote to him explaining that we had no idea how big the part would be, but if it did not matter to whom the headmaster talked, it would be to Mr Pettigrew, the assistant master (it turned out to be a bit of a life-saver for Arthur. He was doing quite well in small cameo parts in films, e.g., *Passport to Pimlico*, but jobs in television were scarce) and dear Arthur joined the team. So excellent was Arthur as downtrodden, bullied Mr Pettigrew that he very quickly became Jimmy's co-star in a kind of Laurel and Hardy relationship.

During one memorable episode, Mr Pettigrew hurt his head due to machinations of the plot and it was wreathed in bandages. The headmaster kept thumping Mr Pettigrew on his sore head to emphasize points, until at one point he bent over his desk to reach something and poor, in-pain Mr Pettigrew broke. He hauled off and delivered a terrific kick to the headmaster's backside. The headmaster lay sprawled across the desk for quite a long time, immobile, while Mr Pettigrew writhed in silent agony. Finally Jimmy rose slowly and faced Mr Pettigrew. 'I wish I was dead!' sobbed Mr Pettigrew. The headmaster said, quietly, 'That can be arranged.'

It was an enjoyable series to write (when it went well). One of the lines I remember fondly was during the early moments of a programme when Jimmy looked out of his study window, outwards and upwards, reacted dramatically to something he saw, said, 'What's that object somebody's hung on the chapel spire?' produced an air rifle, took careful aim and fired. There was a 'ping' followed by the sound of breaking china. Jimmy said to the audience, 'Funny, that. During the war it was the Jerry that shot *me* down!' (Quite true. The plane Jimmy was flying home after towing a glider to Arnhem was shot down by a German fighter plane.)

In another programme there was an inspection of the school account books by a Ministry of Education auditor:

AUDITOR: Can you explain this entry, Headmaster? 'Owed to turf accountant . . .'?

HEADMASTER: Alas, we had to have the first eleven cricket pitch returfed.

AUDITOR: But the entry goes on: 'For my losses on the Oaks, £80.00.' Is the Oaks not a horserace, Headmaster?

HEADMASTER: I don't listen to gossip, sir, I am a man of the Arts. The entry refers to my selling two of our oak trees to a furniture manufacturer who refused to pay up as the trees were riddled with the dread Hungarian gunge beetle.

The auditor is now getting exasperated in face of the headmaster's slippery, confident and clearly bogus answers.

AUDITOR: (*Hotly*) But this entry really does need some explaining, Headmaster. Here it is in black and white, d'you see? 'For Prize-Giving Day. 50 crates.' FIFTY CRATES! You provided *alcohol* at your school's *prize-giving*?

HEADMASTER: No, no, no, no! It was a book prize. I do apologize for Mr Pettigrew's handwriting; grammar-school boy, you know. It's so difficult to get educated staff these days. That's not '50 crates' – it's 'Socrates'.

Another facet of the headmaster's petty conman virtuosity was the smarmy persona he adopted when visiting the Great House where lived the Lady of the Manor, a bit of a battleaxe who happened to be chairman of the school governors. He was usually trying to impress her with his charm and erudition in order to wheedle money out of her or to avoid gaol.

HEADMASTER: (*Closely examining an oil painting on her drawing-room wall*) Exquisite, milady! Quite exquisite! All hand-coloured, I'll warrant?
MILADY: (*Acidly*) It's a Constable.
HEADMASTER   Really? (*He peers closely at the picture*) In plain clothes, I see . . .

Whack-O! was produced and directed by Douglas (Dougie) Moodie, an epicene, very experienced Scot who at one period was directing two programmes a week, *Dixon Of Dock Green* and *Whack-O!*, an impressive feat of organization when each thirty-minute show normally had a whole week of rehearsal to itself.

Dougie had an acid tongue. He loved the stars of his shows but was a bit hard on small-part players. From his seat up in the control box he would shout down the microphone to his floor manager in the studio things like, 'Tell that oily-haired idiot with a face like Colonel Nasser to get out of the bloody way. I need to see the clock!'

It was customary for the writers to turn up and watch the last outside rehearsal, which was usually conducted in a hired drill hall or ice-cold function room, to check that all was well with their beautiful dialogue before the cast went into the studio the next day, endured a camera rehearsal and then went on and did the show.

When Den and I turned up at the last outside rehearsals of *Whack-O!* we were greeted each time with a loud screech from Dougie: 'Attention everybody – Gilbert and Sullivan have arrived!'

Another time it would be: 'Quiet everywhere – Gog and Magog are here!'

Whack-O! was broadcast from a theatre, the Shepherd's Bush Empire. Some time later Denis and I wrote a one-off musical show for Jimmy Edwards (*The Sound of Jim*) to be performed in the theatre. One sketch required a flock of pigeons suddenly to descend over the symphony orchestra which, conducted by Jimmy, was playing a well-loved bird number ('Oh, for the wings, for the wings, of a dooooove') and cause chaos. The producer booked a troupe of performing pigeons for whom this kind of sketch was child's play, and it all went beautifully, the pigeons duly flapped about over the musicians' heads and were comically, if not very wittily, incontinent. Their trainer had brought them down to Shepherd's Bush from Wales by train in baskets, an expensive operation.

When the show was over and everybody was packing up we found the Welsh bird-trainer in high spirits. He had remembered from early days in variety that the Shepherd's Bush Empire's ceiling had a retractable dome and had persuaded the manager to open it up. The bird-trainer then ran up and down the aisles shouting, 'Wow-wow! Off you go! Go on! Home!' and clapping his hands very loudly. The pigeons were puzzled for a while and then realized that there was open air and freedom above them, and in a huge clattering flock they flew up, up and away into the night sky.

'That'll save me a few quid in fares back to Wales!' chortled the trainer.

He spotted at once that we had no idea what he was up to. 'They're homing pigeons,' he explained patiently.

Mounting a farce like *Whack-O!*, which required a realistic production, was not easy on a theatre stage. About the only good thing which came from it was that on the other side of the Goldhawk Road was an excellent little Italian restaurant and bar owned by N. Oddi. It was known to us, naturally, as Noddy's.

Dougie's directing method, an unusual one, was to rehearse his cameras and his actors very carefully so that when the show started there was no need for him to shout at everybody from the control box; his job was done and the cameras and cast knew exactly where to be and what to do.

So while the audience was shuffling into the auditorium, Dougie went with us across the road to Noddy's and enjoyed a medicinal gin and tonic or four. Back in the control box, he would settle himself comfortably into his chair and, now pleasantly relaxed (i.e., lightly befuddled), would quietly enjoy watching his programme.

But at one show, when Denis and I were in the control box, things went wrong. One of the four cameras went down and then there were three.

The cameramen knew all their moves and shots when there were four of them, but with one camera missing their working pattern for the whole show was destroyed. And the show – live, of course – had started. A nasty moment.

Dougie sat up straight and talked to his cameramen quite calmly through his microphone. 'Well, gentlemen,' he said, 'it's fun night! Camera One, could you creep round the table and get me a medium shot of Pettigrew? Meanwhile, Three, see if you can get closer to Jimmy – we're coming to you when Jimmy does the telephone business . . .'

It was a quite extraordinary demonstration of television professionalism. Dougie shook off the effect of his gin and tonics as a spaniel shakes off raindrops, and, ad libbing the shots, talked his camera crews through half an hour of a busy and complicated farce.

As the credits rolled and 'The End' came up, he slumped back in his chair for a moment and then sat up straight again, thrust an elegant hand through the handles of his female vision-mixer's tall, thin, raffia handbag, looked round the control box and said brightly, 'More burgundy anybody?'

Chapter Eleven

AND A NIGHTINGALE SANG
IN TELEVISION CENTRE

The 1960s were years of sudden change for Denis and me with our careers wandering off in unexpected directions.

One evening in 1960 itself, we were at a party in Shepperton given by Bernard Braden and his wife Barbara Kelly at their home, when the Assistant Head of Light Entertainment Group, Tom Sloan, who enjoyed a social glass, fell over and broke a small occasional table. The next morning Tom invited Denis and me to join the BBC Television Light Entertainment Department as advisors and consultants on comedy.

It is not easy, even at this remove when the dust has settled, to spot the connection between Tom splintering a small table and his offer to us next morning of a four-year contract to advise and be available to producers for consultation in matters of comedy. Had the heavy fumes of French table wine (red) lingered on and caused Tom to be visited by demons?

Of course Den and I signed up at once. Although to begin with our office would be a portable cabin on the back of a lorry in the car park, the grand Television Centre building was nearly completed, and in those days to be a consultant was a sinecure. Nowadays 'I'm a consultant' usually means 'I have just been made redundant and am hoping to go it alone', but then it meant that as soon as Television Centre had been completed, we would sit in a pleasant BBC office, with a secretary and a telly, and the canteen and the BBC club bar only a stroll away. And we could get on with our writing work in comfort in the confident knowledge that our privacy would not be disturbed, because any producer of comedy worth his salt would rather be cast naked into a vat of hissing vipers than admit that he needed to take advice on how to do his job from Denis and me.

And this, in the main, proved to be true. Eventually we moved to the fourth floor of Television Centre, read every script submitted and reported on them, meticulously attended departmental meetings and were consulted quite frequently by our two bosses in the Light Entertainment Group, although these informal meetings took place in the bar or in the lift and were more like an exchange of light chat about the department's output than serious professional discussions. For example Tom had a bee in his bonnet: 'Isn't it time we killed off *Dixon of Dock Green*? Jack Warner is a bit old for a police sergeant; he can hardly walk.'

Our advice was: 'No. The fact that he hobbles doesn't matter; unrealistic though Sergeant Dixon and the series may be, it's part of many viewers' lives now. When you kill off the series you'll kill off some old viewers as well.' The series continued with excellent figures for several more years until Jack Warner died, aged eighty.

I find it difficult to recollect any splendid coups we achieved during our four happy years in office. (There must have been *some*. One little one?) But I do recollect very clearly one rather colourful near miss we had.

It was in the 1950s and Denis and I were sent to the USA by the BBC to persuade Jack Benny to come to England and present a big Saturday night television show. In those days weekend television was dominated by 'spectaculars', expensive and long variety shows often starring a big Hollywood name, and Denis and I had to watch shows and tour the agencies. (When we were in the William Morris Agency's offices in New York, Mel Brooks drifted in and we were introduced as the BBC's experts on comedy. He looked at us in awe. 'You mean, you *know*?' he said.)

The daily expenses allowed by the BBC were enough to keep us lightly fed and watered but left little over for fun items, and we were delighted when the BBC office in the Rockefeller Center arranged for us to appear on the big chat show of that era, *The Jack Paar Show*, which would pay us an expense fee of $100 apiece, enough to buy presents to take home to our dear ones.

Just before we were due to fly across to the West Coast to tempt Jack Benny to England we were visited at the Algonquin Hotel by a thin blond man with several twitches going at once, whose name was Rick Something-or-other. He said he was one of Jack Paar's talent co-ordinators, which was not very illuminating. It emerged that his job was to interview Jack Paar's potential victims (Mr Paar was famous for the playfully brutal treatment of his guests when he felt like it), find out what subject the guests intended to chat about on the show, so that Mr Paar, armed with pre-information and a team of writers, could outsmart them, and generally put the guests at their ease. Mr Paar's talent co-ordinator bit his nails.

'Anecdotes! Anecdotes!' he suddenly screamed, like a man bitten by a viper calling urgently for antidotes. 'Stories! Go, go, go!'

His ballpoint was poised above a nasty yellow notepad.

Of course our minds immediately went totally blank.

'Needs thought,' mumbled Denis. 'Can't – just like that.'

'Dunno any,' I mumbled after another horribly long silence.

Rick sighed. 'We got trouble,' he said, sadly. 'It's *Jack*.'

We noticed that everybody in the Paar organization spoke their employer's name in a special tone of terrified reverence.

'*Jack* wants for you to tell anecdotes, right? You don't tell *Jack* an anecdote when he wants for you to tell him an anecdote and you know what he'll do? He'll intrude in the middle of while you're talking and say to camera, "OK, let's take a break here and watch a commercial!" The audience will love your evident discomfiture and shout out, "You tell the limeys, Jack! That's our Jack!" You'll be socially hugh-millated and professionally hugh-millated, and if you're lucky enough to get a table at Sardi's it'll be the one next to the kitchen door.'

Rick clicked his ballpoint shut in a telling gesture. Den and I could see our precious $100 disappearing like mist in sunshine.

'The point is, Rick,' said Denis, rescuing the situation, 'in our long years as Britain's top comedy writers, artistes and entre-preneurs we have amassed a wealth of anecdotes concerning our friends, the superstars of British show business, but we don't just want to blurt them out, willy-nilly. We want to talk them over between ourselves and select for Jack only the cream.'

Rick was visibly impressed by this codswallop.

'I like it!' he said. 'I like it! Good thinking, Dallas.'

'Denis,' said Denis.

'Denis,' he said. 'Right. Now, you're both flying to the coast tomorrow to meet up with Mr Benny, right? Be away ten days, right? OK, that leaves four days before *The Jack Paar Show* recording, so as soon as you get back to New York you call me, right?'

He gave us his card and left for wherever talent co-ordinators go when they have finished co-ordinating for the day.

I raised an eyebrow at Den.

'We'll make up some lies on the plane,' he said.

Los Angeles was different. Jack Benny was kind, gentle and funny. He took us to lunch at The Brown Derby, the famous old Hollywood restaurant shaped like a bowler hat, and we sat quite near, only about fifteen tables away, say 40 yards, from Barbara Stanwyck. The following day he took us to his agent's office, a white colonial mansion set in lawns and full of English antique furniture, and we sat watching kinescopes of his recent television shows. At the end he rubbed his face and said, 'Don't I work *slow*!'

Sadly, we could not persuade him to come to England. He was getting on in years and his main interest was mounting charity shows with symphony orchestras. He made a lot of money for good causes by introducing the music, performing little comedy spots in between orchestral items and playing his violin with cunning incompetence. He seemed to us a very nice man.

Denis and I, making the best use of our time before returning to New York, *The Jack Paar Show* and temporary affluence (or hughmillation), met comedy writers who showed us round their studios and looked after us, and we talked to Carl Reiner, the writer and producer, and generally enjoyed that warm and generous hospitality from our fellow writers which is so much an American tradition.

Stephen Potter called it the American Creative Welcome. He pointed out that in England, when the phone rings, the wife hisses, 'Who is it?' and the husband wraps his hand round the mouthpiece and whispers, 'Those Americans who were so helpful in Corfu when I got that tummy-bug – they're over here for a few days and want to meet up with us!' And the wife says, 'Oh, dear!' and rifles through her diary and says, 'You could ask them to lunch on Thursday week – no, it's one of my coffee mornings – how about three weeks on Tuesday? I could get in some cold meat and knock up a salad.' Whereas when you arrive in New York and telephone friends you get the Creative Welcome. 'Great!' they say instantly. 'Come over right away and we'll have a drink and then send out for some Mexican food!'

But Stephen Potter did also note that when you departed you departed alone: your American friends were busy Creatively Welcoming somebody else.

The BBC office in New York had booked us into the Chateau Marmont Hotel on Sunset Boulevard, Hollywood, a once grand but by then somewhat passé hotel where the great and boozy writers like Hemingway and Scott Fitzgerald once holed up when they were tempted to Hollywood to earn big bucks writing screenplays to order (P. G. Wodehouse, who was one himself except for the boozing, called those lonely, unhappy but rich souls 'the Castaways').

Our ten days sped past swiftly, meeting and talking most usefully on professional matters, and suddenly there were only a couple of days left. The writers urged us to stay on a while as they had organized a day trip by plane to Las Vegas, enough time for a swift look at the gambling palaces, a few goes on the fruit machines and lots of laughter, but we could not linger because we had committed ourselves to appearing on *The Jack Paar Show*.

Then, on our last night in Hollywood, glamour! Excitement! Superstars of Tinseltown all around us!

An old friend and colleague, the writer Michael Pertwee, had worked in Hollywood for years and one of his close, poker-playing friends was the lyricist Ira Gershwin, George Gershwin's elder brother. Michael had written to Ira Gershwin to tell him we were coming over and the good man rang us on our last day, explained that he had just got back from Saratoga and asked us over to his place immediately for an after-dinner drink.

The Gershwin home was long, low and cool; lots of white walls and modern paintings and sculpture. Ira was plumpish, short and white-haired. He took us down to the cellar, which had been converted into a kind of shrine to his brother. There was the old and battered-looking upright piano on which George had picked out 'Rhapsody in Blue', some of George's paintings – he was an enthusiastic, gently gifted Sunday painter – and various bits of memory-jogging memorabilia of George Gershwin's music.

Back upstairs, Ira poured drinks, lit a massive cigar, and we sat at our ease round a white marble table in the centre of which stood a huge Swedish goldfish bowl, shaped like a giant wineglass, not filled with the usual collection of 'My-God-was-that-where-I-was-last-night?' nightclub book-matches but with, oh dear, what seemed to be packets of every known brand of American cigarette.

Now this was the 1950s, when it was a smoker's world and Denis and I innocently puffed away as compulsively as everybody else doing nervy work. But that evening we had both run out of cigarettes. As Ira Gershwin's house was on Sunset Boulevard, as was our hotel, we allowed five minutes to drive there plus five minutes to buy cigarettes *en route*.

Our fatal error was not to realize that American boulevards can go on a bit. The Gershwin residence was indeed on Sunset Boulevard but about 12 miles up it. We had to drive at great speed to get there without being disgracefully late and there was no question of wasting time looking for a shop selling cigarettes.

So there Denis and I sat with the man commonly regarded as the most literate and brilliant lyricist of our century ('Embraceable You', 'I Got Plenty of Nothin'', 'Let's Call the Whole Thing Off', 'Love Walked Right In', 'Long Ago and Far Away', 'Someone to Watch Over Me', 'They Can't Take That Away from Me', 'S'Wonderful', and hundreds more), letting the conversation flag as, desperate for a drag, we gazed beady-eyed at the cornucopia of fags within reach but unattainable.

Other factors contributed to the lengthening bouts of awkward silence. Denis and I can claim a small number of extremely minor social graces: we tend to be punctual and leave the washbasin as we would wish to find it and we are both very tall, but that's about it. As for the important social graces, well, to begin with neither of us has any small talk.

Ira Gershwin did his best, but he was now taking life very easily and his main interests were playing poker and betting on horses, neither of which sciences Denis and I knew anything whatever about. And after a while we realized that Mr Gershwin was skil-fully concealing the fact that he was rather deaf. As my voice is soft and plummy and Denis's is not much crisper, our host had prob-ably not clearly heard a word either of us had said the whole evening. It was awesome. Faced with two inaudible strangers staring fixedly at a Swedish goldfish bowl full of packets of ciga-rettes, like a pair of tall thin fortune-tellers whose crystal ball had gone wrong, Ira Gershwin carried on being an impeccable host.

I managed to sneak a peek at my watch. It was nearly ten o'clock, not really late but late enough if we had to catch an early plane to New York, which we did not have to do as our plane left at midday.

'Well,' I said, rising, 'you've been extremely kind, Mr Gershwin, but we have to leave you in peace now because we have a plane to . . .'

But Mr Gershwin had not heard me so I sat down again.

'Do you know the work of the playwright Lillian Hellman?' he asked suddenly.

'*The Children's Hour*,' said Denis, '*The Little Foxes, Watch on the Rhine* . . .?'

'Lillian's upstairs,' said Ira Gershwin. 'She had some dental work done this afternoon and is having a little rest. Said she'd come and join us.'

Lillian Hellman!

An hour passed very, very slowly. Miss Hellman's dental treatment seemed to have proved more exhausting than had been expected. She did not come down.

'Moss Hart,' said Mr Gershwin some time later.

Denis woke up. 'MOSS HART!' he said.

'Said he'd drop by this evening. I'd like you to meet him.'

'Moss Hart!' said Denis again, sort of breathing the name. '*You Can't Take It with You, The Man Who Came to Dinner, Lady in the Dark* . . .?'

Another hour or so dragged by. Moss Hart did not appear. He had probably forgotten or been kidnapped by aliens or something, but it was now after midnight and Denis and I could not, in all decency, keep this elderly gentleman from his bed any longer. His usual bedtime on non-poker evenings was probably around 8.30 p.m.

'I'm so sorry it's been such a dull evening for you,' Mr Gershwin said. 'It would have been so good if you'd met up with Lillian and Moss.'

The cheerful sound of dance music penetrated the night air.

'The noise is coming from Rosemary Clooney's place next door,' said Ira Gershwin apologetically. 'She's throwing a party there for Frank Sinatra. Hey! Would you like to meet Frank?'

'Couldn't possibly intrude . . . private party . . .' we mumbled, hearts thudding.

'Nyah!' said Mr Gershwin, 'Rosie's really nice and Frankie likes writers. Well, he likes writers who like *him*. I'll ring Rosie, she'll be glad to have you over.'

He heaved himself out of his chair, went over to the phone and dialled.

I looked at Den and Den looked at me.

Mr Gershwin held the phone to his ear and waited. I waited, Den waited, we waited all three.

Eventually, after quite a long time, he carefully replaced the phone in its cradle. 'Waddya know!' he said, chuckling. 'They're having such fun nobody can hear the phone ringing!'

Den and I chuckled with him for a moment or two to keep him company and then drove in silence back to the Chateau Marmont.

When we arrived back in New York and telephoned our talent co-ordinator ('Hi, Rick! We're back!'), we found that while we had been rubbing shoulders with 'our friends the stars' in sunny California, Rick had been fired from *The Jack Paar Show*. And in the American tradition this meant he'd had to relinquish his key to the talent co-ordinators' washroom and his numbered space in the company car park, return to the commissariat the unconsumed portion of his Waldorf Salad and – most important for us – feed into the office shredder the contracts of all the talents he had been personally co-ordinating. Including ours.

So we flew home to England without our lovely dollars. I did manage to scrape together enough dollars and cents and things to present my schoolgirl daughter Sally with a startlingly scarlet, very American plastic sou'wester from Saks Fifth Avenue. Sal has it still. Amazing how long a hat will last if you don't wear it.

On the positive side, back in England we were at once able to rush to the aid of Eric Sykes during rehearsals of the first show of his splendid and long-running series, *Sykes And . . .* in which Hattie Jacques played Eric's twin sister. I think 'rush to the aid' was the important part of our help here. Eric later said that to him the sight of us charging in through the door of the rehearsal room was like the arrival of the US Seventh Cavalry. It was quite a minor blockage he had with his scene and Eric was easy to help; all one did was suggest a line and Eric immediately thought of a better one; it was just a matter of stimulating his own creativity into action.

Our contract allowed us to take a respite from advising and

consulting when a new series of *Whack-O!* was due to be written. When that happened we pinned a card on our door saying 'IN PURDAH' and all the members of Light Entertainment scrupulously left us to get on with our writing undisturbed, unconsulted, advice unsought.

With one exception.

Our Head of Light Entertainment Group (Television) was Eric Maschwitz, author of a great many successful plays, revues (including *New Faces* and *Between Ourselves*), musicals (*Good Night, Vienna; Balalaika; Zip Goes a Million; Carissima, Song of Norway*), Hollywood musical films, and just a handful of songs which our generation cherished as icons of romantic wistful love, of elegance and charm: 'Room 504', 'A Nightingale Sang in Berkeley Square', and best of all, 'These Foolish Things'.

Denis always used to say that if he had written 'These Foolish Things' he would have instantly retired on the grounds that no man should be expected to contribute anything more to the public stock of harmless pleasure.

The lyric had an awkward rhyming scheme because 'things' is difficult to rhyme interestingly, but a contestant in an early *New Statesman* competition for parodies of 'These Foolish Things', even though he borrowed 'clings' from Eric, deserves an honourable mention:

> The smell of cooking close to Earls Court Station,
> Your rabbit curry and then – eructation.
> Oh, how your vol-au-vent clings,
> These foolish things,
> Remind me of you . . .

In purdah Denis and I produced our scripts sitting either side of a desk with our feet on it. We would talk out each line and commit it to paper when it seemed about right.

Eric Maschwitz would occasionally join us. He would just walk into the room and sit down without speaking, clearly escaping from some managerial ennui. He would put his feet up on the desk with ours and sit in happy silence for a while, no jacket, bright crimson braces like streaks of blood on his shirt, nervously pushing his thin hair aside. He was tall, pale and bony. Not bony like a kipper, but like a normal skeleton which has not been given quite enough flesh to cover it comfortably. Then he would reminisce.

Those were most enjoyable interludes for Den and me because Eric was perhaps the last of the great romantics.

'I had a mistress in those days who was a ballet dancer with the Vienna Opera.' (Mistress! Vienna! Ballet dancer with the opera!) 'On one occasion I flew over to Vienna and had a wholly delightful weekend. On the Monday morning, a shade hung-over, I was in a taxi on the way to the airport when I glanced out of the back window and saw that we were being closely followed by a large Alsatian dog pedalling a bicycle with a pipe in his mouth.

'This was unnerving and I almost gave up champagne and the Vienna *corps de ballet* there and then, but the bicycle passed us at a traffic light and I saw that it was actually being pedalled by a small Viennese man in a cap, hidden from our view by his huge Alsatian dog which he had sat in the basket on the handlebars. I am happy to say that I have no idea how the dog came to be smoking a pipe. Some mysteries should never be explained, should they?'

On another occasion, in through the door he strolled, pulled up a chair and arranged his feet comfortably on our desk (now rather crowded with feet and pages of the script we were trying to work on). Scrape, scrape, scrape sideways of hair, then: 'I had this idea for a book, a compilation, which I would call *My Most Memorable Sexual Encounter*.' (The last two words are, of course, a euphemism of the single word which Eric used.)

Eric went on, 'My own contribution would be set during the war when I was in Intelligence and doing a course of something furtive at Woburn Abbey. I was spending most evenings steadily trying to seduce a Wren officer, a delightful creature with promisingly wicked eyes. Eventually, on a beautiful evening after dinner, I took her for a walk in the grounds. Trees and long grass and moonlight. We lay down and I undressed her. With her black silk stockings and white thighs it was like peeling a nut. We were in the middle of pleasure when the ground began to shake.

'"Is the earth moving for you?" she whispered.

'"Yes. But it really *is* moving!" I said. "It feels like a charging bison!"

'Which is what it was. We had strayed into the zoo area of Woburn Park and several tons of angry bison was thundering on its way to deal with us. —

'This was coitus interruptus on an operatic scale. My Wren lady and I semi-dressed in haste and scrambled to safety clutching bits of clothing, all passion spent and never, of course – it never can be – rekindled.'

Another day, with rain pelting down outside, Eric dropped in to tell us about a wartime experience of rain in Regent Street. It was nearly midnight on a warm summer's evening and he, like the few people around at that time, was wearing light clothes. Suddenly down came torrential rain. Eric found shelter in the portico of Aquascutum Ltd. A pretty girl scampered in, an evening paper held over her head to protect her hair and make-up. Eric made way for her so that she could be at the back of the alcove in the dry while he kept watch on Regent Street for a cab. The pretty girl thanked Eric in a Scottish accent for moving and he immediately began to wonder whether a romantic interlude might not be on with this sweet little thing.

A taxi eventually came along with its light on and Eric shot out into the rain waving his arms. The taxi stopped for him. Eric ran back into the alcove and said to the girl, 'Come on, I've got a taxi. Where can I take you?'

'I canna leave here, thank you, kind sir,' said the girl.

'Why on earth not?' said Eric.

She said, 'I'm a wee whore.'

At the regular Light Entertainment Group meetings Eric was terrific value and a fine raiser of morale; he called his eighteen or so producers and their retinues 'my ragged army' and was funny as well as critical in his rundown of the group's activities. As far as we knew he was managing the department extremely well.

Another endearing aspect of Eric as an administrator was that he invented nicknames for many of us. Rather shrill and noisy guitar-playing groups from South America were popular visiting acts at that time and Eric's name for Denis and me was 'Los Layabouts', Dennis Main Wilson was 'Dr Sinister' and Graeme Muir (no relation), a smooth, grey-haired producer of middle-class sitcoms, was 'our resident gynaecologist'.

When considering Eric Maschwitz's achievements in the musical theatre and in Hollywood, and the romantic songs he wrote, it is easy to think of him as a brilliant freelance wit who had drifted into the BBC by accident after the war, but in fact he was an old BBC pro. He had a youthful spell in magazine editing after university and then joined the BBC way back in 1926 (when I was aged six). He edited the *Radio Times* from 1927 to 1933, was a director of radio variety from 1933 to 1937, and after a wartime career in Intelligence and as the architect of forces broadcasting, returned to the bosom of the BBC in 1958 as Head of Light Entertainment (Television).

BBC's Light Entertainment was unique in having a Head who, if he wanted a musical show and couldn't find one he liked, was perfectly capable of writing one himself. Which actually happened while we were there. It was for the August bank holiday. Eric wanted the bank holiday Monday evening's viewing to be built round a happy, very English musical comedy but no suitable script could be found, so Eric sat down with his flat little portable typewriter and tapped one out. It was a musical play which told of a village squire (played by Jimmy Edwards, who led the singing of the champagne finale, 'Fizz, Fizz, Fizz'), and the plots and machinations which resulted in the village, for the first time in its history, winning the annual cricket match against the wealthy neighbouring village's team of weekenders from London.

Eric Maschwitz's assistant, Tom Sloan, was neither a writer nor a producer but a good professional manager. Tom was a rather military figure who had been in the Royal Artillery during the war and had volunteered to become a glider pilot, one of the most dangerous jobs of the war.

The change in management method when Eric left to go on to other things and Tom became Head of Light Entertainment was dramatic. At the first departmental meeting Tom welcomed us all and then said, 'This department has a lot of work to do and we are all professionals so you can forget any "ragged army" nonsense.'

Tom Sloan was keen on things which he felt were due to him like 'discipline' and 'loyalty', but he was professionally adroit at winning money for his Light Entertainment Group from the controllers. He was strict on producers keeping to their budgets and he tried hard to maintain the old Reithean strictures on free thought and language. Like a company chairman who in his career will move smoothly from one company to another and control the destinies of, say, an airline, followed by the manufacture of pills, and then the running of the Royal Ballet, Tom's real interest lay not in the product but in the management of it.

Eric Maschwitz, on the other hand, loved romantic music and

wit and fun and he was much more than the Head of Light Entertainment Group, he was its leader. But then Eric had written 'These Foolish Things'.

Arranging *Whack-O!* for live production in the Shepherd's Bush Empire presented some severe strictures which were no doubt good for our souls, as most things troublesome are claimed to be. There were usually some six to eight scenes in the half-hour show and the programme was performed non-stop on a theatre stage which was a much smaller area than a studio floor.

Dougie Moodie's method was to have a black curtain hung to divide the stage into two halves. Each half had a black front curtain to close it off from the audience's view so as not to distract them when a scene was being changed. The most used scene, the headmaster's study, permanently occupied the left-hand half of the stage, and while a scene was being played in it the right-hand half would be closed off by the curtain and the stage staff would rapidly, and as quietly as possible, set the furniture and props for the next scene. Backstage visitors of a religious disposition would occasionally be discomposed by seeing a large sign reading, 'Have You Got Soft Soles?'

Our responsibility was to write the scenes in Jimmy's study so that they lasted long enough for the scene-shifters to change the other half of the stage; to quote one actual requirement, 'From Lower Fourth's dormitory to a table in the Savoy Grill.'

A live production also raised problems for the actors, such as the peril of eating peanuts. It was quite usual to have a party scene where the actors enjoyed nibbling a salted peanut or two; the problem was that a nut does not disappear entirely when eaten as does a Smartie or a potato crisp. True, the peanuts are ground by the molars into tiny fragments, most of which are harmlessly swallowed down, but a few of them lurk in the dark caverns between the teeth and work their way out later and demand to be chewed smaller. Or worse still, tiny fragments drop down onto a tonsil and demand to be removed, which can only be done by the actor making short high barking coughs.

We first hit the problem when, ignorant of the Peanut Peril, we wrote a scene depicting a staff party in the headmaster's study. Jimmy poured tiny glasses of British sherry for the staff, then went to a globe of the world, opened a hatch in it and pulled out a bottle of whisky.

'There's always something new out of Africa!' he said and poured himself half a tumblerful. 'Cheers!'

Salted peanuts were passed round, thrown up and caught in the teeth and hurled about. Jimmy tossed a handful into his mouth and munched.

A caption card came up on the screen announcing, 'TWO WEEKS LATER'.

We then cut to the other half of the stage to show the drawing room of a noble prospective parent, Lord Portly. The butler ushered in the headmaster who bowed in a grovelly manner.

'Good morning, oh Lord. How gracious of you to grant me a few moments or two of your time to discuss how your elder son – the one with the ginger hair – did in his entrance exam to Chiselbury. By a happy provenance he scraped in. With marks of ninety-nine out of a possible hundred.'

Jimmy unknowingly chewed vagrant fragments of peanut throughout this speech, every now and then putting a handkerchief to his mouth and giving the high-pitched, throat-clearing bark.

Jimmy was rarely fazed by things going wrong during a live transmission, even peanut fragments on the epiglottis. It was often a chance for him to ad lib, such as in the scene of a later programme when the local tax inspector went through the school accounts, tut-tutting, until he came across something deeply suspicious. He put his spectacles down on the desk and rubbed his eyes in a tired manner before resuming his inspection. In the script it said:

> (*While the inspector is rubbing his eyes and cannot see what is going on, Jimmy picks up the whole telephone, reaches across the desk and bangs the telephone down on the inspector's spectacles, breaking the lenses. He picks up the specs, hands the ruins to the now half-blind inspector and says:*)

HEADMASTER: I'm so sorry, I seem to have accidentally dented your spectacles.

On the live performance Jimmy picked up the phone and gave the specs a good thump, but nothing happened to them, so he gave them another thump. Nothing. A couple more thumps. The spectacles showed no sign of injury. The audience was now beginning to appreciate Jimmy's predicament and enjoying it. Mortarboard and gown now askew, tie twisted, clearly sweating, Jimmy thumped the specs all over the desk and finally, exasperated, raised the phone set up in both hands and brought it down with a tremendous bang onto the specs. He picked them up. At last they were twisted and bent and the plastic lenses were broken.

The audience burst into a round of applause.

HEADMASTER: (*Holding out the little mass of twisted wire and bits of plastic to the inspector:*) I'm so sorry, I seem to have accidentally dented your spectacles.

It was a good moment.

Whack-O!, starring Jimmy and Arthur Howard, became an established success, and in 1960 a feature film was made of it called *Bottoms Up*, written up from our scripts by our good friend Michael Pertwee. It was a modest success, but nevertheless a success. *Bottoms Up* can still occasionally be seen on afternoon television when the channel is in need of a filler.

But the film marked a sudden and sad crisis. Arthur Howard was arrested for 'cottaging', the slang word used to describe anonymous homosexual encounters, usually with 'rough trade', in a public convenience.

After a week on remand in Brixton Prison, Arthur came up before the magistrates. Denis and I offered to speak on his behalf and to stand security for his future good behaviour.

The solemn process of the law was not helped by Denis and me trying to enter the small witness box side by side and getting jammed. We broke free to muffled tittering.

The clerk of the court spoke up, 'Are you able to stand surety of one hundred pounds each for the accused's good behaviour over the next six months?'

The court rang with our sincere and confident cries of, 'Oh, yes! And only too happy to, your worships!'

The clerk of the court continued, 'And are you able to stand surety for one hundred pounds each *when all your debts are paid*?'

Our confident cries were replaced by an embarrassed hush.

'Er – yes, sir,' we eventually mumbled. Arthur was fined £50 and put on surety for good behaviour for six months.

Polly and I insisted on Arthur coming down to Anners to convalesce for a week or two and this was a success.

Sally, not yet at boarding school, was entranced by Arthur's ineptitude with his breakfast egg. An adult unable to cope with a boiled egg! Arthur mishit his egg with his spoon, and yolk and white of egg besmirched the tablecloth in huge spots and streaks. We were all astonished at how much egg there was in an egg; it was a lively topic of conversation for weeks.

Arthur's particular homosexual inclination had no connection whatsoever with corrupting young boys, but nevertheless the BBC thought that he could not continue to work in a television series featuring a young cast. So Arthur had to go, and *Whack-O!* had to come to an end.

Jimmy was furious and unforgiving. His successful show had been abruptly ended by what he saw as Arthur's selfish and stupid behaviour.

The ultimate irony was that two decades later, when Jimmy was spending part of each year in Australia, his young male friend of that time revealed to an English tabloid newspaper (for a hefty sum of money) that he was Jimmy's lover and Jimmy was, and always had been, homosexual. Jimmy said at the time, 'I did not "come out", I was booted through the door.'

And so Pol and I offered another colleague and old friend a refuge with us, but in Jimmy's case it was not necessary. He was rehearsing for a pantomime and Arthur Askey and the rest of the cast were understanding and reassuring.

Jimmy's real pleasures were riding to hounds and playing polo, and he was afraid that his county friends would be deeply re-actionary and would no longer even speak to him. But to his great relief he was wrong; his horsey friends were superbly uninterested in his private life. And to the general public, too, the startling revelation that Jimmy Edwards was homosexual passed almost unnoticed. People couldn't believe, or didn't want to believe, that Pa Glum was gay.

Arthur Howard talked to Polly and me about his week on remand in Brixton Prison. His colleagues awaiting trial were mostly thieves and case-hardened, grievous-bodily-harm regulars – Arthur's closest friend for the week had been accused of stabbing his girlfriend in the cheek with a pair of scissors – but they quickly recognized that Arthur was not a threat but a kindly gent in an unfamiliar situation which was only too familiar to them. They protected him, easing his way through the ugly prison regime with such kindnesses as making sure that he had first shave with the morning's communal razor blade while it was still sharp.

Every morning Arthur scoured the newspapers with us for reports on how his new friends had fared when they came up in court. Breakfast would be punctuated by sudden cries from Arthur of, 'Oh, no! They've given Rocky the Horror three months! Just for hitting a Manchester United fan with a fire extinguisher.' Or, 'Oh good! Mick's case was dismissed. He accidentally set fire to his son's school while wiring up the staffroom tea urn. I think he was guilty, but he was very good to me so I'm glad he got away with it.'

A treasury of anecdotes illustrating Arthur's inability to cope with ordinary life could have been compiled.

One weekend he brought his wife, the actress Jean Compton, and their infant son Alan, down to us at Thorpe for Sunday lunch. Arthur was buzzing along happily in their little Morris when halfway up Egham Hill the steering wheel came off in his hands. He turned round in his seat and waved the wheel at Jean, crying, 'Jean, look, the steering wheel's come off!'

'Well, put it back *on*!' said Jean. Which he promptly did.

Next day, when he had the steering wheel checked at a garage, an awed mechanic revealed to him that on that particular model of car the steering wheel was not on a spline but, like an interchangeable camera lens, could only be fitted back in one position. Arthur and his family had avoided crashing by a 1 in 365 chance.

In London one evening, Arthur was walking a little ahead of Jean along Jermyn Street when a lady of the night stepped out of a doorway and murmured enticingly to Arthur, 'Hello, darling!'

Arthur, with his usual impeccable good manners, raised his hat in case she was a family friend he hadn't recognized and said with his warm smile and beautiful voice, '*Hello*! How lovely to see you again . . . !'

Jean accelerated and grabbed his arm: 'Oh, come on, you fool!'

Then Arthur's brief good fortune began to leak away. Jean died and Arthur no longer had his beloved minder to stop him tripping over so many of life's broken paving stones.

Arthur's personal problem seems to have been that he was the least successful duckling of a highly successful brood of achievers. His parents were European refugees originally named Steiner (later Stainer). His elder brother Leslie became a matinée idol of the stage, then an actor and director in films, famously playing Ashley in *Gone with the Wind*.

As Arthur grew up, his mother constantly prodded him to be more like Leslie. 'Why don't you smoke a pipe like Leslie? It's manly.' 'Why don't you read more? Leslie always has a book in his hand.' The consequence of all this, of course, was that Arthur never smoked a pipe and hardly ever read a book.

His sister Dorice Stainer had a successful dancing academy in Ascot and taught dancing at local schools, and his other sister Irene Howard was the casting director for MGM films in England.

Jean also had distinguished relations. Her uncle was the novelist Compton Mackenzie – she was his favourite niece – and her aunt was the actress Fay Compton. Moreover, Arthur's son Alan and his nephew Ronald ('Wink') were both leading actors.

One day Arthur explained to Polly and me what to him was the point of cottaging. At a smart dinner party, where everybody there was more talented and had achieved more in the theatre than he could ever have hoped to do, he would make an excuse, slip away and do his cottaging. And when he returned to the party, he was 'somebody' for an hour or two. He had a secret. He knew something they did not know.

It does seem a pity that life was not just a little kinder to dear harmless Arthur; he was kindness itself.

After the demise of *Whack-O!* Denis and I wrote quite a few series for BBC TV during the late Fifties and early Sixties, including an adaptation of Henry Cecil's book, *Brothers-in-Law*, which did for barristers what Richard Gordon's *Doctor in the House* had done for medics.

I had been impressed by a young actor, Richard Briers, whom I had seen a year or so previously in Lionel Hale's stage play *Guilt and Gingerbread*. Denis agreed he was right and we persuaded Richard Briers to play the young barrister hero. This was, I think, his first starring role on TV.

We had another fortunate piece of casting when one episode required our pupil barrister to settle into digs and come to terms with an awkward landlady. The landlady turned out to be difficult to cast, and then Denis remembered a remarkable performance he had seen in Joan Littlewood's musical, *Fings Ain't Wot They Used To Be*. The actress had never worked in television and was terrified of it; Denis had to spend many hours persuading her that she would be right for the part and there was nothing for her to be afraid of. She eventually agreed and so began the brilliant television career of Yootha Joyce.

Henry Cecil was our co-writer on the series and vetted our stuff for legal plausibility as well as contributing story ideas and dialogue. Henry was a County Court judge (His Honour Judge Henry Cecil Leon), but he also wrote light amusing novels and plays based on crimes and courts. His sense of character was almost non-existent. Most of his cast seemed to have been cut out of living cardboard and they all spoke in the same kind of amusing, exact, witty way in which Henry himself spoke (except for an occasional 'blimey' when the character was a burglar). But as with Agatha Christie, none of this mattered. His plots were ingenious, absorbing and, above all, amusing, the stories rattled along and the books were enjoyed by a large readership.

He used to come to see us at Television Centre after his day in court, driving himself in a no-longer-young Jaguar car and Denis and I would rush him to the BBC club bar where he would enjoy two large, bone-dry Martinis. He told us, 'I'm one of those lucky people. My body tells me when I have had enough.'

Denis whispered to me, 'He slumps to the floor.'

But Henry did nothing unseemly; he was a very good husband, an unpredictable judge (which always disturbs barristers and keeps them on their toes) and a keen writer. And Henry had another rare gift: a genius for hospitality. He loved entertaining and would go to immense pains to make every occasion, from a dinner party to a sandwich, a memorable pleasure.

He invited Polly to sit as his guest on the bench of his court to hear a case (which is apparently a quite acceptable practice) and later invited us both to the first night of one of his plays, *Alibi for a Judge* (Henry wrote an earlier play, *Settled Out of Court*, in collaboration with the Californian/Armenian writer of impetuous, impressionistic prose, William Saroyan; a sobering thought). Our evening began with a drink and smoked salmon sandwiches in Henry's chambers, then on to his play at the Savoy Theatre. Champagne was provided by Henry in the interval, and after the play Polly and I strolled across to the Savoy Hotel for a late supper with the Cecils. A lovely way to spend an evening.

Denis and I found we had a taste for writing about the law (Henry thought we would have made excellent solicitors but dodgy judges) so we followed *Brothers-in-Law* with a new series we devised to tell legal stories from the point of view of the judge. We called the series *Mr Justice Duncannon*.

The idea was partly inspired by the actor we wanted to play our judge, Andrew Cruickshank. Andrew had played a judge for us previously and he was tremendously effective; the beetling brows, the craggy features, the Scots accent, the teasing humour. Henry Cecil was our legal adviser. The series was more light drama than sitcom, but won respectable figures and did its job.

After some 'how-about?' and 'what-if?' sessions, Denis and I settled on writing a new series of seven entirely different programmes, single comic plays really, starring Jimmy Edwards and similar to the parody dramas which were the popular last section of *Take It From Here*. We called the new series *The Seven Faces of Jim*.

Each show had its own subtitle, e.g., *The Face of Power*. That one had Jim as a ruthless Victorian manufacturer of gas mantles with a troublesome labour force (shop steward Ronnie Barker) and a beautiful daughter (June Whitfield). Just when Jim emerged triumphantly as the King of Gas Mantles, some young engineer developed a form of street lighting based on something called electricity . . .

Another of the shows was a topical story based on the first appearance on our streets of minicabs. The story was a parody of aspects of the film *A Matter of Life and Death*, treating minicabs as RAF planes.

Jimmy played the grizzled old wing commander who, now demobbed, had one battered minicab driven by a David Nivenish Richard Briers. June played the girl dispatcher on the microphone who was in love with Richard Briers (as in the film). There was thick fog (as in the film) and Briers was talked safely home by June (as in the film). Her directions over the microphone were so accurate in bringing him safely home that, exactly on time, the minicab crashed through the brick wall of the minicab office and came to rest a few inches from June (not in the film).

The Screenwriters' Guild of Great Britain decided that year to institute an annual ball and present its own professional awards for film and television writing. Denis and I won the first of these. It was a heavy bronze plaque (each), inscribed:

'SEVEN FACES OF JIM'
THE BEST WORK IN BRITISH TELEVISION
LIGHT ENTERTAINMENT SERIES
1961

We wrote another series for Jimmy Edwards called *Six More Faces of Jim* which was gratifyingly successful with viewers (though was not brilliant enough for the Screenwriters' Guild to give us another bronze plaque), and then our four years at the BBC was up and we went back to working in our eyrie high above Conduit Street.

We devised and wrote several sitcom series, including *The Big Noise*, starring Bob Monkhouse as a brash disc jockey, but we found a restlessness setting in. We had been writing together now for seventeen years – writing *everything* together – and our joint product was not a Muir and Norden script so much as a Muirandnorden script, with predictable qualities and weaknesses. There was a good enough demand for the product, but we were getting on a bit as far as comedy writers were concerned – comedy writers were supposed to last ten years – and we had begun to wonder whether there was still an untapped Denis Norden style, or Frank Muir style, which had been muffled by the success of the Muirandnorden magimix.

For one thing Denis, who was interested in all aspects of the cinema, really wanted to write films, which I did not. Making films was a bit too much of a committee operation for me, I wanted to write books.

The fates were kind and we moved relatively smoothly into our solo careers. Denis, through Michael Pertwee, with whom he collaborated on a number of films, met and got on well with an independent American comedy writer turned film producer, Mel Frank. A number of successful films resulted, which Den co-wrote, and he later wrote an original screenplay which was filmed. It was called *The Best House In London*.

When my family was away on holiday I spent a weekend with Johnny Johnson, ex-music publisher and leader of The Keynotes singing group (and sometime wearer in the South of France of papier mâché inner soles made of £5 notes: see chapter nine). Johnny's old music publishing partner, young Bill Cotton, was there. Young Bill, after producing many musical programmes for TV, including his father's, had become a rising figure in the BBC staff hierarchy and was now Assistant Head of Light Entertainment, Tom Sloan's number two.

During the weekend I told young Bill that Den and I were going to have a try at finding out whether we had anything worthwhile left to contribute individually, and Den was now happily into films.

A week later Tom Sloan asked for a meeting. It seemed that the Light Entertainment Group at Television Centre needed a bit of reorganizing because the Assistant Head of Light Entertainment, young Bill Cotton, was a tower of strength where pop music and variety programmes were concerned – and there were a lot of them about at that time (musical shows starring Yana, Ruby Murray, Alma Cogan, Petula Clark, and also *The Black and White Minstrel Show*, *Wakey Wakey!* etc., etc.) – but Bill was less experienced where words were concerned and was overworked. The Head of Television, Kenneth Adam, had proposed that the job of Assistant Head of Light Entertainment should be split in two, and that young Bill should be Assistant Head (Variety) and a new post, Assistant Head (Comedy), should be created. And as young Bill had said that I was available, I should be offered the new job.

I happily accepted; it was the answer to many immediate problems. A devious three-year contract was then haggled over which resulted in my remaining a freelance but 'devoting as much time as was necessary' to do the job (in reality twenty-five hours a day). By this means I could continue doing *My Word!* and *My Music* with Denis for BBC radio, plus the odd commercial.

My first day at Television Centre. The new office smells I would soon get used to; the strangeness of the details of a new environment, e.g., the little slip pasted above the light switch in the loo reading 'PLEASE SWITCH OFF WHEN NOT IN USE'. (?)

I enjoyed the rather tremulous excitement of arriving to take up the first real job I had ever had. I was aged forty-six. But I had no experience whatever of managing anything, not even a car boot sale, and I did not know anybody's name, or far worse, the initials of their jobs on which the whole infrastructure of BBC communications was based, as David Attenborough discovered when he became Controller of the second channel and his wife Jane was greeted at a BBC reception by a keen young man saying, 'How nice that you could come, Mrs C-BBC2.'

I was AHLEG(C)TEL, a slight abbreviation of Assistant Head of Light Entertainment Group (Comedy) Television, which I never used if it was humanly possible not to. It seemed sensible to find an assistant who did know the BBC codes and how the corporation managerial machine actually functioned and let him get on with it, and I had just such a man as my unit manager, an ex-cameraman named Bob Gilbraith who was totally competent at organizing everything.

Penny Sparshott, the secretary Denis and I so prized during our period as advisers (Penny had grown too tall to remain a ballet dancer and was not only beautiful but beautifully competent), had left the BBC. I had to search for a secretary and found the splendid Helen Morton, who proved very good at organizing me. Helen was a talented girl and could well have been a producer, but she sang in the Philharmonia choir, which was very important to her, so at that time she needed as near to a nine-to-five job as she could find.

I had a Script Department along the corridor to read submitted scripts and report to me, write their own shows and generally advise. It occurred to me that they did much the same job that Den and I had once done. This Script Department consisted of two fine and good writers who became my close friends: John Law, a small neat Scot, who was more valuable a co-writer to Michael Bentine than has been acknowledged; he died tragically young. His colleague was the great (in all senses, a barrage balloon in size) Richard Waring.

Richard, brother of the actor Derek Waring and brother-in-law of Dorothy Tutin, really wanted to open his own restaurant and cook all day, or do conjuring tricks, or collect very tatty horror films involving things rising out of swamps, but instead became the writer who, as much as anybody, made middle-class comedy work on television. Previously, most sitcoms featured comically stupid working-class characters or comically stupid aristos, but Waring made ordinary, educated, middle-class people funny in a number of highly successful series, particularly with *Marriage Lines* (starring Richard Briers and Prunella Scales), a bitter-sweet comedy of a young married couple whose relationship was not going all that well (as in Richard Waring's own marriage).

One morning he found himself sharing the lift with Tom Sloan. To break the silence, Richard blurted out, 'John Law and I have been making anagrams of all our names. In the seventeenth century it was used as a kind of character analysis. An anagram of a person's name was supposed to indicate what sort of person he was . . .'

Tom turned and looked at him steadily. Richard wilted but knew that having started he had to finish.

'You came out "Nola Smot",' he said.

My status in the BBC was that of medium-rare management, entitled to park on the gravel forecourt of Television Centre (an important privilege) and to attend the Wednesday morning programme review meeting when all the heads and assistant heads met and rubbished each other's shows.

I could never treat the meetings very seriously and tended to pass remarks. Such as when they were building an extension to Television Centre and our meeting was punctuated by sundry loud and rhythmic bangs. I said to Kenneth Adam, 'Sir, as the knocking outside the meeting is now louder than the knocking *inside* the meeting, should we not adjourn?'

Peter Dimmock, then Head of Sport, made a point of sitting at the bottom of the long table and while others were talking and arguing would conspicuously busy himself sorting papers from a briefcase and signing things, the image of an efficient executive to whom every second was precious. One Wednesday morning when the meeting had guests from abroad I could not find a seat. Eventually I found a spare chair and Peter shifted his briefcase and papers and made way for me to sit beside him at the bottom of the table. When a point on light entertainment arose, the chairman, Kenneth Adam, peered round the table looking for me. 'Is Frank here?' he said.

I piped up, 'Yes, sir, Peter Dimmock has kindly allowed me to sit in his office.'

We were all given copies of the current *Radio Times* to ponder upon. In one meeting I was glancing idly through my copy when I noticed the subtitle of a gardening programme. 'Excuse me, sir,' I said with youthful eagerness to our chairman, who was half listening to a boring argument about studio lighting, '*Radio Times*, sir. Wednesday, seven forty-five p.m., sir. *Gardener's World*. The title of one of the items would make an excellent, sensitive "Wednesday play" about a young couple's tragic inability to fit into the social system: *Tomatoes in a Cold Greenhouse*.'

I was alloted a large office previously occupied by Tom Sloan, who moved a couple of doors along the corridor to a suite of offices in which he could house his staff. I rearranged my furniture and signed for a small coffee table with some comfortable chairs round it so that I could sit and talk to writers and producers on the same level rather than have them stand at my desk.

On my very first day a very important matter of privilege and seniority arose. Tom was Head of Light Entertainment Group and I was only Assistant Head. The head of a group was entitled to a wall-to-wall carpet, an assistant head was not, and my office still had Tom's wall-to-wall carpet.

On my third day in Television Centre, two men in long brown coats came into my office and cut a foot off the carpet.

Chapter Twelve

'DREST IN A LITTLE BRIEF AUTHORITY'

The loneliness of command proved to be non-existent once I had settled in at Television Centre. I often longed for a bit of it.

My door was usually open into the next room, which housed Bob Gilbraith and helpers, and Helen, when they were not in my office chatting, and Tom (Nola) Sloan was through a door on the other side. Tom rarely came in, but when he was having an important meeting with a comedian and wild laughter rang out, I rather enjoyed knocking, putting my head round the door and muttering things like, 'Could you keep the noise down please, some of us here are trying to get some sleep.' And hardly a day passed of my three happy years there when the diary was not liberally sprinkled with meetings, many of them with agents hoping to sell a client. I tried to see them all. However hopeless their mission, it seemed to me that as they had to make a forty-five minute journey out to Shepherd's Bush and then back again, they were entitled to thirty minutes of AHLEG(C)TEL's time.

In the BBC it was customary for the producer of a comedy show also to be its director so that he was solely responsible for the whole thing; it was his baby (in ITV the responsibilities were separated, I think because producers and directors were represented by different unions). So when a BBC producer of comedy ran into a problem he brought his baby to me.

Jimmy Gilbert was a most able producer, who later ran the

242

department and then moved from the BBC to ITV (most of the good producers, Jimmy Gilbert, Duncan Wood, Graeme Muir, Michael Mills, John Howard Davies, etc., eventually ended up at ITV because retirement from the BBC was compulsory at sixty and they could then prolong their careers a few more years by joining one of the commercial stations). Jimmy rang me and said that he had a problem. He was producing an enjoyable series featuring two old men who argued with each other and yet needed each other; it was called *The Walrus and the Carpenter*. Jimmy's problem was that one of his old actors, well-known for enjoying a nip or two, was now taking a nip or two too many and it was beginning to show. Could sir have a quiet admonitory word with the actor?

There was a civilized system whereby a head of department could have a working lunch in his office. An impressive trolley was wheeled in with a range of bottles and glasses, food such as cold salmon mayonnaise was laid out and there was coffee in a thermos. But there was an uncivilized aspect to it: the head's guests at lunch could only be artistes or writers or agents; BBC personnel could not be invited. So I had to fumble my way through my meeting with the actor without Jimmy Gilbert.

I did my best. I appealed to the actor's professionalism; the bad effect he was having on the rest of the cast, etc. No threats, no cajoling. I felt quietly confident that with a bit of luck he would go easier on the sauce from now on after our meeting. When he left to go back to rehearsals he thanked me and shook my hand vigorously.

An hour later, Jimmy Gilbert phoned from the outside rehearsal rooms. 'What on earth did you say to him?' asked Jimmy.

'I just tried to give him confidence to overcome his little problem,' I said modestly. 'Why?'

Jimmy said, 'I stopped on the way back to get petrol and he was out of the car in a flash and into a pub. We're supposed to be rehearsing and I can't get him out of the saloon bar.'

When I first sat at my imposing desk I explored it and found it quite empty except for one lower drawer which contained a small, neatly folded white napkin and a tiny sliver of soap. What were they there for? They seemed a trifle sinister, perhaps to be used in some obscure BBC religious rite. To give thanks when *Songs of Praise* got a better viewing figure than ITV's *Stars on Sunday*? An unlikely event as *Stars on Sunday* had such spiritual and aesthetic delights as plump pink Jesse Yates – Paula's daddy – playing viewers' request hymns on a small electric organ, a huge choir dressed as nuns with glamorous make-up, and celebrities reading the lesson in a scarlet leather wing chair by the side of a (gas) log fire, flanked by rows of eighteenth-century books hired from Books By The Yard.

We seniors had our own dining room with our own waitresses, one of them very Welsh. Huw Wheldon, then Controller of Programmes, used to stride in with vigour and order his lunch in fluent Welsh, which we all thought a bit much, but very Huw. One always hoped to find Young Bill Cotton – AHLEG(V)TEL – having lunch there because he, like Huw, was full of good talk and was a most welcome sight when other production heads were too occupied elsewhere; one could fall amongst administrators.

Gents' suiting in the senior dining room was sombre as in a gentlemen's club, particularly that worn by the administrators. These were decent, amusing fellows who tended to sit together, a little non-riot of dark-grey suits, domestically knitted grey woollen socks and very large black shoes. *Very* large black shoes. There has never been a recorded case of a BBC administrator blowing over in a high wind.

I was acceptable to begin with because my workaday suit was an austere dark green, a tweed fabric seemingly woven from mature spinach. But I tended to do a little light carpentry and house painting in it and not wear a raincoat during showers, so the suit developed a pong. While it was at the dry-cleaner's I made do with dark-grey flannel trousers and a sombre sports jacket with an almost invisible check. On my first entry into the senior dining room wearing this muted ensemble I was greeted by one of the admin group with, 'Hello, Muir, going racing?'

For the first few months I did not have to grub about from scratch to find a whole new schedule of comedy shows, my job to begin with was more to take over and extend the programmes which Bill Cotton had initiated and which were doing well. The comedy series which I think Bill was most proud of having helped to start was Peter Cook and Dudley Moore's *Not Only . . . But Also*.

Peter and Dudley's method of working was strongly reminiscent of the old radio show *In All Directions* with Peter Ustinov and

Peter Jones. Both Peter Cook and Peter Ustinov were bottomless wells of comedy invention, preferably expressed ad lib, and Peter Jones and Dudley Moore made them excellent partners, both far more than 'foils' or 'straight men'.

I went over to Paris where Peter Ustinov was editing a film, and persuaded him to do an *In All Directions* on television with Peter Jones. There was no scenery or costumes. In one sketch Ustinov played a fat American speed cop. He asked the props department for an armchair fitted with good castors, and in the sketch it became his motorbike. He propelled it about the stage with his legs making motorbike and siren noises, and then went into a marvellous accent, brow-beating the unfortunate Peter Jones, an English tourist he had caught speeding.

The final sketch in the radio series was always some swindle attempted by the two Peters playing Morry and Dud, tatty 1950s spivs (the last line of the sketch always ended with Ustinov whispering hoarsely to Jones, 'Morry?' 'Yes, Dud?' 'Run for it!').

The early Sixties was, of course, the period when a breakthrough was made in the language and subject matter considered acceptable in BBC TV. This relaxing of strictures was greeted with delight by progressive liberal minds and with horror by 'Disgusted of Tunbridge Wells' (who was, incidentally, an off-stage character in *Take It From Here*, played by Wallas Eaton).

Those citizens who hankered after the old values were organized into a group by Mrs Mary Whitehouse, an ex-teacher who believed that the BBC rules of censorship as laid down in the *Green Book* all those years previously should be treated as Holy Writ and strictly adhered to. Mrs Whitehouse's reason for nipping at the heels of the BBC seems to have been her belief that the BBC, under its progressively minded director-general Hugh Greene, was to blame for failing to hold back progress and not sticking to Sir John Reith's bleak, granite-like, 1920s-style morality (e.g., no variety programmes or dance music to be broadcast on Sundays).

She thought, overdoing her zeal perhaps, that Hugh Carleton Greene, by supporting such important innovative shows as *That Was The Week That Was* was 'the man who, above all, was responsible for the moral collapse which characterized the Sixties and Seventies.'

Hugh Greene's way of coping with Mrs Whitehouse's attempted

censorship of not only BBC programmes, but also contemporary books and plays in general, was to keep her at arm's length, not recognizing her officially nor replying to her publicly.

I had a slight but much more amicable brush with the DG (oh, those BBC initials) early on in my BBC contract.

After a holiday abroad I returned to find a general election about to happen and the television schedules polluted with party political broadcasts. Incensed by these (and I take a bit of incensing) I wrote a letter to *The Times*, which they printed. I wrote:

Sir, when I was at school and we were coming up to the end-of-term exams I wrote a letter to my headmaster (in brown ink for some reason, which angered him) and gave it as my view that if the purpose of an exam was to test how much information and wisdom had penetrated our natural defences, then swotting to pass the exam was a form of cheating. The Head did not feel able to fall in with this theory, but I believe there is truth in it. By the same reasoning I believe that we should vote for a political party on its proven record not on wild promises for the future made in party political broadcasts which the party has a snowflake's chance in hell of fulfilling. Thus party political broadcasts are quite clearly only another form of cheating.

What I did not know, as I had just returned from abroad, was that a few days earlier the DG had written a keynote letter to the papers saying how important party political broadcasts on television were to the political health of our democracy. What I also did not know, or had forgotten, was that BBC employees were strictly forbidden to write letters to newspapers expressing their personal views on television and political matters.

A memo emerged from the DG's office in Broadcasting House. The memo was kindly, mainly curious how I could ignore such an important rule as the one preventing staff from blabbing to the press. But the memo then descended from one management office to another, the file growing more threatening and larger as it went like a snowball rolling downhill. Eventually it landed with a thud on Huw Wheldon's desk. Huw passed the huge file on to me with a scribbled note attached saying:

You have an unusual contract but it states quite clearly that you will obey staff rules and regulations as laid down in the *Staff Handbook*, a copy of which you were given on joining. Full explanation, please. Immediately. (Or when you are not too busy.)

I replied:

Dear Huw,
I am so sorry to have wasted so many important people's time and I would certainly not have written to *The Times* had I known that it was forbidden so to do. The trouble is I did not read the *Staff Handbook* thoroughly and commit it to memory as I should have done. In fact, I thought the rather slim booklet was my electric blanket guarantee and I filed it away at home under Domestic Items.

But I do think that you should get Mrs Mary Whitehouse to ban party political broadcasts. To this end could you not persuade the political parties to record their promises in the nude?

And that was the last I heard of the matter.

As I began to assemble my schedule of new comedy shows I realized that I had responsibilities which I needed to clarify in my own mind. Pondering over it all in bed, usually at about four o'clock in the morning, half-awake with an Afghan hound puppy fast asleep across my Adam's apple, I tried to focus what thoughts I had.

It seemed to me that a paternalistic attitude was inescapable considering the enormous influence of television, particularly on children. Commercial television's policy was not to give the public what was good for it, which was how the BBC's Reithean attitude of responsibility was regarded, but to give the public what it wanted. Yes, fine, were we in a free-for-all squabble for maximum audiences where diminution of standards was the quickest and cheapest way to popularity, but the BBC was a public service and was not then – and should not be – part of a brawl for audience figures.

The picture was complicated. There was, and still is, the problem of politicians who are incensed because although they vote the BBC its licence fee, they are not allowed to go on the air whenever they feel like it and use the BBC as a personal political loud hailer. And both major parties have always been convinced that the BBC is hopelessly biased politically and infested with activists from the other side.

The complication arose because the Beeb was committed to quality programming and political impartiality, yet winning the exact percentage of the viewing audience was most important. In the Sixties and Seventies, if the BBC's share of the audience rose much above 50 per cent there were howls of rage from ITV companies claiming they had to earn their money from advertisers while the BBC was subsidized by public licence money, which they thought was unfair. On the other hand, if the BBC's audience share of viewers dropped much below 50 per cent there were howls of rage in the House of Commons that MPs were voting public money to a television service which hardly anybody watched.

One of the Comedy Department's responsibilities was to top up the viewing figures so that the BBC could not only have its required quota of viewers, but could also mount quality programmes of minority appeal (which ironically often turned out to be hugely popular successes, e.g., show jumping; *Animal, Vegetable, Mineral?*; snooker; sheep-dog trials; angling).

It seemed to me that a provider of public service television programmes *had* to be paternalistic, and a helpful analogy was to think of programmes as food. If you were to feed your children only with what they wanted to eat, most would want baked beans at every meal. Nothing wrong with baked beans, of course, great taste and full of unattractive-sounding but apparently healthful stuff like fibre – but every meal?

Parents gradually introduce a child to other foods so that the child's tastes are developed and food becomes healthier and a more interesting part of life than being just pabulum.

So perhaps with television. There will always be a need for a few uncomplicated, 'baked beans' series, and I had the very popular *Meet the Wife*, starring wonderful Thora Hird and the excellent Freddie Frinton.

Freddie made a very good stage drunk and his classic music-hall sketch was *Dinner for One* in which he played James, butler to milady, whose husband and friends had expired years earlier. The sketch was an annual celebration party and his one line was, 'Same as last year, milady?' And she would say, 'Yes, James.' Then the butler would plod round the table pouring out glasses of wine for the toasts and then, as there was nobody there to drink the toasts, drink them all himself. Eventually, hardly able to stand, he said, 'Same as last year, milady?' Milady said, 'Yes, James,' and went sedately up the staircase. The butler took hold of a candelabra and staggered up the staircase after her.

Ever since, that sketch has been transmitted on TV every New Year's Eve, as a kind of tradition, all over Europe.

Thora and Freddie's *Meet the Wife* was a most valuable series for me, cheap to produce, with few sets and highly professional writers and cast; it ran for years. The only faint hint of a problem was when Thora, playing a working-class wife, became fed up with wearing plain dowdy clothes every week, so gradually added brighter, more chic items and a smarter hairstyle, until the north country working-class wife she was portraying began to look like a rich divorcée from Las Vegas.

But in my output I was also keen to have several rather more sophisticated popular shows, such as *The Rag Trade*, starring Peter Jones, Miriam Karlin, Sheila Hancock and Reg Varney in a series of stories about a small dressmaking factory and the nonstop problems the owner had with the tiny group of girls who were his work-force. This series was notable for several reasons; it was remade locally by the Scandinavians, the Belgians and the Portuguese. In 1988 the *Listener*, not beating about the bush, called it, 'The most popular TV series of all time.'

It was the first show written for television by the highly reliable team of Ronnie Wolfe and Ronnie Chesney, who later wrote *Meet the Wife*, and was a pre-*Dad's Army* example of how to get laughs from character rather than from jokes, and how to conserve your assets during a long run. For example, one of the sewing-machine operators at Fenner's Fashions was played by Esma Cannon, tiny, wispy, fluttery, white-haired and funny. When Esma had a line she stopped the show, but instead of leaning on this bonus and giving Esma so much to do that her comic twittering became predictable and eventually boring, the two Ronnies used her sparingly, perhaps only two or three times in each half-hour, so she continued to delight for years.

But perhaps the most remarkable success story of *The Rag Trade* is that after some thirty years it is due to be shown on post-apartheid black South African television, and a translated version has become the hit sitcom on Swedish television. *The Rag Trade* may be dead but long live – in Oslo, Belgium and Portugal – *Fredrickssons Fabrics*, *Freddytex* and *Trapos and Compania*.

Among the main courses on my menu I had the near-genius in writing and performance of Galton and Simpson's *Hancock's Half-Hour*, the gentle humour of Harry Worth in *Here's Harry*, and I had Michael Bentine's brilliantly inventive *It's a Square World*, until Mike decided that he wanted more money; not so much a jump in his personal fee as more money for exterior filming and special effects, which were expensive. So I had to let him go to commercial telly, which I hated doing as he was an old colleague. Sadly, it was the time when changing from the BBC to ITV just did not seem to work in comedy. Michael's series on ITV was as brilliant as ever but the figures were not good, and he only did one series before changing direction and working with ingenious electronic puppets on children's television.

Kenneth Williams once said that the most valuable quality a performer could possess was confidence. Tony Hancock's self-confidence ran out at the height of his career. He began to worry that the success of his show was due to Sid James rather than himself, so he dropped Sid from the show. The ensuing, almost one-man shows (e.g., *The Blood Donor*), reassured Tony that he did not need Sid James.

He then worried that the quality of the scripts was the winning ingredient rather than his comedy talents, so he moved from the BBC to ITV, without Galton and Simpson. But he *did* need Galton and Simpson. Without Ray and Alan's complete understanding of his talents, talents which they had developed over the years, the magic seemed to go out of his work and his career went into a slow, sad, terminal decline.

With my Script Department, that haven of help and laughter a few doors away containing John Law and Richard Waring, we reactivated a valuable BBC series of single programmes designed to try out new ideas from established writers and to find new writers, *Comedy Playhouse*. We spread a wide net and the results were excellent (an early find was *Meet the Wife*).

In 1966 a trial script was submitted by John Wraith, a writer unknown to us. The story had a most unusual setting and a neat, clever O. Henry-style surprise ending. The story concerned the thirteenth-century cathedral dedicated to the Blessed Ogg. The cathedral of St Oggs had a crumbling spire which needed repairing, and the bishop discovered that a rich medievalist had willed a large sum of money to the cathedral if a charming old ceremony was revived. In this ancient ritual the bishop was required on Midsummer's Day to ride round the diocese on a white horse and present a pair of white stockings to twenty virgins.

The script's title was *All Gas and Gaiters* and I bought it. We cast William Mervyn as the bishop and Derek Nimmo played the bishop's chaplain, the Revd Mervyn Noote, a charming, naïve young bungler. Robertson Hare ('O, calamity!') played the ancient archdeacon. The thorn in the bishop's side was the dean, played with due severity by John Barron.

Most of the half-hour script was taken up with the unworldly trio bumbling round in search of local virgins. Finding virgins in the permissive Sixties proved a tricky problem. To begin with, it was difficult for three clergymen to bring up the subject at all: 'Excuse me, Miss Hackett, but are you by any chance still a virgin?' would not do.

The three returned at dusk, defeated, with just one virgin out of the required twenty in the bag, and her shy claim was a little at variance with her nickname in the village pub of Dead Cert Deirdre.

There was a professional precision in the way that John Wraith sorted out the plot in the last four words of the stage direction at the very end of the play:

(*A motor hooter sounds loudly outside. The bishop and his crestfallen colleagues idly glance out of the window and then react at what they see. In the courtyard below a motor coach has drawn up and its full load of sightseers are alighting. They are novice nuns.*)

The show was transmitted in the next series of *Comedy Playhouse* and was a success, so I was able to commission a full series, which gave me great pleasure.

Even more pleasure came when I found that 'John Wraith' was a pseudonym adopted by a pair of actors who had become personal friends, Edwin Apps, who played Mr Halliwell in *Whack-O!*, and his wife, the actress Pauline Devaney. It was entirely characteristic of them both that they went to the bother of submitting their first script under a pseudonym so as not to take unfair advantage of a friendship. *All Gas and Gaiters*, written by Edwin and Pauline, ran for five years.

My luck continued with Ray Galton and Alan Simpson putting in a script for *Comedy Playhouse*, a tragicomic, rather Pinteresque story about a trapped relationship between an uncouth, elderly scrap-dealer and his equally uncouth but ambitious son, played, of course, by Wilfrid Brambell and Harry H. Corbett. The show was *Steptoe and Son* and it became one of the most successful comedy series ever broadcast by the BBC.

The caviare end of my menu was enhanced when one morning Alan Bennett's agent turned up and offered me a half-hour comedy script written by Alan. It was marvellous. Not a sitcom but a kind of social revue with wry comments on life in the Sixties and parodies of television programmes, such as a telly celebration of T. E. Lawrence: 'After the war he was, in a way, a lost soul. He would wander along the Strand in his white robes and a curved jewelled dagger in his belt and say to passers-by, "Who am I? Who AM I?" And they would say, "You're Lawrence of Arabia and I claim my five pounds."' Or there was the Northern playwright climbing interminably up a slag heap and muttering things like, 'It's my foonction to get at the reality of life and expose it as a sham. I'm not interested in celebrating the gaudy flower of life, my aim is to take the pith.'

I asked how long Alan would take to write another five scripts to make a run of six programmes. His agent said, 'He's already written them.'

Another happy programme was our adaptation of some of the Jeeves and Bertie Wooster short stories which we put out as a series entitled *The World of Wooster*. I say 'our adaptation' because I was in the thick of it, although it was most ably produced by perhaps the most literary of the department's producers, Michael Mills, and was adapted by Richard Waring. I acted as executive producer, which I suppose was another title for what my job was anyway.

There were huge problems. I thought it important that our series was not dependent upon funny performances by comical actors or on a jokey script but was essentially Wodehouse, otherwise why bother? The solution was simple. The true comedy voice of Wodehouse lay in his similes and his descriptive paragraphs, so I asked Richard to have Bertie narrate the story, voice over. By this device, this important aspect of Wodehouse's genius would not be lost.

Lines such as, 'Jeeves entered – or perhaps one should say shimmered – into the room . . . tall and dark and impressive. He might have been one of the better class ambassadors or the youngish high priest of some refined and dignified religion.' Or, 'His whole aspect was that of a man who had been unexpectedly struck by lightning.' Or, 'Into the face of the young man who sat on the terrace of the Hôtel Magnifique at Cannes there had crept a look of furtive shame, the shifty hangdog look which announces that an Englishman is about to talk French.' Or, 'the unpleasant, acrid smell of burned poetry'.

The method worked well.

Casting was the next problem. The Bertie Wooster we wanted was Ian Carmichael, a highly skilled professional in this kind of deft light comedy. But Ian was in New York about to open in *Boeing Boeing*, a hugely successful stage comedy which had run for years in every theatre in which it had played. We faced a hopelessly long wait. So we turned our attention to finding our Jeeves. We tried a great number of actors – even Robert Helpmann, the ballet dancer turned actor – until somebody suggested Dennis Price, the ex-leading man who went on to become a really good comedy character actor in Ealing comedies.

What happens with casting is that one asks around the BBC bar about an actor one is thinking of employing and directors and producers rave or put the boot in. The word on poor Dennis Price was that he was unreliable and on the bottle.

But *le bon Dieu* looked after us. We wanted Dennis and he was available, so we met him and thought he was exactly right. He lived in the Channel Islands and his companion, we were told, was a lady who had enjoyed a sex-change operation after having previously been a gentleman. We were looking for an actor with an air of reticence and mystery to play Jeeves, and Dennis had both of those all right, so we booked him. He proved to be entirely reliable professionally and his 'drinking' consisted of enjoying a small bottle of Guinness in the morning and one in the afternoon which he brought to rehearsals clinking gently in a British Airways bag.

And then *le bon Dieu* smiled upon us again.

A few days after booking our Jeeves, and now dangerously near our production date, a telegram arrived from Ian Carmichael in New York saying, 'Boeing Boeing opened to disastrous notices and is closing on Saturday. Whatever happened to your idea of putting Bertie Wooster on television?'

The World of Wooster proved to be a most satisfactory series, agreeably well-received by viewers and critics.

A few months later I flew to America to show P. G. Wodehouse, in his home in Remsenburg, Long Island, what we had made of a couple of the programmes. 'Plum' did not normally welcome intruders in the morning because he was devoted to a mid-morning soap opera (how comforting that the great are like us in their dependence on a regular fix of junk TV), but his wife Ethel was a fan of My Word! and persuaded him to let me come.

I took with me two kinescopes (films made of TV programmes; this was before the days of video recordings), and the BBC New York office hired a 16mm projector and a limo to take me from Manhattan right the way down Long Island to Remsenburg. It was a sunny, very hot summer's day and I enjoyed the journey, mostly spent playing with the car's air-conditioning controls. It was all very different and exciting.

At one point we were going quite fast down the highway when we were overtaken by a funeral cortège, a low Cadillac luxury hearse covered in roped-down flowers, followed by a stream of mourners in fast cars. I commented on their speed. My driver kindly explained, 'The more stiffs they plant per day the more dough they make, right?'

Shortly afterwards we were stopped by real speed cops with huge bellies hanging over their belts and guns in unbuttoned holsters. Stepping out of the air-conditioned car was like walking into a wall of hot damp air, but the cops were pleasant and let us go without shooting us.

The Wodehouse residence at Remsenburg was a large white building set in quite a number of green acres. I could hear the barking of many dogs.

Plum (as he asked to be called) apologized for lunching so early (it was midday), explaining that Beulah, who came in to cook for them daily and stir the dust about on Thursdays, had another job to go on to, and hired help was extremely difficult to come by in Remsenburg. Beulah arrived and departed in a huge Plymouth saloon car.

After lunch Plum and I went out onto the patio and slumped into chairs to enjoy a bit of afternoon sun before I showed him the programmes. I asked him if he was considering visiting England after being away for so many years.

'Would I find Dulwich much changed?' he asked. He had been a schoolboy at Dulwich College which had provided him with the sporting and academic stimulations and friendships which had given him the most carefree years of his life.

I did not answer him immediately because I was in agony. A grossly overweight and over-affectionate boxer dog named Debbie had leaped up and was sitting bolt upright, drooling in my lap.

Debbie was one of a large number of stray dogs, each of them either obese, lacking a limb, foul breathed or in some other way socially challenged, who were enjoying the love and full feeding bowls always available at the Wodehouse home.

Plum, then aged eighty-four, was a very friendly man, talking gently and modestly and smiling with pleasure when I managed to slip in a compliment about his work, and worried that arthritis was making typing difficult and painful. He was, I think, the least political man I had ever met, deeply concerned only with his work, boxing and the English public-school cricket results.

We went inside mid-afternoon and the day seemed hotter than ever. Plum sat in an armchair and looked expectantly at the portable screen I had rigged up. Ethel pushed out a smallish table for me to work on and I dumped the projector onto it, only to see with horror that it was a very fine old antique table, probably seventeenth century, its top aglow with uncommon marquetry. I hauled the projector off the table and apologized, but Ethel was not at all disturbed and waved me to carry on. It was very hot indoors.

I laced up the projector and switched on. Oh relief! The picture was reasonable though a bit jumpy and the sound was excellent. Plum sat up and watched keenly. Dennis Price and Ian Carmichael were working well and the studio audience was beginning to enjoy the show. About ten minutes later the film jumped out of the gate and the top reel started to pour film all over the carpet.

I switched off, took out my Swiss Army knife (what a good commercial this scene would have made for those knives) and stripped down the projector gate. As usual with much-used projectors, bits of emulsion from the surface of the film had built up on the chromium gate. I unscrewed the gate assembly and attacked the emulsion with the knife blade. It was a tricky job because the emulsion had set as hard as rock and I had to scrape it away without scratching the gate. I was sweating like a racehorse. Plum went to sleep.

Kindly Ethel said, 'There really is no need to show any more. Plum loved it.'

I fiddled the gate back on, reeled in the film from the carpet and switched on again. The projector purred smoothly into action and the sound came on with a huge loud roar of audience laughter, a live audience laughing, not canned reaction.

Plum woke up. 'What's going on?' he asked, sleepily.

'It's an audience laughing at Jeeves and Bertie,' I said.

Plum said, 'What a lovely way to wake up!'

I showed him the second show and then asked him for his comments. He thought that Dennis Price was without doubt the best Jeeves he had ever seen, and that included all the Hollywood versions with such actors as Eric Blore and Arthur Treacher ('They pulled faces all the time. Awful.').

He thought Ian Carmichael was excellent, although too old for the part (Bertie was about twenty-four and was almost always played by older leading actors in their late thirties or older). And he praised Michael Mills's production. I asked Plum whether he could write all this on a note that I could take back to the BBC, which he did. When I arrived back at the Algonquin Hotel that evening I cabled the words of the note to Tom Sloan, and when I was back at Television Centre I had the note framed and presented it to Michael Mills. I hated parting with it but it was only fair that it should go to Michael.

Flushed with our praise from the great man for our *World of Wooster*, Michael Mills and I decided to have a go at introducing to television Plum's stories about Clarence, the Ninth Earl of Emsworth, the charming, dotty old earl whose passion in life was fattening his prize-winning pig, the Empress of Blandings. His sister Constance was bossy but needed to be to keep the earl more or less socially acceptable. The earl's resident enemy was the dour Scottish gardener, McAllister, who browbeat the kindly earl over important matters like the moss growing on the gravel paths, which the earl liked but McAllister wanted to grub up.

I thought Ralph Richardson would be perfect as Lord

Emsworth. This was a rather ambitious thought – Ralph Richardson in a telly sitcom? – but I knew Ralph well as a fellow member of the Savile Club and we got on, so I could appeal to him personally. Then I had a rather brilliant thought. Ralph's actress wife Mu (Meriel Forbes) would make a splendid Lady Constance.

Perhaps the opportunity for them to work together, a rare occasion, made the difference, but in the teeth of their agent's displeasure, Ralph and Mu agreed to do the series. Michael Mills cast the elderly Scottish character comedian Jack Radcliffe as McAllister. Jack was very good indeed (in a splendidly aggressive ginger wig) and the success of his appearances in the series made a fitting end to his long career.

John Chapman wrote the scripts, adapting six of Plum's short stories; Michael shot the many exteriors in Penshurst Place, Kent; Stanley Holloway played Beach (one of Plum's earliest butlers); Mu played the earl's formidable sister Lady Constance and I, crouched out of sight in a pigsty, played the pig, the Empress of Blandings. I discovered that I am gifted at imitating pigs (and lions, in an emergency). The trick is to snore whilst breathing in and work the mouth into various shapes. After a few seconds it becomes surprisingly painful.

The series, which was called *Blandings Castle*, went out in February 1967.

Ralph was really excellent as Lord Emsworth. In many ways he *was* Lord Emsworth. He needed Mu as Clarence needed his sister Constance. There was the same distaste of formality, the same insights; when Ralph was discussing with our wardrobe lady what clothes he needed to play Clarence, she said, 'An old tweed suit, of course?' Ralph said, 'Oh, yes, but *thin* tweed, I beg you. It should move with the body and do a bit of talking. Working in thick tweed is like walking about in cardboard.'

He worked very hard. He was acting in a play at the time and when there was daytime filming at Penshurst Place he would arrive sitting in the back of a chauffeur-driven Rolls writing out his part on the back of the previous week's script to help him memorize it. And he thought deeply about every aspect of his role and the script.

It was a most satisfactory series, and I was able to write to Wodehouse and say that the programmes had gone well and I didn't think we had let him down. I enclosed a wad of good notices. He wrote back thanking all and informing me that Debbie the fat boxer dog had clearly missed me and had moped about the house in a marked manner since my departure. In spite of her sorrow she had managed to eat well and had put on another stone or two.

About this time the BBC ordered me off on a two-week residential course on management in a huge country house quite near Benjamin Disraeli's grand pile. Polly kindly drove me there, dropping me off at the front door with my suitcase and bidding me farewell with the words, 'Remember, if you haven't "been", ask Matron to give you something.' Then speeding off down the drive doubled-up with mirth over the steering wheel. To her it was exactly like dropping a small child off at boarding school.

But it wasn't quite as funny for me when I delivered Jamie to his prep school, Avisford, near Bognor.

It was the first time he was going to be separated from Polly, Sally, the dogs and his bedroom, and he was going into an unknown life amongst complete strangers. He didn't speak during the hour and a half drive, and we went together into the school building to be greeted by the headmaster, Michael Jennings. I knew that it was best for Jamie if I were to leave as soon as possible and we had an oddly formal, almost silent parting. He was pale and shaking, but he smiled good-bye and I left.

I drove up a Sussex lane for a couple of miles, found a lay-by and burst into tears. It was his courage which I found so moving. Green of face and trembling with nerves, he gave no indication whatever that he would rather go home. No whingeing. No pleading. He seemed to be reassuring me, 'I'll be all right in a moment, don't worry about me.' I was terrifically proud of him.

As it turned out, the school was just right. He was very happy there, eventually became Head Boy, and the senior son of the headmaster's massive family, Luke Jennings the novelist and journalist, became and has remained Jamie's close friend.

Polly took Sally and her suitcase to her boarding school, but it was a serene occasion which held no horrors for Sally. The school, St Mary's Convent, Ascot, was just 6 miles away. Polly had been to school there as had her sister Pidge, who was still there because she was now the Reverend Mother. Sally, like Jamie, made lasting friendships at her school, and to her amazement and amusement was made Head Girl.

On 'going-out' weekends Sal used to bring a friend or two home to Sunday lunch. One of the little girls' favourite lunches was a

Early days of *My Word!* Denis with his partner, the journalist Nancy Spain.
BBC ©

Me with the stunning Dilys Powell. *BBC* ©

1959. *Whack-O!* The dreaded third-form classroom at Chiselbury School.
A school cap has been found adorning the head of William Shakespeare (a
playwright, the headmaster was told to his surprise). The headmaster, cane
at the ready, is Professor Jimmy Edwards, Inter-Ph.D. (Tangiers). Next to
him stands Mr Pettigrew (played by Arthur Howard), the only member of
staff at Chiselbury to have heard of Shakespeare. Mr Pettigrew is, as usual,
silent with terror and trembling. *BBC* ©

1962. Richard Briers starring in a thirteen-week adaptation of Henry Cecil's
book about young barristers in training, *Brothers-In-Law*. With Richard
are his lovely girlfriend, played by the delectable June Barry, and his not-
quite-as-lovely but adequately presentable colleague, played by actor and
writer Richard Waring. *BBC* ©

1966. Peter Jones and Peter Ustinov playing 'Morry' and 'Dudley', two hopelessly incompetent conmen in the two Peters' extraordinarily original comedy series of 'impromptu conversations with illustrations' entitled *In All Directions*. *BBC* ©

This is me, on the set of *In All Directions*, looking a little like Graham Greene on a bad day in Nice. I am playing, as usual, the mug punter out of shot, who ad libs awkward questions to try to trip up the two Peters. I never did manage it. *BBC* ©

The hit show of television comedy in 1965 was *Not Only ... But Also*, with Peter Cook and Dudley Moore. It was semi-ad libbed and consisted of brilliantly original 'interviews' (an aristocrat who is devoting his life to teaching ravens to fly underwater), sketches full of surprises (John Lennon turned up as a nightclub bouncer), and the rambling, face-to-face conversations of Pete and Dud – now copied by almost every pair of TV comics. *BBC* ©

The writers Ronnie Wolfe and Ronnie Chesney had other long-lasting successes before *On The Buses*, including *The Rag Trade*, starring Peter Jones as the distraught owner of a tiny clothing factory trying to cope with his incompetent foreman (Reg Varney), and a whole swatch of fine character actresses, led by Miriam Karlin as their aggressive shop steward ('Everybody out!'). *BBC* ©

All Gas and Gaiters began in 1967 and ran for five highly successful series. There was something charmingly English and irresistible in the stories set around the ancient cathedral of St Oggs, presided over by the bishop (William Mervyn), his chaplain Noote (Derek Nimmo) and his ancient archdeacon, the last part played by the old but much-loved farceur, Robertson Hare ('O calamity!'). *BBC* ©

Ray Galton and Alan Simpson's *Steptoe and Son* joined *Till Death Us Do Part* as another of the BBC's greatest comedy series. *Steptoe* was much more than a knockabout comedy, it was an almost Pinteresque series about an ageing rag-and-bone man with ambitions (Harry H. Corbett), trapped in a relationship with his possessive, unhygienic father (Wilfrid Brambell). The horse was not emotionally involved. *BBC* ©

1965. *The World of Wooster*. Three series of programmes based upon P. G. Wodehouse's Jeeves and Bertie stories, faithfully adapted by Richard Waring and memorably played by Ian Carmichael and Dennis Price (acknowledged by Wodehouse to be the best Jeeves he had ever seen). *BBC* ©

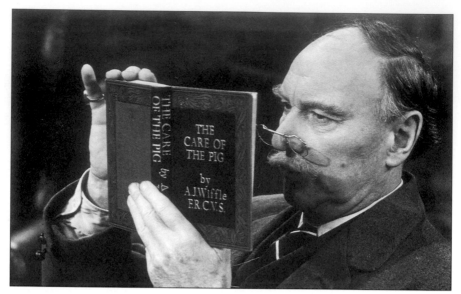

1967. *Blandings Castle*. Sir Ralph Richardson as the dotty old pig-breeding Ninth Earl of Emsworth in a series of six half-hour sitcoms, adapted by John Chapman from the P. G. Wodehouse books. The earl is reading the only book he has read right through in his whole life: *The Care of the Pig*. *BBC ©*

Robert Robinson looking benign and happy. The great Paddy Campbell looking a bit fierce, but then he did a lot of that. When he guessed that a word was a bluff and it was revealed as being true, his eyes seemed to move together as close as cuff links and he would rear up in his chair, rigid with indignation, like an ostrich that has sat in something. *BBC ©*

Warren Mitchell as Alf Garnett, holding the floor as usual in one of the greatest sitcoms ever produced by the BBC, Johnny Speight's *Till Death Us Do Part*. BBC ©

A still from London Weekend Television's *On The Buses*, starring Reg Varney. Simple comedy, not enjoyed by the critics but a huge hit with the viewers for years – and still running in various languages in Europe.
London Weekend Television

Moscow. Being shown round our rooms at the Berlin Hotel by the Russian writer and ex-actor, our dear friend Alexei Kapler.

More Moscow. Three chilly Britons and a more robust Russian (Alexei) on the APN Way. Our friend and interpreter Nina Froud is to the left.
Novosti

A rehearsal at Anners for a thrilling demonstration of army motor-mowing to the whistle at our village fête. The army team of crack mowers, trained to a hair's breadth, are (left to right) Dick Emery, chest thrust out as a sergeant in the ATS; Michael Bentine; Dick Lester in the driving seat; Clive Dunn, and me, trying to look stupid. Oddly enough I found it quite easy.

Another village fête stunt. This year it was a demonstration of *Z-Bikes*, an élite squad formed to combat a bout of daffodil slashing by disgruntled OAPs. The tough, negative-tolerance team consists of (left to right) Graham Stark, Peter Sellers, Bill Kerr, Bruce Lacey, Dick Lester and son, and Clive Dunn. Once again I contrived (without make-up) to look dim.

Sunday Pictorial

Sent up rotten by my Comedy Department at London Weekend Television after what I had hoped was a secret lunch at Buckingham Palace.

The department bending the knee. In the background Tito Burns and Barry Cryer are hovering (unbending). To my right kneels my then secretary, manager, close friend and nanny, Tanya Bruce-Lockhart.

Be it known to all men that on this day, 19th December in this year of Grace 1968, We were most graciously pleased to have our right loyal & trusted servant
F. Herbert Muir
Earl of Stonebridge
for luncheon, & he was delicious.

EIIR

Witnessed:

The manuscript document which the unit put together and presented to me.
I still have it. Of course.

Just after dawn, Dick Lester and a camera crew near Cannes in the South of France, filming me for a Hovis commercial. At one point I asked Dick why he had bothered to bring us all the way over to Cannes. Dick said, 'Would you rather have spent three days paddling round Ramsgate harbour?'

One of my favourite family photographs. Funny how all four of us seem to wear on our heads little tufts plucked from one end or the other of the Afghan hounds' coats. Notice that Sally is cuddling a very, very brave cat indeed.

This is clearly either the School of Naval Architecture's male voice choir trying out a new piano or a BBC publicity picture taken at a recording of *My Music*. Note John Amis's magnificently restrained (for him) striped suit. *BBC* ©

The entire cast of the radio 'anthology' series *Frank Muir Goes Into...*, consisting of my old friend and colleague from wartime shows at RAF Henlow, Alfred Marks, and me. Besides having a strong and true bass-baritone singing voice, Alfred was terrific at any kind of accent and knew every Jewish joke, story and anecdote in the book. These he told from time to time, prudently and superbly. *BBC* ©

A flotation in the lagoon which laps around the St Géran Hotel, Mauritius (a quite wonderful holiday experience). The photograph was taken by Polly and is a model of what a portrait should be of any husband less pretty than, say, Sean Connery. A simple, minimalist composition featuring only toes, nose, hat and pipe.

Interviewing Groucho Marx at the New York Hilton for the BBC's *Omnibus*. Was the film a success? Up to a point, Lord Copper... *BBC* ©

Inducted as Lord Rector of St Andrews University. Being pulled round the town in an open coach by the rugger club, dressed in the students' traditional scarlet gown, stopping everywhere to make a short speech and receive a little present. My tour of duty at St Andrews were three of the most rewarding and happiest years of my life.

Giving a reading for Oxfam with Sir John Gielgud of extracts from Jan Morris's *The Oxford Book of Oxford*. All the fine actresses whom Michael Meyer and I used to invite to our readings were unavailable, but then we realized that the mass of items assembled by Jan Morris were concerned with Oxford when it was still a Catholic religious community, and women were not in the book!

1981. Polly and I on Granada Television, still happily together after experiencing the toughest known tests of a human relationship. Firstly I tried to teach Polly how to drive, and secondly Polly and I worked together, choosing writers and artists for an anthology of new children's stories called *The Big Dipper*. And without one quarrel! No wonder we're looking a bit smug presenting Granada's programme about the book.

complicated, labour-intensive dish which the recipe called Hot American Chicken Salad. One small girl's thank-you letter to Polly began:

Darling, darling Mrs Muir,
Thank you so much for the chicken do-up.

And 'chicken do-up' it has, of course, remained.

Children so often invent better words than the originals and every family must have a collection: e.g., our pair, when very young, referred to waterproofs as 'mackinsops'; and that hot white stuff they ate with beef was 'horse-rubbish'.

A lady in South Africa wrote to me that her son reported to her that in gym that morning they had 'horrors-on-the-bars'.

The actor Eric Chitty revealed that whilst on holiday he went with his granddaughter to find a chemist to make up a prescription. As the nearest chemist was really only a shop which sold tartan sponge bags and smelled of soap they were advised to go to the nearest pharmaceutical chemist, which was quite a long walk across town. They trudged along and when they stopped for a rest, the tired little girl sighed and said, 'Grandpa, it's such a pity we have to find a "far-more-suitable" chemist.'

The BBC management course was well-organized (which was just as well considering its subject). We were a motley crew, a mixture of high-ranking engineers, foreign correspondents, departmental managers, planners and various other members of that shadowy network of functionaries so important to the BBC that one of them, congratulated on his department being housed in a prestigious new building in Shepherd's Bush, was moved to make the now famous remark, 'The BBC doesn't just make programmes, you know.'

As usual in that kind of conference, we were split up into syndicates of about ten assorted members with a chairman, and mornings and afternoons were given to syndicate sessions in which we had to debate solutions to a mixed bag of problems like, 'Where, ideally, would you put the nine o'clock news?' Or, 'Should BBC official vehicles, like radio cars and television equipment lorries, be bought or be hired as required, and if only hired, should drivers be eligible for a sandwich allowance?'

We each had a Toblerone-shaped wooden wedge on the desk in

front of us with our name painted on it. Mine read F. H. MUIR. I objected mildly to the conference organizer, making the point that nobody had called me F. H. Muir since I was at school, so it wasn't really my grown-up name. The organizer was apologetic and blamed the engineers who preferred names to be as formal as possible. I had noted years previously that the BBC engineering department was the Rolls Royce of departments. Their standards were extremely high on all matters of engineering and they held strong views on social matters as well. As Val Gielgud found out. Val, brother of John Gielgud, was a BBC radio drama producer of some distinction. He was wooed into television, took a course in TV production and was given a play to put on.

There were four cameras and when the camera rehearsal began, Val directed his cameras by saying to them, 'Potter, could you move into a medium close-up? Standby for a lens change, Harrison. A little closer, please, Arkwright-Sanderson . . .'

In the control-box the TOM (Technical Operations Manager) leaped to his feet, pulled the switch which cut off contact with the studio and said to Val, 'Sorry, Val, but in engineering we don't address cameramen as though they're gardeners.'

Val explained mildly, 'Actually calling a chap by his surname means you are treating him affectionately as an equal.'

'Dunno about that,' said the TOM. 'I can only say that cameramen should always be addressed by their Christian names.'

'But all four cameramen are named Fred,' said Val.

'Then you address them as Fred One, Fred Two, Fred Three and Fred Four.'

In the evenings we were lectured by such managerial superstars as Dr Beeching (the Dr Guillotine of British Rail services); General Hackett and, by some accident, the wonderful late Michael Elliott, who talked and enthused so effortlessly about Shakespeare that he could have gone on for ever as far as our syndicate was concerned. But next evening we were back to reality with a gentleman from ICI and a stern warning about letting our corporate structures sag. He had pitiless pie charts showing vertical management theory as against horizontal management theory and how it should all be combined into New Management theory, the supreme importance of rigid budget control over all other production considerations. He was very keen (not visibly very keen – he was, in himself, very dull indeed – but *intellectually* keen) on New Management. It was the New Managers, he said finally, showing for the first time a tiny trace of emotion, who were going to save English commerce. He did not mention what they were going to do to creative television.

We conferencees could buy a book of cloakroom tickets after the lectures and exchange them for glasses of beer at a trestle-table. As the first week wore on the queue for warmish beer became like a rugger scrum.

One evening we had an almost inaudible talk from a small, bird-like but famous chartered accountant stressing the absolute necessity of keeping our shows to their budgets, and our last lecturer was the BBC staff doctor who told us how to recognize stress in our staff: the body sits slumped, with the head shrunk between the shoulders. At least I think that is what he said. He was difficult to hear as we were all sitting slumped with our heads shrunk between our shoulders.

My skills as a New Manager were put to the test as soon as the course finished and I arrived back at Television Centre, brimming with undigested facts and theories about something I was not much interested in. I was immediately accosted in the BBC Club bar by one of my producers who had a new series to produce from a successful trial programme in *Comedy Playhouse*, and he had a great idea.

'For the opening credits', he said, 'a helicopter shot of Big Ben, then sweep down to the East End, close-up shot of a lit window, mix through to a crane shot and go through the window to see an elderly couple in bed. Mix to live action in studio and start the dialogue. What do you reckon?'

'But you've already overspent your budget and the series hasn't started yet,' I said.

'Bugger the budget,' said the producer.

'How much would a helicopter cost?' I asked.

He said, 'I could do the shot in an hour, which would cost four hundred pounds.'

It was quite a lot of money in those days. I thought hard. We could amortize the money over the six shows in the series, and it *was* a good, in fact very good, idea for the opening credits . . .

'OK,' I said, 'go ahead with the shot.'

'I'm afraid there's a problem,' said the producer, having the decency to look a bit sheepish. 'The four hundred pounds only stretches to a single-rotor chopper, and in that we are only allowed to fly over the Thames, that is, over water. To fly over land we have to have a twin-rotor job.'

'And how much would that cost?' I asked, starting to breathe heavily.

'The twin-rotor chopper comes out at eight hundred and fifty pounds per hour,' he said. Again I thought hard, and swiftly. There was one hope. Michael Peacock had moved from being Controller of BBC2 to being Controller of BBC1, which 'owned' *Comedy Playhouse*, and I suspected that he had a secret contingency fund for this kind of problem. And I had an idea that as a programme man himself, he would be sympathetic.

'OK,' I said to the producer. 'Go ahead with your shot.'

Then came the double whammy.

'Thanks so much,' he said. 'I knew I could count on your support. The fact is I did the shot last Thursday. It didn't work.'

I went to Michael Peacock, told him a tiny bit of the story and he gave me the extra budget money (and a talking-to about the importance of not letting producers get away with wasteful spending).

So, I had come straight from a senior management conference where I was lectured by money men on the attitudes required of senior management operating in a market economy and I had not benefited at all. Instead I had worked on old-fashioned instinct and instead of firing the producer, obviously the sensible course, I had arranged for him to have more money for his programme. I had managed to drop the mask of being a New Manager before I'd even put it on properly.

But there was another side to the coin. The producer concerned was Dennis Main Wilson. And I knew that Dennis as a producer may have been 20 per cent near-genius and 80 per cent over-enthusiastic, but even when he was in his 80 per-cent mode he was totally devoted and loyal to the show he was producing and would fight to the end for it.

And the series which Dennis was producing turned out to be the great *Till Death Us Do Part*, starring Warren Mitchell as the ranting, right-wing, sexist, male chauvinist pig Alf Garnett, and Dandy Nichols as his placid, toffee-chewing, unimpressed wife, Else, referred to by Alf as the 'silly moo'.

It is impossible to overstate the contribution Dennis made to the success of the show, many times way and above the call of duty;

Dennis did nothing by halves. In the early days he almost lived with Johnny Speight to help get the *Till Death* scripts out on time, and even wrestled Johnny out of Annabels nightclub in Berkeley Square in the early hours of one morning to make sure that there would be a script for rehearsal later that day.

This was the mid-Sixties and permissiveness was touching everything. Johnny was anxious to reproduce as nearly as possible the tough language which Alf Garnett, a docker, would have used. I pointed out that the oaths and sexual swearing which would have made up half of Alf's true conversation would be far too strong for television; the shock effect would be out of all proportion. So I persuaded Johnny to stick mainly to the word 'bloody', which would be startling and strong enough for most viewers.

This turned out to be so. Viewers were shocked in a mild sort of way, but recognizing the truth in the word being used by the sort of character who used it, they were not all that offended. Some were, of course, and a few sat silently through several episodes totting up the number of 'bloodies' and then writing to the DG (and me) giving the episode's count. It was usually between forty and sixty 'bloodies' per half-hour, but the prize for bloody-spotting went to Mrs Mary Whitehouse, who wrote to complain that in the last show she had watched she had counted seventy-eight.

I was quite prepared to defend this and devised a kind of form letter of justification. But I was afraid that part of the hostility to what should have been an inarguable artistic decision came from the way that an actor was tempted to say the dread word. Actors rarely got the chance to say a (then) strong word like 'bloody' on television and when a part came along with two or three 'bloodies' per page there was a temptation for the actor to enjoy the experience and to separate the word slightly from the rest of the sentence and enunciate it clearly. I suggested to Warren that his 'bloodies' should really be mumbled. Alf would probably not have thought of his 'bloodies' as swearing, just making an aggressive noise to strengthen his argument.

Warren saw the point immediately. He was keen on that sort of thing because he had become interested in method acting, at which he was very good indeed.

During one rehearsal, Warren had embarked on one of Alf's tirades against Arsenal Football Club, the Labour Party, the Asian grocery shop on the corner which was taking the food out of the mouth of the saintly Lord Sainsbury, and so on, when Dandy Nichols, who had been leaning against the wall by the fireplace, straightened up, wandered past Warren and sank into an armchair.

Warren was furious. 'Dandy!' he said. 'What did you move for? Right in the middle of my speech you wander vaguely right across me. You had no motivation for moving, Dandy. None. If you'd looked chilly and had seen a woolly on the chair, then right, we'd have known what was in your noddle. But to just wander across me . . . You were at position A and you moved, all of your own accord, to position B. Why?'

Dandy said, 'I was at position A and I farted, so I moved to position B.'

Till Death Us Do Part ran for nine years and became one of the most profitable comedy shows (in terms of viewing figures and prestige) the BBC had ever transmitted.

They were long and busy days, but from *Comedy Playhouse* came some good programmes and the discovery of good new writers, including two ex-cartoonists – Brian Cooke and Johnnie Mortimer – who only wrote a mildly successful caper about the diplomatic service for me, but went on to write success after success for ITV, retiring young and, I hope, rich.

The best writers I found were John Esmonde and Bob Larbey, who began well and steadily improved.

When Michael Peacock moved to BBC1 and David Attenborough became Controller of BBC2, David asked me to find him a game show which would be right for BBC2.

This was far from easy. Most formats submitted were hyped-up versions of established successes such as *Twenty Questions* or *Wheel of Fortune*. They demanded a set like a bingo hall from hell with a screaming audience, flashing lights and a pretty, lightly-clad girl to manoeuvre the contestants onto their camera mark (a piece of sticky tape on the floor). The suggested compères tended to be not very successful or elderly comics who were now wisely seeking a change of career.

None of these programmes was suitable for BBC2, or for that matter BBC1 (or ITV), so I let it be known amongst the agents that I was interested in looking at kinescopes of available American game shows.

At least the American compères did not look like ex-comics. They looked like ex-human beings. Their uniform was a dark-blue blazer with an enormous badge on the pocket, hair (if any) dyed shoe-polish ginger, and a tremendous number of teeth winking and blinking in the lights. They were jolly men and when they read out a one-liner joke from their idiot board, the audience, anxious to help, yelped like an overexcited posse of American Indians galloping round John Wayne on their ponies.

And then I found what I was hoping to find: an American game which had capability for entertaining British BBC2 viewers.

The show had been adapted from a parlour game and the copyright was now owned by the two great impresarios of American televised game shows, Goodson and Todman. There was no copyright on family games, but there was copyright in the format of a game show which had been adapted for television.

Messrs Goodson and Todman hit upon this happy state of affairs and worked their way steadily through a great number of old parlour games, mostly British, adapting them and then selling licences to produce them to other countries. Early Goodson and Todman adaptations included *Twenty Questions*, *What's My Line?* and *The Name's the Same* (Denis and I served our time as panel members on all of those).

But not all Goodson and Todman shows were hits. They had a go at adapting one old English parlour game called *The Dictionary Game*. It was played by a player selecting an obscure word from the dictionary and giving three definitions of the word, one of which was true and the other two bluffs. The other contestants had to guess which definition was true.

Goodson and Todman's television version was named *Call My Bluff* and was very American in style. The question master was the usual late-middle aged teenager with his blue blazer and dyed hair, but instead of having professional broadcasters as contestants, ordinary members of the public were invited up from the studio audience. It was all a bit of a shambles, mainly because bluffs from amateurs were so obviously false that it was painfully easy to spot the trues. The show proved not to be to the taste of American viewers and only lasted one season.

I have always found that British viewers appreciate a programme which they suspect is slyly educating them, and it seemed to me that if I could jack up the IQ of the show sharply and use well-known people as contestants, it could well be the programme David Attenborough was stalking.

The alterations I proposed to make were not greeted with much enthusiasm by Goodson and Todman's London agent, Philip Hindin, probably because he was worried that it might loosen his office's grip on the copyright, but it was a case of making the changes we wanted or no deal. Happily Philip preferred to make the deal.

Choosing the words was a vital part of setting up the shows; the word had not only to be obscure but to yield two bluffs which were more plausible than the truth. I booked Peter Moore as our compiler. Peter was an old friend, Sally's godfather, an occasional contributor of odd original sketches to *Breakfast with Braden* and a lover of words.

As Peter chose a word because it yielded a pair of good bluffs, it made sense for him to make a note of those bluffs for the contestants to develop and put into their own words. So after a camera rehearsal, the teams went off to their captain's dressing room, the words and Peter's cards were delivered by the producer in a sealed envelope, and with their captain's help the contestants worked on Peter's suggested bluffs and plotted their strategy to confound the enemy.

The result of this system was that *Call My Bluff* became easy to play but extremely difficult to win.

We began to find out what kind of guests worked well on the show. Viewers seemed to enjoy seeing faces which were familiar to them for doing something else, like newsreaders and dramatic actors and actresses. Our most reliable contestants were the new breed of *Beyond the Fringe*-style comedy actors who were witty ad libbers, e.g., Peter Cook, Alan Bennett, Jonathan Miller, and witty actresses and writers such as Joanna Lumley, who was so good at the game that we booked her for every series we made.

We learned to be wary of booking comical comics. They tended to keep slipping into their act and trying to inject their personal comedy into the game instead of extracting fun from the game itself. Some of the biggest laughs came when the next word to be defined appeared on the board above our chairman Robert Robinson's noble head and he, with precision, read it out.

Our audiences and viewers took a pride in the eccentricity of the English language and consistently found it hilarious. Hardly surprising when one considers the wonderful words which Peter Moore found buried in the *Oxford English Dictionary*.

Here are some samples of the words hand-picked by Peter, with their true meanings:

BONZE:	An impolite but not necessarily offensive Portuguese word for a Japanese clergyman.
BEARLEAP:	A Tudor housewife's large shopping basket.
POLLYWOG:	Dialect name for a tadpole.
MOLOCKER:	An old, but renovated, top hat.
COMSTOCKER:	An American affronted by nudity.
ABLEWHACKET:	A naval card game not unlike whist played by able seamen, which was called ablewhacket because, when an able seaman lost, he held out his hand and the winner whacked it.
BANDOLINE:	A hairdressing made from quinces.
MERROW:	An Irish mermaid.

Some twenty years later, Mr Goodson of Goodson and Todman was in England staying at the Savoy Hotel when *Call My Bluff* came on the television screen in his suite. He thought it was a wonderful show, rang Young Bill Cotton at Television Centre, who was by then Head of Light Entertainment Group, and asked whether he could buy the American rights. Young Bill, relishing the moment, pointed out to Mr Goodson that Goodson and Todman owned the programme, the BBC merely had a licence to broadcast our version. What had happened was that the American version had lasted for only one season twenty years previously and Mr Goodson had forgotten all about it.

Our first chairman of *Call My Bluff* was Robin Ray. At David Attenborough's command I was captain of one team and Robert Morley was captain of the other.

We used to do two programmes per show day, one live and then one pre-recorded. This was a good thing as it enabled our guests to earn two small fees instead of one (one would hardly have been worth starting the car for).

Most things that could go wrong did so and usually on the show which went out live. Such as when Lord David Cecil suddenly discovered that all his bluff and true cards had disappeared from his desk. Robert Morley, not of lissom build, managed to crawl underneath, and found that Lord David Cecil, in a moment of deep concentration pondering which of the opposition's definitions was true, had absent-mindedly dropped his cards one by one onto the floor. Robert scooped them up and, when the cameras were on my team, rose into view again like a flushed but triumphant porpoise.

Strangely, of all our various contestants, academics, authors, industrialists, journalists, weather forecasters, musicians (André Previn was excellent), it was the actors who were the most nervous.

Jimmy Villiers was a good example of horror descending upon an actor on suddenly realizing that he had to speak without a script. He had only seen *Call My Bluff* a couple of times and was not all that familiar with it.

At the camera rehearsal, Jimmy, a man of ancient lineage, asked in his superb voice (with vowels mown and rolled for 300 years, like the lawns of Magdalen College, Oxford), 'When it's my turn to choose our opponents' true definition, what do I do?'

Robert said, 'You just say a few words dismissing the two definitions you reckon are bluffs and then say why you believe the one you've chosen is true.'

Jimmy looked appalled. Then he stood up – a long way up as he is very tall – and said, 'Sorry, heart, don't ad lib.' And made for his dressing room.

Happily his wife was there and she had a little talk to Jimmy and he agreed to have a go at chatting as required and, of course, he was excellent.

An actor's worry at 'being himself' without even a funny voice or costume to hide behind was exemplified by Donald Pleasance, the villain in hundreds of stage, TV and film productions, even sinister arch-enemy of James Bond. And here was Donald in the *Bluff* studio pleading with our producer to let him wear a moustache. 'Just a *tiny* one would do. *Please?*'

Wearing a moustache, however near-invisible, would have given Donald confidence because he would have acted Donald Pleasance with a small moustache and not had to be his naked self. But on the show he too, as himself, was excellent.

One evening the female guest on my team was a beautiful American actress. Halfway through the show she laughed so much at Arthur Marshall's definition of a word that the retaining brooch on her blouse flew open and a breast popped into view. Happily for her, the cameras were on Arthur Marshall at the time and she was able to restore her modesty so swiftly that the viewing millions had no idea what a delightful crisis they had missed.

After the recording the good lady told me she was driving to Norfolk to spend the rest of the weekend with friends and could she have a quick bath in the tiny bathroom attached to my dressing room? Of course she could. What is more, there was to be no more accidental immodesty. The lady carefully closed the bathroom door, then opened it slightly and pushed out into the dressing room the most aggressive 8 ounces of white miniature poodle I have ever seen. This Guardian of Virtue did a quick warning run at our ankles, nipping those within range, barked like a falsetto, demented Dobermann pinscher and settled comfortably on the carpet by the bathroom door, giving us all a steely stare which clearly said, 'Come on, punks. Make my day.'

Towards the end of my three-year contract with the BBC my working life was beginning to become uncomfortably demanding. *Bluff* took up many evenings, as did recordings of *My Word!* and *My Music* and warming up the audience for the first show of all my new comedy series. When I managed to get home at a reasonable hour there were shows I felt I should watch, and my days were very full with meetings and duties like reading unsolicited scripts. How I wished I could have dealt with them as Disraeli is said to have done. In a fine example of subtle ambiguity he would reply to the would-be author, 'Thank you for sending me your manuscript. I will lose no time in reading it.'

I had realized early on that running a variety department was like flower arranging. You chose and bought your expensive, eye-catching blossoms and your job was to display them in a good setting, jiggling them around so that they showed to best advantage.

But if you were running a sitcom department you were not just flower arranging, but in the nursery business. You had to plant new untried writing talent, nurture it, take care of it and hope it would grow. Good shows, in this country anyway, are originated by writers not by executives. Ideas are sometimes the easiest part and frequently are not the reason for a show's success; it is the other factors, the handling of character, the quality of the dialogue, the originality of the stories, happy accidents of casting, which matter.

Steptoe and Son was not fun and games with a couple of rag-and-bone men, it was a series about a trapped relationship between a father and his son. Ray and Alan could just as well have set the show in a railway station or a postal sorting office, but I have always had a feeling that they set it in a junkyard to muck up their producer, Duncan Wood – writing out the week's list of props must have taken him at least two days a week.

Tom Sloan once proudly told me of a programme idea he had just had. He called it *Circle Line*, and to a non-writer it might have looked promising. In the series, an underground train stopped every week at a different Circle Line station and on the crowded escalator a story began to unfold. One week, perhaps, a tragedy; the next week a funny piece; then a love story, and so on. Each programme could be any kind of drama from any kind of writer and would surely make a colourful series. What did I think of the idea?

Well, not much. I explained to Tom that his idea of using the Circle Line as the continuity between independent half-hour stories amounted to offering a piece of string and saying, 'If you thread a ruby on this piece of string, then perhaps a diamond, then a pearl and so on, you would end up with a valuable necklace.' The faulty reasoning is that if you acquire a fine ruby, and a valuable diamond and a beautiful pearl, and so on, you don't need the piece of string. And until you have the jewels, all you *do* have is a piece of string.

One evening, in the middle of a series of *Call My Bluff*, I arrived home dog-tired and Polly said, 'Aren't you overdoing it? You look a hundred.' And I felt a hundred. But I could not duck out of the next week's show because one of my guests was an old friend, a young American film and TV director, Richard Lester, who was working in England on off-beat TV comedy shows mostly starring Peter Sellers and/or Spike Milligan (Richard later made the Beatles' films and a stack of other big-screen successes). Richard was nervous of being in front of the cameras and I had to coax him into performing, assuring him that as his team captain I would be there to hold his hand.

At the weekend I began to feel awful, tired, miserable and wobbly. By Wednesday, the day of recording, I was clearly not well. As usual, my team had gathered in my dressing room for our conference and I suddenly found breathing difficult. I asked somebody to find the producer and the duty matron and tell them I thought I might be rather ill.

Matron arrived and asked me to take some deep breaths, which I managed. It was like inhaling broken glass.

'You've probably got pleurisy!' said matron cheerfully. 'You'd better go home immediately and get your own doctor to do what he can.'

The producer phoned Polly to get our doctor to stand by at home and arranged for a car to take me home.

And so, on Dick Lester's first personal appearance on BBC2, his team captain on whom he was relying so much, white-faced, whimpering and trying not to breathe, was carried briskly out on a stretcher.

As it was Christmas, Dr Sam thought I should stay at home in bed. 'You can't spend Christmas Day in a teaching hospital,' he said. 'All that jolly fun. They'd kill you.'

I do not recommend pleurisy. Have something else if you can. Pleurisy lacks charm; there is nothing to enjoy and much to endure, but my pleurisy changed next day – Christmas Day – to pneumonia, which was not nearly so nasty. No pain, just both shivering and overheating at the same time, an odd experience. The only really bad moment was when I realized that my father had died at the age that I was then, forty-seven. And of pneumonia, too. But we now had antibiotics.

Polly cooked the turkey, but it was enormous, so she and the children ate what they could and then, whilst I lay in bed upstairs steaming like a Christmas pudding, buried the rest of the cadaver with suitable ceremony in the garden.

I had a few comfortable weeks in University College Hospital getting better. There wasn't a lot to do in my little room, I found it difficult to concentrate on reading or watching television, but I had regular visitors who dropped in for a (mercifully) few minutes on their way home in the evenings. My most regular visitors were Denis and Ralph Richardson, both of whom lived in North London. It was marvellous to get all the chat and gossip from Den to keep me up to date.

Ralph and Mu had recommended me to a lung specialist who was excellent, so Ralph had a kind of proprietary interest in my progress. He brought me those expensive glossy magazines like *Apollo*, which seemed to consist largely of advertisements from antique shops in Edinburgh offering small occasional tables for £2,000 a leg. And Alan Bennett sent me a postcard which read, 'Be wary of New Zealand nurses. They are so strong that when they tuck your sheets in they break your ankles.'

Then my specialist said that he thought a little champagne would be good for me, so when friends rang asking whether I would like them to bring me grapes, or would I prefer a book? I replied in a wistful croak, 'I am permitted a little champagne . . .'

As I hoped, within days my room was awash with the stuff. The fridge became full of half-bottles, and nurses made a habit of dropping in for a glass when going off-duty. I suddenly became *the* most popular patient on the wing.

I left hospital, white and wobbly, with a ratty little beard which made me look like a cross between Robin Cook the politician and Iago. Polly said it must come off within twenty-four hours. We then went off to Tenerife to convalesce for a few days, the nearest area certain to be warm and sunny as early in the year as February. And beautifully warm and sunny it turned out to be, too.

We have three strong memories of Tenerife. Firstly the beaches, which consisted not of the normal yellow sand but what looked like a mixture of coke and coal dust. The second memory was of our excellent waiter, who was living and breathing for the following week when he would be taking a not inconspicuous part in Tenerife's street carnival. At every meal he would turn over a plate on the table and while he dreamily honed our knives on the rough pottery ring on the bottom of the plate would tell us about the excitements of the annual carnival, which would last three days and which he would spend, as usual, dancing and prancing about, without sleep, dressed in spectacular drag. He showed us a photograph of himself in his costume; he resembled a narrower Hispanic version of Barbara Cartland. He was unmarried.

And then a man in the British consulate's office presented us with two tickets for the local bullfight, apparently a great treat. We went and found the matador to be about eighteen years old and, when lurching at the bull, entirely lacking in the skill to demonstrate the beauty in death so admired by *aficionados* such as Ernest Hemingway and Ken Tynan. The young man severed one of the dead bull's ears with his sword and flung it bleeding onto Polly's lap. Polly, teeth gritted, was congratulated by all around us on being chosen for this charming traditional gesture of honour.

I am squeamish even when in robust health, but I managed to survive the afternoon because, before leaving the hotel, I swallowed the only thing I could find in the sponge bag which looked helpfully medicinal: a couple of air-sickness pills.

The BBC, patient and generous as ever over illness, gave me a driver for my car and let me work half days for a while, half days turning out to be ten o'clock in the morning until five at night. We continued to find good new shows. I persuaded Kingsley Amis to let us set up a television series based on the hero of his novel *Lucky Jim*. We called it *The Further Adventures of Lucky Jim* and it starred Keith Barron, then at the beginning of his television career, and was written by a new team at the beginning of their writing careers, Dick Clement (then a producer in the department) and Ian La Frenais.

One day I was having lunch at the Savile with Kingsley to discuss various production problems when, to my delight, he blew the gaff on Denis Norden.

It seems that Kingsley and Denis were at public school together, the City of London School. Denis was very active politically and was secretary of the Peace Pledge Union and an activist on behalf of the United Nations and all those pre-war peace movements. He was reckoned to have a fine, sensitive, academic brain and Kingsley reckoned that Den would probably end up writing the definitive monograph on a fourteenth-century French poet nobody had ever heard of. What, I ask myself, went right?

I woke up with a jolt one day to realize that my three-year contract with the BBC was almost up. At the same time I realized that I did not really want to stay – not that anybody had asked me to. It had been a marvellously productive period but to stay on would have meant repeating the same thing over again. What should and could have been altered in the way the Comedy Department dealt with writers and comedy ideas had been altered; there was nothing more that I felt needed changing, so another tour of duty would mean merely consolidating, which was not nearly so much fun.

Then one evening Michael Peacock summoned me for a little talk. He asked me whether I knew much about the reallocation of commercial television licences which was about to take place. I knew nothing, of course, so he explained. The word was that Associated Rediffusion, which broadcast to London and the Home Counties, might be replaced by two companies, one to run weekdays and the other to cover weekends. Michael had given in his notice to the BBC and had been invited to be managing director of a consortium which was going to try for London's weekend licence.

There were already two teams being put together. David Frost had promises from a sparkling assembly of talent, including Peter

Hall the director and Galton and Simpson, while Aidan Crawley had put together a mix of politically balanced figures and City money-men. The trouble was that neither team had experience of actually producing a television schedule. Michael was trying to combine the two teams by losing a few of those members obviously included for window dressing and taking on board some experienced programme-makers. Would I join him as potential Head of Entertainment?

It was not exactly joining, there was nothing to join, it was more like being given a ticket in a lottery where the prize was a job yet to come into existence. Polly and I decided that there was no harm in accepting a free lottery ticket so I did. I wrote my brief manifesto for the application, laying out my approach to light entertainment production ('to make shows which are not only popular but are also worth making'), and we virtually forgot all about it except that I saw the Head of BBC TV Personnel and told him I would be leaving when my contract was concluded.

He seemed a bit thunderstruck. '*Leaving*?' he said.

'Well, nobody's asked me to stay,' I pointed out, reasonably.

'We took it for granted!' he said.

It was, I suppose, a compliment.

But there was no time to worry about trifles, there was the urgent question of what I was going to do in a few months' time when my BBC contract was up and I would be out of gainful employment. I had an idea for a book and I began to research for it. I also built a small brick wall which curved round in front of the house. Still does.

Jamie was at school at Ampleforth in Yorkshire, and Polly and I drove up for the annual Exhibition Weekend to watch, glowing, as he collected the Art Prize. On the drive home down the A1 (by now the car was an elderly Alvis) we suddenly heard the announcer say on the car radio, 'And here is the nine o'clock news. It was announced today that Associated Rediffusion has lost its commercial television licence and the new companies taking over in the London area will be, Monday to Friday, ABC Television headed by Howard Thomas, and London Weekend Television headed by Aiden Crawley and David Frost.'

I slowed the car down, slid into a lay-by, and Polly and I tried to work out all the implications of the news.

'What have we done?' we wondered.

Chapter Thirteen

CROSSING THE CHANNEL

When commercial television first came on air it was jocularly referred to as 'Cad's Television', particularly by BBC personnel. There was a pride then in working in public service broadcasting and in the generally high quality of BBC programmes, and a great many employees felt a surge of loyalty to the BBC when a colleague left to do the same job for more money in Cad's Television.

One deeply BBC-minded man was Tom Sloan. Tom was cut to the quick when, in a break from recordings of *Steptoe and Son*, Harry H. Corbett took part in a play for ITV. 'Has he no feelings of loyalty?' cried Tom at what he took to be Harry Corbett's base act of ingratitude. 'After all the BBC's done for him!' Tom did not for a moment consider what Harry Corbett had done for the BBC.

When a BBC staff man or contract star, however well-liked or successful, moved across to ITV, there was no farewell party thrown for him, at least not in our group. To Tom the traitor had put himself beyond the pale and was treated with remote politeness as though he or she had developed a sinister blister on the lip. How Tom would have recoiled from the situation today when the BBC is legally required to buy a proportion of its programmes from independent production companies, many of which have silly names which Tom would have loathed.

A compromise between the old ethical differences of BBC and commercial programme-making was foreseen without optimism many years ago by Donald Baverstock when he was Controller of BBC1. He called the impending merging of creative minds 'a process of cross-sterilization'.

It would be about four months until my new employer, London Weekend Television, had any premises and the BBC did not want me hanging about recruiting their staff (they claimed), so they paid me my four months' money in a lovely lump sum and asked me to clear my desk and leave Television Centre at once.

A sudden four months of paid autumnal holiday was a treat indeed, although unwarranted, I was not planning to poach BBC staff. Several of my producers had come in for a chat to find out the possibilities and ask my advice and I told them to stay put, if only because I had nothing I could offer them. Meanwhile, I enjoyed a bit of gardening at Anners and made Sally a coffee table (which she wanted to be the same size as an opened-out copy of the *Observer*).

One of LWT's directors was Arnold Weinstock, Chairman of GEC, who reads balance sheets with as much pleasure and hope as other people read menus. He lent us some offices in which to start up at GEC's head office in Stanhope Gate, off Park Lane.

At the first meeting in the autumn of 1968, we heads of production departments sat bunched tightly round a huge but still slightly too small mahogany table. There was Jimmy Hill, Head of Sport, who came to us from Coventry City where he was manager; from the BBC came Doreen Stephen to run religious and educational programmes; Joy Whitby, Executive Producer of children's programmes; Humphrey Burton, Head of Music and the Arts. I was called Head of Entertainment, which managed to give the impression that my colleagues' output was for information only. There was so little room round the table that at one point I said frostily to Humphrey Burton, 'Would Drama, Music and the Arts kindly take its elbow out of Entertainment?'

Apart from the BBC Mafia a number of the production staff came from Associated Rediffusion, the London company we replaced, including our Controller of Programmes, Cyril Bennett. And we had a few more from Granada, notably the excellent Derek Granger, our Head of Plays, who later went back to Granada and produced several series of sensitive rural love stories, a genre which might be termed the 'Sex and Sensibility' school. He titled his series by borrowing a neatly apt Shakespearean bawdy pun, *Country*

Matters. Later still, Derek was responsible for producing the monumental, massively successful *Brideshead Revisited*.

I was given a colleague whose responsibility was the tricky specialist job of booking singers and variety performers, then a substantial part of weekend programming. He was Tito Burns, who once had an accordion band but gave that up to become a wily (and funny) agent. Joining us was a case of gamekeeper turning poacher.

LWT took over a new tower block of offices, Station House in Stonebridge Park, close to Wembley studios which was to be our temporary production centre, but whilst work on our open-plan offices was being completed we worked from a clutch of little offices in Old Burlington Street.

We were a hectically busy band of brothers and sisters during those first few months of getting a television station on the air from scratch; I think our state of mind at the time could be fairly described as hopeful, happy and terrified.

There was so much to do so quickly. It was not only having to make bricks without straw, but also seemingly without clay and during a drought. It seemed to me to be impossible to produce a full schedule of sitcoms and variety shows in the few months I had before we went on the air. Where to start? Where to get hold of a few seed potatoes and bulbs to plant and bring on?

It was all very different from life at the dear old BBC where there was terrific back-up. They had everybody's phone number and address so you could get in touch with anybody; there was a newspaper library and music libraries, classical and pop; press cuttings were photocopied and circulated; relevant newspapers and weeklies were available. Legal advice was to be had, there was a car park, canteen, a matron and a club bar.

And in spite of my built-in resistance to being made into a money-obsessed manager when I believed other considerations were more effective in working with gifted people, I must confess that during my three glorious years at the BBC I willy-nilly learned three valuable skills: how to stand at a superior's desk to be reprimanded and read his correspondence upside down; how to write a critical memo which deeply impresses those who get copies but avoids upsetting the recipient; how to yawn at meetings with mouth closed.

In the middle of this sudden wave of nostalgia, my old colleague and friend Michael Mills rang and asked me to meet him for a drink in the Television Centre club bar, the first time I had been invited back since the estrangement. I agreed immediately, but driving there I was suddenly overcome by a strange fear – a sort of daymare – that once inside the building I wouldn't want to come out again. It would be like a return to the warmth and safety of the womb, and I would rush up to the office of the producer of *The Epilogue*, seize him by the lapels and cry, 'Sanctuary, oh, sanctuary! I wish to eschew the hurly-burly of Cad's Television and rest here for ever in the quiet curved corridors of Television Centre, heart of public service broadcasting which I know and love!'

But when I arrived at Television Centre my fears that I would have an emotional comeover turned out to be groundless. The reception desk wouldn't let me in.

Things began to move in Old Burlington Street.

Thanks to *My Word!* and *My Music* being heard all over the world, Denis and I had become used to writers and performers from the Commonwealth, even from America, coming to see us when they landed in England so that we could brief them on what was going on in radio and television, the possibilities of employment and so on.

There was Richard Lester and Dick Vosburgh from the USA, Bernie Braden and Barbara Kelly from Canada, also Eric Nicol from Canada. The same thing happened when Oxbridge graduates came down looking for work. We tried to help on their way such talents as Leslie Bricusse, Frederick Raphael and John Cleese.

Also, because Denis and I had worked in Australia, Antipodean singers, comics, conjurors, musicians, almost anybody wanting to work in radio and television tended to make a beeline for us on landing at Heathrow. One lad who turned up to see me at Old Burlington Street was a young, curly-haired producer, writer and director of good, off-beat comedy whose name was Maurice 'Mocker' Murphy. He was a kind of Ozzy version of Dennis Main Wilson. Maurice was over here to get directing experience in Britain. This ambition was a little tricky to help along as I was still regarded by old-time executives at Television Centre as though I was a disgraced step-uncle who had left the family to embrace Islam, but I wrote to old friends and Mocker was called to a few interviews.

A couple of weeks later Mocker was back. He was offered one or two comedy things to direct but he turned them down. This was rather brave as he and his producer wife Margaret were hoping to stay a year and then have saved enough money to go home via the USA. It seems that he did not like the 'civil service' feel to the BBC which still lingered, and he found that artistic decisions were made too high up the ladder and too remote from the coalface. I warmed to the lad. Unfortunately LWT had absolutely nothing to offer until we moved into our studios in Wembley and began production; I said I would try to do something then.

Meanwhile I had an idea for an Anglo-Russian exchange of comedy plays. It came about when I went to a lecture given by the distinguished Russian screenwriter, Alexei Kapler. Alexei's speech was simultaneously and brilliantly translated by the literary agent and linguist Nina Froud. Via Nina, I asked Alexei whether he would write a comedy play for us. Nina persuaded Alexei that earning a little hard currency could not be bad.

Alexei almost immediately produced the outline of a delightful satirical comedy of modern Moscow. The action was set in one of those tiny ancient wooden houses which still crouch, gently falling apart, at the foot of Moscow's concrete high-rise offices and vast ministerial blocks. It was a semi-detached bungalow, one half occupied by a failed priest (to be played, I hoped, by Ralph Richardson) with nobody attending his services, and the other half housing a failed science master in a local school (Warren Mitchell) whose pupils take no notice of him. The priest fakes icons to earn an extra rouble. He also brews *kvas*, a highly popular, very Russian drink. The priest mixes up his icon-faking chemicals and accidentally spills some into his friend's *kvas* before leaving the beaker out for him on the balcony to enjoy his usual end-of-day swig. When darkness falls, the science master finds he has developed a bright shining halo. It stays until daylight renders it invisible.

I was thinking that Joan Sims would be just right as his girlfriend, and we could have a scene with Joan, flushed with desire, rushing round the room switching out the lights while the science master, fearful of his halo becoming visible, rushes round the room after her switching them on again.

The development of the plot was how the two men could use the halo to their advantage. Scientifically? Like filling the science master's empty lecture theatre with citizens eager enough to pay a large fee to see the dull little science master with a halo? Or should the priest take a swig of the *kvas* and fill his church and become a famous miracle and a television celebrity?

My scheme was to produce Alexei's play for LWT and then produce, in exchange, a television comedy set in London which Alexei would screen in Moscow.

Michael Peacock was in favour of the project and agreed that I should go over to Moscow for a week to meet Alexei, discuss production problems and so on, and sort out a contract with the relevant government agency (this was a very chilly period of the Cold War when you couldn't officially sneeze without permission from a government agency).

Michael allowed me to take a small team of two with me, namely the indispensable Nina Froud, who spoke perfect Russian and had been in Moscow only a few months previously helping one of her authors research his biography of the great Russian bass singer, Chaliapin, and Polly. Polly, having a French mother, was bilingual, English/French, and Alexei, most surprisingly for a successful and popular Soviet public figure and professor of cinema with his own television programme, had come from a bourgeois Jewish family, had been brought up by a French nanny and was bilingual, too, Russian/French.

So on Saturday 3 February off we went to Moscow.

The word was that the temperature there was 18 degrees below zero so I had hired an enormous fur-lined coat and fur hat from Moss Bros (Polly and Nina had their own sheepskin coats). In a photograph taken by BEA of me standing on the aircraft's steps waving, I resembled a nervous yeti.

The flight was calm and pleasant. There were only ten passengers in our huge BEA aircraft, so we paying customers congregated at the back of the plane and the cabin crew lay down and slept or played cards up in empty seats at the front end. They left the drinks trolley next to us and told us to give them a shout when we wanted lunch. It was like having one's own enormous private jet.

Polly had sensibly invested some time in learning the Russian alphabet so she could at least prevent me being arrested for wandering into the Ladies. While Polly was having a session with Nina on pronunciation and I was having a tentative stab at the crossword in my complimentary copy of *The Times*, I was joined by a genial burly man. He was helpful with the crossword because he had finished his before the aircraft's wheels were up.

He was a senior BEA engineer. His job was to be flown to Moscow, supervise the refuelling of the aircraft, then get back in it and be flown home.

'Watch your ears,' he said.

'Not easy,' I said, ever ready with a merry quip.

'Well, you'd better keep an eye on them somehow, frostbite is cumulative,' he said. 'Builds up without you knowing it. A few months ago I was on the wing of an aircraft checking the tank and my fur ear flaps were up. I was bitten. The remedy is rubbing them with brandy, so I called out to the chief steward and he came running with the bottle. I took one look at the label, gave the bottle back to him and said, 'When I need brandy, Adrian, I expect you to bring me Courvoisier VSOP not rotten tourist class Three-Star!'

He honked with laughter all the way back down the aisle.

The seat across the gangway was occupied by three ample ladies. Two of them chattered away happily to each other for the whole flight, and the third, who had a large magnifying glass harnessed to her formidable bosom, worked silently on a piece of *petit point* embroidery which Polly managed to glimpse and told me was a reproduction of a Landseer painting of animals lying in the heather, bleeding.

A steward whispered to us that two of them were titled, but he had no idea which two.

I had a nasty twinge of panic when the aircraft came in to land. Painted on the front of the Terminal building in huge letters was the name of the airport, MOCKBA.

'It's not Moscow!' I hissed to Polly. 'We've been hijacked!'

'Pull yourself together,' said Polly, collecting her hand luggage peaceably, 'Mockba is Russian for Moscow.' One does feel such a fool.

When the aircraft came to a complete stop the three elderly ladies were the first to disembark. Adrian the head steward joined us as we stood watching the ladies picking their unflurried way down the aircraft steps, wincing but not dismayed by the sudden bitterly cold air.

'Aren't they marvellous?' I said to Adrian. 'Makes you proud to be British.'

'Absolutely,' said Adrian. 'Do you know they shifted fifteen mini bottles of gin between them?'

Snow was falling on the parked aircraft, the roofs, the roads. The cold was intense and I quickly put on my Moss Bros fur hat. It was so huge and heavy that I felt I looked like a toffee apple. Milling all around us in the arrivals lounge were fur-hatted, snowed-upon Russians looking for each other, and young soldiers with smooth round Asiatic faces looking lost, like new recruits reporting for duty with a Tartar horde. The air was heavy with spoken Russian which we had never realized was such a musical, beautiful sound.

We felt a long way from home and in a very alien country and this feeling was not dispersed when we were told that the modern, bang-up-to-date, concrete barn of a hotel we had booked into was required by the authorities for some workers' jolly and we had been summarily off-loaded to an old Edwardian establishment (actually rather famous) called the Hotel Berlin.

But Alexei Kapler was waiting for us at the arrivals barrier, which cheered us up. He was fifty-fiveish, lots of grey hair, plump-ish and happy to see us.

We piled into his little car, cuddling our luggage, which was too big to go into his boot, and he drove us to Moscow. Most of the way was through miles of silver birch trees, behind which loomed the dark shapes of firs.

We passed a concrete memorial commemorating a famous heroic occasion during the last war when a small unit of Russian soldiers on a farm held up the entire German invasion force for several valuable hours.

Alexei explained with some glee what had happened. It seems the colonel commanding the small garrison manning the farm was a mean-spirited man who suspected the general commanding this stretch of front line of disliking him and wishing to do him down. When the Germans began their invasion and the tanks were rolling, the general sent a radio message to the farm commander telling him that the German army was on its way and ordering him to evacuate the farm and retreat immediately. 'Aha!' thought the idiot colonel. 'I know his little game. It's only a platoon of Germans on a scouting recce. If I retreat he'll arrest me for cowardice and I will be reduced to the ranks, which is what he's always wanted!' So he commanded his tiny garrison to man their mortars, load their rifles, position their machine-guns and repulse the small scouting sortie at all costs.

The German army suddenly found itself being fired upon and the mighty advance was halted and a worried meeting was held at German Brigade Headquarters. Intelligence had assured them that there would be no serious resistance until they were nearer Moscow, but had the Russians outwitted them and was the main Russian army dug in and waiting to annihilate them ahead? It was too risky to chance, so the German invasion halted to consider tactics and the Russians won a valuable day in which to build up their defences. The lucky garrison commander won himself a statue.

We zinged along in Alexei's car which was a little like Alexei, friendly, slightly battered-looking and lots of surprises. The seats were once very comfortable. Alexei kept reaching down to the floor and producing things to show us. He talked away in his excellent French and Polly translated for me when she felt I was being left behind.

Moscow was a dramatic sight. Huge snowflakes were drifting down, but the city's wide main roads were being efficiently cleared; snowploughs and bulldozers were pushing the snow into heaps in the gutter as it fell. Another machine with steel arms embraced the snow and slid it onto conveyor belts which lifted and dropped it into the back of a queue of lorries.

When darkness fell, the snowy roads continued to be cleared all night by a more traditional Soviet system. An army of quite old, fat women, wrapped in rusty quilted black clothes, emerged from somewhere with picks and hacked away at the nobbles of ice on the pavement which a multitude of feet treading on snow at 20 degrees below had produced. In the freezing cold these fragments of ice and the massive snowflakes still falling were shovelled up into wheelbarrows by the women and carted off by them into the darkness. As the authorities were so right to point out, they had no unemployment problem in Moscow.

Alexei took us to the Hotel Berlin and made sure we were properly registered. We liked the hotel immediately. It was a relic of a different world with decor about as baroque as anyone ever got.

As we peered into the gilt, mirror-lined dining room Polly suddenly gripped my arm. 'There's a waiter fishing!' she said. And indeed there was. At the far end of the room there was a small circular pool surrounded by a brass rail. An ancient waiter was leaning on the brass rail dabbing at the water with what seemed to be a large shrimping net. He straightened up and made his way on painful feet to the kitchen with a wriggling trout in his net dripping onto the carpet.

We were given what the lady on reception insisted was the hotel's de-luxe suite. It consisted of a tiny salon, a minute bedroom with twin beds and a bathroom. The loo did not work, or more accurately it never stopped working. But I found it was possible to staunch the flow cleverly, even when seated, by reaching behind into the cistern and punching the ballcock. The manoeuvre might have been even cleverer had it occurred to me to roll up my sleeve first.

Alexei returned later to take us to dinner at the Screenwriters' Club. Escorting him downstairs we had to pass close by the two black-clad ladies on duty at a desk in a corner of our corridor. They eyed us suspiciously as we passed, making us feel like escapees sneaking out of a government house of correction.

On the way downstairs we also had to squeeze between a lady wearing furs and a picture hat in earnest conversation with a gentleman in striped pyjamas. The hotel foyer was dimly lit. Near the door was a television set which was difficult to see as the uniformed hall porter was sitting right in front of it and about 6 inches from the screen. Reception did not seem to be at all good but occasionally the crackling noises stopped and the screen went into sharp focus, whereupon the hall porter rose, fiddled at the back of the set and mucked the picture up again to his satisfaction.

It was very hot in the foyer and very cold outside. Through the glass door I could see a furry, assassin-like figure on the pavement gesticulating for me to come outside. What did he want? To enroll me as a secret agent? To bum a cigarette? To steal my hat?

Consumed with curiosity, I befurred myself, let down the flaps of my hat and went out into the aching cold. 'Psssst, man!' said the assassin in a slightly American accent, quickly looking over both shoulders to make sure the coast was clear. 'Wanna buy a glass cutter?'

It wasn't even one of those glass cutters which incorporated a chip of diamond, it was the sort with a little rusty wheel, which in my experience was about as efficient a method of cutting glass as scribing it with a knob of butter. I politely declined the offer and nipped back into the warm foyer of the hotel.

It was the fiftieth anniversary of the Red Army and that evening the entire membership of the Moscow Screenwriters' Club seemed, understandably, to be pissed (which a great many Muscovites appeared to be every evening).

While we were waiting for our table we had an odd conversation with a thin merry man who for quite a long time had been trying to light a broken cigarette. He did not seem to be speaking any language recognized by our party. When something amused him, and almost everything did, he dropped down and squatted on his heels, enjoyed his laugh and then reared up again with a cracking of knees to a standing position. Alexei said that in daylight he was a military historian.

We were joined at supper by Alexei Bolokon, a publisher, with his wife and his daughter Natasha, who spoke excellent English which she used almost exclusively to list for us the recent cultural and humanitarian achievements of the USSR.

We had a splendid meal which began with what seemed to be a selection of about fifty hot Russian hors-d'œuvres followed by delicious Georgian chicken – a small chicken hammered flat with a cleaver until it resembles a recently run-over frog.

Alexei's blonde wife Julia was a poet. On the way back to the hotel, Nina told us that during the war Julia had fought in the Army as a private and now washed her hair every night for the sheer pleasure of being able to.

As Polly and I lay in bed, too exhausted to sleep after what might reasonably be termed a busy day, we decided that the smell of a city is the smell at night of its petrol fumes. Moscow petrol smelled of bubblegum.

The following five days in Moscow were so action-packed that they made our day of arrival seem in memory like a day off. I had somehow to make a deal with a government agency appointed 'to look after Professor Kapler's interests', which in reality meant blocking any deal which required Alexei's presence outside Russia in case he had it in mind, which he certainly hadn't, to defect to the West.

Alexei must have been quite a worry to the authorities. He began as an actor in silent films in 1920 and worked for a while in Leningrad with the splendidly named Eccentric Actors' Factory. In

1928 he turned to screenwriting and became a leading writer of film scripts, working with such directors as Eisenstein. Then, whilst working in Moscow, he met and fell in love with Stalin's daughter Svetlana, and she with him. It was a gentle love story of a highly intelligent man of forty and a sensitive schoolgirl and was beautifully described by Svetlana in her book, *Twenty Letters to a Friend*. Alexei is letter sixteen.

The affair had no future, of course. Stalin was strongly anti-Semitic and Alexei was Jewish. Alexei was arrested and sent to exile in a Siberian mining village for five years. He was ordered to stay away from Svetlana and to make no attempt to contact her ever again. When his five years were up he went back to Moscow and immediately telephoned Svetlana, was arrested again and sent 'north' for another five years. And that was that. Svetlana married (her husband was Jewish) and Alexei got on with his career, but the police must have amassed a thick file on Alexei down at the old Lubyanka.

The government press agency with whom I had to make the deal was called APN (Russia's use of acronyms almost equalled the BBC's). Every morning at about ten, Polly, Nina and I briskly stepped out from the hotel to APN's offices, a fair trot up Gorski Prospect (which we renamed the APN Way). At ten thirty every morning we had a brief meeting with APN's senior man, who told us that the Minister of Culture, who had to authorize every detail of our deal, was at a meeting and would we come back at four fifteen? Then, every afternoon at four fifteen we returned, and as I tried to discuss Alexei's fees and role as supervisor of the production the agency man would fidget and then blurt out that the minister had gone home. Would we please come back at ten thirty tomorrow morning?

During our walks to and from APN, we managed to cram in a bit of shopping and sightseeing, not easy as the streets were thronged with the 2 million visitors from other republics of the USSR who were always trudging round Moscow trying to buy a wedding ring. Queues for wedding rings curled out of the jewellers' shops, went round the block and curled back in again. Customers lined up according to the initial of their surname, i.e., those whose names began with A–D queued up on Mondays, E–H on Tuesdays, and so on.

Those of the 2 million not queueing for wedding rings seemed to be trudging along the pavement very slowly in front of us.

Restaurants, for which lengthy queueing was the norm, were mostly ethnic. We had lunch in the Sofia, a Bulgarian restaurant. The only part of the meal I can remember is the coffee. Our Bulgarian coffee was exactly like Turkish coffee except that the grounds floated on top.

One day Alexei collected us from our morning disappointment at APN and drove us on a sightseeing tour round the city. It was amazing how Alexei managed to turn up in his car just when we wanted him, and he was hardly idle at the time: as well as setting up a co-production deal on a film to be made in France, he was trying to get a visa for Julia to read her poetry at a Brussels literary festival, he had a daily lecture to give to his students and he had his weekly television show about films.

Alexei's car was not a massive government limousine. It was a small dented saloon of some age, yet every time we stopped and parked Alexei carefully removed the windscreen-wiper blades and locked them away in the glove compartment. 'Is there much petty theft in Moscow?' I asked him.

He grinned. 'Who knows?' he said. 'It's not reported in the newspapers!'

About every mile Alexei shot out of his seat with a stifled Russian oath and hit his head on the roof. The spring in his seat was broken and every so often it ripped through the upholstery and hit dead centre.

On Sunday we stood at the back of a Russian Orthodox church which was crammed full of devout elderly people and equally devout young soldiers. Just inside the door stood a huge battered roll-top desk at which two old ladies sat selling candles, gossiping quite loudly with friends and entering up account books.

We had lunch back at the hotel. As I could not understand the menu, even when Polly translated the words, we stuck to what we knew and lived on bortsch, or smoked salmon and blinis, or caviare, with a flask each of vodka. It was a tough way of life, I grant you, but it was only for a few days so we gritted our teeth and endured it.

Unfortunately, when I was about to demolish a small mountain of Beluga caviare, Alexei spoiled my lunch by announcing that he had arranged for me to give a lecture at three o'clock to English-speaking students on the subject of humour in English literature. It was to take place in the unconvincingly named House of Friendship.

At three o'clock there were sixty or seventy quiet and respectful students of both sexes and many ages sitting on hard chairs with pencils and pads at the ready. Also present was the British Cultural Attaché who asked Polly if she would phone his mother when we got home.

Alexei introduced me in Russian. As I had no idea what he was saying I tried to adopt a look of nonchalant amusement to give the students hope. I gave them about forty minutes of tedium, waving my arms and leaping about to keep them awake, and then it was question time, always a relief to all. The students were only really interested in why I had not made more of Charles Dickens (clearly a Party hero in Russia) and his fight for the betterment of the working classes. To liven things up I pointed out that although Dickens was against nasty employers he was not very interested in put-upon employees, and I challenged the students to name one major serious Dickens character who was an ordinary worker, not a servant or a clerk. I pointed out that Dickens himself began as a working-class lad in a blacking factory, but managed to pull himself out of squalor and become a member of the well-off middle classes, where he intended to remain.

Afterwards I found the lecture and the bickering about Dickens (whom I enjoyed reading but didn't really know much about) had been recorded for playing on Moscow radio that evening. I was then interviewed by a delicate man with beautiful English and a sound recorder the size of a suitcase. During the interview, to be broadcast that evening as a trailer for the lecture, I gave London Weekend Television a terrific build-up, possibly the most useless bit of public relations ever perpetrated.

The interview had just finished and I could see Alexei struggling towards me through the Dickens fans with a restorative mug of vodka when a rather beautiful lean lady in black with her hair scraped back, like a character from a Chekhov play – I had noticed her smiling and nodding all through my lecture – came up very close to me, still smiling and nodding, put her hand gently on my arm and said, 'You should be in the cinema, Mr Myer, you are so *plastique*.'

Well, *I* think it was a compliment.

We were now in the rhythm of life in Moscow which consisted

largely of struggling out of boots, fur coat and hat in enormous vestibules, then eating, or talking, or watching something, and then struggling back into boots, fur coat and hat to brave the icy pavements again. The tiny cloakroom lady in APN's vestibule had got used to the weight of my coat and did not attempt to lift it from the counter but slid it along the floor to a vacant hook.

That evening we saw a witty and imaginative production of *Turandot* which had been running for three years. This was the reproduction of a commedia dell'arte version orginally staged in Moscow in 1929. Afterwards, Nina took us to a supper party given in a high-rise flat belonging to a friend of hers, a young painter who restored icons (honourably) for a living. Also present were a cheerful bunch of young actors, actresses, writers, an architect and a huge puppy called Philip Morris. With the exception of Philip Morris, they all spoke fluent English.

Our artist host unfortunately did not believe in possessions so there was no furniture. We dined upon a large framed religious painting laid on trestles and when we sat down on our beer crates the 'table' came up to chin level.

As the Armenian brandy flowed, the beautiful young wives and girlfriends sang sad Russian songs, danced ancient dances of submission before their lords and offered them gherkins. At something of a loss how I could reciprocate for England I finally got up and sang them 'Miner's Dream' with actions.

'You are beautiful,' said a small actor.

I was a little disconcerted by this until Nina whispered to me that in Russian the word 'beautiful' also meant 'red'. Our host kindly opened the door on to the tiny iron balcony, and in seconds the room was agreeably cool and I was no longer at all beautiful.

About midnight we went back to the Hotel Berlin by taxi. The driver was very drunk and at one point, with a couple of loud thumps and the scraping of branches against paintwork, drove us at speed across a landscaped traffic island.

Next day we asked Alexei whether there was much drunkenness in Moscow. He smiled. 'Who knows?' he said. 'It's not reported in the newspapers!'

Finding ourselves with an hour to spare we did a quick run round the Kremlin Museum. Perhaps 'run' is the wrong word. As a sensible rule to preserve the fine old parquet floors, we added our shoes to the other clobber we handed over in the vestibule, put on huge slippers made from old bits of domestic carpet, and shuffled past such glories as the Tsars' collection of Fabergé eggs and King Charles II's golden coach like a very old couple trying to find the bar in a health farm.

And there was the State Circus. Superbly groomed ponies pranced about the red-carpeted ring. The great Russian clown Popov was excellent, but a reminder that continental clowns don't skimp on their time, usually doing a routine that runs for about two hours. Chocolate cake was served in the interval on a piece of beige unperforated loo paper. The queue – there was always a queue in Moscow – was as kind as ever and as soon as they heard us speaking English waved us to the front. All the women looked at Polly's shoes. They weren't knee-high, scarlet, plastic startlers, just decent shoes, but as such envied.

Polly's shoes were envied again when we went to the Bolshoi Theatre to see a performance of *Prince Igor* and joined the crowd strolling along the grand first-floor promenade between acts. We were seated in the third row of the stalls, not in tip-up seats but in separate and very elegant *fauteuils* on a gleaming parquet floor. It was a suitable way to see *Prince Igor*, particularly in the spectacular production we accidentally booked for. There was a cast of hundreds; the chaps continually broke into gruff and emotional song, real horses galloped at speed about the huge stage, and when the Tartars attacked, the outer fortifications burst into real flames (well, they looked real).

The performance was slightly spoiled for us by Natasha, the publisher's lovely Soviet daughter, giving us a loud, politically correct running commentary on the action on-stage. And the principals had rather faint voices. Nina thought the first company was probably on tour and we were seeing the third or fourth company.

Success with Alexei's contract was in sight. I had upped the money which seemed to have helped. We paid our last visit to APN and the manager handed me the signed contract in a glossy blue folder marked 'Fiftieth Anniversary Of The Revolution'. The hand-over was photographed by an APN staff photographer as though I had won the pools.

Alexei drove us back past the silver birches to the airport and there produced presents from deep down between his car seats; little jars of caviare for me and a huge engraved walrus tusk, a genuine scrimshaw from Siberia, for Polly, which he had brought back as a reminder of his ten-year exile. Polly tried not to take it as it was clearly of great sentimental value. Alexei insisted. 'What is the point of giving a present unless it's something you'd really like to keep for yourself?' he asked.

Alexei, being a professor, was allowed to come onto the tarmac with us to the aircraft. It was suddenly intolerably sad having to say goodbye. His bear-hug crushed my ribs and his face was surprisingly bristly. 'See you in July,' I managed to say, and Polly, Nina and I climbed into the aircraft and sat silent with our thoughts as we took off into the evening sky.

A British Embassy man was immensely impressed on hearing about my deal with APN. He said that to get what you wanted signed in Moscow in five days might be a world record, but not so. Alexei's play never happened. Nina said afterwards that she thought APN never had any intention of letting it happen.

A few weeks before Alexei was due to come over to England to start work with us he telephoned Nina – for some reason he could telephone from his *dacha* without the call being bugged – and told her that if in the near future somebody claimed that he was ill, she must not believe it and worry. On the contrary, he was in very good health.

Sure enough, a few days later the Russian Embassy in London contacted Nina regretting that unfortunately Professor Kapler was ill with a virus infection and all his overseas commitments had to be cancelled.

Polly and I wanted to thank Alexei and assure him that he was still much in our thoughts. We were trying hard to think of something rather more fun that just writing him a letter when we came across an American advertisement for mail-order fruit cakes which they would send anywhere in the world (and probably anywhere in space by now).

What intrigued us was that the bakery was in a city in Texas named Corsicana (probably because of the influence the pioneer democracy of eighteenth-century Corsica had on the thinking behind the founding of American independence; e.g., Thomas Jefferson called his house Monticello), and we knew Alexei would enjoy the thought of getting a large, rich, American fruit cake stuffed with pecan nuts and fruit, all the way from Texas by post. And it worked; the cake arrived in Moscow safely and was much enjoyed. In return, Alexei sent us a portfolio of thirty watercolour prints of costume designs painted by his friend and colleague Sergei Eisenstein, who was a theatrical designer before he became a film director.

It seemed wrong for us to keep the prints hidden away in a file, they were colourful, exuberant and amusing, so we had them framed simply and, via Godfrey Smith's column in *The Sunday Times*, offered to lend them free to any theatre putting on a Russian play who could use them to decorate the foyer. Eventually they toured all the theatres that wanted them, so what should we do with them next? It was the time that the Groucho Club in Soho was opening its doors to media people and we presented the prints to Groucho's on permanent loan. They now hang on the walls of the staircase leading downstairs from the reception desk. At least they can now stimulate and inspire authors and publishers and rock stars as they clamber their way down to the loo.

When Alexei died a year or so later, our 'quality' newspapers gave him fulsome obituaries, but they did not mention that when he was walking in the woods, birds settled on his shoulders.

Shortly after we arrived home, London Weekend Television moved into its high-rise building (it swayed in a strong wind) just off the North Circular Road and near its Wembley studios. Entertainment Department was open-plan, which was a new experience. It meant that I had to hide the (illegal) portable bar-in-a-suitcase given to me by Jimmy Edwards, which I kept to comfort disconsolate visiting writers, and it was peculiarly difficult to tick somebody off in a whisper, but the open-plan design promoted an all-in-the-same-boat feeling which was good.

One afternoon I had just been comforting one of our secretaries who had run into trouble with her love-life – she had been at a concert of the Deep Purple pop group and, emotionally stirred, had grabbed her companion's arm and breathed, 'I've 'ad all of them, one by one.' Unfortunately her companion was her new, although from that moment on her ex-, boyfriend.

She thanked me for my wise advice (what on earth could I have said to her?) and I replied, 'Any time, Marlene. My door is always open.' And she said, 'You 'aven't *got* a door!'

Happily I had a super secretary to guide me through this comforting old grey-haired-uncle role, a part of the job of being head of a unit about which I had not been warned but rather enjoyed. At our very first LWT get-together meeting at Stanhope Gate, the bottles of fizzy water and the pencils and pads were arranged on the conference table by a most attractive temp named Tanya Bruce-Lockhart. Months later Tanya rang me at home and said, 'LWT begins as a company in September, which is quite soon, and before that I have to find you a secretary. What would you like me to do? Advertise the job, then arrange interviews and board applicants? Or will *I* do?'

So Tanya was my secretary at LWT right from the start. That meant she was the department's unofficial queen bee. Tanya was very keen on keeping up standards and this was the era of tights and very short miniskirts. On occasional mornings, as the girls were bent over their filing cabinets, Tanya's voice would ring out, rattling the open-plan dividing panels, 'Marlene – you've forgotten to put on knickers again!'

Tanya was very bright, too bright really for the job, but she was marvellous at getting me to settle down and do my correspondence, almost without me noticing. The trouble was that her shorthand speed was much speedier than my thinking speed – dictation was a task which was new to me and I loathed it – and on the many occasions when I was struggling for the right thing to say, Tanya would helpfully break the silence with something like, 'Is that a spot coming up on your nose?'

Eventually I managed to have her promoted to Location Finder, a job which needed considerable initiative. From there she worked her way steadily upwards, eventually becoming an important asset to Humphrey Burton's Arts programme, *Aquarius*.

One sympathetic but occasionally awkward character trait which ruled Tanya was a love of animals. The previous year, on holiday in Spain, Tanya had found a dog on the beach which had been deserted and was starving. She fed him, failed to find his owner, christened him Ricky and brought him back to England with her, paying for his six-month quarantine and visiting him almost every day. Ricky was a large dog, vaguely Alsatian, friendly but odd-looking. Every day Tanya brought him to Station House and he lay under her desk dozing happily.

Unfortunately there was a house rule that no dogs were allowed in the building and Tanya was sent a memo by the premises manager reminding her of this rule and asking her not to bring Ricky to the office any more.

Tanya was devastated and told me frankly, 'I'm sorry, but I go where Ricky goes. How can I leave him all on his own in a flat? If he has to stay at home, so will I.'

I knew the manager was not personally anti-Ricky, he had to play to the rules to cover himself. I needed to give him a reason to overlook Ricky and to have an excuse for Ricky's presence in the unlikely event of the dog getting overexcited and biting the property company's chairman on the ear, or being unsociable on his carpet.

I eventually wrote back, 'I am grateful to you for reminding me of the legal position of Miss Bruce-Lockhart's popular pet which spends its day snoozing under her desk in my department. Happily, I am able to assure you that the animal is not affected by your wise house rule of no dogs in the offices because Ricky is not a dog. Miss Bruce-Lockhart rescued him from a Spanish beach under the impression that he was a dog, but an inspection by a zoologist (the famous one on television) has revealed that he is an Andalusian, hornless, short-haired mountain goat, an uncommon breed which is perfectly harmless to humans and carpets . . .'

Ricky stayed. And so did Tanya.

In an LWT programme conference it was decided that LWT's first programme, to go on early Friday evenings, would be a series reflecting the change from weekday programming to a more care-free weekend schedule. The perfect title would have been *The Weekend Starts Here*, but Rediffusion had already used that. It was decided that the series should not be another pop-music show but would go for humour, and its provisional title was *We Have Ways of Making You Laugh*.

To produce the series, I had one of the best producers who came to us from Associated Rediffusion, Humphrey Barclay, who was young, extremely bright and inventive. We decided that we did not want to start the weekend with an anarchic romp, but with a cheerful, unpredictable, bitty sort of show which viewers could join at any point and then leave at any point to put the potatoes on.

We had the producer and the title, we now wanted the presenter. To my horror and delight (emotions which frequently coincide in television), Humphrey Burton argued strongly that I should present the show. I accepted. It was not all that much of an interruption to my work as unit head once Humphrey Barclay had got things organized.

We put together a team of writers and performers, and

writer/performers. Ken Cope, the writer, actor (*Randall and Hopkirk (Deceased)*) and restaurateur, wrote and performed a weekly five-minute piece to camera as the manager of a none-too-successful restaurant (foreshadowing Harry Enfield's Stavros?); Dick Vosburgh, superb writer of topical one-liners and well-known beard, sat at the back with a clipboard and the most bulging briefcase in television, writing his odd funny comments and passing them forward; the then almost unknown Eric Idle did some excellent bits and pieces; Terry Gilliam, an American artist and cartoonist, now director of extraordinarily imaginative Hollywood movies (*Brazil, The Adventures of Baron Munchhausen, Twelve Monkeys*), sat in the studio happily drawing what was going on and the camera zoomed in on his work from time to time; and Barry Cryer, Benny Green and others popped in with pieces.

As well as introducing *We Have Ways of Making You Laugh*, I contributed material, such as thinking up things to say which would enable us, since it was a live show, to bring it down exactly on time. I sometimes needed a long piece of waffle and sometimes a short piece, and thinking up various lengths of waffle enlivened the tedious daily drive to and from Wembley. The items were like (short waffle):

Surrey Constabulary have asked me to broadcast the following message. Yesterday afternoon at approximately 3.10 p.m., a police vehicle backing out of the forecourt of Woking Police Station was hit by a police vehicle backing *into* the forecourt. Nobody was hurt but both vehicles were extensively damaged. If any member of the public witnessed the incident – *please* shut up about it.

Another idea I had was for star comedians to do a bit of their original audition routine, or their first stage or radio act. These turned out, as I had hoped, to be bad, but considering how the comedians had grown in stature over the years, very funny.

Max Bygraves was the first. His original act was so brash and feeble that he could hardly get through it without corpsing. Dick Bentley was also very effective. He did the warm-up routine which he had done every week for over ten years to cheer up the studio audience before *Take It From Here*. Most of it purported to be a letter from his mother in Australia giving him the family news. I remember (how could I forget?) such lines as:

Your Great-Aunt Maude called in on Wednesday. What a marvellous old lady she is, ninety-six and not a grey hair on her head. Completely bald.

And:

Your Aunty Cissie came home drunk again on Thursday, bashed over one of the brick gateposts, flattened a flower bed and crashed into the rear wall of the garage. Thank God she wasn't in a car.

The letter always ended:

Must close now as Granny wants the Biro to do her eyebrows.

One Friday evening, 2 August 1968, *We Have Ways of Making You Laugh* made an almost illegible blur on television history as the first programme of the new station LWT. The show went marvellously, the full audience laughing and clapping their appreciation. The series never went so well over its subsequent fourteen weeks' run, but that was not surprising as the first show's audience consisted almost entirely of friends and investors.

Glowing with sweat and pleasure at the end, I was leaning against a camera feeling happily tired when Humphrey Barclay came up and said, 'I have the most rotten news. The show didn't go out.'

I couldn't believe it.

'The unions pulled the plug just before we went on air,' Humphrey said. 'I took the decision to let you do the whole show in case they plugged us back on, but they didn't. The technicians have called an indefinite strike.'

The cameraman beside us, who had much enjoyed doing the show, tore off his headphones and flung them to the ground in fury. I found myself in the ironic position of comforting a union member – 'Now come on, don't take it too badly, we'll do the show again sometime' – whose union had killed our transmission.

The weeks that the unions were out on strike were, in fact, most helpful to me, and I began to build up some potentially interesting shows.

Ronnie Wolfe and Ronnie Chesney offered me a sitcom series they had devised about a small-town bus driver and his family. This the BBC had turned down as they doubted how many laughs the boys could get out of oil leaks on the bus-depot floor. This was about as sensible a criticism as worrying how many laughs Galton and Simpson could get out of two rag-and-bone men and a horse.

The Wolfe and Chesney series was *On the Buses*, with Reg Varney as the cheery bus driver. It was hated by the critics and ended up being one of the longest-running sitcoms ever shown on ITV.

A quite different kind of programme was a smart domestic sitcom series, *Never a Cross Word*, written by Donald Churchill for Paul Daneman and Nyree Dawn Porter. It was our first big success. In the opening programme of the series the part of a shy awkward Welsh student who was their lodger was played brilliantly by the young John Alderton, previously a doctor in *Emergency – Ward 10*.

When I was at the BBC, a young man named Terry Jones was heavily recommended to me as a potential director and I wangled him onto a BBC directors course. The end-of-course exercise required the student to find a suitable sketch, get an actor to perform it for nothing and then shoot it on tape so that his directing skills could be assessed by the tutors.

Terry wrote his own sketch and it was played by his good friend, an unknown would-be actor/writer named Michael Palin. The sketch was very well played and directed and Terry passed his course.

Then, out of the blue, Terry and Michael turned up at LWT with a wild six-part comedy series which they called *The Complete and Utter History of Britain*. Humphrey Barclay would produce. It was a totally original piece of work for which we needed the right unconventional-minded director. I remembered 'Mocker' Murphy, the young Australian, and with a great deal of cunning string-pulling I managed to get him.

There was one episode which gives an idea of Terry's and Michael's approach to history. The commentator said something like:

VOICE-OVER: In those early days, Britain was a rich target for marauders from less fertile lands and was subject to wave after wave of invaders who proved difficult to cope with.

(Cut to beach. A modern naval officer in gumboots and holding a loud hailer is addressing unseen invaders.)

NAVAL OFFICER: Right, Jutes, come on in! Finger out, Jutes, haven't got all day! Saxon hordes, hold off until I tell you, then follow the Jutes onto beach four. Sorry, Vikings, that's all for today! Can you come back first thing in the morning, say nine thirty sharp?

Another good thing was a series written by Ken Cope about an amiable, mischievous old-age pensioner known to everybody as Thingummybob, which was the name of the show. Stanley Holloway starred as Thingummybob.

The show had great warmth with some good lines (on the price of an air ticket to Paris: 'If God had meant us to fly he would have given us the money'). I even managed to get Paul McCartney to write the signature tune. But the show was hampered by being forty-five minutes long instead of the accepted thirty minutes. This was at the request of Tom Margerison, a senior management figure, though exactly what he managed I never knew.

Tom was a very agreeable, softly spoken, ready-to-smile journalist who specialized in scientific matters (at an earlier stage in his career he had introduced computers to local papers in Reading and Hemel Hempstead). At the beginning of LWT he seemed to be principally concerned with convincing me to make all sitcoms last forty-five minutes (I tried, but they suffered because writers, in fact everybody, was so used to the half-hour length that forty-five-minute shows came out as thirty-minute shows with padding). He also strode about carrying plans and considering whether our new studios being built on the South Bank should have glass walkways going through them so that visitors to Dear Olde London Towne could watch a television show being recorded.

Another really good script was brought to me. I was the writers' second choice, but didn't mind when the writers were John Esmonde and Bob Larbey. It was a series to be proud of, set in a comprehensive school in a tough area of London. It was Esmonde and Larbey working well, the pupils were beautifully delineated and the staff were a recognizably funny lot. The central character, the young teacher, was slightly awkward and gauche but fundamentally tough enough for the job, and remembering the Welsh lodger in the first *Never a Cross Word*, we cast John Alderton as 'Privet' Hedges.

The BBC had been offered the series and had turned it down because one of the pupils was 'educationally subnormal' and they thought it was wrong to make fun of afflictions. This was a curious lack of confidence in the tact and taste of the writers. In fact the character in question, Dennis, was handled very well. The other members of the class protected him and he became a popular part of the show to viewers. *Please Sir!* had a long, highly successful run, followed by a spin-off, *The Fenn Street Gang*.

Then I managed to persuade an old friend, Richard Gordon, to let me have the TV rights to his *Doctor in the House* books. John Cleese and Graham Chapman – a writer who was also a doctor – wrote the pilot script for the series and several episodes. Another pair of writers on the series were Graeme Garden – also a doctor – and Bill Oddie (both were later Goodies).

A well-balanced, reasonably happy unit of real television people is a formidable machine, capable at a pinch of swinging into action with breathtaking speed and resourcefulness. My unit had all those qualities and they displayed them to me on Thursday 19 December 1968.

At breakfast a few days earlier I had nearly bitten a lump out of my coffee cup when I opened a letter to find it was an invitation to lunch at Buckingham Palace. It seems that the Queen held random 'Thursday lunches' at the palace, so that she and other members of the royal family could meet and chat about this and that to a selected few citizens.

The Queen and the Duke were to be there, as were Prince Charles and Princess Anne. There were eight of humble us, a cross-section, but of what? We consisted of Lord Rothschild, Professor Asa Briggs, Mr Grima the jeweller, Sir Matt Busby, Sir Michael Tippett, Michael Green the editor of the *Daily Telegraph* and

Victor Sylvester, who looked odd sitting quietly in a lounge suit rather than standing upright in white tie and tails, undulating and waving a baton.

It was all rather heady and splendid. Excellent food and plenty of conversation. For me, anyway. I was seated next to the Duke of Edinburgh who had a bee in his bonnet about studio audiences at comedy shows (this was before canned laughter), and he would be pleased if I got rid of studio audiences so he could enjoy his comedy unprompted by squeals.

I was stoutly opposing the Duke's point of view (it's always more fun) when the Queen rose to lead us into another room for coffee. We all immediately rose with her and followed her towards the door, the Duke arguing fiercely with me on a good point about studio audiences being so excited at being present at a recording that they were not a natural audience.

I suddenly realized I was in trouble. The Queen had arrived at the door and was waiting for the Duke to catch up with her, but I was with the Duke and he had what he believed to be a killer argument and was only halfway through it and going strong. What should I do? Rudely break off the argument just when the Duke was in full gallop and retire to my proper place at the back in the queue, or go in with him?

I went in with him. So the little procession weaving its way towards coffee was led by the Queen, after whom came the Duke of Edinburgh and Mr Frank Muir (a peasant), and following them came Princess Anne, Prince Charles and the rest of the guests.

The coffee was served by footmen and then the equerries got to work. Like hyper-intelligent sheepdogs they nudged each of us in turn to the Queen's side for a five-minute chat and then detached us, without us really realizing it, to make way for the next guest.

The Queen and the Duke had had a bad press after visiting South America and the Queen asked me whether I believed what I read in the papers. I said that I didn't *believe* what I read, but because it was in the papers it gave the event or whatever a kind of importance. I said that it was rather like advertisements. One didn't *believe* what was claimed for the product, but because it was advertised it put the product into a more prominent category in the mind than other products.

And the Queen said, 'Oh, yes, I see what you mean. If I bought an electric drill I'd buy a Black & Decker.'

I had gone to great lengths to keep this lunch appointment a secret from my colleagues at LWT, so I had booked a hire car to take me to St James's Street to lunch in the fish restaurant there, and redirected the driver to the palace later. There were no mobile phones then, so there could be no leakage from the car of the secret destination.

And yet, I underestimated television folk. When I returned to Station House and stepped out of the lift, I found my whole department on one knee in a mock-humble welcome. Purple crêpe paper made a special carpet to my desk where I was presented with a gold (coloured) sceptre and a crown, heavily bejewelled (wine gums), and a scroll recording the lunch in ancient script on vellum (wrapping-paper). The wording concluded:

> We were most graciously pleased to have our right loyal and trusted servant F. HERBERT MUIR for luncheon, and he was delicious.

Well, the exact phrase to describe that little welcome home was 'sent up rotten' and I remember being so sent with great happiness.

Everything now in LWT seemed to be going so well. My department had the usual complement of failures, but also some stunning successes, three of the shows ran for years and there were plenty more in the pipeline. Tito's variety bookings for Saturday nights were excellent and we had not yet been eighteen months on the air.

Then the whole thing suddenly fell apart.

On Monday 5 September 1969, the available unit heads in the building, Doreen Stephens, Terry Hughes, Humphrey Burton, Derek Granger and I, were summoned to an urgent meeting at 6 p.m. that evening at our chairman Aidan Crawley's fine home in Chester Row. Mr Crawley informed us that the directors had that morning sacked Michael Peacock. And our new managing director, chosen to turn round the company's fortunes with an iron hand was – we held our breaths – Tom Margerison.

We were dumbfounded.

Dr Tom Margerison! The gentle, solid-state physicist, sometime science correspondent of *The Sunday Times*?

Our first question was of course, what on earth did the board have against Michael Peacock?

Aidan Crawley's answers were lame, vague and somewhat

evasive, as all the directors' answers to the question were to be, e.g., 'It was time for a change . . . Peacock did not get on with the board . . . there was a fall off in advertising revenue . . . faulty purchasing of programmes . . .' And the board of directors' trump card: 'The managing director must carry the can for what the board considers to be poor company performance. It is rightly in the board's power to hire and fire its managing director when it feels it necessary.'

Next day we unit heads met and discussed what to do. There was not a lot we could do at that stage except to protest vehemently and try to find out what the directors' panic move was really about. The most likely truth was the complaint that Michael 'did not get on with the board'. One of the board once said to Michael, 'Could we have more swimming programmes on Saturday afternoons? My daughter likes swimming.'

Had Michael been a well-trained, docile managing director who knew his place, he would have said something like, 'What a splendid idea, sir! Why didn't I think of that! I'll have a word with Jimmy Hill right away!' And he would have immediately forgotten all about the idea (as would the member of the board). But Michael was not like that; he had no smarm, was totally professional and he brushed off the director's request by pointing out that programme content was the responsibility of the Unit of Sport, thank you.

The board was mainly composed of professional financiers, courteous kindly men who were highly regarded pension-fund managers, building-society executives, a sugar magnate, a merchant banker, knowledgeable chaps in putting millions of pounds of people's savings to work but – whether or not to have more swimming on Saturday afternoon telly they were not in any way equipped to judge.

We met the senior members of the Independent Television Authority (now renamed the Independent Broadcasting Authority). Seeming not to know much about LWT's crisis, or even wanting to know much about it, we found the IBA massively unhelpful. Trying to persuade them into some kind of action was like pushing a finger into a lump of lard. When the finger was pulled out again there was no trace of the finger ever having been in there.

Was our present crisis really how the business world successfully operated? To we programme-makers, who had left good, well-paid jobs with the BBC and Granada for the excitement of starting up something new and ambitious with an ethic, LWT was *our* station.

Many, many BBC comedy series – from *Take It From Here* upwards – began badly with poor figures and a poor press, but were kept going by the BBC's faith in them, and many became successes. When we at LWT went on air some of our programmes disappointed the press, but might well have improved greatly if given the care and time that the BBC gave to nursing new shows. Most commercial television companies short-sightedly did not bother to do this. The accountants regarded new programmes with low initial viewing figures as financial losers to be chopped as quickly as possible.

We, the programme-makers, knew that our names were paraded at the IBA when the application was being submitted and that that was one of the reasons, even perhaps the major reason, why our group won the licence. Financial backing had been organized, a task in the days of 'licences to print money' about as difficult as organizing rabbits to become involved with a lettuce. In effect, the silken rope was lifted and a few privileged City men were permitted to scramble under it and grab a hunk of LWT's equity shares, an almost sure-fire investment.

Unbelievably to me, a total innocent in the business world, once the company was formed, *our* company we thought, it then belonged to the directors, who, it seemed to me, knew as much about running a television company as I knew about copper futures (promotion in the police force?). And they could do what they wished, sack our leader or any of us if the financial return was not swift and to their liking.

There was no contact at all between the board and the creative side of the company; the programme-makers were not represented on the board or even consulted by the board.

In a brilliant *aide-mémoire* written by Humphrey Burton, he summed up our attitude: the company was no longer the company we joined, its objectives were different and were not ours; we had lost all confidence in the board of directors, they had plenty of integrity and were kind to animals and all that, but they had no idea how to run a television company and no sense whatever of show business; it seemed to us that to many board members LWT was regarded as a prestige toy.

What could we do? We persuaded the board to meet us and discuss the crisis, and a sub-committee of directors, headed by the vice-chairman, Lord Campbell, came to Burlington Street.

Lord Campbell told us that in his experience all management was the same. 'You unit heads may think that managing talented producers and performers raises special problems,' he said, 'but I have been in sugar all my life and I can assure you that the management of people in television is precisely the same as the management of sugar workers.'

It was clear that no bridges were going to be built with him, so we tried yet again to find out why these people had chucked Michael.

Lord Campbell thought a bit. Then he turned to me and said, '*You* will know what I mean, Frank, when I say that he "lacks synthetical propensity".'

As it happened I did know what the line meant, but milord seemed so patronizing that I remained silent. If his assumption was that the other unit heads would never have heard of the phrase it was insufferably insulting.

The phrase came from a fairly well-known letter written by the Revd Sydney Smith to his co-founder of the *Edinburgh Review*, Francis Jeffrey. Jeffrey's literary reviews were growing increasingly crabby and vicious and Smith wrote urging him to make his criticism more constructive, and he accused Jeffrey of lacking 'synthetical propensity', i.e., the urge to build up rather than tear down (which is what the phrase means, I think. I must check with a sugar-cane cutter). Anyway, to accuse Michael Peacock of lacking ambition to build up his company and lead it forward would have been ludicrous.

Our group met later and discussed what we could possibly do to retain the old company; the unions met and overwhelmingly voted to retain the *status quo*, but without us getting some official backing from the IBA, which they were not prepared to give, our case was hopeless. So regretfully, and sorrowfully, we handed in our resignations.

The press had a field day. It was huge headline stuff (anything that happens backstage in television always is) and took up most of the front pages of the *Daily Mail* and the *Guardian*.

It was a horrible time. My unit begged me to stay and I had to say, 'You are children asking me not to leave you alone in the dark, but the roof's on fire.'

I found a copy of the prospectus I had written for our company's application for the LWT licence, a brief description of what I hoped the unit would achieve in comedy. I pinned it up on the unit's cardboard wall and wrote underneath:

And we did it.
Grateful thanks to you all.

I had to start thinking about what I was going to do about money. My shares in LWT would almost certainly mature at a huge profit, but I couldn't in all conscience resign on a matter of principle but keep the money. With a pang, I sold the shares back to the company at face value.

Both children were at fee-paying schools, the ancient matchwood farmhouse staircase at Anners was sagging with age and we had rather rashly gone heavily into expensive pine for a new staircase and new interior doors and fireplace. I had also ordered a new car.

When the papers reported that 'The Six' were being implored to stay, Jamie sent me a postcard. It was a reproduction of the colour painting of young Napoleon campaigning in Italy, heroically flourishing a banner in one hand and a pistol in the other. Jamie had superimposed a colour photograph of my face over Napoleon's. It came with the message, 'Don't weaken, Father'.

I talked it over with Polly, who was quite unfussed and insisted that I must do the work I wanted to do, not bust a gut in the wrong job.

The family's unanimous attitude was wonderfully encouraging and made me realize that, although being freelance must always be financially dodgy, real solid security lay in having a family like mine behind me.

I packed up my portable bar, swiped all the paper-clips, rubber bands and Biros in sight (real freelance behaviour), endured tearful farewells, made a statement to the press that I would now seek employment in some capacity which did not involve boards of directors, which seemed to boil down to the Methodist Church or burglary, and went home for ever.

A couple of days later Dr Margerison's secretary rang to ask would I come into Burlington Street, Dr Margerison wished to see me on an important matter.

With some trepidation I made the journey up to London

wondering what on earth the new managing director wanted to see me about; the offer of a directorship? A highly paid job as his comedy consultant?

Tom was as gently amiable as ever. 'When the company started up', he said after some pleasant chit-chat about the traffic, 'you were lent a television set so that you could watch LWT programmes at home. May we have the set back, please?'

Months later Polly and I were flying to Paris where I was giving a speech and the deal included first-class air fares. In the departure area I saw one of the LWT directors, David Montagu the banker (now Lord Swaythling) and his very nice wife. David Montagu was clearly furious about something. He kept striding about and telephoning from the BA desk. I said to his wife, 'What's up with David?' She said, 'Oh, there's no room left in first class so he's been put into tourist – and he's a director of British Airways!'

I said, 'Tell him to loiter near the curtain and when we're airborne I'll pass him through a free glass of champagne.'

I spent the first weekend of freedom at home, theoretically researching for the book I was working on, but mostly just staring at the beautiful pine door and the new car (both as yet unpaid for), and doubting miserably whether after five years on the wrong side of a desk I was still employable as a writer.

On Monday morning the phone rang. It was Richard Lester, film director and friend whom I had last seen sitting rigid in my dressing room at *Call My Bluff* as I was carried out past him on a stretcher.

Dick had a feature-film script he was due to shoot for United Artists, a very good adaptation by the playwright Charles Wood of the first of the *Flashman* novels, but Dick – and United Artists – wanted a funnier treatment.

Dick had read about the walkout at LWT. Would I do a quick rewrite of the script, beginning immediately?

Chapter Fourteen

Harold Ross, founder/editor of the *New Yorker*, told his writers, 'If you can't be funny, be interesting.' So:

AN INTERESTING CHAPTER

Having a film script to work on urgently was the boost I needed when I reverted to being self-unemployed.

Richard Lester was stimulating to work for, laconic and funny. He knew exactly what he wanted and I spent quite a time driving swiftly to and from Twickenham Studios, mercifully only about twenty minutes from home, bearing the rewrite of a rewrite of a rewrite of a scene.

The character of Flashman, the bully boy of *Tom Brown's Schooldays*, later in life to have a highly successful public career in the Army whilst remaining in private a coward, bully and lecher, was the egregious anti-hero of George Macdonald Fraser's series of *Flashman* novels. Flashman seemed to me to be the perfect and timely alternative to James Bond.

Both Dick and I thought that John Alderton would make a terrific Flashman; he was young, tall, good-looking, rode well, was athletic and an excellent comedy actor.

United Artists in Hollywood had, of course, never heard of John, who had worked mainly in British television, so Dick had to shoot a screen test of John, who worked well, especially when the bed he was lying on in the scene collapsed and he ad libbed brilliantly in character. United Artists were quite happy to go along with John, and the script, when finished, was pronounced 'a knock-out' by somebody in far away sunny California.

A slight hitch came with a request from the United Artists' accountants to cut a million dollars from the production costs of the film. This seemed a lot of dollars to me, but Dick said the traditional way to soothe the accountants was to have the script retyped with much narrower margins and less space at the top and bottom, which would impressively reduce the number of pages. We did this and then met for a weekend at Dick's house in France and cut some scenes.

But it was the Alexei Kapler project all over again. Dick had found locations in Spain for the Afghanistan scenes and was on the point of casting when there was a 'palace revolution' at United Artists in Hollywood and the Head of Film Production, a great admirer of Dick's work, was promoted to running the company's chain of supermarkets or whatever and was replaced by the United Artists Head of Production in Britain, who did not like Dick's style at all. So off this executive went to Hollywood where one of his first moves was to cancel the *Flashman* film.

We were paid, of course, and I was not at all dismayed, in fact faintly relieved, because I had no real ambition to be involved in the movie world, I was far more interested in the book world. I think the unfortunate loser was John Alderton. If ever it was a case of the right actor finding the right part and then losing it through no fault of his own it was John. And there was a whole shelf of the superb *Flashman* novels as source material. Ah, well, that's show business. The wrong side of it.

Earlier, when Dick was still directing unconventional, quirky television comedy in England, mainly with Spike Milligan and Peter Sellers, Polly and I saw more of him and Deirdre. It had become traditional that I found 'openers' for the Thorpe village fête, which meant exerting moral blackmail on a star, and also from time to time thinking up a stunt as a surprise item for the fête.

I still had my sit-on Dennis motor-mower, so one year I decorated the huge grass box with military insignia and stencilled on it, 'MAX SPEED 40 M.P.H.' Comical friends decided it was a fair enough way of spending a June Saturday afternoon so 'army motor-mowing to the whistle' was demonstrated by an élite, drilled-to-a-hair squad, consisting of Michael Bentine, Clive Dunn (in a huge moustache and looking 104), Dick Emery (in drag as an

ATS sergeant), and Dick Lester (in skid-lid and racing goggles) as the driver. I was dressed as a second lieutenant, so that I could tell them what to do next through a microphone.

An interesting point arose when I – illegally, the mower had not been licensed as a vehicle – drove the mower back home along Village Road, our main road. It was Ascot Gold Cup day and there was a steady stream of Daimlers full of punters being driven back to London. There, taking up a fair bit of the narrow road and having to be passed with care, was a regimental motor-mower being driven by a second lieutenant in the uniform of a Grenadier Guardsman. Nobody gave me a second glance.

That lack of curiosity about people behaving in a peculiar way was echoed later in France; again it concerned Dick Lester. I was taking part in a commercial for Hovis bread directed by Dick. The plot required me to be a cross-Channel swimmer (in a painful, woollen, Edwardian, knee-length costume which shrank a little at every wetting). In the commercial, when my swimming began to flag, a slice of buttered Hovis was fed to me on an oar and, revitalized, I struck out in a rapid crawl for the horizon. The next scene was in the public gardens on the Croisette at Cannes, in the South of France. There is a large fountain there in the middle of a round pond. I had to submerge myself completely in the pond, count to ten and then rise up, dripping, in my now almost obscene striped woollen costume, push up my goggles, look round me with amazement and then stride off in a purposeful English manner towards the town.

As I emerged from the water and looked round I saw that a few feet away from me was an elderly French gardener watering the shrubs with a hose. He glanced up at me. 'Bonjour,' he said. He did not give me a second glance.

The army motor-mowing wheeze was successful, so the following year we tried another. A kind friend lent us an ancient five-seater bicycle, so our demonstration that year was called *Z-Bikes* (which dates it). In the programme it claimed to be a demonstration of how new technology has been called into use by the modern constable to fight crime in our village if and when any should occur.

The five constables were played by Graham Stark, Peter Sellers, Bill Kerr, Bruce Lacey (eccentric artist, prop-maker and actor), Clive Dunn (looking 105) and, because Dick had just acquired a baby and would not be parted from it, Lester & Son. I was the inspector again, so that I could bawl at them and tell them what to do. It went well enough.

There was plenty of work about at this time, and being freelance once again after the LWT débâcle meant that I could go back into *Call My Bluff*.

This time I was opposite Patrick Campbell, who hated losing and was jauntily smug when he won ('It's only a game, Frank, only a game, lad!'). Paddy was wonderful. His stammer was a bother to him – he was a natural talker – but when he unthinkingly embarked on a word beginning with an 's' and got stuck, he would rear up in his seat like an ostrich which had sat in something, eyes close together like a cuff link, and he would struggle until he had got the word out, banging the desk and muttering to himself, 'Come on! Come ON!'

Margaret Drabble said that Paddy was a great help to all stammerers because he displayed the mechanics of stammering and dared anyone to pity him.

When Paddy died he was replaced by Arthur Marshall, a cuddly old humorous writer and performer of great charm and intelligence. The producer instructed me to work up the same kind of steely animosity that Paddy and I enjoyed. Steely animosity with dear old Arthur? On his first show he lost five nil and was laughing so much that he couldn't say good night to the viewers.

My Word! and *My Music* were soldiering on. I also had a new BBC radio series, a programme which was a comedy anthology on a different subject each week, e.g., *Frank Muir Goes Into . . . Food.* The series, and the subsequent books, owed almost everything to our producer, now novelist Simon Brett. My co-star in the show, in fact he was the rest of the cast, was 'Alfredo', my very old friend from RAF Henlow's old time music hall, the multi-talented Alfred Marks.

A new kind of work which I enjoyed and which grew with the years was after-dinner speaking. The requirement was about thirty minutes of comedy material disguised as a speech. I soon found that I could use the same speech, with minor modifications, for all occasions. The trick was to avoid jokes; the audience might have heard them. My speech was lightly autobiographical and I had worked in a number of funny incidents based on real happenings. Such as the pig routine.

The pig was in all my speeches and it never failed in its long life. I worked it into a speech I made to the American Booksellers Association's annual conference when my first big book was published. It was in Chicago and the pig went wonderfully, so much so that I was invited back to Georgia a year or so later to make a speech at that year's ABA Conference banquet. Naturally I worked up a new speech. The committee was almost in tears afterwards. 'Why didn't you do the *pig*?' 'What happened to the *pig*?' It was a lesson that the familiar, even in comedy, can be more welcome than the new.

I have been telling the pig story for many years. When my son Jamie was still at school a long time ago he said to me, 'You're not *still* doing that old pig routine, are you?' Indeed I was – and was still doing it until quite recently, in all something like twenty-five years.

In case any reader should be fired with the need to know what this seemingly bullet-proof, humdinger of an anecdote story actually is, I will now tell it.

I first came across my pig – a true story – in a letter to a newspaper forty years ago. It was from a woman and I worked it into my speech as a useful example of how men underestimate women in areas where their macho instinct demands that they predominate. As in driving a car. A good man might admit, reluctantly, that his girlfriend or wife was quite a good driver; he might, in a warm moment, tell her that she was as good a driver as he. But how many of us are saintly enough to admit to our womenfolk that they are better, shrewder drivers than we are?

And yet, and yet.

I don't know how well you know St Anne's Hill in Surrey, whose sharp corners and gentle slopes (before the motorway was built) carried the motorist up from Thorpe and down into Chertsey, but I was taking that rural route one morning in my old, fifteenth-hand Lagonda. I was 'think' driving, driving idly well on my side of the road, hoping that a bright idea might alight like a mustard seed on the damp flannel of my brain, when round the corner ahead came a woman driver at speed, in a clapped-out, dented Morris Minor. She missed the wing of my beautiful Lagonda by a centimeter, wound down her window furiously and yelled at me, 'PIG!'

'Women drivers!' I snorted, drove on round the corner and hit a pig.

NB. Anybody using my pig story without saying where they got it from will be hounded through the law courts of Europe.

Working at home was wonderful. I had a study to work in and there was no dismal rush-hour driving. In the morning I just enjoyed a cup of coffee and a read of the papers and strolled to work through the drawing room at about nine thirty.

I am not sure that the arrangement was all that wonderful for Polly. When I started to live at home I was amazed that I knew so little of the busy constructive life she led, which over the years included doing the rounds with a trolley of Red Cross library books at St Peter's Hospital, Chertsey (fully experienced in hill starts and reversing solo through swing-doors), manning the phone as a Samaritan, acting as a dispatcher for the voluntary CARE organization, as well as enjoying classes in graphology and French literature. And now her leaf of lettuce and a yogurt at midday did not seem adequate for a male to share, so a tedious interruption to her busy activities in order to knock up a more substantial meal seemed inevitable.

This unfortunate turn of events was encapsulated in an old saying: 'I married him for better or for worse but not for lunch.'

According to Eric Partridge in his *Dictionary of Slang*, the phrase was popular with Australian wives when their sheep-shearing husbands retired. It was quoted, with less relevance perhaps, by the Duchess of Windsor in her autobiography, *The Heart Has Its Reasons*.

It seems to me that when we grow old, we either cannot be bothered much with food, or meals become the high points of our existence. I am a 'cannot be bothered' man, perhaps because I have a limited sense of taste and smell due to years of taking snuff and also having a colony of polyps resident in my nasal plumbing.

I gave up cigarettes and pipe for snuff quite easily after many years of smoking but snuff-taking brought its own problems. The good side of it was the beauty of snuffboxes themselves, particularly old ones, and the elegant, slightly theatrical routine of tapping the box, taking a pinch, sniffing it up and then lightly dusting the superfluous snuff off the nose with a spotted red handkerchief.

The bad side was that it was a filthy habit. What goes up must come down and the snuff was not absorbed by the nose but just hung in there for a while and then fell out over whatever lay beneath it, such as a clean shirt-front or a plateful of food or Polly being kissed good night. And if the snuffer wore a moustache, as I do, humiliation was inevitable. Snuff is tobacco leaves and stalks roasted until bone dry and brown and then milled into powder. And when the brown powder got into my moustache I could not entirely wash it out, so when I dried my face on a snow-white hotel towel, or snuggled down in bed amongst the sheets, traces were left. I reached the stage of not being able to stay in a hotel twice. I even thought seriously of ringing the offensive beige stains with a felt pen and writing, 'Actually, it's snuff.' But instead I gave it up.

My sense of taste and smell did not return, so Polly and I, for something like the last twenty-five years, have settled for the sort of simple lunches which we both really enjoy. Our favourites are a salad with the boscage wrenched up only minutes earlier from the kitchen garden, or slices from a fresh Hovis loaf toasted and buttered, a chunk of cheddar cheese and a jar of Polly's home-made marmalade.

I drool whilst writing this.

As Jamie and Sal were away at school so much and Pol and I had busy working lives, we relished our holidays. At first we all trailed off to Broadstairs where we had installed my mother in a bungalow, but after swimming in the waters of the Indian ocean at the temperature of warm milk, Polly found the grey and chilly sea and the boisterous bracing breezes of East Kent less than user-friendly.

Our next move was to take to the canals. There is quite a choice of places to visit as there are about 2,000 miles of 'cuts' and most of them interconnect.

We caused to be built, with the help of a yacht mortgage, *Samanda*, who was 31 feet 6 inches long, the regulation 6 feet 10 inches wide, so that she could be manoeuvred in and out of narrow canal locks, and flat bottomed so that we could navigate almost anywhere where there were a few inches of water.

The five family summer holidays we enjoyed on *Samanda* were physically demanding yet refreshingly peaceful. There were the locks to work, frequently a strenuous job, but canal cruising would be boring without locks, and we glided through the backyards of towns and farms and the heart of the countryside, our metabolisms slowing as life itself slowed to a walking pace.

And we met canalside folk who are our friends still. We had to get a dud dynamo replaced, so we tied up for a few days at The Boat Inn, Gnosall, Staffs, kept by Stan and Ros Marshall. Stan's mother ran the inn when it was an overnight stopping place for working boats, a different kind of function from selling a couple of shandies and a packet of cheese and onion crisps to townsfolk on a hire cruiser. One memorable night old Mrs Marshall heard banging and cursing and found the drunken crew of a narrow-boat trying to push their shire-horse up the narrow staircase to their bedroom.

Stan kept a parrot in a cage in an inner room. When Stan or Ros rapped sharply on the bar, a voice rang out, 'Cum in, ya booger!' When the bird was asked his name he piped up, cheerfully, 'Tommy Tight-Arse!' What with the parrot for conversation and Ros's home-made pickled onions to crunch upon – possibly the best pickled onions in the world – they were great evenings.

What finally drove us away from canal holidays was the uncertainty of the weather. Rain and cold winds did not bother Polly and me all that much, we put on more clothes, and anyway the boat was worked from a centre cockpit which had a moveable roof and side curtains, but it was tough on Jamie and Sal who had nothing much to do except punch each other in their tiny cabin up front.

When the rain was falling drearily and we were chugging our way through Birmingham, trying to avoid the submerged boughs of trees, the bloated bodies of dogs and sheep, we felt our family holiday was being spent not so much messing about in boats as boating about in mess.

The fates once again smiled upon us. Denis and I were taken briefly rich by appearing in a television commercial for Mackeson's milk stout and I decided to blow the lot on taking the family for a month's summer holiday in a Mediterranean hotel, with a hire car, after which I would cease to be even slightly rich. We chose Corsica as I had been there briefly the year before as the captain's guest on a Royal Navy destroyer (that's the way to travel) and I liked Corsica a lot; a violent but oddly heart-warming history, granite mountains, ancient hill villages, and away from the beaches it is almost uninhabited.

The hotel was on a rock in the port of L'Ile-Rousse on the north-east coast, and from the hotel we had a good view of the medieval villages of Monticello and Santa Reparata which, like most

Corsican hill villages, clung a prudent 600 feet or so up the mountainside to give the villagers a head start when the Corsairs and Saracen pirates came raiding.

We were on the beach or in the sea most of the day, but when it began to grow cool in the early evening we took to driving up to Monticello and having a drink in the bar of its small hotel. This had just been converted into a hotel from two or three houses on the square and was owned and run by the Martini family, whose real work up to then had been milking their *troupeau* of sheep to be made into Roquefort cheese.

Polly and I were much taken with the Martini family and Corsica and the little stone village of Monticello, so when the Martinis invited us to the *langouste* lunch celebrating the official opening of their Hôtel A Pastorella, and we found a sign in front of a house across the square reading, '*A VENDRE*', we asked if we could look round. Fatal, of course.

Very few houses in Corsican hill villages stand apart from their neighbours, the general impression is of a congealed bag of boiled sweets. The property for sale was called A Torra ('the tower') and belonged to Pierre Martini and his wife, who had put together some ancient semi-ruins, including the top of a medieval watch-tower, to make up a self-contained dwelling. The entrance on the *place* was by a wrought-iron gate, beyond which were forty high stone steps each of which seemed to grow higher every year.

There was a Parisian family, the Gustins, staying at the same hotel as us down in the port. They were very chic, with a holiday house in St Tropez, and we proudly showed Madame Gustin round A Torra to see whether she agreed with us what wonderful potential it had.

Unfortunately, running water had only just come to the village and A Torra's drain was connected to the main drains at the bottom but open at the top, waiting for a bath or a loo or something to be installed over it. It had a bit of rag stuffed in it to shield us from the smell of the main village sewers. It was not an efficient shield.

Hurrying Mme Gustin through the noxious area we saw her looking disapprovingly at the not-very-even cemented floors which had been painted with cardinal-red paint. 'How much are they asking for this, this . . .?' said Madame Gustin, hanky to nose. We told her. It proved to be almost exactly what we got from selling our canal boat.

'Much too much for Corsica!' cried Madame Gustin, forcefully. 'I could buy a tiny place in St Tropez for that sort of money!'

In reply, Polly opened the far door. Beyond it was a small ancient stone bridge which led to the tower. We walked through. The tower room had black and white tiles and a vaulted ceiling. Then we walked out onto the little balcony and looked down 600 feet to the port of L'Ile-Rousse and the impossibly blue Mediterranean.

'Take it!' said Madame Gustin (in French).

We took A Torra over thirty years ago and have been back every year. Jamie and Sally went there first as schoolchildren and now go as parents. The village has only one shop, a grocery and 'everything' store kept by ample Janine Canava, and the hotel has been added to and improved and is now popular with English tourists with its busy bar and impressive menu. The English are liked as guests as they are grateful for everything, especially the food, unlike the French on holiday from the Continent who tend to count the chips.

There was a fair amount of work to be done every holiday. The tower ceiling was high up and vaulted to make redecorating a stimulating challenge in the middle of a heatwave. It was painted with a very French, very white emulsion paint called Vinyl-Soixante. When this stuff was attacked from the rear by damp seeping through the stone walls, the paint gently buckled, flaked and came away in beige petals so fine that they clung to clothes and skin and refused to be brushed off.

The lady in the house below us was Dutch and was most helpful in our many crises, except that her English, though charming, was rather opaque. She caught us lunging at the ceiling with putty knives lashed to broomsticks.

'Stop!' she cried. 'I haf a stepcase in my cello!'

True enough, she did have a stepcase (stepladder) in her cello (cellar) and she lent it to us, which was a help. But getting rid of the fine flakes of paint from ourselves was quite a problem. Polly took to wearing a paper bag on her head and a strange tent-like garment which she had made to change beneath on the beach. I worked naked, except for a plastic shower hat nicked from a hotel (the only use I have ever found for those little elasticated bonnets).

We have many good memories of those early years in Corsica, such as Sally meeting an English girl on the beach and finding that they were both about to go to the same school; going on a quick tour and finding that we would rather be in Monticello than any-where else on the island; Jamie having a sword fight down in the *place* with a small Corsican boy who lost his temper and screamed at Jamie, '*Merde! Merde!*' And Jamie replying coldly and loudly, 'Cow-shit, cow-shit.'

And in with all these we have one particular memory to be cherished. It was during that baking-hot June holiday which Polly and I spent scraping the tower ceiling. It was not the scraping we look back on with affection, it was the golden hour in the evening when the sun was still warm. We took glasses of wine out onto the terrace, lay down on our mattresses and, like a couple of old bonded gorillas, groomed each other, intently easing off with chisels the delicate flakes of old Vinyl Soixante still sticking to our salient features.

My first close encounter with the book world, in which I was really interested, came when the publisher Geoffrey Strachan of Methuen took Paddy Campbell and me to lunch (which resulted in the quenelles episode reported for posterity in chapter five). The purpose of the lunch was to get us to write a book version of *Call My Bluff*. Geoffrey also asked us to illustrate our definitions, an interesting suggestion as we did not know how to draw. But incompetence had never held either of us back from accepting an offer of gainful employment so we signed on.

It was quite a short book dealing with just one word per page, with three paragraph-long definitions of it illustrated on the opposite page. Paddy stayed with us at Anners for a week while he and I worked on the book. We immediately settled into a steady routine.

We would start work about half-past nine. About eleven, Paddy would get a bit restive and would say, 'If you happen to have a bottle of champagne in the fridge, don't you think a wee glass each would speed the prose? One glass each should be quite enough to do the trick.' So we had just one glass of champagne.

About half-past twelve Paddy would be overcome with the need for a Bloody Mary – just one. Then we had lunch, a piece of fish helped down by a glass or two of Chablis. We worked in the afternoon until about six when Paddy had another Bloody Mary or two, a bath, then we had supper with an accompanying bottle of red, followed by a sprightly evening of conversation from Paddy with the whisky bottle by his elbow.

By the end of the week I was white and shaking and felt that I had donated my liver to literature, but Paddy was serene and cheerful. He did not binge but drank a fairly large amount in a steady but entirely civilized fashion. In all the years I knew him I never saw him even the slightest bit squiffy.

What a week that was. The book did quite well, too.

My work on the 'Big Book' had gone beyond the enjoyable research, and I now had to buckle down and write the thing between all the other briefer commitments, like writing a book about Christmas with (in fact almost wholly by) my son Jamie, who had just got his degree at London University and was, by profession, unemployed. And Polly and I had persuaded some very good writers and illustrators to contribute to a children's anthology of new work we were putting together for Heinemann called *The Big Dipper*.

I called my major project the 'Big Book' because it was a substantial volume, the first original book I had written, rather than one inspired by, or looted from, one of my radio or TV series, and it took me five years to write.

There was at the time, and probably still is, a dining club consisting of very important people; owners of newspapers, advertising tycoons, media millionaires, chaps of that speed, who met regularly for dinner at Claridges. It was just before Christmas and the honorary secretary of the club, a publisher named Timothy Benn, asked me to make the club's pre-Christmas dinner a howling success by honouring them with an after-dinner speech. He spoke like that; he had enormous enthusiasm and gave the impression of a man who got to his office early in the morning, pinned himself to the wall, span round like a Catherine wheel giving off sparks until 6.30 p.m., and then unpinned himself and went home. He was a very nice man.

Claridges! Media tycoons! I worked hard polishing up the old speech, honing every little routine, positioning my pig in exactly the right place, making the whole thing smarter, slicker, suave.

It went very well. Feeling rather pleased with myself, I was making a move to go home when Timothy Benn shot over, beaming with delight, shook my hand vigorously muttering, 'That was wonderful! Great! Superb! Thank you so much!' He drew me to him, went on tiptoes to get near an ear (he is not a tall man), and said, 'Your speech – I hadn't realized that you talk so *simply*.'

I restrained the impulse to maim him.

He went on, 'A *child* could understand your every *word*! Have you ever thought of writing a children's book?'

I had never thought of doing so because I knew it was a highly specialized area of writing of which I knew nothing, but over the following few weeks Timothy Benn was so keen on the idea that my only way of stopping him fizzing with excitement down the phone every hour was to give in and write him one as swiftly as possible.

I always found with my stories on *My Word!* that those based on truth, however faintly, worked better for me than stories which were wholly inventions, and as I had told a great many stories based on the behaviour over the years of our various cats and dogs, I decided to have a go at writing Ernest Benn Ltd a story about our latest problem animal, an Afghan puppy that was the scruffiest of a litter which had arrived a few months earlier in the space under the stairs.

Afghan puppies are not quite what they seem. An adult Afghan is a very handsome dog, like a greyhound in a fun fur. This fun fur is about two sizes too big, so when an Afghan breaks into a run its body travels about 6 inches before the fun fur starts on its way, which results in a beautiful rippling motion of the silken coat.

But Afghan puppies do not look like Afghans until they are the equivalent of teenagers, they are very woolly and their puppy coats collect a great deal of assorted debris. They are almost impossible to train as, affectionate as they are most of the time, they are not afraid of you, nor do they particularly want you to pat them and coo over them, so it is very rare indeed to see an Afghan puppy – or even a senior Afghan – walking in public beside its owner without being on a lead.

A bitch's pleasure is to pee on the lawn and kill huge circles of grass; a male Afghan's aim in life is to jump over the gate and find out what's happening on the far side of the world.

One lady in the village who owned a male Afghan was telephoned one mid-morning: 'Are you the owner of a cream Afghan hound?' asked a voice. 'Yes,' said the lady, 'why?' 'This is the signalman at Sunningdale railway station speaking, madam. Your dog is at this moment preceding the eleven fifteen on the down-line to Guildford.'

I gave my fictional puppy the noble pedigree name of Prince

Amir of Kinjan, but because he was so scruffy, everybody on see-ing him said, 'What a mess!' so he thought that What-a-Mess was his real name.

Timothy Benn spent many months trying to find the right illustrator. It seemed that illustrators who could draw well rarely had much humour and those with humour could not draw. Then one afternoon Timmy rang and said, 'May I come down and see you?'

He arrived, bursting with excitement. 'I'll say nothing,' he said, and with a flourish opened up a folder of drawings. And there *was* What-a-Mess. Exactly right, smiling engagingly as though he was as beautiful as his mother, his coat a refuge for rose clippings, bits of eggshell, paint, compost and a small duck resident on top of his head. The artist was the wonderful Joe Wright, a gentle giant of a man who drew a vigorous comic line and crammed every picture with inventive detail.

Joe and I produced seventeen *What-a-Mess* books which three times became TV cartoon films, one of them made in Hollywood. The books were translated into fourteen languages and it was interesting to see how the various translators coped with the diffi-cult job of translating the name 'What-a-Mess'. Some examples:

WEST GERMANY:	O-Schreck-lass nach
NETHERLANDS:	Wat-een-Troep
SOUTH AFRICA:	Bollie-Blaps
FRANCE (BRILLIANT):	Okeloreurrr!

I am not equipped to comment on how well the Japanese and Israeli translators managed.

1974 was our silver wedding anniversary and Polly and I decided to celebrate it by spending a whole month on the island of Mauritius, where Polly was born and to which she had never returned since coming to England at the age of twelve.

Mauritius is one of those islands, like Fernando Po, which most Britishers have heard of but few can point to on a map with one confident stab of the forefinger. The island is about the size of our own dear Isle of Wight, lies in the Indian Ocean, a whisker inside the tropic of Capricorn and an inch and a third to the right of Madagascar (ref: *Philips Modern School Atlas*).

The staple crop of Mauritius was sugar and the 8-feet-tall sugar canes seemed to cover the whole island except for some of the main roads and the middle of the airport runway.

There were only one or two hotels on the whole island then (the beaches are lined with hotels now). We booked a package tour to the Troux au Biches, a beach hotel of thatched bungalows. It featured a kind of semi-self-service; guests occupied a bungalow with a bedroom and a kitchen, which had a few cooking facilities and a great many cockroaches and ants. There was a shop where food could be bought and taken back to the bungalows and cooked up for lunch (and shared with the bungalow wildlife). The hotel provided a proper dinner in the restaurant but, perhaps to make us Brits feel at home, although we were in the middle of the Indian Ocean, the menu did not offer curries and mangoes and paw paws and fresh pineapples but roast lamb and two veg.

Polly had no relations left on the island and most old family friends had retired to England, but enough were left to feed us some wonderful curries and generally mark our cards. Perhaps worse than the shortage of hotels was an almost total lack of independent restaurants. The answer for having lunch out, we were advised by Polly's old friends, was to make for a Caltex petrol station, most of which had a perfectly good restaurant round the back.

At the beginning we hired a car and whizzed ourselves about the island, but driving inland was a bit overexciting. Villages of sugar-workers had grown up alongside the roads and on hot nights the whole village population, in pitch-black clothes, played cards, gossiped, ate, practised football, took a siesta, repaired the car and meditated, all in the middle of the road.

Other driving hazards included just missing a goat sitting placidly in the middle of the highway from the capital Port Louis steadily eating its way through a newspaper; a large lorry with a happy grinning worker sitting on the tailboard strap-hanging from the tail of a cow; bullock carts of cut sugar cane suddenly crossing the road ahead at a speed of 0.5 m.p.h., and tiny Honda motorcycles putter-puttering along the road, ridden by small entrepreneurs in large crash helmets, laden with wares for sale such as iron pots and pans, blankets, a guitar, a mattress, and also, usually, a large glass display cabinet roped sideways to the carrier, full of necklaces and earrings on cards.

We found that owing to a hiccup in the economy it was cheaper to hire one of the cars outside the hotel complete with its owner/driver than rent a self-drive car. But that facility, too, presented the occasional problem.

It was dusk and we were going to have dinner with friends in the small town of Curepipe. We climbed into the taxi/car and the driver asked us very politely if he could stop at his village *en route* to collect something. The something turned out to be a huge torch, and as the sun sank, the necessity for the torch became apparent: when he braked all the car's lights went out. Undismayed, he shone his torch through the windscreen and accelerated out of danger.

What did not help to soothe his increasingly nervous passengers was a large and pretty green and red toy parrot which dangled from the driving mirror. When the direction indicator was operated the parrot's relevant eye lit up and blinded the driver.

It was a wonderful month. We went up to the teak and ebony forest, happened upon a colourful and impressive Hindu Ceremony of Light at the huge lake of Grand Bassin. We walked along the beach when the tropical sunset so swiftly arrived; one moment the sun would be shining, the next moment it would be setting, all pinks and mauves, behind the range of extinct volcanoes; the next moment – darkness.

The return to Mauritius was a little bitter-sweet for Polly; much had changed, inevitably, and did not match her childhood memories. But it was exciting to go back; there were old friends still there and the island was so beautiful anyway that it made for a superb celebratory holiday.

The second half of the Seventies proved to be a busy demi-decade. I was invited to be President of the Johnson Society, Lichfield, for 1975–1976. There were no time-consuming duties attached, but a presidential address had to be written on an aspect of Samuel Johnson and delivered at the society's annual banquet in the Guildhall at Johnson's home town of Lichfield.

The theme of my paper, 'Samuel Johnson and his Search for the Wild Guffaw', was that letters from his friends showed that Sam Johnson was a much funnier and jollier man than Boswell's biography allowed him to be, and he had a nice touch of irony (when a silly young man tried to impress Johnson by claiming that he had, alas, lost all his command of the Greek language, Johnson nodded in sympathy and said, 'I believe it happened at the same time, sir, that I lost all my large estate in Yorkshire.' And when Adam Smith overdid his praise of the beauties of Glasgow, Johnson interrupted him with, 'Pray, sir, have you ever seen Brentford?').

But a sense of humour only became a desirable quality in modern times. In Johnson's eighteenth century a gentleman could pee on the lawn, salute a gentleman friend with a kiss, cry in public, but it was vulgar and simply not done to be seen laughing heartily. Swift proudly stated he had only laughed twice in his life, Lord Chesterfield warned his son, 'Frequent laughter is the characteristic of folly and ill-manners,' and Alexander Pope claimed he had never laughed in his life. Plays and books of the time went in for 'sentimental comedy', which was genteel and called not for a healthy guffaw, but for what the poet Robert Southey called 'a silent and transient simper'.

Boswell almost certainly suppressed the playful joking side of Johnson's nature because he knew his hero would be regarded by eighteenth-century society as having a serious character defect.

The audience at the Guildhall listened to me in silent and transient boredom, but the paper was printed in the society's *Transactions* and it was read by members all over the world, provoking some lively letters.

A little earlier, my working life was changed by a lurch in yet another direction: backwards; that is to say back to performing rather than writing. Michael Elliott, the theatre director, was the driving force behind a new theatre-in-the-round being erected inside the great Cotton Hall of the old Manchester Exchange. To raise funds to complete this, his (and my dear and good) friend Michael Meyer had put together a funny but informative anthology of acting and theatrical history entitled *Rogues and Vagabonds*, which was to be given a reading at the Old Vic Theatre, London, in June 1975. They had assembled a terrific cast, Edith Evans, Wendy Hiller, Polly James, Edward Fox, Tom Courtenay, Albert Finney, with Michael Flanders as compère. I was asked to join the team to read some of the comical bits.

At the rehearsal, still an uncured ham as far as theatrical appearances were concerned, I flung myself into my bits and gave them my all. After a few minutes Michael Elliott took me aside out of hearing of the others.

'You're *acting*!' he said. 'I don't advise it.'

'But . . .' I said, 'surely . . .?'

'No, please don't *act*,' he said. 'Get the feel of the character, make yourself familiar with the lines and then just *say* them. The audience will do the rest of the work.'

Wonderful advice to an enthusiastic overactor.

Then a few days before the show was due to go on, Michael Flanders died. I admired his work enormously, I think he was one of our best light lyricists, but I did not know him personally. As the show now had nobody to do the linking, the two Michaels asked me to take it on as well as non-acting my acting bits. I was happy to do the compèring as I enjoyed semi ad libbing appearances.

The Old Vic was full on the night. It turned out to be Edith Evans's last public performance, and what a performance she gave, playing the pioneer feminist Millamant to Edward Fox's Mirabell in the famous my-conditions-for-marriage scene from *The Way of the World*.

In the Green Room where we all gathered before the show, Edith Evans said to Michael Elliott in that wonderful voice, indicating us, 'Are all these people going to be on the stage while I am acting?'

'Yes,' said Michael.

'Oh, dear!' said Edith Evans.

When she and Edward Fox stood up to play their scene, she went forward and explained to the audience, 'The part I am about to play is Millamant, who is very young and very pretty. I am neither of those things.' Then she began the scene and Edith Evans became before our eyes both of those things. Almost as soon as the little, very old lady in her pink, nightdress-like garment stood up, glared at her lover Mirabell and started putting him in his place, she completely changed into a strong-willed, beautiful girl in her twenties. Magic.

Then a BBC arts programme came up with an irresistible offer. They wanted me to go to America and film three one-hour conversations with the last surviving three great American comedians: Groucho Marx, Jack Benny and Bob Hope. The notion was to discuss with them professional matters of comedy and their formative experiences.

The first programme was to explore the comic genius of Groucho Marx. Before flying off into the great blue yonder I phoned Kenneth Tynan who had worked with Groucho. He said that Groucho loved singing and it was a good way to relax him.

The producer and I took Groucho to dinner at Sardi's restaurant to find out his speed of talking, etc., and to establish what rapport we could for the following day's shoot.

Groucho wore a houndstooth-patterned raincoat and a navy-blue beret throughout the meal, in fact every time we met him. We ate soft-shelled crabs (a mistake), and afterwards I jollied Groucho into singing. He gave us his version of Will Fyffe singing 'Roamin in the Gloamin'. He had toured England's music halls with Will Fyffe back in the mists of time.

Then we got on to Gilbert and Sullivan and Groucho really began to enjoy himself. Spurred on by me he gave the diners at Sardi's his fine, stirring and surprisingly loud version of 'A Wandering Minstrel I'. By the time we had demolished between us 'Poor Wandering One' and 'Three Little Maids From School Are We', the other diners were applauding and the drunks were singing along with us.

The BBC had hired a suite at the Hilton for the recording and had booked in a New York camera crew to film the show. Groucho arrived (a tiny figure, still in his raincoat and beret) and we and the crew crammed into the lift. There was a young secretary there, and on the way up Groucho gave his famous leer and said to her, 'I like your tits.' She was horribly embarrassed. The crew went wild with excitement. 'Ain't Grouch the wittiest!?' said a crew member, pummelling my arm. 'Well, no,' I said, 'not on present form he isn't.'

It was a difficult interview. My inexperience as an interviewer – a subtler craft than it looks – didn't help, and Groucho was not at all interested in talking about the Marx Brothers or comedy. At one point he admitted that he would have switched to making rain-coats if there were more money in it.

During the interview, moments of real charm did break through and he made one or two very quick and funny ripostes, but on the whole he relied on his one great Groucho trick, which was to take one's breath away (as he did to the girl in the lift) with remarks of numbing effrontery.

He suddenly said to me on camera when I was asking him about the old days of Hollywood, 'Nelson Eddy was a homosexual, did you know that? Everybody thought he was laying Jeanette MacDonald, but he was a homosexual, and she was a lesbian.'

Groucho wore thick spectacles which were also hearing aids. His red-haired girlfriend/manager took him off to the loo when there was a break to load film and gave him one of his pills. He returned with a springier step and was sparkling for a few minutes before gradually slumping again until it was time to load another film into the camera and another pill into Groucho. We ended up with two hours of filmed interview from which the producer just managed to put together an *Omnibus* programme. But only just.

We had left the whole project about ten years too late, the three old boys were too rich and successful. And private. American showbiz stars had their personal stock of oft-used, safe comical anecdotes which their chat-show hosts were expected to trigger off; the great comics didn't want the boat rocked by having to talk seriously about their work.

After the filming, we were walking the frail figure of Groucho through the foyer of the New York Hilton towards the limo when he suddenly stopped. He looked up at me and said in his gentle slow voice, 'Nelson Eddy wasn't a homosexual, and Jeanette wasn't a lesbian. I think they were a little in love with each other. Now what made me say that?'

Well, yes. Quite.

My Big Book was due to be published in 1976 and I had severe title trouble. The book was a social history of six subjects: music, food and drink, education, literature, theatre and art, from the early Greek to modern times, heavily illustrated by quotations from citizens who were alive at the time and did not like what was going on. This, I hoped, made for a lively and informative book which was also funny.

But what to call it? I thought of *Pieces of Hate*, but then discovered that the title had already been used for a collection of theatre reviews by the American critic George Jean Nathan. Eventually, in despair, Roland Gant of Heinemann and I settled on a feeble and embarrassing main title with a subtitle to do the real work, so the book was published as *The Frank Muir Book: An Irreverent Companion to Social History*.

The publication of the book in South Africa, Australia, New Zealand and the USA before it was published in Britain meant a great deal of global dashing about; personal appearances, book-shop signing sessions, literary lunches and radio and TV interviews throughout 1976. Then in the late Seventies and early Eighties I had more books published which meant more tours. As I have done so much of this author-touring game, I consider myself something of an authority on it.

It is at least a differently daunting experience from writing. I met Kingsley Amis on a train once coming from a book signing and he told me he looked upon it with pleasure as a day off without guilt. So if the saying is true (and I hope to heaven it isn't) that everybody has a book in them, then the following notes on how to survive your own tour might prove helpful.

Very few literary lunches are really literary, most are just social. A bookshop chain or local newspaper might set up a series of literary lunches in a town. They do a deal with a local hotel to provide lunch for £15 a head and start selling tickets for £20 a head. There will be a few genuine book buyers, but many of the tickets are taken up for corporate entertaining; the Midland Bank would probably take a table for ten of its good customers, and so on.

The publicity departments of publishers would be contacted for the free entertainment, a ten-minute speech from you and perhaps up to three more authors who also have a book out. After you have made your ten-minute speech – and try to make it friendly, domestic and jolly; the less literary the better – the authors are shown into another room with desks for them to sit at and a pile of their books to dedicate to eager buyers. You will find that none of the ladies who queue up for your book wants to read it, it's to give to somebody else. 'Will you please make it out to Mavis on her dread fortieth, with warmest regards from Aunty.' There is always one author who has nobody forming a queue and just sits there, fiddling with his Biro in lonely humiliation.

The classic signing-session story is of Monica Dickens in a bookshop in Sydney, Australia. A lady picked up a copy of the book, peered at it and handed it to Monica who opened it, fountain pen poised over the title page.

'May I dedicate it to someone?' Monica asked, as usual.

'Emma Chisset,' said the lady.

'Is Chisset spelled with a double "s"?' asked Monica.

The lady looked puzzled. 'Emmuch *iss* it?'

Light dawned. 'Thirty-two Australian dollars,' said Monica.

No sale for Monica but a story which has become a book-publicity legend.

And there will be a certain amount of signing autograph books to be done. Try and sit down for this with the book resting on a surface so that the signature does not come out like Guy Fawkes's after torture.

The collecting of signatures has always seemed to me to be an odd hobby, a kind of celebrity version of train-spotting. To what use can the collection be put? What happens to all those scrawled names, mostly illegible, which were written standing up with the writing arm being jogged by other collectors, often in pouring rain? Such is fame that after a few years, months even, the legible names attract the comment, 'Who on earth was he?'

A cautionary word. I was once doing a book-signing session in Leeds. The large bookshop had been constructed from three old Georgian houses knocked through, which meant that the shop was actually a warren of tiny rooms. I was stuck up on the third floor with a pile of books and a Biro, and nobody knew I was there.

Every ten minutes or so a girl's voice was heard on a very crackly Tannoy system saying, helpfully, 'Mr Frank Murr is in room (CRACKLE) on the (CRACKLE) floor signing copies of his book *The* (CRACKLE) *Book; an Irreverent Companion to Social* (CRACKLE). Thank yew.'

My loneliness was relieved from time to time by the head of a lost book-lover peering round the door. 'Birthday cards?'

'Ground floor, back of the shop.'

'Cheers.'

Or, 'Occult?'

'Two floors down. Through Gardening and turn right.'

'Cheers.'

Then a lady towing a tartan shopping trolley trundled in, realized there was no through door and trundled out again. There was a pause and then, as in a cartoon film, she slowly backed back into the room, peering at me.

'You're, er, you know, what's-his-name on the telly, aren't you?' she said.

'I have that honour,' I said.

She fumbled in her handbag and produced a ballpoint pen. 'Would you?' she said.

For the first time that morning I joyfully reached for a copy of my book.

'No, no,' she said. 'I can't afford those things, I just come in to see my friend on the till. Just sign a bit of paper for me, luv, that'll do nicely.'

I searched my desk and pockets and my fan searched her handbag, but neither of us had a bit of paper.

She rummaged in her tartan shopping trolley and triumphantly produced a half-pound packet of Anchor butter. 'There you are!' she said. 'Would you make it out to Mrs Potter?'

Nota bene: It is not possible to autograph half a pound of butter with a ballpoint pen, it merely makes a dent in the shape of your name. I suppose that when she arrived home Mrs Potter could have poured molten lead into the dent, cast my signature in hot metal and printed from that, but it would not have done the butter much good.

Denis had an experience in Bond Street which further demonstrated how baffling is the behaviour of autographarazzi. Denis was stopped outside Aeolian Hall by a young woman proffering a shiny autograph album and a pen.

'Would you, for my daughter?' she said (a question which Denis has always enjoyed).

He took the book and the pen, and while he was writing a friendly message the lady chatted away. 'My daughter loves your show,' she said. 'She's very good at guessing which is a bluff and which is true.'

Denis stopped writing.

'You've got the wrong one,' he said. 'You want Frank Muir. I'm Denis Norden.'

The lady went thoughtful for a moment and then said, 'Well, you might as well carry on signing. She can't read yet.'

The most enjoyable time I had on my author tour of *The Frank Muir Book* was when I was driven from one session to another by Heinemann's publicity director, Nigel Hollis, and he and his wife Sarah very soon became close friends.

It was somehow good fun being driven by Nigel up the M6 in belting rain, squeezed between a coach doing 90 m.p.h. marked 'REGAL LUXURY COACHES – Edinburgh to London – £2.40 Return with toilet', and a vehicle marked 'SCHWEINHUND-BLASTEDROTTENTRANSPORTGEFUNKEN – HAMBURG'. Nigel seemed to know all about the great houses up on the hills and who lived in them and was totally incapable of being boring about anything.

Tragically, Nige died in his mid-forties. He was a modest man ('I was the worst scholar Balliol ever had.') but in fact he was highly intelligent, had an inquisitive and witty mind and I still miss him very much.

My first coast-to-coast author tour in America, without Nige and all on my own, was rather different. The book had been bought by Stein and Day, good, small, literary publishers but, I later learned, having cash-flow problems.

In a brief but moving ceremony at the Gotham Hotel, New York, I was handed a batch of internal airline tickets; an itinerary which listed which cities, hotels, bookshops and radio and TV studios I was to get myself to, and when; a considerably slimmer wad of dollar bills for taxis and dinners (the itinerary did not allow for lunch) and a genial handshake, all from very likeable Sol Stein.

I glanced through page one of the itinerary and then shot down to the bar and had a swift beer. Page one was a list of commitments for the first day of the tour, Milwaukee. It began with a television interview at 6.45 a.m. (not my time of day at all). Then came a dash across town for a radio programme, then a visit to a down-town bookshop, a live television discussion programme (about American politics) from 11.15 a.m. to 12.30 p.m., another radio interview at 1.15 p.m. (in depth, the itinerary said: a lie), an inter-view with the *Milwaukee Journal*'s columnist at 2.15 p.m., signings at three more bookshops and take-off for Minneapolis at 6.55 p.m. I was delighted to note that my first engagement the following morning in Minneapolis was a radio programme at the ludicrously late hour of 7.45 a.m.

In twenty working days I survived seventeen newspaper inter-views, twenty-nine radio programmes, twenty television appear-ances, fourteen bookshop signing sessions and an after-dinner speech to the American Booksellers' Association (as already noted *re* pig story) in Chicago.

Most of the Midwest lunchtime radio and TV hostesses were either important local matrons without a nerve in their body who resembled wealthy prison visitors, or nervous ex-actresses looking like retired hookers who crouched behind their make-up smiling fiercely at nothing in particular. During the whole tour, some of the researchers had read the book but none of the interviewers, with the honourable exception of the lady on *Good-Morning America* back in New York.

The feminine radio interviewers ranged from an incredibly beautiful Norwegian girl in Cincinnati, who was so intelligent and humourless that she treated everything I said as the babblings of a problem child, to a very funny and massive black lady in Chicago who wore a long black dress with *Dallas*-width shoulder pads and a mass of frizzy hair dyed beige. It was during a heatwave and as she floated down the corridor towards me, shimmering in the heat like Omar Sharif approaching on his horse in *Lawrence of Arabia*, she looked like a beautiful pint of draught Guinness. But a great interviewer.

My problem with most of the male radio interviewers was trying to get a word in edgeways. 'May I ask, sir, how you came to write this thoughtful and fascinating book?' 'Well, I have an interest in social history which—' 'Well, how about that! I majored in history and I have always thought . . .' (fourteen minutes).

One man in a small Los Angeles local radio station interviewed me for an hour and a half during which I failed to complete a sentence. When the red light went out to signal the end of the ordeal, he wrung my hand, his eyes damp with emotion, and swore that it was the most gracious interview he had ever conducted (what *do* Americans mean by 'gracious'?).

An all too important element of my author tour was taxi cabs. In New York most cabs were yellow and all were dented. Just before my first visit the cabs had been adapted to make the driver less open to being bopped on the head by a social malcontent. The protective device was a bullet-proof steel mesh which took up much of the space previously occupied by the passenger, so anybody taller than 5 feet (and I am 6 feet something) had to fold up on the back seat in a foetal crouch.

New York cabbies are inquisitive ('You're foreign, ain't ya?' one said to me. 'You French?'), and much time, when not spent curled up, was spent kneeling painfully on the coconut matting talking to the driver through his square of steel mesh. It was like riding around New York in a very expensive mobile confessional.

Perhaps the worst aspect of the tour, but one which I solved rather brilliantly I thought, was the problem of personal laundry. None of the hotels in my itinerary had enough stars to guarantee that a suit would be pressed, or a shirt washed, overnight, so I bought a tiny travelling iron and a packet of detergent and worked out a system.

The problem with washing small clothes in the bedroom was that the plugs in American hotel washbasins were not made of rubber but metal and they did not seat properly, so my suds slid down the drain before I had begun.

My method was as follows. In America, bathroom waste-paper bins were made of white plastic and were watertight. So my routine (which rapidly became an obsession, but an obsession can be a comfort when you are travelling alone) went thus. All internal flights in America seemed to take an hour, so I booked into the hotel usually at about eight in the evening, exhausted and crumpled after a long day's work in the previous town and too tired to eat in the hotel restaurant.

Most American restaurants equated chic with darkness, so not only did I usually measure my length on the carpet on the way to the bar, which had a step round it which I could not see, but I also could not see the other diners, if any, or the food. Nor could I read the metre-square glossy menu once brandished at me in the gloom by a giant blond Swedish student who said, 'Hi, I'm Carl, your host for the evening,' and disappeared into the darkness never to return. So I always went straight up to my room and rang room service for a club sandwich and a beer. 'Comin' up right away, sir!'

Next thing was to unpack. Not a long job as a suitcase was too bulky and time-wasting to take on a plane, so 'luggage' meant simply an under-the-seat piece of hand baggage and one of those zip-up 'suiters' which crush the suit inside and have a hook sticking out of the top which catches in fellow travellers' pockets when rushing to board the plane.

Found the plastic waste-paper bin in the bathroom and filled it with hot water from the shower. Tipped in a handful of washing powder, knickers and shirt and left them to soak.

Stripped off, with the exception of socks (the shape of the human hand makes it impossible to wash socks properly when they are hand-held). Enjoyed a hot shower, soaping socks thoroughly (which, note, simultaneously cleaned the feet within them). Took the day's used handkerchief and trod it in shower, scrubbed it with nail-brush, rinsed it and plastered it to the wall of the shower using edge of hand as squeegee.

Next morning the handkerchief peeled off the wall IRONED.

Dried self and pummelled knickers and shirt in waste-paper bin until water went grey. Poured off and refilled with clean water.

Repeated until water remained transparent and hung garments to dry over shower rail. Plugged tiny travelling iron into bedside point, laid suit out on a towel and gently urged away the concertina creases which had developed behind the elbows and knees. Hung up suit and got into bed.

The entire laundering operation took exactly twenty-four minutes. Six minutes later room service ('Comin' up right away, sir!') arrived with my club sandwich and can of Budweiser.

I dined.

After my solo tour across the USA I made a point of not going abroad without Polly to act as a kind of manager, to make sure I ate enough to keep me from toppling over from nervous exhaustion, and to block last-minute demands for unscheduled speeches and interviews.

As more of my books were published, we made more author tours together, South Africa, Australia and New Zealand, America and Canada, and we had some good moments.

I admired the protective attitude towards his books adopted by a bent-with-age bookseller in Auckland, New Zealand, who had not quite got the hang of the recent fad for author signing sessions. He greeted me with, 'Well, I dunno, mate. You can sit in my shop for an hour if that's what you want to do, but I don't want you defacing my books by scribbling in 'em.'

New Zealand had only two television channels then, perhaps still has, and I recorded a variety-cum-interview show on one of them, only to find that on the evening it went out I was booked to do a 'serious' interview, live, from a university lecture room, which would go out at the same time as the recorded show. So for one glorious hour New Zealand TV viewers had the choice of either watching Muir or switching off and making a pot of tea.

Halfway through the live interview it began to get too serious, i.e., boring, so to cheer myself up I said to the camera, 'If you're fed up with looking at this suit, switch over to the other channel, I'm in a tweed jacket there.'

When the show finished, the programme's executive descended upon me, white with fury. 'We're in competition with the other channel!' he said, 'and what do you do? Tell our viewers to *switch over to the opposition*! It's unbelievable! In all my years . . . !' He was led away.

*

Back home to Anners at last, and a few weeks later there was more excitement of a different kind. At about midnight a young Scot telephoned. He sounded a little in wine, or more probably in single malt whisky, and he was ringing on behalf of the Kate Kennedy Club of St Andrews University, Fife: would I stand for election as the university's next lord rector?

I asked him whether it was a jokey thing or if there was a job to be done. He assured me that it was not a joke, it was really up to me what I made of the job.

I discussed it seriously with Polly for about thirty seconds and accepted. I was duly elected rector by the students and enjoyed a three-year tour of duty, 1977–1979, which I will always look back on with misty-eyed pleasure.

My installation as rector was the excuse for a number of ritual celebrations. On 27 April 1977 I was met at the entrance of the town, made a member of the student body by being wrapped in a St Andrews scarlet gown (which centuries ago divinity students had to wear so that they could be spotted nipping into brothels), pulled round the town in an open coach by the university rugby club, stopping frequently to be welcomed with presents.

The gifts included an engraved pewter quaich (neither did I. It's a two-handled, Gaelic drinking cup) from the district council; a most useful silver-handled, very sharp paperknife from the Royal and Ancient Golf Club; from a hall of residence came a mobile made from bars of Cadbury's Fruit and Nut (which I had advertised on television for eight years); and from a girl's hall of residence a pink plastic elephant which emitted a charming but very shrill whistle when squeezed. I managed to get everything home eventually and still have most of the items. The pink elephant is a favourite of the grandchildren at bathtime as they can get it to blow vulgar bubbles.

The only formal duty of the rector was, as father of the university, to chair the monthly meetings of the university court, the governing body which has to approve everything before it becomes university practice. The rector was not involved with the educational side of things, this was the responsibility of the senate (which has to report to the court).

As I had never in my life chaired anything, the university court was daunting. I was saved by having next to me at court meetings the university secretary of that time, David Devine (who wrote thrillers in his spare time and was a Good Thing).

'It's getting a bit boring,' I would whisper anxiously to David out of the side of my mouth.

'It's quite an important issue,' he would whisper back, 'give them a few more minutes and then take a vote.' Eventually I acquired confidence, and on a discussion as to what the court should do about a modern statue lent to the university by the Scottish Arts Council, consisting of a number of bent welded railway lines which students fell over lurching back to their residences late at night, I was able to say, cheerfully, 'Right, gentlemen, time for one more philistine joke all round and then we really must get down to a policy.'

The professors and other members of the court were immensely forbearing with their amateur chairman and I never felt any personal animosity. Perhaps this might have been because they were all busy men and hoped not to have to go back to court for another session in the afternoon. During my three years I always managed to bring the meeting to a close by lunchtime.

Flying BA shuttle once a month up to Edinburgh then picking up a hire car and driving to St Andrews for a long weekend in that lovely stone town with its own private weather, promised to be the perfect escape from the headache-inducing research I was doing for my next book. I imagined having quiet meals all by myself, a steak of Tay salmon perhaps at the Old Course Hotel, a stroll round the town, read for an hour or so . . .

The reality of my monthly 'leisure breaks' was a little different from that vision of delight.

The students elected from one of their number an assessor whose job it was to represent the rector in the university and arrange a programme for his monthly visit.

The university had changed its cooking arrangements and had just moved over to having a central kitchen with a professional chef; the food was fast-frozen and had to be skilfully thawed out. The system had yet to settle down and I was usually greeted by my assessor with, 'You're having a quick lunch in a hall of residence which thinks it's being poisoned. Then I've got down a list of eight students who've got problems and want to see you. Dinner with the girls of University Hall who want to watch their rector eating, and you've been invited to a party after dinner to celebrate an engagement (a lot of St Andrews students seemed to marry each other). It'll be a late night but I said you'd stay on and make a speech at the end.'

I was officially installed in office at a ceremony in Younger Hall where I had to make a rectorial address. In the old days this was all the job amounted to. The distinguished personage, elected for having done something notable elsewhere, such as Rudyard Kipling, Earl Haig, Andrew Carnegie, Sir James Barrie, delivered a powerful address, had a couple of whiskies with the vice-chancellor and that was that for another three years.

Barrie took a villa in the South of France for a month or so to compose his address, a magnificent message to youth which was admired and reprinted all over the place. His theme was courage. Typically, my predecessor-but-one, John Cleese, gave a reasoned address on the usefulness of cowardice.

My address was entitled 'Rectorshipdom'. In it I explained that I was the first rector they had ever had with no qualifications whatever, no letters after my name, I did not even pass a driving test as they did not exist when I started driving, no degree, not even an O level, the most I ever hoped for was a crack at the school cert – and she got married the term I arrived (a little joke to help things along).

The rectorial robes, of medieval design, were enormously heavy, and during the banquet that evening I tilted my chair and very nearly somersaulted backwards.

But a pair of students gave me a warm welcome on my first working weekend. Polly, who loved the town, came with me. Just as we were driving slowly past a hall of residence, a window was thrust up, two carroty heads appeared, yelled in unison, 'FRANK THE WANK!' and dropped out of sight, chortling.

John Cleese with his mocking of Barrie's famous address on courage had broken up the old ground and had set out not to be the Establishment figure that had previously been elected. I felt that my contribution during my three years should be to sow a few seeds in John's broken-up ground and find out whether there was a real job for a modern working rector, and quite what the job was.

I quickly realized that what students wanted above all from their rector was availability. They wanted to see him wandering about the town and they wanted to be able to talk to him, be bought a drink and have a moan in the pub with him. So I put the dates of the court meetings in my diary as soon as they became known and tried hard, unsuccessfully of course, not to miss even one. I had to miss six in my three years, but they assured me this was some sort of a record. A bad or a good record never emerged. And I put a permanent advertisement in the student newspaper, *Aien*, giving my home phone number and address for the benefit of students who had a problem which they thought I might be able to help them with. Not a day passed in those three years without at least one letter thudding in postmarked Kirkcaldy, always by second post for some reason.

Problems varied hugely: a geography expedition to Greenland asked me to arrange for them to have some portable food which was a bit of a treat as well as being nourishing, so I persuaded Cadburys to provide a half-pound bar per man per day of their Fruit and Nut.

A girl student from Belfast working for her finals dearly wanted to work in an English bookshop but did not have the time or the money to tour the country for interviews. I spoke to Peter Giddy, manager of Hatchards in Piccadilly, and he took her on sight unseen. She was a success and went on from Hatchards to become a publisher's rep.

There were students uncertain of their sexuality who could have gone to the perfectly competent university's gaysoc, but did not want to be seen going, so wrote to their dear old white-haired rector for help. I usually recommended a visit to the Catholic chaplain and his nun helper who were very good at this kind of advising.

And there was a round robin from a feminine hall of residence pleading for Rector to arrange for them to have soft loo paper. I wrote to the warden of the hall who explained that the soft kind of loo paper was too wasteful as the girls used it in handfuls as face tissues for removing make-up, polishing their specs, cleaning their shoes, et cetera. I didn't see much harm in that, but the warden was adamant, so I got in touch with the customer care officer at Andrex, luckily a woman, and explained the position. She sided with the girls, as I had hoped, and sent them up, as a free gift, a packing-case full of rolls of Andrex (very soft) loo paper and a huge woolly Andrex toy puppy.

Students wrote wanting advice about finding jobs, and how to get a novel published, and how to make some money reasonably legally, and would I write a speech for the writer to deliver at his aunt's wedding . . .

Then there was the persuading of friends and colleagues to travel up to St Andrews to take part in events with no fee attached. One of the first of these duties was to supply a speaker for a public lecture series which the university wanted to revive. I asked Robert Morley to do it. '*Must* I, dear Frank?'

'Yes, please, Robert,' I said and arranged to meet him at London airport and escort him up.

Although Robert looked like the comfortably plump chairman of a building society, I knew that he actually leaned strongly to the Left and was quite a rebel. He sat on the edge of a table on the stage in Younger Hall and just talked brilliantly. He described being seduced when a young man by a beautiful older woman, of his playwriting days, of Hollywood, and he told his audience that they would learn little worth learning at university, and the sooner they got out into the real world and started living their lives the better. The students cheered him for a long time.

The university held an arts festival every three years and one was being organized when I was elected, so I had to act as a talent procurer for two festivals. For the first of these my friend Michael Meyer dusted off spare copies of his 'entertainment about actors and acting' which he called *Rogues and Vagabonds* and directed and compèred it for the festival. I managed to talk Peter Ustinov and Dame Wendy Hiller into joining us on stage.

Peter was, and is, probably the cleverest actor in the world at performing this kind of fragmented, character acting in many accents and he was on top of his form.

Dame Wendy wore a terrific dress for the performance, colourful and dramatic with a train long enough to be trodden on. Before we went on stage, as I was goggling, Wendy rather apologetically asked me if I would hand her to her chair as the skirt was very full and quite difficult to manoeuvre. She wore the dress because she thought the girls in the audience would want to see her wearing something theatrical and glamorous. And of course, as we learned afterwards, Wendy was absolutely right.

It was a wonderful evening.

Shortly after, Michael and I put on *Rogues and Vagabonds* at the Edinburgh Festival.

So began for me a tiny sub-career as a platform performer (highly enjoyable but unpaid, which is so often the way). Michael compiled two more programmes: *He and She* about love and marriage, and *Fun and Games* about leisure and sporting activities (my favourite quotation, Max Beerbohm on rowing: 'Eight minds with but one single thought – if that'). We did, in all, four Edinburgh Festivals, but many more performances all over the place for theatre charities.

We almost always performed on a Sunday when actors would be free. We met in the afternoon and had a read-through, did the performance (just over an hour) in the evening and then went home. Those who gave up their Sunday to appear with Michael and me over the years included, in addition to those already mentioned, Alan Bates, Judi Dench, Alec McCowen, Dorothy Tutin, Freddie Jones, Polly James, Brian Cox, Miranda Richardson, Edward Fox, Michael York, Stephen Fry, Robert Powell and Paul Eddington.

Searching in my memory for some spicy sleaze, some kiss-and-tell liaison with a famous star which would make these memoirs headline news and earn an expensive serialization in the *News of the World*, I drew a blank for a long while and then remembered: in our many performances of Michael's *He and She*, Dorothy Tutin and I played a scene from Congreve's *The Old Bachelor*. I played Heartwell, the old bachelor, and Dottie played young Sylvia, in the scene where Sylvia seduces the reluctant old man into kissing her. I know I may be branded the rat of Thorpe, but my wife and family will stand by me when I confess that I much enjoyed kissing Dottie. What is more I enjoyed kissing Dottie Tutin a little more every time we played the scene.

For me the most memorable of these platform performances was a special show about Oxford compiled by Michael from Jan Morris's *Oxford Book of Oxford* and performed in Oxford in aid of Oxfam.

We had great difficulty trying to find an actress who was free on that particular Sunday until I realized that we did not need one. Oxford dons and almost everybody else quoted in Jan's book were celibate in those earlier days and there were no lines for an actress even if we had one. Then came the great *coup*: Michael managed to persuade Sir John Gielgud to join us.

He was wonderful, of course. That voice. His instant grasp of character, or rather the dozens of characters he had to play, which many actors found difficult under the rough-and-ready, instant-theatre conditions of platform readings, and his instinctive sense of comedy. There was one passage which needed livening; we played two rather dotty old dons rubbishing a colleague, but the dialogue was not quite funny enough (a frequent problem in compilations), so I suggested to Sir John that we do that old people's habit of repeating the last half of what the other one has just said while the other one is still mumbling away. We had a lovely meandering sequence, both talking at once and neither listening.

In between the monthly weekends at St Andrews and dealing with the daily letters postmarked Kirkcaldy and the consequent phone calls and meetings, I was able to fit in some work. Besides *My Word!* and *My Music* on radio and *Call My Bluff* on the telly, I was beavering away on my *Oxford Book of Humorous Prose*.

In 1974 an editor of the Oxford University Press, Bruce Phillips, had written to me saying that in their series of Oxford books they had not as yet tackled an *Oxford Book of Humorous Prose* and would I care to take it on.

There are certain difficulties in anthologizing humour, not the least of which is that as soon as you label something funny, readers instantly want to find it unfunny because you are telling them what their sense of humour should be, and everybody's sense of humour is an extremely personal thing not to be tampered with by others.

I wrote the OUP an argument as to how I thought the book should be approached. I suggested it should be subtitled *A Conducted Tour* and aim at being a representative selection of humour in prose illustrating how it had developed in the 500 years from Caxton to P. G. Wodehouse.

Furthermore, there was a problem in setting the extracts, which would necessarily be torn out of context. I suggested that I introduce each piece by explaining something about the author and how he came to write what he did and why it was found highly amusing at the time (although perhaps not now). So I had a tremendous load of research to get through, which suited me as I could work happily at home and the London Library posted me the books I needed.

There then followed a serene run of years from the late Seventies through to the late Eighties. Home life was even better than usual; our medieval granite tower in Corsica did not need repainting and Jamie had got his degree, spent a while in rescue archaeology wallowing about in Thames mud with a 4-inch trowel helping to uncover a length of Roman river frontage just along from the Mermaid Theatre, and then changed career slightly by going into making television arts programmes, first as a researcher on

Humphrey Burton's *Aquarius*, then as a freelance director and producer.

Sally, after working happily at Hatchards, wanted to get away from London, so got herself a job in Kettering with J. L. Carr, the novelist and compiler of county maps which had little to do with geography but a lot to do with odd local characters and happenings and cricket scores. Then she met Joanna Osborne, a PA at Granada Television who wanted a different kind of life. Together the girls bought a second-hand knitting machine (one of those strips of busy little bits of metal which look like a Chinese typewriter) and, without benefit of art-school training, working from Joanna's bedroom, set up as designers and manufacturers of fashion knitwear, available for sale to the discerning public from a barrow in Covent Garden craft market on Thursdays.

And they won. Their breakthrough was their sheep jumper (the V and A has one in their permanent collection of contemporary designs). The jersey showed a flock of white sheep on a red background with one black sheep. The luck came when Lady Di, as she was then, was given one of the jumpers and wore it to Smiths Lawn polo ground in Windsor Park whilst leaning across a Land Rover. The resultant colour picture was so delightful that just about every glossy magazine in the world used it on their cover.

The girls now had a small but well-established fashion jumper business, Muir and Osborne, selling mostly to America, with a posse of freelance knitters working away in their homes.

Then, out of the blue, a trio of glittering prizes came my way.

In 1978, in the middle of my stretch of rectoring, St Andrews decided to make me an honorary Doctor of Laws (LL.D.). Even more pleasing was that the presentation was to be made during term time so that students could be present, which it seems was a rare honour at St Andrews.

Then, in 1982, Kent University decided to honour one of its local sons, me, with the honorary degree of Doctor of Letters (D.Litt.). This took place during the usual graduation ceremony held in the cathedral in front of a full congregation of students, parents and family friends. It was customary for one of those who had obtained their degree the easy way (i.e., honorary) to elect one of their number to make a brief speech from the pulpit. I was elected to do this. I could find no way of including the pig story.

Anyway, when the talk is of theatres notorious for being the graveyard of comedians and somebody says to me, 'It's all right for you, you've never played Glasgow Empire on a wet Tuesday afternoon,' I can say, 'Well, no – but I've played Canterbury Cathedral in the middle of Help The Aged week.'

In 1980, between the two degrees, came the bestowal of a different kind of honour. The beige envelope had a portcullis insignia on the flap and a nice letter inside asking whether I would accept if Downing Street recommended the Queen to appoint me a Commander of the British Empire.

A few minutes later Denis telephoned and said, 'Have you had your letter?'

Denis was quite troubled about accepting the honour because he thought that people in the entertainment industry tended to be overpaid and honours should be otherwise distributed, but eventually he accepted.

Off we went with our families to Buckingham Palace on the great day, Den and I in correct morning suits but hatless: wearing top hats made us both look like stilt-walking undertakers. It was very splendid being driven in our hire car through the palace gates, underneath an archway and into the central courtyard.

A police sergeant instructed our driver, 'Open the boot of your car and wait for the explosive dog.' After a while a constable arrived with an eager dog which leaped about all round the car and in and out of the boot, tail wagging furiously.

We went upstairs as directed to the 'waiting area', a reception room divided up into squares with red silken ropes threaded on stands, like a tremendously chic cattle market. Most of the roped-off areas were fairly full of chalk-faced, middle-aged citizens (like us) shaking with nerves, but Den and I managed to find a square which contained only a handful of potential heart attacks. We stood there shaking away with the others when I saw my old friend Johnnie Johnston, he of our Boxing Day lunches in Windsor Great Park and now in his capacity as comptroller of the Lord Chamberlain's Office, working his way towards us and looking anxious.

It seems that Den and I were in the wrong enclosure. We were in the area reserved for those about to be knighted. Johnnie extricated us and took us away to a room where he rehearsed us in how to bow so that our quite small Queen could get the CBE medal on its ribbon over our heads. It involved bending our heads forward and gazing stolidly at the floor like Chinese bandits awaiting beheading by sword.

In the event we managed it quite smoothly, marching forward when our turn came without banging into each other and bowing together, only to let ourselves down during our brief conversation with the Queen.

'How long have you two worked together?' the Queen asked.

We answered confidently, in unison:

'Twenty-three years,' said Denis.

'Twenty-six years,' said I.

'And is your work mainly for the radio?' asked the Queen.

'A certain area of it is,' I said.

'No,' said Den.

And so on for what seemed like four hours, but was actually about a minute and a half.

The CBE medallion was heavy and colourful and it came with a pink moiré ribbon with a buckle so that the device could be adjusted to dangle just below the knot of the tie. Unfortunately for its proud owners, it should only be worn on very formal occasions with full evening dress.

Again, although the rule book says that honorary degrees are full degrees and should be regarded as such, in practice they are rarely used except in academic circles. Soon after the investiture I had a letter from St Andrews University addressed to Dr Frank Muir, CBE, LL.D., D.Litt. I found our local postman examining the envelope suspiciously, 'This isn't *you*, is it?' he said.

Denis was right in saying to the Queen that his work was no longer mainly in radio. It has been said that power should only be given to people who don't want it, and perhaps it can also be argued that the only people who should be allowed to go on television regularly are those who don't want to. And Den is a good example: he hates being on telly, but he is very good indeed at what he does on it.

I suppose I must have influenced him into performing against his instincts because when we began working together I loved being 'on' and producers wanted to use *us* as a team, not just me.

Denis began work as a trainee manager for the Hyams Brothers, good, old-fashioned showmen who ran a North London super-cinema, the Kilburn Empire. Their successful philosophy, which I think had a lasting influence on Denis, was, 'Charge the customer

sixpence and then give him ninepenn'orth of entertainment.'
Certainly ever since I have known him, Denis has been extraordinarily thorough in everything he has taken on.

When we began to work separately, Den was asked to be the
presenter of *Looks Familiar*, a quiz/nostalgia/chat show about
earlier television which ran for years, due as much as anything to
his painstaking preparation before each show. And then began his
extremely successful (and very funny) series of film clips of actors
forgetting their lines, walking into the furniture and generally
falling down on the job, which has been winning huge audiences
for years and on which Den works very hard viewing clips before
making his final selection and writing his links. The show was, of
course, *It'll Be Alright on the Night*.

Ironically, as Denis appeared more and more on television I
appeared less and less, which was a good thing for me because my
next book was approaching point of lay and was very time-
consuming. I had chosen humorous pieces from over 200 authors
and was very busy writing up the commentary when my blissful
three years as Rector of St Andrews came, usefully but sadly, to an
end.

Usefully because I was astonished at how much more time I
suddenly had to work on the book. No more monthly shuttle trips
to Scotland, no more letters from students in the second post, no
more doing the hundred and one tiny things which the job
required. Sadly, because I had so enjoyed it all and hated the
thought of not being rector any longer.

I could have returned for several events shortly after leaving but
Polly thought that would be a mistake. She insisted, wisely, that I
should leave the new rector to settle himself in and keep well away
for a while. In fact we did not go back to St Andrews until 1993.
The occasion was the graduation ceremony at which honorary
degrees were to be conferred.

The vice-chancellor, Professor Struther Arnott, invited Polly and
me up to St Andrews for the ceremony to help him give the Dalai
Lama a hot meal afterwards. It was a good lunch. His Holiness the
Dalai Lama was great company, wide interests, strong sense of
humour, so deeply holy that he did not need to constantly demonstrate it. A remarkably impressive and likeable man.

Although study-bound, forefingers stabbing at the word-
processor keys most of the day every day, I still went on the

occasional exhausting author tour. In 1980 Pol and I went to Australia and New Zealand yet again. It was two or three more weeks of only seeing the insides of taxis and radio studios and bookshops in those lands of natural beauty, but we had a pleasant happening in Sydney one very hot and sunny morning.

We had a free hour – very rare – and were walking past a huge department store in Sydney when we saw a notice saying that Robert Morley, who was on tour with a play, was inside signing copies of his latest book.

Pol and I joined the queue.

I was on my way to a telly interview, so I was wearing my donkey-coloured tropical suit. As we got near to Robert I noticed that he was wearing khaki shorts. When it was our turn to face the author he saw us and said, 'Good God!'

I said, very loudly, 'I am shocked to see that you've gone native, Robert, and abandoned a proper British suit for a beachcomber's tatty shorts.'

Without a pause, Robert replied cheerfully, 'You must remember, Frank dear, the chief scout, Lord Baden-Powell, laid it down that fresh air wafting around the genitals is beneficial to health.'

My next trip abroad was three years later, sadly without Pol, when the Hong Kong Arts Festival, money coming out of its ears, invited the whole *My Music* team, including the producer and the engineer, to Hong Kong to record one (one!) *My Music* programme as part of their festival.

We had quite a colourful landing at Hong Kong's notoriously difficult airport. We dropped down between the skyscrapers, so close to them that we looked through the windows at the flickering blue of the residents' television sets, and then, because of mist over the runway, the BA pilot aborted the landing and gunned the mighty Jumbo up into the sky again as though it was a fighter plane.

'Sorry about that!' he said cheerfully over the speaker system. 'Took a lot of petrol, but no worry, we've got enough for another go. If we still don't make it we'll go across to China and spend the night in Canton.'

But we made it.

It was then the same old grind for a few happy days; corruptingly luxurious hotel, Denis being taken to the races and being advised by his host which horse was going to win (not which horse *might* win, which horse *would* win), a formal dinner with the governor amid a selection of distinguished and extremely rich Hong Kong businessmen. Industry and movie-making in the city in those prosperous days was perhaps epitomized by a grey-haired Hong Kongian at John Amis's table tilting back his chair and calling across to a friend at another table, 'Hey! Thank you for the million!'

Ah, well, saved the cost of a stamp.

And then it was an author tour of the USA. The American novelist and publisher Sol Stein much enjoyed good hotels and took a suite at the Connaught Hotel on business trips to London. When he sent me on my way across America coast-to-coast he warned me sadly that American hotels did not match up to the standard of British hotels (surely not many British hotels match up to the Connaught, either). But Sol was wrong.

By the time I had worked my way across the Midwest (Sol said only the Midwest could read) I arrived exhausted in Los Angeles to find that Stein and Day Inc's publicity girl had booked me into a downtown Hilton for a weekend in the smog. This was not on. I rang the splendid Beverly Hills Hotel and explained all. They found me a room and I moved out of the smog and up into this slightly old-fashioned hotel – all the best British hotels are slightly old-fashioned, too – with its famous Polo Bar and the one swimming pool in California to be seen at, not swimming but lying on a mattress in the sun pretending to read a film script. And the really 'in' thing was to be paged on the poolside telephone, which demonstrated not only that you were still alive but somebody actually wanted to talk to you.

There is an old and rather sweet Hollywood story about a much-liked small-time agent whose ambition it was to be called to the poolside phone whilst sunbathing. He never achieved it, but when he died his many actor friends raised a fund and paid the hotel to have him paged by the pool every morning for a year.

I am happy to put on record that I was paged by the pool.

A day or so before I left England to do the USA tour, I did an urgent rewrite for an old friend and one-time BBC colleague, Patrick Garland (I had managed to get the BBC's Music and Arts Department to let me borrow Patrick to produce and direct the Alan Bennett comedy series, *On the Margin*. Persuading another department to release one of its producers and then getting the

Head of Light Entertainment, Tom Sloan, to accept the borrowing was, I think, an exercise in guile which was probably my greatest achievement in BBC managementship).

Patrick Garland had become Director of the Chichester Festival and was having a little trouble with a Feydeau farce he was putting on starring Rex Harrison. A couple of scene endings needed a tickle up, which I managed to do in time and then drive up to London and read them to Patrick and Rex Harrison before I flew off to the USA and began my coast-to-coast trudge for Sol. And blow me, at the end of the trudge, sitting by the Beverley Hills Hotel pool was Rex Harrison. I had a copy of my book with me, and I asked him if I could take a photograph of him holding it.

'It won't be used in an advertisement, will it?' he asked, warily.

I assured him not and I still have the photograph in the loo at Anners. It is framed with another photograph, so I have pictures of two rather different kinds of friend clutching copies of *The Frank Muir Book*, an elderly Corsican, Dominic Orsini, the first Corsican Polly and I really got to know when he was building a café/restaurant with his own hands on a L'Ile-Rousse beach, and Rex Harrison.

Then, whilst talking to Rex Harrison by the Beverley Hills Hotel pool, I was paged. Paged at the Beverley Hills Hotel pool!

'Mr Muir, please – telephone!' piped the page-boy, carefully picking his way through the mattresses and scripts and expensive jars of suntan cream. 'Telephone for Mr Muir!'

Reality returned and I realized that I had no idea how the pagee was supposed to react when paged.

'What do I do?' I asked Rex, feebly.

'Answer the phone!' he said. 'Don't hurry, it makes you look anxious about your career. The phone is in the far corner there, just stroll over with a light confident smile, waving intimately to one or two recumbent figures on the way.' I think Mr Harrison was enjoying himself.

The call was from Brits working in Hollywood, John Barry, the film-music composer, and Ian La Frenais, the writer. They had heard me on a local radio interview and invited me to a British lunch the following day, a Saturday.

When I booked into the Beverly Hills Hotel on the Friday afternoon and unpacked, I found that the coast-to-coast slog across the USA in a heatwave had played hell with my pale donkey-coloured tropical-weight suit, so I rang down to reception and asked if there was any hope of getting the thing pressed as I was flying back to New York on Sunday night for a rather important early morning interview on *Good-Morning America!* and I wanted to look cleanish and tidyish.

Reception deeply regretted, but hoped I understood that Juan the valet was off at weekends. I understood. Then half an hour later there was a tap on the door and a burly young man introduced himself as Juan the valet. 'I live in a bungalow in back of the hotel,' he said. 'I ain't planning to go noplace tomorrow. You give me your suit and I'll do what I can.'

The next morning my suit was laid out on the other bed in the room, beautifully sponged and pressed. No question of touting for a big tip, just wanting to help.

My experience of Los Angeles included, suitably, a shoot-out near a radio studio. I wasn't shot myself, but I saw the drama happening, live.

It was the Saturday evening after my lunch with John Barry and Ian La Frenais and I was doing an interview at a radio studio, which like most similar low-cost enterprises in the USA was a breeze-block building in the middle of a cinder car park. Surrounding it was a bungalow development; it also had some bushes in which I saw fireflies for the first time in my life. Very beautiful and exciting.

After the interview I waited in reception for my hire car to arrive and take me back to the hotel. The interviewer had gone home to her children and I sat in silence with an elderly uniformed security guard. The whole evening was getting very boring when suddenly there was the sound of gunshots from the bungalow area followed by flashing lights and shouting. I rushed to the window and saw two beefy policemen hauling a tiny malefactor out of a bungalow window. He was wriggling like an eel and they dropped him a couple of times, but eventually – perhaps he gave up and bowed to the inevitable – they flung him into the back of their police car, one of them, ironically, protecting the malefactor's head carefully with a hand so that his skull would not hit the top of the car doorway.

The elderly radio-station security guard did not react at all, almost certainly because he was too deaf to hear the shots. A minute or two later the entrance door crashed open and a vast fat man, also in a security uniform, staggered in, clutching his arm as though if he released his grip he would spurt blood all over the ceiling. He blurted out in an extraordinarily high voice, 'Hey, Al, did you see that asshole with the gun? Fired at me, the bastard!'

He slowly withdrew his hand from his arm revealing a tiny round Elastoplast on his elbow.

'Must have been a small bullet,' I ventured.

'He missed me!' he squeaked. 'When he started shootin' I flung myself to the ground and scraped my arm on the brick wall.'

Then it was back to England, Anners, radio and TV recordings, after-dinner speeches, voice-overs and head down on the *Oxford Book of Humorous Prose* for a year or two, before any more excursions abroad.

The last of these was in 1989, a two-week long semi-holiday/semi-session of nervy hard work in Tokyo, giving a short series of one-man shows for the Tokyo British Club to raise money to help the Tokyo British School build up a library. Nervy because I did not happen to have a one-man show to give.

I had stumbled through something of the sort in a theatre in Hong Kong. It was at short notice – a kind of thank-you to our hosts – and consisted mainly of my after-dinner speech with every remembered variation, spoken slowly (the pig lasted about twenty minutes). It was reviewed, in a baffled kind of way, in *The South China Morning Post*, which I read on the flight home. The reviewer did not think my piece was all that comical but found it oddly fascinating. He thought it unpredictable and difficult to describe, but then he pulled himself together and finished agreeably by saying that nevertheless he had enjoyed the evening very much.

This is what the Brits stalwartly endured for several performances in the Tokyo British Club's little theatre. The shows were, to my great surprise, rather successful, which was gratifying as I was not a stand-up comic and only agreed to do what I could to make some money for the British School library.

When it was time to go home the club gave Polly and me a rather emotional send-off (known in Australia as 'a farewelling'). The club handed over to the school governors a cheque for £10,000, and the school library was formally started off by the presentation of a copy of *What-a-Mess* autographed by Margaret Thatcher (who happened to be in Tokyo at the time although our eyes never crossed).

Pol and I have strong memories of Tokyo. Arriving at the Capitol Tokyo Hotel, ordering two coffees and finding they were £6 each. Watching from our hotel-room window, high up, when it was going-home time and seeing a million thin black-and-white clerk-ants streaming out of offices and walking briskly to the tube stations. Black and white because they all wore black trousers or skirts and brilliantly white shirts or blouses.

It was an unnervingly hygienic city. Many cyclists wore gauze masks over their mouths, not to avoid breathing in noxious fumes, but because they thought they might have a cold and did not want to spread their germs. Until recently, if you went upstairs in a department store, a girl with a duster went ahead of you polishing the brass handrail.

The city was free of petty crime (although troubled with the usual organized urban heavy crime). You could leave a bicycle or a purse anywhere and it would still be there when you came back to look for it.

Our richest experience was taking the 'bullet' train to the ancient capital Kyoto to catch a glimpse of the old Japan.

We needed briefing by our Brit hosts as all the signs on the rail-way were, of course, in Japanese. We successfully bought our tickets from a complicated machine by watching what the travellers in front of us did to it. Our tickets gave us our seat numbers and told us that we were in carriage Q, so we did as the Brits instructed and joined the orderly queue on the part of the platform marked out with parallel white lines and labelled Q. Sure enough, bang on time the train hurtled in and hissed to a halt with the doorway of carriage Q exactly opposite us.

The seats were airline-like and comfortable and the train steady and almost silent at speed – which I think approached the 200 m.p.h. mark. Girls in kimonos, bowing a lot, came round pushing trolleys offering bowls of sushi and cups of green tea (extremely nasty tea I gathered from Polly unless you were inexplicably keen on it).

We had worried how we would know when we reached Kyoto, because the train went on further south. Our friends asked, 'When are you supposed to arrive there?' We said, 'Four-seventeen.' 'Right,' said our friends, 'keep an eye on your watch and when it says four-seventeen, walk out onto the Kyoto platform.' Which is what we did. The train, whispering through the air like a guided missile on rails, was on time to the second.

Our hotel was a small but quite famous traditional Japanese inn dating back to 1818, the Hiragiya Ryokan. The receptionist showed us our room, double futon on the floor, paper sliding doors, rice mats and the alcove which once enshrined a samurai's sword and now displayed a scroll and an ikebana flower arrangement. She asked us not to disturb the holy corner which was part of the great Japanese love of tradition, then gave us our electronic remote control which opened and closed the curtains and switched on the heated loo seat in the bathroom.

The maid allocated to us arrived. She was almost exactly half my size, a bit older, and she took a deep dislike to me, eyeing me venomously when serving supper, mainly because I could never leave my shoes pointing in the right direction. It was customary to keep taking your shoes off when wandering from one room to another and going to the loo, and there was a traditional direction they should be left pointing in, which I never managed to grasp.

Our meals were taken in the Japanese style, legs stretched out under the 9-inch-high table, praying not to be seized with a sudden spasm of cramp, lying on the futon with one elbow propped up on a device remarkably like one of those round china stands used in delicatessens to carve ham upon.

Next day we ordered a car to take us to see the Golden Temple. It was beginning to rain heavily. Our Japanese driver spoke very good English because he had been an insurance broker in the City of London and told us we were experiencing the tail-end of a typhoon. The rain got worse; we arrived back at the inn soaked to the skin and Polly had to blow-dry our clothes with her portable hairdryer.

On the way back in the 'bullet' train in even worse rain, the storm clouds parted for a moment and we had a clear sighting of Mount Fujiyama. A quite emotional moment.

A nature note completes our Tokyo memoirs: total number of animals sighted by Polly during our two-week stay; eight dogs, one cat (on a balcony in Kyoto), five cows (seen from our train window) and some sacred bantam chickens pottering about the Shinto Shrine in Tokyo. Not a lot, really. Are pet animals not liked in Japan? Eaten?

It was good to get home again, as ever.

The following year, 1990, my family and friends celebrated my seventieth birthday and *The Oxford Book of Humorous Prose* was published.

A good year. A kind of culmination.

Coda

(A FEW LATE-FLOWERING *PENSÉES*)

Apart from increased sales of my books, there was another product of all that dashing across shopping precincts and making speeches at endless literary lunches and dinners and rushing from one interview to another and enduring long-haul flights across the world. It would have been great experience for an ambitious and athletic young author, but it was not all that wise an activity for an old gent in his seventies.

So in 1992 I had a stroke.

The night before it I had a severe headache, most unusual for me, and in the morning I realized that something was not quite right. No pain, but I could not make sense of the morning papers, and when a policeman came to the door I asked him what he wanted. He told me that I had sent for him to advise on burglar alarms, of which I had no recollection at all. Polly sent for the doctor who arranged for me to go immediately into a hospital in Windsor and for me to be seen by Dr Daffyd Thomas, the neurologist.

At the Windsor hospital they inserted me up a torpedo, switched on a huge electro-magnet inside it which whizzed round me at speed for some thirty noisy (and very expensive) minutes and the resultant print of my poor brain was handed to Dr Thomas.

'You've suffered a TIA,' said the good doctor.

'That's Spanish for "aunty", isn't it?' I said (brain still working well. Or rather, normally).

'Well, the bad news', said the doc, 'is that the 'I.A.' stands for an ischaemic attack. The good news is that the 'T' stands for transient. In other words, you've had a stroke which we hope was too brief to do lasting damage.'

Once again, I had been one of life's lucky ones, but nevertheless the TIA changed my life. I am on six varieties of pill, thrown to the back of the throat three times a day at mealtimes, seventeen colourful baby Smarties in total per day. There is one mischievous little red devil, Persantin (six a day), which lurks in a stiff plastic bubble. I have an old friend, hotelier Hugh Neil, who is on the same regime as me, and his one ambition in life is to thumb his day's ration of Persantin out of their bubbles without one of them flying out of the window.

Since the attack I have become nervously apprehensive about almost everything; meeting people, travelling, performing. All these have now become stressful activities and I am only too grateful to myself for having accidentally arranged my affairs so that at this stage of the game I can stay quietly writing in my study, all dashing about done.

A melancholy aspect of giving up making speeches was having to bid farewell to my pig story, which I do now, formally, by quoting the only poem I know describing the sad parting of a man and a pig (I rather think the little anon verse began life in America or Ireland as a recitation):

> One evening in October,
> When I was far from sober,
> And dragging home a load with manly pride,
> My feet began to stutter,
> So I laid down in the gutter,
> And a pig came up and parked right by my side.
> Then I warbled, 'It's fair weather
> When good fellows get together,'
> Till a lady passing by was heard to say:
> 'You can tell a man who boozes
> By the company he chooses!'
> Then the pig got up and slowly walked away.

*

In his book *Letters from Iceland*, W. H. Auden quotes the longest word in the Icelandic language, It might be worth memorizing as it could well come in useful. The word is:

Haestarjettarmalaflutunesmanskiffstofustulkkonutidyralykill.

It means 'a latch key belonging to a girl working in the office of a barrister'.

*

In early American B-pictures they used to indicate that a character was English by making him say, 'Pip-pip, old fruit!' an expression made popular by P. G. Wodehouse, but originally, according to Partridge's *Dictionary of Slang*, 'A hue and cry after a youth in striking bicycling costumery'. Presumably the phrase mocked the youth's little warning hooter and his colourful clothing.

The French (and the Corsicans) keep another archaic phrase alive by still raising their glass to an Englishman in a bar with the salutation '*chin-chin!*'. This was originally an Anglo-Chinese expression of greeting meaning in Chinese, 'please-please'.

The point is that, when in the Far East, it behoves one to exercise caution when using old English colloquialisms.

In Japan, we were told, '*chin-chin*' is slang for 'little boy's penis'.

*

When I was at the BBC working on the Jeeves and Bertie Wooster series, the family had to go off on holiday to Corsica without me for a few days and the producer Michael Mills, who was spending that weekend with his mother in her cottage on the south coast, kindly invited me down with him.

I took with me a small box of hand-made chocolates as a little pressie for Mrs Mills. She was delighted.

She lightly prodded the chocolates in turn. 'I'll give that one to Mrs Potter,' she said. 'Jane would love that one, and this one I think I'll give to Mrs Turner who loves chocolates and never gets them, poor soul. And this one . . .'

'Oh, really, mother!' said Michael. 'Frank gave them to *you*!'

'Yes, he did,' said Mrs Mills, 'but he didn't impose conditions. He gave them to me as a present, so they are now mine to do what I like with. Eat them, deep-freeze them for Christmas, give them away to friends. Surely, enjoy them in any way I choose?'

Polly and I were so struck with this entirely sensible and honest approach to gifts that ever since, when we find that a present we have given has been lost by the recipient, or sold or thrown away, it hasn't bothered us one jot. 'It's the Mrs Mills story!' we say.

*

During the Suez crisis, when petrol rationing was imposed, I bought a motor scooter and rode to London every day on it until it slipped away from under me one rainy evening in Curzon Street and I was helped to my feet by an elderly tart.

Soon after I bought the bike I was in The Red Lion at home when a local village character, Long Charlie Fimbo, said, 'I saw you riding that foreign bike thing o' yours. You look like a swan on a piece of cheese.'

What an extraordinary expression.

*

When Nigel Hollis first worked for William Heinemann the publishers, he lived in Barnes with his wife Sarah and their two boys and cycled to his office in the West End. Quite a few publishers used to cycle in those days, but most of them eventually came adrift from their bikes round Hyde Park Corner and went back to buses and taxis.

The Hollis family lived in a typical London tall thin house, and breakfasted in a smallish kitchen in the semi-basement. The boys were still at school and would occasionally bring a friend home with them for the weekend.

Sarah said that breakfast in the tiny kitchen doing a fry-up for small boys and their guests, particularly in winter when the heating was on as well as the cooker, was like being in Little Hell. Rain poured down outside, condensation streamed down the windows inside and Nigel had to be got off to work in good time so that he did not have to pedal like mad in and out of the King's Road traffic.

Sarah was trying to cope during one such frantic Monday morning breakfast, with the bacon beginning to burn, the toast really burning, the temperature in the kitchen about 150 degrees centigrade, and Nigel, late, searching for a lost bicycle-clip under the table, when Sarah found her skirt being gently tugged by the small boy guest, a judge's son, whom her boys had brought home for the weekend.

'Do excuse me, Mrs Hollis,' he whispered discreetly, 'but you appear to have forgotten the butter-knife.'

MORAL: Never underestimate the British middle classes, even when they are only schoolboys.

*

Never underestimate the British grandchild, either.

I was seized with a wish for my grandchildren to address me as

Grandpapa. The word has an elegant ring to it – a hint of Proust? Gigi?

What a hope.

It is the grandchildren themselves who decide the word they will use to summon us.

Abigail Wheatcroft had a sporting go at saying 'grandpapa' but just couldn't make it, so she reduced 'grandpapa', via *Barbar the Elephant*, to 'bummer'. When we are, say, gathering foodstuffs in a Bath supermarket, her little voice will cry out, loud and clear, 'I'm over here, Bummer!'

Her younger brother, Gabriel, who has just discovered the joys of talking, goes at the problem with energy but as yet little finesse. He has heard how his sister addresses me and has simplified it to, 'Hey, Bum-Bum!'

*

Denis and I had to finish a script which meant missing lunch. Then in the evening I had to go to the Odeon cinema, Leicester Square, to watch a film in the *Doctor* series which had somebody in it we were thinking of using in a programme, and I missed dinner. Feeling very hungry by then I bought the most substantial nibble I could find on sale in the cinema foyer, a 1-pound box of Meltis New Berry Fruits. Devotees of eating during films will know that these fruits are soft pastilles filled with a sweet fruit-flavoured syrup and rolled in sugar.

During the film I unthinkingly munched my way through the whole top layer, i.e., a full half pound of Meltis New Berry Fruits.

Nothing alarming happened until I was driving home to the village of Thorpe in Surrey and just past the airport I came over peculiar. I slowed down the car to walking pace and concentrated on driving in a straight line. I was clearly in the way of the car behind me which turned out to be a police car.

It suddenly rang its bell; that dreadful, heart-stopping clangour which police cars made in those days, like the fire-alarm gong going off in a Tibetan monastery. I pulled into a lay-by, palpitating.

Oddly enough, I was to pull into that same lay-by some four years later, also after coming over peculiar. On that occasion I was on my way home from one of those odd anniversaries so beloved by the BBC, the nineteenth and a half anniversary of Radio 3 or something. It was at the Guildhall and after dinner the waiters plied the guests with small glasses of neat whisky and neat brandy, which could not easily be differentiated. The evening became suddenly jollier and voices and laughter a touch shriller.

I found myself standing next to the Archbishop of Canterbury, the Right Revd Michael Ramsey, a tremendously imposing figure with a mane of white hair, the only male in the room not clutching one or more small glasses of whisky/brandy. I felt an overwhelming impulse to tell the archbishop a religious joke to help him to lighten up a sermon or two.

'Archbishop, sir,' I said, 'here's a good one for you. There was this epicene young hairdresser who'd never been to a Roman Catholic service, so one Sunday morning he took himself off to the Brompton Oratory and picked an end seat in the pew. As the procession passed down the nave he was alarmed to see a priest swinging a censer from which emerged little puffs of smoke. The hairdresser, feeling he should do something, leaned across as the priest passed close to him and whispered urgently, 'Excuse me mentioning it, madam, but your handbag's on fire.'

The archbishop did not even smile.

On the way home I remembered telling the Archbishop of Canterbury the joke and was so ashamed that I came over peculiar and pulled the car into a lay-by for a little private palpitate.

Remembering that occasion reminded me of an even worse instance of self-reproach, a real scarlet-cheeked memory. In this one I palpitated in another lay-by, the small car park on the edge of Thorpe Green.

Over the years my family and I enjoyed the most pleasant custom of having lunch on Boxing Day with friends who lived in Windsor Great Park. Fast-forwarding to 1976, I had just had a book published, *The Frank Muir Book: An Irreverent Companion to Social History*, which had climbed to being the number one bestseller the week before Christmas. On that fateful Boxing Day I had given a copy of the book to our hostess, who had most kindly left it prominently on a side table.

Our hosts had over the years invited those members of the royal family who wanted to get away from their young watching telly at the castle to have a before-lunch drink on Boxing Day.

On Boxing Day 1976, Her Majesty the Queen, Prince Philip and quite a few of the rest of the family turned up. I suddenly spotted that the Queen's equerry had picked up my book and was glancing through it, but what is gloriously more, he was LAUGHING. I casually shot over to his side.

'What is that you're reading?' The queen asked the equerry.

He saw me. 'Oh, it's a book by – er – Frank Muir here. Be very useful for writing speeches!'

The Queen said to me, smiling, 'Then we should have a copy.'

It was at that point that, nerves strung tight as a bowstring, I cracked. 'Don't you buy one, ma'am,' I croaked. 'I'll send you one. I get a third off.'

It was on the way home that the tattiness of saying such a shabby thing to the pleasant lady, who was not only my monarch, but also one of the richest ladies in the land smote me and I had to pull into the small car park on the edge of Thorpe Green and have a right royal palpitation.

To return to the original Meltis New Berry Fruits-inspired palpitation, I steered into the lay-by with great care and got out of the car. I found standing up difficult so I hung on to the door and the fresh air helped. A police officer swiftly joined me from the squad car, putting on his hat.

'Is this your vehicle, sir?' he said (why do they always say 'vehicle' and never 'car'?). He was not much concerned whether it was mine or not, it was just the police equivalent of saying, 'How do you do.'

'It will be in two years next September,' I said, rather wittily considering the circumstances.

'Had a little drink, have we, sir?' he said.

'No, I haven't,' I said.

'We've been following you for seven-tenths of a mile and your driving appears to be on the unconventional side.'

He leaned forward and sniffed me. This was before breathalysers. 'It's unusual in this kind of incident, sir,' he said, 'but you smell of oranges.'

I pointed at the box of sweeties on the passenger seat.

'Meltis!' he said. 'May I?' He selected one with care and swiftly crunched it up. 'Blackcurrant!' he said. 'My favourite!'

'I have not been drinking,' I said, 'nor come to that have I been eating. I came over hungry in the cinema and bought these Meltis Fruits. I ate rather a lot of them.'

'That's it!' said the officer, holding the box and gazing at the pastilles longingly.

'Do have another,' I said.

He popped three into his mouth. 'Your stomach experienced a

quick intake of an excessive amount of sugar, sir, that's what you done. On an empty stomach you get what medical science calls "the collywobbles". It's a well-known side-effect.'

He probed the box with a stubby forefinger, seeking another blackcurrant.

'*You'll* get the wobbles if you carry on eating those things,' I said.

'No I won't, I've just had me tea,' he said. 'Well, you're in the clear so off you go, sir,' he said, banging the top of the car in dismissal.

I drove on home. My last glimpse of the law in the driving mirror was of him standing by the kerb, clutching my box of Meltis New Berry Fruits and munching steadily.

*

I had collected a plastic bag full of books from Hatchards in Piccadilly and was strolling past Fortnum's when a tiny middle-aged couple, from south-east Asia I would have thought, emerged. They were clearly filthy rich; the lady was elegantly clad in mink (this was some twelve years ago) and diamonds glittered here and there upon her person. She came up to me, smiled delightfully and said, 'You have the most beautiful trousers I have ever seen!'

Now this happened to be welcome news. Polly had recently told me that all the clothes I had ever bought were in a shade of donkey (Polly occasionally comes out with these confidence-shattering observations. When we were driving to a restaurant on my fiftieth birthday, she suddenly said, 'I never realized you had such cruel eyes'), so I asked Doug Haywood, my tailor and an old friend, to construct me a pair of non-donkey-coloured trousers. These he made from a highly coloured, almost phosphorescent tweed in the sort of strong design which used to be called bookmaker's check.

I was a bit worried about them so when the nice lady asked if she could see the trousers in motion, I obligingly prinked up and down Piccadilly, smiling enigmatically like a supermodel and non-chalantly swinging my plastic bag of books.

The lady said, 'Beautiful! Beautiful!' Then when I had come to rest, laid her hand on the left cheek of my behind, cupped it for a moment in the manner of a Far-Eastern housewife estimating the weight of a mango, and gave it a strong and painful pinch. As my eyebrows shot up, she smiled her sweet smile again and said, 'In my country we always give a pinch when we give praise!'

I was intrigued whether my pinch was a widespread piece of

folklore practice or a sudden sexual urge, so I wrote a letter to *The Times* describing what had happened and asking what was the significance of the event. The subject obviously appealed to readers because letters in reply were printed for weeks afterwards. What emerged from the printed letters was that it most certainly *was* a widespread practice.

Mrs Audrey Jones of Ealing wrote that it is well known in Jewish domestic circles, and pointed out that for a child to be praised for being artistic and intelligent and beautiful and then to have a cheek painfully pinched was one of the terrors of having a Jewish grand-mother; particularly, it seems, if she came from Russia, Poland or Latvia. Mrs Jones described these immigrants as 'the feared matri-archs of Maida Vale'.

On the other hand, Mrs Tomlinson of London NW8 remem-bered that when she was a girl in Scotland it was customary to give a schoolfriend wearing new clothes a hard pinch on the upper arm 'for luck'.

Mr P. J. Barlow from Argyll thought that I had got off lightly. He pointed out that had I been an Arab or a Spanish gentleman of the old school I would have been honour bound to whip off my trousers there and then and present them to the lady.

The facts of the matter were explained in a letter from Dr Jacqueline Simpson, honorary editor of *Folklore*, who wrote that my alarming experience simply illustrated the misunderstandings which arose when people who did not traditionally believe in the evil eye encountered those who did. It seems the belief is quite common in India, the Near East and primitive bits of Europe. Its core is the notion that if anyone or anything is praised, this will arouse the envy of a malevolent onlooker with magical powers who will 'cast the eye'.

Dr Simpson's letter to *The Times* went on, 'If nothing had been done to counteract the praise, such as bestowing a powerful pinch, Mr Muir's fine trousers would undoubtedly have met with some dire accident – some soup perhaps, or too hot an iron. Maybe even the anatomy within would have withered under the glance of the unknown eye.'

Phew!

I was also sent a *Folklore* magazine which listed some of the counter-charms traditionally employed by peasantry in the Balkans. It seems that Balkan ploughmen, plodding their weary way homeward, on suspecting that there was a malevolent sprite about, protected themselves from the eye by exposing their organ of manhood.

Suddenly a pattern began to emerge. The use of 'chin-chin' in Japan to describe the infant version of the Balkan ploughman's counter-charm ties in with a European use of the expression. So when a Frenchman (or a Corsican) in a bar raises his glass in your direction and says 'chin-chin!', do remember that he is actually protecting you against the evil eye with the French verbal equivalent of a quick flash from a Baltic ploughman.

*

Back in the Eighties I had a letter from the artist, John Bratby ARA, inviting me to sit for him.

It was an odd letter. He emphasized that I would not be asked to buy the portrait, that was not his point in inviting me to sit; it was to be one of a number of portraits he was painting to make up an exhibition for the National Theatre of contemporary figures of fame and influence (you see what I mean by calling it an odd letter). Already on canvas were the faces of many of my friends, including Dilys Powell, John Cleese and Johnny Speight.

I knew Mr Bratby's work. He had a deserved success at Academy exhibitions with vigorous and colourful paintings of backyards seen through the kitchen window, that kind of thing. I had also seen some of the portraits he had already painted for this new exhibition. There was the familiar Bratby vigour and colour and the use of lots of paint, and a thumb here and there, but they seemed to me to be all the same face.

The rather crumpled face belonged to Johnny Speight, the writer. His portrait by Bratby hung on his wall (all my friends seemed to have bought their portraits) and it was an excellent likeness, but if you didn't look like Johnny Speight Mr Bratby's portrait didn't look like you. John Cleese looked like John Cleese doing an impression of Johnny Speight and Dilys Powell looked a little like Johnny Speight's aunt, but not much like Dilys Powell.

I accepted Mr Bratby's invitation because I had never sat for an artist, I wanted to meet him and the whole thing was intriguing.

I sat for only one afternoon at his studio in Greenwich. He stabbed away at the canvas with his brush (and his thumb) and chatted all the while. It was not a conversation because that suggests an interchange of dialogue and Mr Bratby spent the three hours asking lots of questions, but not listening to the answers because he was busy painting. A weird experience, like being interviewed by somebody who was deaf and had forgotten to put in his hearing aid.

As I left for home he again stressed that there was no pressure on me to buy the portrait, but almost as soon as I arrived back, a Polaroid of the portrait arrived with a thank-you note saying that the picture was mine for £400.

Next day I had to lunch at the Savile Club and I mentioned to the chap next to me, an accountant, that I had been painted by John Bratby, who was offering me the picture for £400. The accountant, with investment in mind, said, 'Buy it.'

I passed him the Polaroid.

'Don't buy it,' he said.

The face in the picture did not look much like me because I do not look like Johnny Speight. If anything, I looked in my portrait like the BBC sports presenter Desmond Lynam after he had been run over.

The final word came from our dear 'daily', Rene Hayes. I showed her the Polaroid of the portrait and said that it was mine for £400. What did she think? Mrs Hayes took it to the window, turned it upside down and sideways, held it at arm's length and then made her judgement: 'Seems a lot of money for a photograph.'

*

One evening Polly and I were lolling on the sofa, semi-watching some pretty awful television. I looked up *Radio Times* and there was no escaping to a better channel, all channels were offering pretty awful television.

It occurred to me that in the fifty years that I had been on and in and in front of television it had changed a great deal. It had to, of course, but so much had changed for the worse.

I was only thinking of programme quality. The curious belief by the present BBC that 'management consultancy' is the mystical answer to the difficulty of making better entertainment is understandable; 'management structures' are mainly about measuring things and doing sums and writing memos, which are not difficult tasks and 'management consultancy' is a comfortingly self-perpetuating, inexact science which manages to get itself paid enormous fees (it is altogether a much more sensible career to put a personable, intelligent, totally ungifted son or daughter into than making TV programmes).

The basic problem is that there are now too many TV stations, and what is more there are a great many more to come soon due to wonderful digital TV (worked by finger?). Miserably, I think it is probably inevitable that, as Kingsley Amis said about education, 'More will mean worse', and the BBC's public service ethos will be abandoned as it chases the chimera of multi-channel digital plenty. There is simply not enought talent to go round. Not only performing and writing talent but creative production and directing talent, and what exists now will have to be spread even more thinly in the years of 'progress' ahead.

The Americans ran into this problem years ago and met it by rationing talent, which is expensive stuff, and making do instead with talent-substitutes; good humour rather than humour, formulaic comedy, the use of young producers and directors trained to work by the book and produce a show which was good or bad but was, more importantly, on time and within its budget. I speak of American television as a whole, not just the excellent comedy shows we import, which are the lilies on the dungheap of an enormous and mostly unattractive national output.

We see this talent-substitution in operation now in Britain with the rise in importance of the presenter. Alan Titchmarsh, once the ace gardening presence on *Pebble Mill At One* we now see interviewing showbiz folk and presenting this and that all over the place; attractive weather girls, perfectly competent at reading their autocue and making odd but pretty hand gestures, turn up in front of programmes which have nothing to do with the weather. Ex-Radio 1 disc jockeys present jokey game shows, and journalists front everything from chat shows to travel programmes. Perhaps the best example of this use of an unusual presenter to beef up an otherwise not very original programme idea was a long series about the history of painting presented by Sister Wendy, an enthusiastic nun.

Another discovery by TV chiefs was that popular cheap programmes could be made without using any talent at all, by making 'people shows', programmes which did not feature an expensive star but the antics of the general public. This was another American idea, pioneered by the radio broadcaster Alan Funt. Many years ago he devised *Candid Microphone*, a radio show in which a hidden microphone recorded people being hoodwinked into making fools of themselves. The programme then moved over to TV as *Candid Camera*, orginally presented in Britain by Jonathan Routh and later revived using Jeremy Beadle. Jeremy Beadle was also used to present another American idea which exploited the widespread use of home camcorders. This was an even cheaper way of putting on a half-hour programme than *Candid Camera* as the public took the pictures and just sent the tape in to the programme. If their film was used they were paid a small copyright fee.

This was yet another programme idea which fed the viewing public's keen pleasure in watching somebody else being humiliated. The difference with this one was that the humiliations were not brought about by complicated traps devised by the production staff as in *Candid Camera*, but were supposedly real slip-ups which happened during family filming. And slip-ups was what they literally were. In 99 per cent of the 'funny' clips, an adult, or more frequently a toddler, came out through the French windows and fell over. Sometimes the victim reached the shrubbery before falling over, sometimes started to climb the fence before falling over, but eventually, and usually quite swiftly, the victim fell over, sometimes quite painfully.

On 'humiliation' programmes, the victims have to sign a clearance chit approving the transmission of their moment of misery, but this is rarely a problem. As Andy Warhol might have said, soon everybody will be on television for two minutes and a great number of keen viewers would willingly have a leg off on film if it meant that they might appear on the nation's telly.

A grander programme appealing to the same ignoble pleasure in watching others suffer was the BBC's *Auntie's Sporting Bloomers*, presented by Terry Wogan, a brilliant and witty radio broadcaster who shifted to television, but after a few good years curiously faded in appeal, apart from keeping us all awake with his excellent cheeky commentary on the annual *Eurovision Song Contest*.

Auntie's Sporting Bloomers was simply another version of the very good *It'll Be Alright on the Night* and the naff Jeremy Beadle amateur videos, but this time with blood. Toddlers falling into puddles was no longer enough so rally cars slid into rivers, pole vaulters' long poles snapped beneath them, racing skiers suffered horrendous crashes or ploughed into spectators, young women fell off jumping horses. (Denis told me that on *It'll Be Alright on the Night* he has a rule that if the victim who falls over doesn't get up, they don't use the clip.)

To a regular viewer these personal disasters induced no more than the normal nervous laugh, yet the companies' excuses for screening them were that they were highly comical. 'They're only fun,' was the defence. So the inherent sadism and loss of human dignity had to be presented as hysterically funny entertainment, which brings us to the nub of this rather long moan.

Among the technical innovations which have proved a great help to television, such as machines which record programmes, and the autocue which enables newsreaders (and, of course, presenters) to read prepared pieces whilst looking into the lens, there was another technical device which to my mind has proved the most destructive and dishonest influence ever on television comedy: manipulated laughter.

Laughter added to a show later – a little 'sweetening' as it is known in the trade – was originally done by using a laughter tape. This is still done, but it is not too successful. Firstly, because the sound doesn't ring true. A live audience bursting out laughing is the sound of audible pleasure growing which is not the same sound at all as the volume control being turned up in the middle of a tape of recorded laughter, and live laughter dying away is a quite different sound from recorded laughter being faded out. And all programmes seem to use the same two or three laughter tapes. The most recognizable has a woman horribly close to the recording microphone who has a continuous cackle (do they audition the laughers?), and in the background is a random squeal of uncalled for shrieking, whooping and whistling.

The second problem is that producers and directors do not seem to know how to handle canned laughter. They use the tapes, of course, to paper over the fact that the show is not as funny as it should be, but then they get carried away and dub howls of laughter over any kind of movement on the screen even if there is nothing whatever going on which would prompt such a reaction.

Producers then moved on from the crude taped-laughter system and devised what they believed was a totally justifiable and efficient method of 'sweetening' a show. This was to record the studio audience laughing at something else, perhaps a smutty joke routine from a comedian warming up the audience before the recording, and then mix this laughter into the actual recording at key points.

The next development was to make sure that the audience provided loud enough hysterical laughter, whoops, whistles and so on. This is now done, particularly on give-away, 'yoof' and game shows, by skilful assistants who train the audience for a long time before the actual recording to make the required noises. The audiences (carefully selected by 'researchers') are only too happy to oblige.

One of the small but real pleasures of watching bad television is when an incompetent producer has dubbed on gales of hysterical laughter but has forgotten that the next shot is a reaction shot of the studio audience, and the audience is slumped silently in its seats, half asleep.

*

In winter I suffer, mostly in heroic silence I must point out, from a boring item known to doctors as Raynaud's Disease (or if they are in private practice, Raynaud's Phenomenon), a widespread little bother where the fingers go white and dead when the weather is cold or the sufferer stays in the water too long when swimming. To relieve this harmless but unhelpful and sometimes quite painful infliction I sent off to a mail-order company for a pair of newly invented hand-warming sachets. They turned up the statutory twenty-eight days later. Happily the weather had turned viciously cold, and as I had to go to London to a *Punch* lunch, it was a good moment to road-test my Mycoal Grabber Hand and Pocket Warmers (Odourless, Non-toxic, Dry, Clean and Disposable). They looked exactly like tea bags.

Obeying instructions, I tore them (with some difficulty) out of their stout plastic envelope and massaged them, whereupon by some scientific miracle they swiftly grew comfortingly warm, almost hot. They stayed so all morning, one in each coat pocket, keeping my hands pink and cosy as I shopped in icy London.

At lunchtime the hot tea bags were still going strong. As I passed the entrance to Hamley's the toyshop, I was pulled up by the sight of a vagrant slumped in the doorway. Not a young, *Big Issue*-selling vagrant but an old-fashioned tramp, elderly, covered in many overcoats and bits of plastic. He had a beard like rusty barbed wire and he was filthy.

On an impulse I took out one of my hot Grabber hand-warmers and pressed it into his very cold and grubby hand. 'This might help to warm you up,' I said cheerfully.

'Giss a quid,' he said.

At the *Punch* lunch I was seated next to Lady Olga Maitland, the slim elegant journalist and politician. I showed her my remaining hot tea bag, explained its magical workings and presented it to her. Lady Olga took it with a charming smile and slipped it down her cleavage.

It would be difficult to think of two more diverse resting places for my pair of Mycoal Grabber Hand and Pocket Warmers (Odourless, Non-Toxic, Dry, Clean and Disposable).

*

People often stop me in the street and ask, 'With your white hair and feeble moustache and vague air of wanting to be somewhere else, why have you never been knighted?'

Actually, not all that many people have stopped me and asked that. To be brutally honest *nobody* has stopped me and asked that, but should somebody ever stop me and ask why I am not Sir Frank, I have a full answer. I blotted my copybook with Prince Philip at a fund-raising dinner in the ballroom of an exclusive (a tabloid newspaper adjective meaning expensive) London hotel.

There used to be a story about a high-born epicene young Guards officer who had somehow survived the First World War and was asked what trench warfare on the Somme was really like. He said, 'Oh, my dear, the *noise*! The PEOPLE!'

That is how, now that I work at home, I tend to feel when I have to go to London. One evening some years ago I arrived home from London tired and tetchy as usual in time to see the nine o'clock news. The lead story was Prince Charles's maiden speech in the House of Lords. The newsreader said, 'Prince Charles began his speech with the quotation, "As Oscar Wilde said, 'If a thing is worth doing, it is worth doing badly!' " (much respectful laughter).'

A good modest introduction to a speech, but unfortunately the line was not written by Oscar Wilde but by G. K. Chesterton. Ascribing it to Wilde suggested it was nothing more than a witty *bon mot*, one of those amusing Wildean inversions such as, 'Work is the curse of the drinking classes.' But coming from G. K. Chesterton meant it was a more thoughtful observation. In Chesterton's work his humour arose from a serious thought, as an oyster was prompted into action by a gritty grain of sand. What Chesterton was saying (in a piece about playing croquet) was that playing a game simply because you enjoyed playing it, perhaps hoping to get better at it in time, is a worthy enough reason for playing it however badly.

In my tetchy mood I lost my cool for a moment, telephoned *The Times* newspaper and left a message for the editor of The Diary column explaining how important I felt it was that the quotation was given its proper author.

Next morning *The Times* made the Prince's speech its front-page story. It began, 'Last night the Prince of Wales began his maiden speech to the House of Lords by saying "As Oscar Wilde said, 'If a thing is worth doing, it is worth doing badly!'" (laughter).'

Then came an asterisk, and at the bottom of the page was its twin asterisk and, in nasty black type, '**Mr Frank Muir pointed out last night that the Prince had opened his speech with a misquotation. The line was not written by Oscar Wilde but by G. K. Chesterton.**'

And then other newspapers began telephoning for follow-up stories . . .

Worse happened. A year or so later I found myself in the Crystal Room of London's 'exclusive' Grosvenor House Hotel having pre-dinner drinkies with the formidable committee who were mounting the evening's ball, which was an early exercise in prising money out of the rich and good for the World Wildlife Fund. I was there to give my after-dinner speech.

Also speaking was the Duke of Edinburgh. I found myself beside the Duke in a quiet corner of the noisy room. He was looking a bit bored, so I felt it incumbent upon me to put him at his ease.

'Oh, sir,' I said, 'I feel I must apologize for correcting the Prince of Wales on the misquotation in his maiden speech to the Lords. But, sir, I felt rather strongly about it. You see, sir, it wasn't a joke, but a philosophy which I happen to agree with. It is the opposite view to the American cult of winner take all. If your child does not come top of the class does that mean that it is a useless human being? No, of course not . . .'

As I warmed to my theme the Duke closed his eyes several times, presumably in order to concentrate on what I was saying, but as I talked on I remembered that both he and Prince Charles had been to stern Gordonstoun school where, it was rumoured, those pupils who did not come among the top three in exams were shot (only a slight wound in a fleshy part of the thigh, I understood, but still . . .). After something like a quarter of an hour I brought my little apology to a close by saying, laughingly, '. . . anyway, sir, I would have thought the blithering idiot who gave Prince Charles the quotation would have had the nous to check it first!'

The Duke looked at me levelly. '*I* gave him the quotation,' he said.

*

If only Polly and I had been less shy in the early days we might have been younger grandparents and not found it all quite so exhausting, but in our seventies we find that racing after a runaway three-year-old in the garden, or bending down and picking up 200 small, vitally important broken toys from the floor at bedtime is getting to be quite an effort. Even lifting Gabriel out of the bath made Polly long for a domestic fork-lift truck on loan from the district nurse.

The senior Wheatcrofts had to go off somewhere and for the first time left Abigail in our care for a whole week.

Afterwards Polly and I booked into a health farm for four days.

*

Omar Khayyám wrote the wistful lines:

*   Alas that Spring should vanish with the rose,
    And youth's sweet, scented manuscript should close.

For those readers who are worried whether they have reached the stage when their spring has disappeared, their aromatic manuscript is completed and they are about to be dead-headed, Denis and I have isolated some foolproof symptoms. You are beginning to be truly old when:

You do not kneel down unless you have first spotted something you can grab to pull yourself up again.

You get into a car by backing your bottom in and then hauling your legs in by hand.

You have given up eating toffees, stewed figs (the seeds), and anything with nuts anywhere near it.

* I remember those lines from the *Rubáiyát* because in the 1930s they were painted on a wall of the Omar Khayyám Café, next to the Royal Hotel in Albion Street, Broadstairs. They might still be there.

*

Before we oldies can enjoy the great pleasure of cuddling and/or tripping over our grandchildren, there is an interesting intermediary stage: our children have to acquire mates. Neither Jamie nor Sal rushed into marriage. Friendships, yes, but total commitment was not undertaken lightly. Sal met Geoffrey at a party and from then on his name seemed to crop up more and more in conversation. She seemed to be seeing him so frequently that we asked her when she was going to arrange for us to meet him. 'Probably never,' Sal said a little loftily, which was a clear pointer that things were getting serious.

In 1990 I had my seventieth birthday and Sal brought Geoffrey to the party and we liked him very much. After the party the two of them went off to Paris and when they arrived back Geoffrey met me at the Garrick Club for a drink and told me that in Paris he had asked Sal to marry him and she had agreed.

Geoffrey and Sal seemed to spend most of 1990 getting married.

They had a civil ceremony at an off-licence (as Denis and I like to call register offices) in Bath, where Geoffrey lived, then later we all trooped over to Siena where Geoffrey's friend, Jasper Guinness, had arranged a church wedding in an ancient Protestant chapel, conducted by an elderly English vicar from Florence who spent much of his time clad in scarlet leathers happily roaring around Chiantishire on a motorbike.

Back to Bath in mid-summer, the wedding breakfast was held; a joyous party. The temperature outside was in the nineties and inside the marquee it was like a vast mixed sauna.

Theoretically, Sally could have brought into the family a nice kind water-diviner or a non-ferrous metal welder, in which case conversation over Christmas dinner might have been a little difficult to maintain on a sprightly note ('Divined anything interesting recently, Ronald?' 'Do tell us again about the trouble you had fusing copper to brass in the cold spell, Sidney').

But Sally augmented our family to the good with the much respected journalist and author, Geoffrey Wheatcroft, columnist, opera correspondent, writer of newspaper 'think pieces', and author of, amongst other books, *The Randlords*, the riveting story of the gold and diamond barons of South Africa and, more recently, *The Controversy of Zion*, about the founding of the Jewish independent state. And if that was not enough, Geoffrey cooks superbly and is father of Abigail and Gabriel.

Jamie, too, did the family proud. A few months after Sal's wedding, he married Caroline Robertson, an extremely attractive girl who had modelled for the painter John Ward ARA, but when we met her was an editor with Penguin Books. She has since taken a degree in paper conservation and works with museums. Jamie and Caroline have added a daughter, Isobel, to our grandchildren's Christmas-present list.

Caroline's father, John, who was with British Steel before taking early retirement so that he could do what he had always wanted to do, become an antique dealer and whizz about the country with bits of Georgian silver, solved for me a difficult problem of relationship.

I am not very good at that cat's cradle game of who is whose ninth cousin twice removed and where step-grandnephews fit in – it seems to be a game exclusively enjoyed by one's wife – and I could not work out what my relationship was to the father of my son's wife.

The problem was resolved when the good man telephoned me soon after Jamie and Caroline's wedding. 'Hello, Frank?' he said. 'It's me, John-in-law.'

*

In Egham High Street, a frail old man stepped carefully out of the door of Mr Mullan the pharmacist. The old man saw me and halted.

'I know you from the telly,' he said. His face went sad. 'I used to like you,' he said.

*

Mr Mullan the pharmacist came to Egham from Belfast and is a fellow parishioner with Polly of the Catholic church. I know him well as I get my pills from him. Mr Mullan's grey-haired, benign, avuncular appearance belies a swift-thinking and occasionally wicked turn of mind.

I had put in to my health centre for a renewal prescription, but it had not arrived when I noticed that I was almost out of Persantin tablets, which I was told were vital to stop me from slumping occasionally to the floor. A friend advised me to go to my friendly pharmacist and borrow a couple of Persantin to keep me vertical pro tem. So off I went to Mr Mullan.

'Mr Mullan,' I said, 'I have been a foolish virgin . . .'

'Boasting again?' he said.

*

Going through this manuscript, that is to say toning down the adjectives and trying to cut out a hundred or so 'very's, I was very struck by how random and wayward the finger of Fate seems to have been in my life, and presumably everybody's. A coherent plan did not seem to have entered into her thinking; she had clearly not been on a planner's course or had a session with the management consultants.

Theoretically one makes one's own decisions, we are free spirits, but looking back I have been about as much in control of my progress as a plastic duck in a jacuzzi.

The fact is that the major hinges in life are hidden. When I think of the jobs years ago which Denis and I hoped so much to get, and in hindsight can only say – thank *heavens* we lost that job of writing musicals on ice for Harringay Arena, and the deal which fell through of moving to America to write a version for their TV of *Whack-O!*, a comedy about an English public school whose customs and values American viewers were not in the slightest bit familiar with. And how invisible are the tiny hinges which swing us into our really important human relationships and career moves.

Nearly fifty years ago, when Charles Maxwell took Denis and me to lunch at Frank's, the Italian restaurant in Jermyn Street, and suggested that we might get together and have a go at writing a radio series for Jimmy Edwards and Dick Bentley (which turned out to be *Take It From Here*), we were both so busy already with (small) commitments that we could have strolled along to St James's Street, exchanged pleasantries about the meal, then I could have said something like, 'Interesting offer, but, like you, I'm a bit full up at the moment. Shall I give you a ring in a month or so and see how we're placed then?' and turned right at St James's Street to find my parked car and drive home. And Den could have turned left and gone back to his office.

But we didn't; we both went back to Den's office together. From that day on we wrote everything together for nearly twenty years, radio shows, theatre revues for George and Alfred Black, scenes for films, sketches for summer shows, and so on. And when that stopped we performed in *My Word!* and *My Music* together for many years, and then we had our television shows. Nowadays, now that I am taking things a little more calmly, we make do with phoning each other two or three times a week.

These are pleasant phone calls; Den and I exchange physical symptoms, unpick the previous evening's TV and recount to the other some bit of observed idiocy, knowing that the other is probably the only person in the world who will wholly appreciate the story.

We are quite different people, which is probably why the partnership worked so well. Producers bought the product of two minds; it was an additive process not one comedy approach divided (like the fee) into two.

Denis was a revelation to me. His mind is a fascinating mixture of intellectual rigour and showbiz flair. He is a worrier, alarmingly intelligent, a very hard worker, doodler of complicated geometrical patterns when thinking, a reader of everything, hopeless at doing anything complicated with his hands like putting a refill into a ball-point pen, but with a keen and original mind for comedy and a love of musicals and good 'flicks' (rather than 'cinema').

Perhaps one reason why we never had a row in all those years, apart from both being good at 'rubbing-along' and never having enough nervous energy to spare for squabbling, was that we hardly ever saw each other outside our office. During the day we were with each other longer than we were with our wives, but then, when we had finished for the day, Denis went home to North London and I drove back to Anners, Thorpe. Polly and Avril Norden have an enjoyable lunch together twice a year; Den and I are always faintly worried what they talk about.

A year or so ago Antonia Fraser threw a drinks party in her garden in Camden Hill Square. Afterwards Polly suggested that all four of us might wander across the road to the Pomme d'Amour, a Mauritian restaurant. While we were menu-studying I said to Den, 'I've suddenly realized this is the first time we four have had dinner together since we were in Australia twenty-five years ago.'

Den said, 'I hope you're not thinking of making a habit of it.'

*

I had ordered from Harrods a made-to-measure venetian blind (we had found to our dismay that for quite a few years Polly and I had tottered stark naked up and down the stone stairs of A Torra in Corsica on our way to the shower in full view of anybody walking across the square below).

The department at Harrods was on a lonely floor, and was empty of customers when I arrived to collect my bespoke blind. The only inhabitant was a young assistant. I gave him my chitty for the venetian blind. 'Sorry, but I'll have to keep you waiting for a few minutes,' he said. 'I have to find your blind in the stockroom on the next floor up.'

Left alone amongst shelves of yard-long bolts of curtain material I suddenly realized that this was a wonderful opportunity to fulfil a childhood ambition – to 'flip-flop' a bolt of cloth noisily along the counter and unwind a length of the material as I had seen so many haberdashery shop assistants do in my childhood. I reached behind me, took out a board, over which was wound blue curtain material, and laid it on the counter, noting with pleasure that there was a yard-long brass measure let into the countertop. 'Flip-flop' the bolt of material went as I flipped it over deftly. In my exhilaration I soon flipped it to the end of the counter and had to stop.

I looked up in my moment of glee and saw that there was an elderly lady standing at the customer's side of the counter looking at the curtain material with interest.

'Have you by any happy chance got it in green?' she asked.

'I'll have a look, madam,' I said.

I *had* got it in green.

'Eight and a half yards, please,' she said.

I slid the bolt of cloth off the shelf and onto the counter and flipped it over, flip-flop, flop, flop, flop. I measured 8½ yards against the imbedded ruler and cut the material with a massive pair of scissors I found lying by the till, folded up the cloth and stuffed it into a dark-green plastic bag.

'How much is that?' asked the lady, fumbling with her purse.

I suddenly went chill. Now that money was involved my little romp could easily turn nasty. The assistant could well take the view that I was a thief and call the store detective . . .

And the assistant was suddenly there, standing by the till clutching my venetian blind and watching.

I gulped. 'This lady asked me for eight and a half yards of the green so I sold it to her,' I said defiantly.

'Cheers,' said the assistant.

*

On the matter of the power of hidden hinges as against one's own control over events, it was certainly no cunning stratagem, nor any feeling of destiny which made me decide one day to wander down the stairs and grab a quick lunch at the BBC canteen in Aeolian Hall, where I stood behind that blonde with a lovely voice, a tray of beans on toast and an apple.

That was forty-nine years ago (as I write) and I still stand behind my blonde with the musical voice when we go to buy the birds' peanuts at Lynne's the ironmongers in Virginia Water on Saturday mornings, and Polly and I will soon be enjoying the rigours of our golden wedding anniversary.

Denis and I wrote a joke once in *TIFH* that being in love is only a temporary mania which after marriage changes into something much more lasting – hatred (not a very jolly joke). As far as Pol and I are concerned, being in love certainly developed into something more lasting – love. And love is altogether a much deeper, give-and-take, *affectionate* relationship than being 'in' love.

Polly and I confirm our feelings towards each other every night along with prayers for the rest of the family and Sal's Dalmation Dotty, and our cat Cinto (named after the tallest mountain in Corsica, such a sensible name for an Abyssinian cat), so should a feminist journalist from a women's page telephone me today and ask me how often I have told my wife that I love her, I will reply (after a quick arpeggio on the calculator to check), roughly 16,822 times. And I spoke the truth every time.

Pol and I are on paper reasonably incompatible, so important an ingredient in a good partnership. Polly seems to me to have rather over-fastidious views about personal hygiene, such as when one has been greasing the motor mower, nature's method of wiping the mess off one's hands quickly is on a guest towel (normally so rarely used) or a drooping bit of the tablecloth. This sort of *ad hoc* solution to a problem is not encouraged by the management.

Polly enjoys eating pasta. To me, with my diminished sense of taste, pasta tends to be like eating bits of blotting-paper. And Polly has always loved the flower garden and the vegetable patch. When I was more spry I used to labour quite a lot in the garden, but it was only labouring. To me flowers and vegetables were a foreign country, I could never remember their names or recognize them. It was all right when the edible bit appeared and I could name it as a cabbage or a stick of rhubarb, but when it was just green foliage I couldn't tell one plant from another.

A really shaming incident occurred when daughter Sal, aged about six, was in bed slowly recovering from flu. Polly had to go out shopping and she asked me to dig her some potatoes. I toured the kitchen garden and could not see any potatoes. I thought they might hang down from a bush like gooseberries, or hang upwards and sideways like corn on the cob, but there were no potatoes to be seen dangling anywhere.

If I failed to dig the potatoes it would lead to tremendous loss of face, harsh words, and a coolth would develop with Pol which might last for weeks. Frantic, I thought hard and came up with the answer. There was somebody in the house who knew a great deal about nature and in a flash could point me in the direction of potatoes. I rushed upstairs, wrapped little flu-stricken Sal in an eiderdown, staggered downstairs with her, and methodically waved her over the kitchen garden, face downwards, like a metal detector. She was coughing a bit, but soon located the row of Murphys and I was saved.

When brother Chas and I were teenagers our granny decided to give us signet rings. I hated the idea of wearing jewellery and so she gave me something else.

It was coming up to our forty-seventh wedding anniversary and Polly asked me if there was something I would like to have as a keepsake, and suddenly I knew exactly what I wanted. I said, 'Please may I have a wedding ring?'

Polly was very surprised. She said, 'Tell me why you suddenly want a wedding ring after all these years and you shall have one.'

'Well, I wanted to be sure first,' I said, the sort of slick half joke inappropriate for a rather emotional moment, but it gave me time to think. Most readers who have reached this far in the book will know exactly how I feel towards Polly.

The weaker the little jokes which I make at home, the more Polly laughs, which is a thoroughly good sign. We do a fair bit of laughing. And Pol is very sensible, and common sense is becoming a much underrated quality. Polly, above all, is kind and good and unselfish and strong, all the things which her Roman Catholicism has encouraged.

I find it quite impossible to visualize what life without Polly would have been like. Finding Polly was like a fifth rib replacement, or 'the other half' we search for to make us complete in the process which Plato called 'the desire and pursuit of the whole'. It was a wonderfully successful process in my case.

I asked for a wedding ring so that I could wear it as a symbol of the happiness my marriage to Pol has brought. Now that I work at home it is so good just to know that Pol is somewhere around, even though invisible, perhaps bending down picking white currants in the fruit cage and swearing gently, or upstairs shortening a skirt for a granddaughter.

The happy thing is to know that Pol is near.

*

Finally (Oh, happy word to read? Only equalled, according to the poet Robert Southey, by churchgoers nodding through the sermon and suddenly hearing the vicar declaiming '. . . in the name of the Father, the Son and the Holy Ghost . . .').

Finally, a word from Dilys Powell.

When the novelist Arnot Robertson died in the early years of *My Word!* her replacement as my partner was the doyenne of British film critics, Dilys Powell.

Our daughter Sally met Dilys when the whole team came to Anners for a quick snack before we all went off to record *My Word!* at our local hospital. Sally was still at school and began writing to Dilys. The correspondence, and the friendship, went on for years (Sal also had other pen-friends – 'pen-pals' does not seem appropriate to describe Sal's list of quite elderly and distinguished correspondents, which included the county court judge His Honour Judge Leon, and the glass engraver and poet Laurence Whistler).

Then we found that Dilys, twice widowed and getting on in years, spent Christmas alone in her house in London, so we invited Dilys down to be our honorary granny.

It was a huge success and Dilys spent Christmas with us for the next nineteen years, latterly quite old and physically slow, but mentally as brisk and stimulating as ever; although she'd had two happy marriages she warned Sal not to jump into it. 'Do not marry unless you cannot possibly live without him,' was her advice (actually her command) to Sal.

Then one weekend after dinner, Dilys was now in her early nineties, I told her about beginning these memoirs. She asked me whether I regretted anything. I said that there were no deep regrets; I had been helped along so often by sudden shafts of good fortune that life, like democracy and walking, had been a constantly interrupted fall forward.

'Just one mild bleat,' I said to Dil. 'Nowadays young comics in their late twenties and early thirties have their own production companies and control their video sales and so on, and several are millionaires. Den and I did a bit of useful pioneering in the beginnings of radio comedy and then of telly comedy, but pioneers don't make that sort of money. It would have been nice for me, still the breadwinner in my late seventies, to have emerged from the struggle just a little bit rich.'

Darling Dil's reaction was extraordinary. She banged the table, eyes blazing. 'What on earth are you talking about! You ARE rich! You're a very rich man! Just look at what you've got. You have

Polly as your wife, you have worked happily for years with Denis as partner, and he is now your closest friend, you have two gifted children with good marriages, three delightful grandchildren, you've had a most successful career, you have written bestsellers, your voice is recognized all over the world, you have Anners and Corsica . . . you are rich in everything worth having. How DARE you wish you had more!'

Well! That was telling me.

And of course Dilys was right.

*

It seems that few famous last words were actually uttered by the departing, at least not at the time of their departure. I was assured by a courtier who was present at the bedside that King George V did not expire saying, 'Bugger Bognor,' although apparently it accurately reflected his views. Nor, sadly, did the eighteenth-century pioneering traveller and poet Lady Mary Wortley Montagu review her life and pass on with the words, 'It has all been most interesting.' It seems the phrase was invented for her in a biography, *Portrait of Lady Mary Montagu* by Iris Barry. But what a superbly aristocratic attitude! As though life had been a pageant, like the Coventry Mystery Plays, trundled past on carts to amuse her ladyship.

So, what better way for me to end these memoirs than to adapt the splendid Lady Mary Wortley line which I like so much, and, with dear Dilys's comments ringing in my ears, change just one word of it so that my own summing-up reads:

'It has all been most enrichening.'

Index